IMPLICIT MEMORY:
New Directions in Cognition, Development, and Neuropsychology

IMPLICIT MEMORY: NEW DIRECTIONS IN COGNITION, DEVELOPMENT, AND NEUROPSYCHOLOGY

Edited by
PETER GRAF
University of British Columbia
MICHAEL E. J. MASSON
University of Victoria

LEA LAWRENCE ERLBAUM ASSOCIATES, PUBLISHERS
1993   Hillsdale, New Jersey   Hove and London

Lawrence Erlbaum Associates, Inc., Publishers
365 Broadway
Hillsdale, New Jersey 07642

Library of Congress Cataloging-in-Publication Data

Implicit memory : new directions in cognition, development, and
    neuropsychology / edited by Peter Graf, Michael E.J. Masson.
        p.   cm.
    Includes bibliographical references and index.
    ISBN 0-8058-1115-X(cloth) — ISBN 0-8058-1116-8 (paper)
    1. Memory. I. Graf, Peter, PhD.
    [DNLM: 1. Cognition—physiology. 2. Memory—physiology.
    3. Neuropsychology. WL 108 I34 1993]
    QP406.I555   1993
    612.8'2—dc20
    DNLM/DLC
    for Library of Congress   93-959
                                                                  CIP

Printed in the United States of America
10 9 8 7 6 5 4 3 2

Contents

Preface

In the last decade, research on memory for recent events and experiences sprouted a new branch and we now distinguish between two modes of using memory, called implicit and explicit, respectively. Explicit memory is the mode used in those situations in which recent events and experiences need to be recollected in a deliberate, intentional manner, and implicit memory covers situations in which the same events and experiences influence performance in the absence of specific intentions to recollect them. Several core observations on similarities and differences between implicit and explicit memory were reported in the early 1980s and then interest spread in an explosive manner, so that today this topic can fill entire journal issues and hold center stage at major conferences.

The immense growth of research on implicit and explicit memory is making it difficult to keep up with new methods and findings, to gauge the implications of new discoveries, and to ferret out new directions in research and theory development. Keeping up is especially difficult because research is ongoing in parallel in several domains, including mainstream cognitive psychology, lifespan developmental psychology, neuropsychology, personality, and social cognition. Thus, with research all abuzz around us, we are in danger of losing the forest for the trees. The present volume is intended to counteract that danger. Its purpose is to provide a status report of work on implicit and explicit memory in the three areas that have contributed the bulk of what is known about this domain: cognitive psychology, lifespan developmental psychology, and neuropsychology. In each area, the volume highlights developments in methods, critical findings, and theoretical positions, and it outlines promising new research directions. By so doing, we hope to provide the reader with a multidisciplinary perspective on implicit and explicit memory and thereby enable the cross-fertilization of ideas and research.

The chapters that make up this volume were written by experts on the topic of implicit and explicit memory. We invited them to write about their area of research, to outline its theoretical and empirical roots, to emphasize new developments and fundamental issues, and to speculate about implications and about promising new research directions. But unlike other collections of chapters that report the latest findings from various research labs, the contributors to the present volume were asked to write for a broad audience—to give a tutorial introduction and overview—for their colleagues from allied disciplines, for new researchers, for graduate students and for advanced undergraduate students, to help them gain a comprehensive overview of the mushrooming research on this topic, grasp the most fundamental empirical and theoretical issues, and focus on new research directions.

We thank the chapter contributors for following our directions, and for reading and reviewing each other's chapters, and we thank Lawrence Erlbaum for showing patience despite several broken deadline promises. Grants from the Natural Sciences and Engineering Research Council of Canada to both editors made this volume possible.

Peter Graf
Michael E. J. Masson

IMPLICIT MEMORY:
New Directions in Cognition, Development, and Neuropsychology

1

Introduction: Looking Back and Into the Future

Michael E. J. Masson
University of Victoria

Peter Graf
University of British Columbia

Our objective in this introductory chapter is, first, to briefly trace the history of observations, research, and ideas that have led to the differentiation between implicit and explicit memory and to the current intense investigation of this domain. The emphasis is on the contributions from each of the three areas that are represented in the separate parts of this book: cognitive psychology, developmental psychology, and neuropsychology. Our second goal is to discuss what makes the study of implicit and explicit memory important and exciting, and to justify why we chose to focus this book on three particular research domains.

HISTORICAL ROOTS IN METHODS AND BEHAVIORS

The distinction between explicit recollection of recent events and instances in which memory for the same events affects behavior in the absence of conscious recollection has resulted from a confluence of observations and ideas contributed by various interacting but usually independent fields of study. In his historical review of the literature on implicit memory, Schacter (1987) identified major contributions from psychical research, neurology, psychiatry, philosophy, and experimental psychology. Thus, we see no need here to duplicate Schacter's effort; instead, our aim is to identify and discuss events drawn from the three research domains that are represented in this volume. We begin by considering developments at the turn of the 20th century, and then outline how they evolved into currently debated issues and theories.

Many contemporary cognitive psychology investigations of implicit and explicit memory are rooted in the work of Ebbinghaus (1885/1913). Much has

1

already been written about Ebbinghaus' influence on bringing memory research into experimental psychology and making it scientifically respectable. Among his many other contributions, Ebbinghaus also gave us a broader conceptualization of memory than that held by his contemporaries (see Nelson, 1985). The received view of memory in Ebbinghaus' day was that articulated by James (1890), who regarded memory as involving the conscious recollection of an event, accompanied by awareness of its prior occurrence. By contrast, Ebbinghaus generalized the concept of memory so as to include test performance influences due to prior events that occur in the absence of such awareness. He argued that "the vanished mental states [created by prior events] give indubitable proof of their continuing existence even if they themselves do not return to consciousness at all, or at least not exactly at the given time" (1885/1964, p. 2).

Ebbinghaus' contribution is especially interesting and critical because he also gave us a method to index and quantify influences due to memory for prior events that occur in the absence of conscious recollection. This method involves relearning a set of materials after some retention interval and computing "savings"–the difference between the number of trials needed initially to memorize the materials and the number of trials needed to relearn them later. The savings in relearning was intended to capture not only that which can be consciously recollected, but also that which is unavailable to consciousness. Ebbinghaus' expectation concerning this latter feature of the savings measure was validated by much later research in which significant savings on a relearning measure were found even for items that subjects failed to recognize (Nelson, 1978). The sensitivity of this measure is also underlined in a case study reported by Burtt (1941) in which meaningless Greek passages were read to a 15-month-old child. Some 13 years later when the child attempted to memorize these and comparable new Greek passages, reliable savings were observed for the familiar passages.

At the time when Ebbinghaus was writing about savings as a method for investigating a form of memory that occurs in the absence of conscious recollection, there were reports of a number of critical clinical demonstrations that are the historical precursors of recent neuropsychological investigations of spared and impaired memory functions in amnesic patients. Of particular interest are reports involving amnesic patients who are seriously impaired in their ability to consciously recollect recent events and experiences. Korsakoff (1889) observed that although amnesics are not aware of memory for prior events and experiences, they nonetheless retain weak memory traces that can be revealed in the absence of awareness and that can continue to influence behavior. To illustrate, Korsakoff described a patient to whom he had given an electric shock. When he later displayed a case that contained the shock apparatus the patient was unable to remember receiving a shock. Nevertheless, upon seeing the case the patient inferred that Korsakoff planned to give him a shock, even though he could only know the function of the case and apparatus by having some form of memory for the original episode. A similar incident was reported by Claparède (1911/1951), who used a pinprick during an initial handshake to make an amnesic patient wary of shaking hands with him at a subsequent meeting, despite her inability to recollect their original introduction. In Claparède's view, this division between conscious recollection and preserved memory for events represents a dissociation of the ego and the memory trace.

More recent demonstrations of selectively preserved memory functions in amnesic patients have come from experiments on perceptual-motor skill learning. For example, studies with the patient H. M. have shown that he can acquire a number of skills, such as mirror tracing and rotary pursuit, despite being unable to recollect having engaged in such tasks (Corkin, 1968; Milner, Corkin, & Teuber, 1964). The pioneering work of Warrington and Weiskrantz (1968) helped to generalize and show the breadth of selectively spared memory functions in amnesia. In their experiments, subjects initially read a list of words and then were presented with word fragments in which pieces of the printed letters were missing, thereby making the letters and words difficult to identify. The probability of successfully identifying word fragments was higher for those items corresponding to previously studied words versus nonstudied new words. More critical, the magnitude of the advantage on studied versus nonstudied words was similar for amnesic patients and control subjects, thereby indicating that some form of memory for the original experience had been preserved at a normal level.

By contrast with neuropsychology and cognitive psychology, where we can easily identify at least some of the landmark events that provided an impetus for recent investigations of implicit and explicit memory, such events are more difficult to identify in the developmental literature. The reason may be that in early development, learning and memory that occur in the absence of conscious recollection are the norm rather than the exception, and the focus of investigations was more on understanding the development of an explicit form of memory. Consistent with this idea, Piaget (1952) posited two memory systems, one of which develops later than the other. In a paper first published in 1945, the Russian psychologist Istomina (1975) discussed how a later, explicit form of memory grows out of an earlier form. Istomina proposed that during infancy and the early preschool years memory processes are neither distinct from other ongoing process nor operating under the child's voluntary control. Rather, memory processes were viewed as being involuntary and integrated into other ongoing activities, and thus, at this stage, the use of memory is guided by the nature of the ongoing activity. In the later preschool years memory processes become differentiated as the child develops the ability to formulate plans for independently initiating and guiding intentional recollection. This view of memory development is consistent with the current distinction between implicit and explicit memory. The recruiting of memory processes by other ongoing activity enables implicit influences of memory on behavior, whereas the ability to formulate plans for using memory is a prerequisite for the emergence of explicit memory.

RECENT FINDINGS

The observations and ideas discussed in the preceding section yielded a constant trickle of research across the years, but when they were brought together in the early 1980s the trickle swelled into a stream, so that today, after only one decade of research on implicit and explicit memory, an entire book is required to gain an overview of the major findings and explanations. The wealth of findings that makes up the current data base on implicit and explicit memory is summarized in the various chapters of this volume. In this section, our goal is to highlight three general findings (one from each part of this book) that have had a strong influence on the theoretical accounts that have been offered to explain similarities and differences between implicit and explicit memory test performance.

Many of the major findings on implicit and explicit memory come from studies that are built on the pioneering work of Kolers (1975, 1976) (see Levy, Chapter 3, this volume). Kolers required subjects to read and after a delay reread text that was spatially transformed in some way (e.g., displayed upside down). His goal was to examine how the first reading of a text influences its second reading, when the text was displayed in the same format on both occasions or when it was displayed differently on each occasion. The main dependent variable—the decrease in time required for the second versus the first reading—is akin to Ebbinghaus' savings measure. Kolers found (a) that the greatest rereading benefits occurred when texts were displayed in exactly the same manner on both occasions, (b) that changes in text typography or in the presentation modality between the first and second occasion reduced the rereading benefit, and (c) that rereading benefits can last for as long as a year. Such findings led Kolers to propose a general view of memory (outlined later in this section) that emphasized the specific processing operations engaged to encode and retrieve to-be-remembered items.

Kolers carried out most of his landmark studies in the 1970s, and the focus of his research was on issues other than the distinction between implicit and explicit memory. However, the conclusion that memory is mediated by the specific processing operations engaged to encode and retrieve to-be-remembered items is consistent with many findings that have emerged since then. We now know, for example, that a change in the modality in which words are presented for study and test, or a change in the font in which they are typed, influences test performance, and this influence tends to be much larger on implicit than explicit memory tests. Other experimental manipulations produce the opposite pattern of effects—that is, they have a larger influence on performance of explicit than implicit tests. The chapter by Roediger and Srinivas (Chapter 2, this volume) summarizes much of the relevant evidence. That chapter highlights the general finding that specific encoding and retrieval manipulations influence memory test performance, and that implicit and explicit test performance are often affected by different kinds of manipulations.

Several of the first implicit/explicit memory studies with amnesic patients were also inspired by and modeled after Kolers' work, and they contributed findings that shaped and continue to shape theoretical developments. To illustrate, Cohen and Squire (1980) examined amnesic patients' ability to read words presented in a spatially transformed display. They found that the amnesics could learn to read transformed words at the same rate as normal control subjects, despite the fact that the patients were unable to consciously recollect the words they had read or even that they had ever been asked to read transformed words. Other studies, modeled after the work of Warrington and Weiskrantz (1968), presented subjects with a list of words and then assessed memory with an explicit memory test or an implicit memory test. The general finding, discussed in the chapters in the neuropsychology part of this book, is that across a variety of study and test conditions, amnesic patients can show entirely normal performance on implicit memory tests despite being severely impaired on explicit memory tests.

An additional general finding that has shaped theoretical advances comes from lifespan developmental studies. The relevant literature is reviewed in the developmental part of this book, and the critical finding is displayed in Fig. 8.1 of Mitchell's chapter (Chapter 8, this volume). The figure shows that implicit memory test performance remains invariant across the lifespan, whereas explicit memory test performance increases in early childhood and then declines in late adulthood.

These general findings from cognitive psychology, neuropsychology, and developmental psychology have provoked two kinds of theorizing, with one explaining similarities and differences between implicit and explicit memory test performance by appealing to various cognitive processes and the other by postulating two kinds of memory systems. In the next section, we briefly discuss each approach.

THEORETICAL ALTERNATIVES: PROCESSES VERSUS SYSTEMS

The processing perspective is founded, first, on Kolers' notion that memory is best understood in terms of the cognitive operations or processes that are engaged by different study and test activities. Kolers maintained that a task such as reading a word or sentence, for example, requires a particular set of sensory-perceptual and conceptual analyzing operations, and that engaging these operations has the same effect as practicing a skill—it increases the fluency and efficiency with which they can be carried out subsequently. A second foundation of the processing perspective is the concept of transfer-appropriate processing (TAP) (Morris, Bransford, & Franks, 1977), the notion that performance on a memory test is determined by the degree of overlap between study and test processing. From the combination of these ideas it follows that performance on a memory test will be facilitated to the extent that it engages the same set or a similar set of cognitive operations as that used for a preceding study task.

As pointed out elsewhere (Graf, 1991; Graf & Ryan, 1990), the general idea that performance is determined by the degree of overlap between study and test processing, in the absence of an independent index of processing, is consistent with any experimental outcome, and thus cannot by itself explain similarities and differences between implicit and explicit memory test performance. For this reason, researchers who have espoused TAP have treated it as a general framework for theorizing about memory, and then postulated specific kinds of processes that mediate implicit and explicit memory test performance.

Roediger and his colleagues, perhaps the most ardent advocates of TAP in the domain of implicit and explicit memory (see Roediger & Srinivas, Chapter 2, this volume), focus on the distinction between perceptual and conceptual processing. They have argued that implicit memory test performance is mediated primarily by study to test overlaps in perceptual processing, whereas explicit test performance is mediated primarily by study to test overlaps in conceptual processing. Other researchers have explained similarities and differences between implicit and explicit memory test performance in terms of different processing distinctions, including integrative versus elaborative processing (e.g., Graf, 1991; Graf & Mandler, 1984; Light, 1991), interpretive versus elaborative processing (Masson & MacLeod, 1992), and environmentally driven versus subject-guided processing (e.g., Craik, 1983). These different TAP-based views were introduced to explain specific subsets of the findings related to implicit and explicit memory tests, and thus they were not necessarily intended to be mutually exclusive alternatives. Instead, future research and theorizing are likely to reveal them as variations on the same theme—options that focus on different but complementary aspects of study and test processing.

In contrast to these processing accounts, several chapters in this volume show that the distinction between implicit and explicit memory can also be framed in terms of independent memory systems that are associated with different brain structures. Systems accounts begin with some assumptions about what constitutes a memory system, for example, a collection of correlated memory functions that are served by (at least some) anatomically distinct brain structures. One early account of this type was introduced by Cohen and Squire (1980), who emphasized the distinction between *knowing how* and *knowing that*. They suggested that *knowing how* to do something like solving a puzzle or reading a spatially transformed word involves perceptual and motor procedures or operations of the sort discussed by Kolers, whereas *knowing that* an event has occurred at a particular time and place involves another form of memory representations (e.g., propositional), which can be expressed verbally. Squire (1986) postulated the existence of two independent memory systems corresponding to these two kinds of knowing: procedural memory and declarative memory. The procedural system is assumed to be spared in amnesic patients, permitting normal acquisition of skills, whereas the declarative system is damaged, resulting in impairment on explicit memory tasks. Other researchers have postulated different types of systems to explain amnesic patients' spared and impaired memory functions, including habit versus memory (Mishkin, Malamut, & Bachevalier, 1984), semantic memory versus cognitive mediation (Warrington & Weiskrantz, 1982), and presemantic perceptual versus episodic (Schacter, 1990; Tulving & Schacter, 1990).

The separation of memory into differentiated systems is consistent with the developmental scheme proposed by Istomina (1975) and Piaget (1952) and also fits neuropsychological theories of memory development (e.g., Hirsh & Krajden, 1982; O'Keefe & Nadel, 1978; Schacter & Moscovitch, 1984). In a number of these formulations, it is proposed that the memory system available to newborns enables only incremental learning that underlies the acquisition of habits and skills. This system does not support intentional recollection of prior events. A later-developing memory system is assumed to enable intentional recollection of specific events and the contexts in which they occurred. The neurological substrate assumed to be responsible for this developmental change is the hippocampal formation. Evidence suggests that this structure develops in humans between 18 and 36 months of age (Jacobs & Nadel, 1985), and damage to the hippocampus is related to amnesic syndromes in which conscious recollection is impaired but the ability to acquire certain skills is preserved (Cohen & Squire, 1980). The observation of *infantile amnesia,* in which normal adults typically are unable to recollect events that occurred during their first few years of life (e.g., Moscovitch, 1984), is also consistent with this scheme.

Some of the chapters in this volume show a partiality to either a systems explanation or a processing explanation for similarities and differences between implicit and explicit memory test performance, but most highlight the fact that these perspectives are not mutually exclusive and that they can complement each other in various ways. When we enter the debate surrounding systems versus processes, it might be useful to reflect on the fact that a similar debate was also waged three decades ago with the introduction of information processing models that differentiated between short-term memory and long-term memory. At that time, researchers who favored systems could point to a wealth of performance dissociations between short-term and long-term memory, and those who were against systems (and in favor of learning theory) could find evidence for continuity between them (see Melton, 1963). The outcome of this debate can be found in the literature where systems and processing accounts for short-term and long-term memory phenomena live happily alongside each other. The point to remember is that theories are tools, that we use different tools for different purposes, and that our purpose is to gain a better understanding of similarities and differences between implicit and explicit memory test performance.

THE EXCITEMENT ABOUT IMPLICIT
AND EXPLICIT MEMORY

What is exciting about the distinction between implicit and explicit memory, and why has this distinction moved to center stage of memory research in less than a decade? A partial answer can be gained from a survey of the recent literature, or by inspection of the proceedings from a recent conference. In either case, we find that the distinction between two forms of memory[1]—one implicit and not mediated by conscious intentions and the other explicit and consciously controlled—is relevant to a wide range of topics. Until the 1980s, some of these topics were taboo (or at least neglected) as investigations focused primarily on recall and recognition of recent events and experiences. But as we know now, explicit memory is only a small part—the conscious tip of the iceberg—of how memory for recent events and experiences influences us in our daily activities. The submerged and much larger part of the iceberg is the domain of implicit memory, and its rediscovery (after Ebbinghaus) in the mid 1980s opened the floodgates to feverish prospecting.

The implicit/explicit memory-research rush began mainly because of the finding that some memory functions are spared and others are impaired in patients with anterograde amnesia (see Neuropsychology, Part III, this volume), but it has now spread well beyond this domain. Today, investigations are examining the relationship between memory and consciousness (see Parkin, Chapter 9, this volume), exploring the connection between memory, learning, skill acquisition, and problem solving (see Lockhart & Blackburn, Chapter 5, and Kirsner, Speelman, & Schofield, Chapter 6, this volume), and constructing new links between memory and reading skill development (see Levy, Chapter 3, this volume). Beyond the limits of traditional cognitive psychology, developmental psychology, and neuropsychology, the discovery and legitimization of research into the unconscious underbelly of memory has also engendered investigations in allied fields, including social psychology where experiments are examining the basis for preference (for people, objects) and decision making, and in clinical psychology where experiments probe into how a phobic individual reacts to spiders, for example. Research on implicit and explicit memory has also found a home in school psychology and in marketing research where it is used, for

---

[1]Other labels are sometimes used to mark the distinction between implicit and explicit memory, including *procedural* and *declarative* memory. The differences among these labels are important. The terms implicit and explicit memory usually denote two different ways of using memory—one implicit and not mediated by conscious intentions, and the other explicit and consciously controlled. By contrast, procedural and declarative are theoretical terms used to denote two kinds of memory systems. In this way, implicit and explicit are concerned with different forms or functions of memory, and these distinct functions may be explained either in terms of cognitive processes or in terms of memory systems.

example, to ask questions about what kind of advertisement is most effective in shaping consumers' purchasing decisions.

But the realization that implicit memory is implicated in many different cognitive activities and everyday situations may be only part of what fuels the recent rapid expansion of research. Another major influence is the exchange of ideas, findings, and methods among fields of research that previously operated independently of each other. One of the first examples of this kind, produced by the finding that implicit memory is selectively spared in amnesic patients, is the question of whether implicit and explicit memory can function completely independently of each other. This question was picked up quickly by cognitive psychologists who examined the circumstances under which implicit and explicit memory can become dissociated, and by developmental psychologists who began to study how the two forms of memory develop across the lifespan (see Lifespan Development, Part II, this volume). This flow of questions across domains is continuing, and, more importantly, it is paralleled by the import and export of methods and by systematic attempts to replicate and generalize findings with different subject populations. Thus, an important reason for the excitement about implicit and explicit memory comes from the fact that it has made researchers interact more closely with each other. The three research domains that are featured in this volume provide outstanding examples of this interdisciplinary activity; the various chapters are a testimony to the value of this enterprise, and they illustrate the benefits of a cooperative striving toward a common goal.

REFERENCES

Burtt, H. E. (1941). An experimental study of early childhood memory: Final report. *Journal of Genetic Psychology, 58,* 435–439.

Claparède, E. (1951). Recognition and 'me-ness.' In D. Rapaport (Ed.), *Organization and pathology of thought* (pp. 58–75). New York: Columbia University Press. (Reprinted from *Archives de Psychologie,* 1911, *11,* 79–90)

Cohen, N. J., & Squire, L. R. (1980). Preserved learning and retention of pattern analyzing skill in amnesia: Dissociation of knowing how and knowing that. *Science, 210,* 207–209.

Corkin, S. (1968). Acquisition of motor skill after bilateral medial temporal lobe excision. *Neuropsychologia, 6,* 255–265.

Craik, F. I. M. (1983). On the transfer of information from temporary to permanent memory. *Philosophical Transactions of the Royal Society of London, B302,* 341–359.

Ebbinghaus, H. E. (1913). *Memory: A contribution to experimental psychology* (Trans. H. A. Ruger & C. E. Bussenius) New York: Teacher's College, Columbia University. (Original work published 1885)

Graf, P. (1991). Implicit and explicit memory: An old model for new findings. In W. Kessen, A. Ortony, & F. Craik, (Eds.). *Memories, thoughts, and emotions: Essays in honor of George Mandler* (pp. 135–147). Hillsdale, N.J.: Lawrence Erlbaum Associates.

Graf, P., & Mandler, G. (1984). Activation makes words more accessible but not necessarily more retrievable. *Journal of Verbal Learning and Verbal Behavior, 23,* 553–568.

Graf, P., & Ryan, L. (1990). Transfer-appropriate processing for implicit and explicit memory. *Journal of Experimental Psychology: Learning, Memory, and Cognition, 16,* 978–992.

Hirsh, R., & Krajden, J. (1982). The hippocampus and the expression of knowledge. In R. L. Isaacson & N. E. Spear (Eds.), *The expression of knowledge* (pp. 213–241). New York: Plenum Press.

Istomina, Z. M. (1975). The development of voluntary memory in preschool-children. *Soviet Psychology, 12,* 5–64.

Jacobs, W. J., & Nadel, L. (1985). Stress-induced recovery of fears and phobias. *Psychological Review, 92,* 512–531.

James, W. (1890). *Principles of psychology.* New York: Holt.

Kolers, P. A. (1975). Specificity of operations in sentence recognition. *Cognitive Psychology, 7,* 289–306.

Kolers, P. A. (1976). Reading a year later. *Journal of Experimental Psychology: Human Learning and Memory, 2,* 554–565.

Korsakoff, S. S. (1889). Etude medico-psychologique sur une forme des maladies de la memoire [Medical-psychological study of a form of diseases of memory]. *Revue Philosophique, 28,* 501–530.

Light, L. L. (1991). Memory and aging: Four hypotheses in search of data. *Annual Review of Psychology, 42,* 333–376.

Masson, M. E. J., & MacLeod, C. M. (1992). Re-enacting the route to interpretation: Enhanced perceptual identification without prior perception. *Journal of Experimental Psychology: General, 121,* 145–176.

Melton, A. W. (1963). Implications of short-term memory for a general theory of memory. *Journal of Verbal Learning and Verbal Behavior, 2,* 1–21.

Milner, B., Corkin, S., & Teuber, H. L. (1964). Further analysis of the hippocampal amnesic syndrome: 14 Year follow-up study of H. M. *Neuropsychologia, 6,* 215–234.

Mishkin, M., Malamut, B., & Bachevalier, J. (1984). Memories and habits: Two neural systems. In J. L. McGaugh, N. M. Weinberger, & G. Lynch (Eds.), *Neurobiology of Learning and Memory* (pp. 65–77). New York: Guilford Press.

Morris, C. D., Bransford, J. D., & Franks, J. J. (1977). Levels of processing versus transfer appropriate processing. *Journal of Verbal Learning and Verbal Behavior, 16,* 519–533.

Moscovitch, M. (Ed.). (1984). *Infant memory.* New York: Plenum Press.

Nelson, T. O. (1978). Detecting small amounts of information in memory: Savings for nonrecognized items. *Journal of Experimental Psychology: Human Learning and Memory, 4,* 453–468.

Nelson, T. O. (1985). Ebbinghaus' contribution to the measurement of retention: Savings during relearning. *Journal of Experimental Psychology: Learning, Memory, and Cognition, 11,* 472–479.

O'Keefe, J., & Nadel, L. (1978). *The hippocampus as a cognitive map.* Oxford, England: Clarendon Press.

Piaget, J. (1952). *The origins of intelligence in children.* New York: International Universities Press.

Schacter, D. L. (1987). Implicit memory: History and current status. *Journal of Experimental Psychology: Learning, Memory, and Cognition, 13,* 501–518.

Schacter, D. L. (1990). Perceptual representation systems and implicit memory: Toward a resolution of the multiple memory systems debate. *Annals of the New York Academy of Sciences, 608,* 543–571.

Schacter, D. L., & Moscovitch, M. (1984). Infants, amnesics, and dissociable memory systems. In M. Moscovitch (Ed.), *Infant memory* (pp. 173–216). New York: Plenum Press.

Squire, L. R. (1986). Mechanisms of memory. *Science, 232,* 1612–1619.

Tulving, E., & Schacter, D. L. (1990). Priming and human memory. *Science, 247,* 301–306.
Warrington, E. K., & Weiskrantz, L. (1968). New method for testing long-term retention with special reference to amnesic patients. *Nature, 217,* 972–974.
Warrington, E. K., & Weiskrantz, L. (1982). Amnesia: A disconnection syndrome? *Neuropsychologia, 20,* 233–248.

I

COGNITIVE PSYCHOLOGY

Cognitive psychology is a vast and multifaceted enterprise that covers memory, perception, problem solving, reading, and other topic areas. In the past decade, researchers in each of these topic areas have begun to examine implicit and explicit memory, and their combined contributions constitute the largest portion of what we now know about the similarities and differences between these two forms of memory. For that reason, this part of the book is the largest. It includes six chapters that collectively (a) summarize core findings that have emerged from a decade of research and (b) delineate the theoretical implications of these findings. Each of the first four chapters deals with a different subdomain of cognitive psychology, including memory, affect and memory, reading, and problem solving. The fifth chapter invites us to broaden our perspective and consider the relationship between implicit memory and the extensive literature on learning and skill acquisition, and the final chapter illustrates the use of computational models that can accommodate the combined findings from implicit and explicit memory tests.

The chapter by Roediger and Srinivas provides an excellent overview of research on implicit and explicit memory; it introduces the distinction between implicit and explicit memory, and highlights many of the empirical and theoretical issues that have motivated and/or are motivating research in the area. Roediger and Srinivas begin by outlining the classic evidence from studies of amnesic patients that have promoted the idea that implicit and explicit memory tests tap structurally different memory systems. In contrast to a systems view, Roediger and Srinivas favor an approach that focuses on processing, or, more specifically, *transfer-appropriate processing*. In support of this approach, they summarize a large body of evidence showing that the influence of an encoding episode on a later implicit memory task is highly specific, that priming effects are reduced or eliminated when certain aspects of a stimulus are changed between study and testing.

In the second chapter, Levy traces the history of a line of research that predates the contemporary work on implicit memory, but whose issues/questions have become important to investigators interested in implicit memory. Unlike the majority of the studies described in this book, in which a single object such as a word or a picture constitutes a stimulus event, the work explored by Levy deals with the reading of texts. The critical questions of this research concern the basis of fluent rereading of text. Evidence regarding contributions of memory for conceptual and perceptual information is reviewed, and Levy argues that these two types of text information are integrated in a holistic manner to form the episodic memory that mediates rereading fluency. In the last section of the chapter Levy discusses research in which these ideas have been examined in the development of skilled reading in children. Issues regarding word recognition and comprehension skills are addressed using tools from research on rereading fluency with adults.

The next two chapters explore the role of implicit memory processes in two intriguing domains: affect and memory, and problem solving. Macaulay, Ryan, and Eich employ the transfer appropriate processing framework (cf. Roediger & Srinivas, Chapter 2, this volume) in their review of research on mood dependent memory. The connection between affect and cognition has been investigated in only a few studies, but Macaulay et al. provide convincing evidence that mood may operate in the same way as other aspects of context to influence memory encoding and retrieval. They show that when the affective context that was present at study is reinstated at the time of retrieval, memory test performance is enhanced relative to situations in which encoding and retrieval contexts vary. Both implicit and explicit tests of memory are sensitive to changes in mood between encoding and test, although the effects are most clear when memory tests involve subject initiated/guided information processing. The authors also consider theories of emotion as a source of insight regarding the influence of particular emotions on cognitive processes, opening the possibility of an alternative, interdisciplinary approach to the study of cognition and emotion.

Lockhart and Blackburn consider the relation between implicit *learning* and implicit memory in problem solving. Implicit learning is defined as referring to the acquisition of a novel rule or knowledge about some form of regularity in the environment in a manner that does not depend on the ability to articulate the rule or regularity. They explore the hypothesis that implicit learning may enhance procedural processes in problem solving. The evidence they review, however, suggests only a limited role for implicit learning that possibly is restricted to cases in which problems depend on the acquisition of rules that are captured by simple frequency or contingency relations. Lockhart and Blackburn also consider the possibility that implicit memory for conceptual processing operations may influence the accessibility of critical information needed to solve problems. There is limited evidence in favor of this proposal, but it has been difficult to draw firm conclusions because of the possibility that the effects of prior experience on solving a problem may be mediated by conscious recollection rather than memory operating without awareness. The task now is to develop problem-solving paradigms that are designed to convincingly isolate the contribution of implicit memory processes.

In the final two chapters of this section two different attempts are made at building alternative frameworks within which implicit memory phenomena may be understood. Kirsner, Speelman, and Schofield argue that implicit memory may be viewed as an aspect of a more fundamental psychological process—learning or skill acquisition (cf. Levy, Chapter 3, this volume). They take the position that retention of encoded episodes and their impact on implicit memory tests can be interpreted as points on a more global learning function that adheres to the basic principles of skill acquisition, such as the power law of practice. This argument is developed in the context of research on word identification and the modulation of priming effects by word frequency. A critical implication of this view is that there is good reason to use data from skill acquisition and implicit memory paradigms to test a common set of models, derived from general learning theories.

The other approach to framing issues associated with implicit tests of memory involves the development of computer simulation models. Wiles and Humphreys provide a tutorial on the computational modeling approach, as instantiated by neural network models. They illustrate how some of the critical aspects of these models can be used to account for context effects in various types of explicit tests of memory. These tools are then used to demonstrate how implicit memory might be modeled as the learning of a mapping between modality-specific representations and conceptual representations. Rather than offering a particular model, a case is made for specific features that likely will have to be included in a successful model. A small simulation is provided to illustrate the power of some of these ideas in accounting for the quintessential implicit memory result—the powerful impact that a single presentation of a familiar stimulus can have on its subsequent identification.

2 Specificity of Operations in Perceptual Priming

Henry L. Roediger III
Rice University

Kavitha Srinivas
Boston College

First a test: Look at Fig. 2.1 and try to identify the object in the scene. We suspect that virtually all readers of this book, graduate students and professors in psychology or related fields, will be able to name the object in the foreground almost immediately. This scene has been celebrated in so many textbooks written for introductory psychology, cognitive psychology, and perception courses that most readers now see the dalmatian with little time or effort expended.

For each of us it was not always so. The first time a person examines Fig. 2.1 often it takes minutes, not milliseconds, to identify the object, and may require numerous hints and descriptions (even outlining) before the scene coalesces.

Why does this difference occur between the practiced and the naive observer? We argue that the difference reflects a form of perceptual memory like that tested in numerous experiments described in this volume and elsewhere. The rapid identification of the dalmatian reveals long-lasting priming of perceptual procedures that most readers have used repeatedly. To remind yourself of the difficulty of identifying so data-limited a display, try to name the objects shown in the four panels of Fig. 2.2. These picture fragments were first used in experiments reported by Weldon and Roediger (1987), which will be described later, and we have used them in more recent research. To us they are as easy to resolve as the dalmatian in Fig. 2.1, but we suspect that most readers will find them quite challenging. (Readers may exhibit some priming even on these items because most pictures in the Weldon and Roediger [1987] experiment were taken from the familiar Snodgrass and Vanderwart [1980] picture norms.) In recent terminology, facility in perceiving the dalmatian in Fig. 2.1 reflects priming on an implicit memory test. We now need to define these terms.

FIG. 2.1. The famous scene created by R. C. James showing the diffi-culty in recognizing a data-limited display. Reprinted by permission of R. C. Jones.

IMPLICIT AND EXPLICIT MEASURES OF MEMORY

Explicit measures of memory are those that involve conscious recollection, most typically recall or recognition (Graf & Schacter, 1985; Schacter, 1987). If we posed the question, "Can you recall the first time you saw the scene in Figure 2.1?" that query would represent an explicit test of memory, with the scene as the retrieval cue. *Implicit measures* of memory are those in which no act of conscious recollection is necessary to accomplish the task (Graf & Schacter, 1985). Asking a person to name the object in Fig. 2.1 functions as an implicit test of retention,

FIG. 2.2. Picture fragments used in the experiments of Weldon and Roediger (1987).

because the task can be accomplished (at least potentially) when the exact item has not been seen previously. In implicit memory tests, subjects are instructed to perform the task at hand as well as possible. If the person has had relevant prior experience, such as naming the degraded object before (or perhaps seeing the intact scene), then naming the object is easier. Implicit memory is reflected in priming, the difference in performance on a task (such as naming fragmented pictures) when one has either had relevant priming experiences (seeing the pictures beforehand) or not (seeing pictures unrelated to the fragments).

There are by now at least a half dozen standard procedures for studying implicit memory (for reviews of the literature see Richardson-Klavehn & Bjork, 1988; Roediger & McDermott, in press; Schacter, 1987; Shimamura, 1986). A typical procedure is for subjects to study a long list of words (e.g., *elephant*) and then, after some filler tasks, to be given a test under an instructional set that tells them to respond with the first word that comes to mind when (a) seeing a series of word stems, such as ele_____; (b) seeing a series of word fragments, such as e_e__a_t; or (c) seeing the entire word presented too rapidly for accurate perception (around 15–30 msec). In each case, priming is observed: A greater proportion of studied words is named, relative to nonstudied words. We refer to these tasks as word stem completion, word fragment completion, and word identification, respectively. Several other verbal tasks have also been used as implicit memory tests, especially the lexical decision task (deciding if a string of letters is a word), category production (generating members to a category name, such as *Animals*), and answering general knowledge questions (What animal helped Hannibal cross the Alps in his attack on Rome?). However, for purposes of this chapter, we consider data from only three verbal tasks, word stem completion, word fragment completion, and word identification, which seem to behave similarly under several manipulations (Rajaram & Roediger, in press).

Nonverbal implicit memory tests, such as naming the fragmented pictures in Figs. 2.1 and 2.2, have been less thoroughly studied than verbal tests, but in the last few years this omission has been remedied in numerous research reports. A later section of this chapter is devoted to the review of what is known about priming of nonverbal stimuli. To anticipate, we argue that such priming reflects perceptual operations that are often highly specific. Before turning to our review, we provide a brief overview of the origins of implicit memory research and our approach to explaining differences among memory measures.

IMPLICIT MEMORY AND MEMORY SYSTEMS

The origin of psychologists' current fascination with the distinction between explicit and implicit measures of memory lies in neuropsychological studies of amnesic patients (e.g., Warrington & Weiskrantz, 1968, 1970; Graf, Squire, & Mandler, 1985; see Shimamura, 1986, for a review). These patients typically have suffered damage to the hippocampus and other limbic areas, which renders them extraordinarily forgetful on most standard measures of memory. On explicit tests such as free recall, recognition, and cued recall, amnesic patients are quite poor when compared to matched controls. On the other hand, immediate memory (such as the ability to recall a series of digits just after presentation) is intact, as is general knowledge about the world acquired before the brain injury (semantic memory). The deficiency seems to lie in what Tulving (1972) called episodic memory, the events and experiences of one's life, after these events have receded into the psychological past (i.e., after they have vanished from what James [1890] termed primary memory). Indeed, around 1970 the guiding idea in the field was that amnesics could register information in a primary memory system but could not represent it more permanently in a secondary, or long-term, system, because of a failure in consolidation or some other transfer mechanism between the two systems (e.g., Baddeley & Warrington, 1970).

The new studies of implicit memory showed that the starkest form of this failure-of-consolidation idea was unsound. After studying a list of words, amnesics could not remember them, but they showed perfectly normal priming on implicit memory tests such as completing word stems (Warrington & Weiskrantz, 1970; Graf, Shimamura, & Squire, 1985). The study of words must have had a long-term impact on the cognitive system for this to occur, even if the experiences could not be consciously recollected. The original processing of the events was not obliterated as they faded from primary memory, as the proponents of the consolidation failure idea would seem to assert.

The preservation of experience in amnesics, exhibited so convincingly in many experiments using implicit memory measures, argued for preserved memory systems to complement the damaged ones. The original idea was that the general faculty of memory could be fractioned into a small number of subsystems, such as declarative and procedural memory (Cohen & Squire, 1980) or episodic and semantic memory (Tulving, 1983). However, data from both normal and amnesic subjects has caused the number of putative memory systems to grow, so that now most researchers working within this framework would agree that at least half a dozen memory systems are needed to explain the dissociations between tests and the number may extend to about 25 (see Roediger, 1990a, for a listing).

In a number of prior articles and chapters we have argued that the continued postulation of memory systems to account for dissociations between tests may not be the most fruitful approach to explaining test differences (e.g., Roediger, Rajaram, & Srinivas, 1990) and have offered an alternative framework, transfer appropriate processing. We consider this approach now.

TRANSFER-APPROPRIATE PROCESSING

Implicit measures of retention employ the logic of transfer of training experiments: Subjects are given various types of experiences, and the influence of these experiences is measured by transferring them to another task. Entrained experiences that produce facilitation relative to some control or neutral baseline condition are said to produce positive transfer; those that harm performance produce negative transfer. Implicit measures of retention examine positive transfer; priming is positive transfer.

The defining features of implicit measures of retention are that the criterial task used in the test can be accomplished without requiring subjects to consciously recollect the prior study experiences, and subjects are not instructed to remember the prior experiences in performing the task.[1] As mentioned, several tasks (both verbal and nonverbal) have become popular measures of implicit retention. However, the tasks studied so far are only a small sample of those that might be used, because virtually all performances of humans (or other animals) can be affected by prior experience and meet the defining criteria of implicit memory measures. Studies of classical conditioning, operant conditioning, observational learning, motor skill learning, concept learning, and learning of sets in problem solving (among others) meet the definition of implicit retention. In fact, one welcome dividend arising from the new interest in implicit memory is to return these venerable topics to the forefront of concern among cognitive psychologists, although other developments (such as the rise of connectionism) have aided this movement. It may be that all these other forms of learning themselves represent (or are underlain by) separate memory subsystems, which is in fact Squire's (1987) proposal (see too Squire & Zola-Morgan, 1991). Surely, these various types of learning differ in many ways, but Sherry and Schacter (1987) have argued that unless different "laws" exist (sets of empirical relations between independent variables and dependent variables measuring the different forms of learning), it is premature to postulate a separate system (see Roediger et al., 1990).

We believe that one general principle does unite the various forms of learning—transfer-appropriate processing: Tests of retention will benefit (there will be positive transfer) to the extent that the processing operations at test recapitulate or overlap those engaged during prior learning (Kolers & Roediger, 1984; Morris, Bransford, & Franks, 1977; Roediger, 1990b). The same general idea is embedded in the concepts of primary and secondary stimulus generalization in studies of conditioning, in Thorndike's (1903) identical elements theory of transfer, and in Tulving's (1983) encoding specificity principle, among other ideas. This principle seems to apply at a general level across many different forms of learning, evidenced in organisms as distinct as slugs and humans, although the basis of the transfer may differ in the various tasks and organisms.

---

[1]Implicit memory tests may be contaminated by explicit remembering: Subjects may use word fragments or word stems as retrieval cues to recall items from the list. Schacter, Bowers, and Booker (1989) discuss this issue and suggest solutions to the problem, which have been used by others (e.g., Roediger, Weldon, Stadler & Riegler, 1992). Jacoby (1991) suggests a different method for accomplishing this end.

Within human learning and memory, Roediger (1990b; see also Roediger & Blaxton, 1987b, and Roediger, Weldon & Challis, 1989) proposed that one important distinction is between perceptual bases of transfer in some tests and semantic bases of transfer in others. We followed Jacoby's (1983) lead in saying that such tasks as word identification, word fragment completion, and word stem completion seem *data-driven*, because changes in the surface form of studied events affected priming on these implicit memory tests. The form of data given in prior learning greatly affects transfer. For example, alterations in modality (visual or auditory) produce large effects on priming on all three of these visual tests, with about half as much priming arising from words presented auditorily as for those given visually (Donnelley, 1988; Kirsner, Dunn & Standen, 1989). The basis of transfer seems perceptual in nature on these tasks and, for reasons given later, we now refer to these as perceptual tests, rather than data-driven tests. (Other implicit tests, such as producing instances to category names and answering general knowledge questions, are generally not affected by perceptual variables.) At any rate, on several standard implicit tests, the basis of transfer seems perceptual in nature; the more the test recapitulates the perceptual processing during learning (or training), the greater is transfer or priming.

On the other hand, the basis of transfer on most explicit memory tests (and some implicit tests) seems conceptual or semantic in nature. Matching or mismatching the meaning of the same nominal event gave rise to many of the experimental results taken as evidence for the encoding specificity hypothesis in explicit memory. One example is the effect of meaningful context on recognition memory: Study of *traffic jam* produces better recognition of the word *jam* in the semantically similar context of *log jam* than in the different context of *raspberry jam* (Light & Carter-Sobell, 1970). The same semantic specificity principle holds in cued recall, too (Roediger & Adelson, 1980).

Returning to the case of implicit memory tests, Tulving and Schacter (1990) have argued that three different neural systems account for the findings to date. A word form perceptual representation system underlies priming on verbal implicit tests, a structural description perceptual system underlies priming for pictures and objects, and a semantic memory system underlies priming on conceptual implicit memory tests such as producing instances to category names, a task more affected by manipulations of meaning than by perceptual variables (Hamman, 1990; Rappold & Hashtroudi, 1991; Srinivas & Roediger, 1990).

In earlier papers (e.g., Roediger & Blaxton, 1987b) we criticized the notion of there being broad distinctions between a small number of memory systems (e.g., episodic and semantic memory), because experimental results were inconsistent with this proposal (Blaxton, 1989). However, with the postulation of additional memory systems, the findings that were problematic for earlier systems theories can now be accommodated. The result is that the theories postulating memory systems and those endorsing a processing viewpoint have moved closer together. From a processing perspective, a memory system may be defined as "whatever neural processes underlie performance on a particular memory task." We agree with Schacter (1990) that the transfer-appropriate processing and the memory systems viewpoints might most fruitfully be considered as providing complementary rather than competing perspectives on task differences at this point in time. In particular, the proponents of memory systems accounts often tie their findings and theorizing closely to what is known about brain anatomy and function. This approach may sometimes illuminate findings and puzzles that seem difficult to understand from a purely behavioral level, as we demonstrate at a later point in the chapter (borrowing from Schacter, 1992).

In the next sections of the chapter, we first briefly review past work indicating striking perceptual specificity in some types of verbal implicit memory tests. Then in the main part of the chapter we consider demonstrations of perceptual specificity on nonverbal tests. In particular, the form of study experience often greatly affects the amount of priming on tests such as naming fragmented pictures. We next consider two classes of exceptions to the forms of specificity that we claim. We consider each in turn and try to reconcile differences in the literature. We cap the chapter with a section summarizing our conclusions and providing a perspective for future research.

SPECIFICITY OF PRIMING ON VERBAL PERCEPTUAL TESTS

Numerous investigators have emphasized that certain forms of learning are affected by specific perceptual characteristics of the learning experience and how well these match perceptual features of the test. Kolers (1975, 1979; see Kolers & Roediger, 1984) was the first to do so through his studies of reading and recognizing passages of text in various orientations. Following his lead, many others have shown effects of perceptual specificity, including Craik (1991), Graf and Ryan (1990), Jacoby (1983), Jacoby, Baker, and Brooks (1989), Kirsner and Dunn (1985), Masson (1989), and Tulving and Schacter (1990), among others. We consider here results from only a few experiments and tests, mostly those done in our lab. Many other experiments could be added to reinforce the points made.

We confine attention in this section to three tests that seem to rely on some form of perceptual operations in the verbal system, or on lexical processes (or the visual word form system). As mentioned previously, word identification, word fragment completion, and word stem completion all seem similarly affected by manipulation of independent variables. This conclusion is supported by reviews of the literature based mostly on cross-experiment comparisons of the three tests, especially as the tests are affected by modality of presentation (Donnelly, 1988; Kirsner et al., 1989). However, some details may differ between the tests, because (for example) much less cross-modal (auditory to visual) priming seems to occur in the word identification test (Jacoby & Dallas, 1981) than in the word fragment completion or word stem completion tests (see Roediger & Blaxton, 1987a, and Graf et al., 1985, respectively). One cannot know if these apparent differences between tests are real unless the tests are evaluated under similar conditions within one experiment.

Rajaram and Roediger (in press) had subjects study blocks of items in one of three conditions prior to receiving an unspecified test. Some items were presented as words that were read, some given as words that were heard, and some were given as pictures. Other items were not studied, to serve as the baseline on the implicit memory tests. (Items were counterbalanced across study conditions over subjects.) Subjects rated each item for its pleasantness on a seven-point scale during its presentation, thereby encouraging meaningful processing. After presentation, subjects were engaged in some distractor tasks before they received one of three implicit memory tests: word fragment completion, word stem completion, or perceptual identification. The same target items and distractors were presented on all tests, and the only changes made between tests were those necessary to create the three types of test. Before each test, subjects were given implicit memory instructions, that is, they were told to complete the task as well as possible by guessing the identity of the words and no mention was made about explicitly remembering items from the earlier phase of the experiment. (Rajaram and Roediger included other study and test conditions in addition to those described here.)

The basic results from the experiment are shown in Table 2.1. The scores represent priming, the difference between proportions of studied and nonstudied items completed in each of the tests. The nonstudied base rate for each test is given in parentheses at the bottom. The results are straightforward: The greatest amount of priming in each test occurred from visual presentations of the words during the study phase, next greatest from auditory presentations, and least from the pictorial presentations. Therefore, the three tests seem to behave similarly as

TABLE 2.1
Performance on Three Implicit Memory Tests as a Function of Study Conditions*

	Type of Test		
Study Conditions	Word Fragment Completion	Word Stem Completion	Perceptual Identification
Word–Visual	.15*	.16*	.10*
Word–Auditory	.06*	.05*	.04
Picture	.04	.01	.03
Nonstudied	(.30)	(.31)	(.43)

Note. The scores reflect priming (studied - nonstudied rates of completion) with the nonstudied base rate for a test given in parentheses at the bottom of each column. An asterisk indicates reliable priming. Results of Rajaram and Roediger (in press). Reprinted by permission of the American Psychological Association.

a function of the relation between surface features of study and test events. Words given visually produced more priming than those presented auditorily, confirming the Kirsner et al. (1989) conclusion that priming on these tests involves both modality-independent and modality-dependent processes. Slightly greater priming occurred from auditory than from pictorial presentations, because auditory presentation of words engages lexical processes partially similar to those used in reading words, whereas encoding of pictures does not require such lexical processing.[2] The critical role of lexical processes in these tests has been emphasized by Weldon (1991), who pointed out that the term *data-driven* used to characterize these tests by Jacoby (1983) and by Roediger and Blaxton (1987b) may be a misnomer. The processes that must overlap to produce good transfer lie at a higher level than implied by the term data-driven process, which often indicates low-level sensory processes.[3] However, the main point to be taken from Table 2.1 is that the three verbal tests are similarly affected by the manipulation of surface variables and, in this sense, seem perceptual in nature (if we include processing of the lexemes or word forms as perceptual).

The word fragment completion task has been studied more systematically in a series of experiments in our laboratory, with the impact of various study manipulations compared under similar conditions. The results from a number of experiments are summarized in Fig. 2.3, which is reprinted from Roediger and Blaxton (1987b). The amount of priming from the various study manipulations on a visual word fragment completion test is shown on the ordinate, ordered from left to right in terms of decreasing similarity between study and test experiences. The greatest priming occurred when the studied word was given visually in the same typography as the fragment on the later test; changing the typography between study and test produced a slight but significant decrease in priming, and changing to an auditory presentation reduced priming further, as already described (see

---

[2]None of the differences between priming from words given auditorily and priming from pictures is statistically significant, although the same trend occurs on each test and in other cross-experiment comparisons. Priming from auditory presentations is lower here than in most other experiments (see Kirsner et al., 1989). Indeed, priming rates are generally lower in this experiment than in others. This may be due to our using relatively familiar (high frequency) concepts, because we had to have pictureable items. Less priming typically occurs for high- than for low-frequency words in priming tasks (Jacoby & Dallas, 1981; MacLeod, 1989; Roediger et al., 1992; Scarborough, Cortese, & Scarborough, 1977; but see Tenpenny & Shoben, 1992).

[3]Another reason the term data-driven was a misnomer can be derived from reflecting on the processes involved in resolving Fig. 2.1. The point made by this figure in textbooks is that higher level (top-down) processes must be used in recognizing such displays. In all likelihood, retention of these procedures produces the long-term perceptual priming effect, not lower level (data-driven) processes. In verbal tests, the processes are likely lexical, or involve the visual word form system (Nelson, Keelean, & Negrao, 1989; Tulving & Schacter, 1990; Weldon, 1991); in nonverbal tests priming may result from processes in a "geon assembly layer" (Biederman & Cooper, 1991) or a structural description system (Tulving & Schacter, 1990). The point is that the processes that are primed are not as low level as is implied by the term *data-driven*.

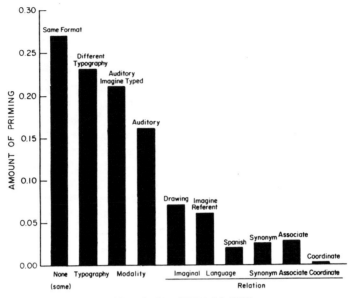

FIG. 2.3. Format of presentation affects perceptual priming. Priming
on the word fragment completion test declines with decreasing similarity between perceptual features encoded during study and those
used in word fragment completion. The data in the figure are drawn
from several reports. Roediger and Blaxton (1987a, Experiment 1) provided data for columns 2, 3, and 4 from the left. The data for the fifth
column came from Weldon and Roediger (1987, Experiment 1); those
for the sixth and seventh columns from Durgunoğlu and Roediger
(1987); and data for the last three columns from Roediger and Challis
(1992, Experiment 1). Data in the first column represent a composite
score across the experiments. From Roediger and Blaxton (1987b).
From Roediger and Craik (1989). Reproduced by permission of Lawrence Erlbaum Associates.

columns 1, 2, and 4 from the left in the figure). Interestingly, if people were
given an auditory presentation and instructed to form an image of what the word
would look like when typed, priming was boosted (see column 3). Showing
people a picture produced a small amount of priming (column 5), but providing
the item in a different language to bilinguals did not (column 7). However, if the
word were given in the second language and subjects were told to imagine the
referent of the word, then priming was enhanced almost to the level of prior
study of pictures (column 6). Finally, presentation of synonyms, associates, and
category coordinates of target words produced little or no priming on the tests, as
can be seen in the three rightmost columns of Fig. 2.3.

Two small provisos should be added to the presentation of Fig. 2.3. First, the data came from several different experiments employing different subjects, materials, and designs, so no strict claim can be made about comparability. This point is ameliorated somewhat by the fact that all the experiments were conducted using the same general procedures within the same lab and the priming score takes overall base rate differences among experiments into account. Second, some of the data have not been replicated yet in other experiments so, for example, the comparability between the amount of priming from drawings and from forming images to words in the bilingual experiment might be treated with caution pending further research. Nonetheless, the data in Fig. 2.3 lead to the conclusion that primed word fragment completion is quite sensitive to the type of processing encouraged by the format of the priming event. The regular drop revealed in Fig. 2.3 represents a kind of generalization decrement, where the relevant dimension is similarity of perceptual processing between study and test.

A more serious problem with the results portrayed in Fig. 2.3 is that there is no good method to determine similarity of procedures between study and test, a priori. In studies of stimulus generalization in classical and operant conditioning, the relation between the stimuli used in training and testing can be indexed by physical measures (e.g., wavelength for light or frequency for tones). However, no similar physical metric exists for indexing similarity of processes or similarity of information in more complex situations. Indeed, Medin (1989) has argued that similarity is poorly defined in many applications and is often used in a rather post hoc fashion. Construction of Fig. 2.3 was attempted after the data were in hand and so the problem of defining similarity independently of the amount of priming produced still exists as a problem for future research. Nonetheless, the dimension underlying the abscissa in Fig. 2.3 seems to capture some expression of similarity between study experiences to testing on a fragmented word form.

One aspect of Fig. 2.3. seems ironic in 1993, but did not when the figure was first created in the mid-1980s. It is the leftmost column, labeled *Same*, indicating our belief (Roediger & Blaxton, 1987b) that maximal priming on the word fragment completion test would occur when an intact stimulus (the word *elephant*) was studied and then the fragment in the same typography was provided at test (e__e__h__nt). We never stopped to ask if there were priming conditions that, according to the principle of transfer-appropriate processing, should cause greater priming than studying the intact word. There are. Gardiner, Dawson, and Sutton (1989) found conditions that enhanced priming above the "Same" condition. They had subjects either generate (aloud) words from a conceptual and perceptual clue during study, such as *single unmarried man*—B___E_OR, or read the intact word (BACHELOR) following the phrase. In the later word fragment completion test people were given the same fragment (now out of context). The results showed that greater priming occurred from prior generation of the target from the fragment than from reading the word intact, .41 priming in the former case to .28 in the latter. This makes perfect sense according to the principle of transfer-appropriate processing: The procedures involved in naming a fragmented word during the study phase, relative to those used in reading its intact version, transfer better to the fragment completion test. Interestingly, Gardiner et al. (1989) showed that this enhanced priming was highly specific to solving the exact fragment at both study and test. If one letter were added or subtracted from the fragment at test, then priming was at about the same level as in the Read condition (a mean of .31 priming). Hayman and Tulving (1989) provided similar evidence for specificity of priming on the word fragment completion test.

The evidence we have reviewed here indicates specificity of processing on priming in three (visual) verbal implicit memory tests. However, we would be remiss if we left the impression that the results on this point are entirely consistent, because they are not. Although radical shifts in form of presentation between study and test (auditory to visual word form, picture to visual word form) produce consistent differences in priming, changing features within the written mode produce inconsistent effects. The results in Fig. 2.3, taken from Roediger and Blaxton (1987a), showed that more priming occurred when a studied word and test fragment appeared in the same typography (relative to different typographies). Jacoby and Hayman (1987) and Masson (1986), among others, have reported similar findings. However, exceptions also appear in the literature. In the experiment by Rajaram and Roediger (in press; see Table 2.1), a manipulation of typography was included in the visual study conditions for the three tests we examined. In none of the three cases did similar typographies at study and test reliably enhance priming, relative to the case when typographies were different. (Data are combined across this dimension in the top row of Table 2.1.) It is unclear when manipulation of surface features between study and test for visually presented words will affect priming. Graf and Ryan (1990) found that such surface manipulations affected priming only when subjects' attention was carefully focused on the surface form of the words, which was not the case in the Rajaram and Roediger experiment. This problem, too, represents a challenge for future research. At present, much evidence in (visual) verbal implicit memory tasks indicates that priming depends on similarity of processing between the form of the studied event and the visual cue given at test in word identification, word fragment completion, and word stem completion tests, although there are some exceptions. We turn now to consider specificity of priming on nonverbal tests.

SPECIFICITY OF PERCEPTUAL PRIMING IN NONVERBAL TESTS

Most tasks used to study implicit memory have been verbal in nature, but recently a number of investigators have begun to examine priming on nonverbal tests. Priming has been observed in tasks (a) requiring the naming of pictures (Durso & Johnson, 1979), (b) requiring the identification of degraded pictures (e.g., Warrington & Weiskrantz, 1968), (c) requiring the identification of briefly presented pictures (e.g., Warren & Morton, 1982), and (d) requiring a decision about whether or not a given object is "structurally possible" (Schacter, Cooper & Delaney, 1990), among others.

These same tasks that are now included under the rubric of implicit memory tests have, of course, been used for years to study processes involved in perceptual learning and recognition per se (e.g., Gollin, 1960; Leeper, 1935), a practice that continues to the present day (Biederman & Cooper, 1991a). Studies of perceptual priming have revealed both striking examples of specific effects and cases of generalized transfer. In this section we consider cases of specific transfer effects and turn to examples of general transfer in a later section, where we also try to rationalize the two sets of findings.

One example of specificity in both nonverbal and verbal perceptual priming comes from Weldon and Roediger (1987, Experiment 4). They presented subjects with a long series of pictures and words and then tested different groups of subjects on one of two implicit tests. One group was given word fragments and told to guess the word that would complete the fragment; the other group was given fragmented pictures such as those in Fig. 2.2 and told to guess their identity. The results are shown in Fig. 2.4, where specificity of priming is clearly evident. Words produced considerable priming on the word fragment completion test, but small effects on the picture fragment naming test. On the other hand, pictures produced considerable priming on the picture fragment naming test, but little priming on the word fragment completion test. This pattern is similar to results of Durso and Johnson (1979; see too Durso & O'Sullivan, 1983), among others. Obviously, in these tasks the processes involved in studying pictures do not transfer well to those involved in completing fragmented words, whereas those involved in studying words do not recapitulate those involved in naming fragmented pictures.

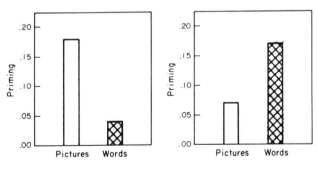

FIG. 2.4.   Results of Weldon and Roediger (1987, Experiment 4). On two fragment completion tests, prior study of items that engaged the same perceptual operations as required in the test produced considerable priming, but prior study of the same concept in the alternate form produced little priming.

Some cross-form priming (words to picture fragments, pictures to word fragments) is also evident in Fig. 2.4, although it was only significant in the picture to word fragment case (also, see Table 2.1). One interpretation is that priming from pictures on the word fragment completion test reflects covert labeling of the pictures during study, but experiments designed to test this hypothesis failed to confirm it (see Roediger & Weldon, 1987). A second interpretation is that the fragment naming tests are sensitive to conceptual as well as perceptual factors, albeit at some low level (Weldon, 1991). In order to test this idea, Weldon, Roediger, and Beitel (in preparation) conducted another experiment to determine if the amount of priming could be boosted in the cross-form case by spaced repetition of items. Spaced repetition has a large effect on performance on conceptually driven episodic tests such as free recall and recognition, so examination of this variable on the priming tests should prove informative (see Roediger & Challis, 1992). In this experiment, subjects studied a long list of words and pictures that instantiated one of five conditions: (a) words presented once, (b) pictures presented once, (c) words presented twice, (d) pictures presented twice, or (e) a word presented once and the corresponding picture presented once. (In this last condition, items were counterbalanced so that half the time the word appeared first and half the time the picture was given first.) Finally, another group of items was not studied, but served as a baseline against which to measure priming. Items were rotated through conditions over subjects, so that all items contributed equally to means in each condition. The lag between items in the three repetition conditions was seven to nine other items.

After studying the items, subjects took one of several different tests, three of which are of present interest. (Study conditions were manipulated within-subjects, test conditions between subjects.) One group received an episodic recognition test in which they were to select previously studied words and pictures from lures; subjects were given only words at test, but told to judge them *old* if they corresponded either to a studied word or to the name of a studied picture. The recognition test was included to show that conceptual factors were at work in these study conditions—pictures should be recognized better than words even on a word recognition test (see Madigan, 1983), and repetition should also improve recognition performance. The other two tests were word fragment completion and picture fragment naming, where some items corresponded to studied items and some to new items. The question at issue was whether the conceptual factors thought to be at work in this situation, particularly repetition of an item in the cross-form mode, would have an effect on these tests. (Repetition effects of an item in the same mode—word-word or picture-picture—could arise from either perceptual or conceptual analyses, so the cross-form condition is of greater interest.) If cross-form repetition effects occurred, then the fragment completion or fragment naming tests would be seen to be partly conceptually driven (contrary to the claims of Roediger et al., 1989, and Tulving & Schacter, 1990).

The results are shown in Table 2.2, with study condition represented in the

TABLE 2.2
Performance as a Function of Study Condition on One Explicit Memory Test (Episodic
Recognition of Words) and Two Implicit Memory Tests Believed to Be Largely Perceptual in
Nature (Word Fragment Completion and Picture Fragment Naming)

	Type of Test		
Study Conditions	Episodic Recognition	Picture Fragment Naming	Word Fragment Completion
Word	.40	-.01	.13*
Picture	.59	.13*	.05
Word + Word	.50	-.02	.08*
Word + Picture	.68	.12*	.13*
Picture + Picture	.70	.15*	-.03
Nonstudied	(.11)	(.20)	(.29)

Note. Recognition scores are hits minus false alarms (in parentheses at the bottom); scores on the other tests are priming (studied - nonstudied proportions, with the latter provided at the bottom). An asterisk indicates reliable priming. Results of Weldon, Roediger, and Beitel (in preparation).

rows and three tests in the columns. The recognition scores (hits − false alarms) in the left column show that (a) pictures were better recognized than words, and (b) repeated items were better recognized than items presented once. These results replicate past findings, but are important here because they show that conceptual factors are operating in this situation. The picture superiority effect may be credited to pictures being encoded more quickly or richly in terms of meaning than are words (e.g., Nelson, 1979). The cross-form repetition effect indicates that information from two different surface representations aided recognition of the concept.

The main interest is whether these conceptual factors affected the word fragment completion and picture fragment naming tests. The answer is no. The relevant data are in the second and third columns of Table 2.2, which represent priming from the various study conditions relative to the nonstudied baseline given at the bottom of the table in parentheses.

In the picture fragment naming test there was no priming from words presented either once or twice. Similarly, repetition had no effect on the amount of priming, whether in the form of two pictures being presented or a picture and a word. Single presentation of a picture produced priming, and the other manipulations had no additional effect whatsoever. Similarly, in the word fragment completion test there was little evidence of priming from prior study of pictures, whether presented once or twice. In addition, presentation of a word twice did not enhance priming relative to presenting it once (although see Greene, 1990, and Roediger & Challis, 1992, for different outcomes). Finally, presenting a picture in addition to a word (the picture's name) did not produce more priming than just presenting the word, unlike the case in episodic recognition. This last

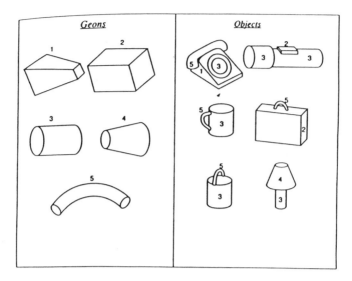

FIG. 2.5. Component parts of objects (geons) that are used in identifying the objects, according to Biederman's (1987) recognition-by-components theory. From Biederman (1990). Reproduced by permission of MIT Press.

finding confirms a result of Roediger and Challis (1992), who found no influence on word fragment completion of following a target word (such as *elephant*) with a synonym (*pachyderm*), associate (*tusk*), or category coordinate (*hippopotamus*). Word fragment completion seems largely insensitive to conceptual repetition (although see Smith, 1991, for an exception).

The previous experiments have shown priming from study of pictures to later naming of fragmented pictures. However, as we noted earlier, the greatest facilitation on the naming of fragmented pictures should be found from prior study of the fragmented pictures themselves rather than the intact versions of the fragmented pictures. The remainder of the experiments reported in this section formed part of a doctoral dissertation by Srinivas (1991) and were motivated in part to test Biederman's (1987) recognition-by-components theory of object recognition in perceptual priming (see Srinivas, in press). They are included here because they show highly specific transfer effects between different fragmented versions of the same pictures.

According to the recognition-by-components theory of object recognition, people identify objects through component parts that are simple geometric primitive volumes (*geons* in Biederman's term); see Fig. 2.5 for an example of the geons that can be assembled to form several objects). Priming is a result of enhanced facility in recapturing the geons that compose the object. Therefore, as long as the intact studied pictures allow recovery of the same geons as the tested

Butterfly

FIG. 2.6. A sample of the pictures, recoverable fragments, and nonrecoverable fragments used by Srinivas (1991).

Butterfly

Recoverable

Butterfly

Nonrecoverable

fragments, maximal priming should occur. If the studied items do not allow access to the same geons as the tested fragments (such as study of words or different exemplars of the same picture), priming should be reduced. There is evidence supporting some of these predictions, as reviewed here and in Biederman and Cooper (1991a). However, the recognition-by-components theory also predicts that as long as two different primes (e.g., intact pictures or fragmented pictures) permit recovery of the same geons, they should produce equivalent priming on later naming of fragmented pictures. This basic prediction was tested by Srinivas (1991, Experiment 2).

In this experiment, two different fragmented versions were constructed for each complete picture. One of the fragmented versions was created so that it would allow access to most of the geons present in the complete picture. In Biederman's terminology, this would be called a *recoverable* fragment (see Fig. 2.6 for an example). The other fragmented version was created so that it would allow access to a misleading set of components that did not exist in the complete picture (in Biederman's terms, these are *nonrecoverable* fragments). These two fragment types were then normed for their recoverability using a criterion specified by Biederman (1987).

In the study phase of the experiment, subjects saw the pictures in one of three conditions—intact pictures, recoverable fragments, or nonrecoverable fragments. In each case, subjects were provided with the name of either the intact picture or the fragment, so that items could be identified in all three conditions. This study phase was followed by a test phase where subjects were required to identify brief presentations of recoverable and nonrecoverable items. Some of the fragments had been studied earlier, and others had not. Performance on the nonstudied items provided the baseline measure for priming.

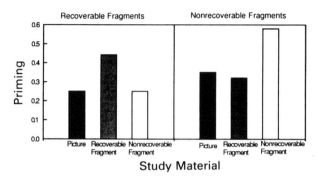

FIG. 2.7. Results from Srinivas (1991, Experiment 2). If subjects had seen the relevant picture fragments (and their names) during the study phase, greater priming occurred during the test on the same fragments, relative to studying intact pictures (and names) or the other type of fragments (and names).

Figure 2.7 shows priming on the naming of recoverable and nonrecoverable fragments as a function of whether the items were presented at study as pictures, recoverable fragments, or nonrecoverable fragments. The results show the greatest facilitation on later naming of fragments when the same fragment was presented at study. When either the intact picture or a different fragment was presented at study, priming dropped to about half the level. These data indicate that priming is mediated by a match in perceptual processes used in identifying the pictorial forms during study and test. However, these results do not support the idea that priming is mediated by an abstract representation of the common geons between study and test pictures, although such processes may be partly responsible for priming. Note that Srinivas' (1991) results in Fig. 2.7 provide a similar demonstration to those of Gardiner et al. (1989) with words: Priming on a fragment naming task is greater from the prior experience of deciphering the relevant fragmented form of a studied event (picture or word) than from examining the completed form during study.

Taken together, the results in this section show that nonverbal perceptual priming can be greatly affected by the specific match of perceptual features between study and test. However, in the next two sections we consider exceptions to our claims of specificity in nonverbal perceptual priming.

EXCEPTIONS TO SPECIFICITY OF PRIMING

In this and the next section we consider two classes of exception to our claims that perceptual priming shows highly specific transfer of the perceptual operations between study and test. The first class of exception, considered in this section, comes in the form of research reports showing results apparently inconsistent with the foregoing claims.

Brown, Neblett, Jones, and Mitchell (1991) used speed of naming pictures as an implicit memory test and measured transfer from prior study of words or pictures (both of which were named during the study phase). In previous work, they had found that picture naming showed robust priming effects that persisted for a week (Mitchell & Brown, 1988). The interesting new finding to emerge from several experiments was that pictures only produced greater priming than did words on picture naming when the pictures and words were mixed together during a prior exposure phase. When a between-subjects design was used, Brown et al. (1991) reported just as much priming from words as from pictures. They pointed out that most findings taken as support for transfer-appropriate processing (e.g., Durso & Johnson, 1979; Weldon & Roediger, 1987) had used within-subjects presentation of material prior to the implicit memory test. Although Brown et al. (1991) offered no explanation as to why the type of design should so greatly affect amount of priming in the cross-form (words to picture naming) case, they did point out that manipulation of variables within or between subjects often affects performance in cognitive tasks (e.g., Begg & Snider, 1987; McDaniel & Einstein, 1986; Poulton, 1982).

The Brown et al. (1991) findings are of present interest because they seem to reveal a case where transfer is general, not specific: Prior study of words generalized to a picture naming implicit test as well as did prior naming of pictures, as long as only one type of material was exposed in the study phase. Besides the nature of the design, there were at least two other differences between the research of Brown et al. (1991) and the work reported here. One was in the choice of the dependent measure; in our research subjects named fragmented pictures and proportion correct was the measure, whereas in theirs subjects named intact pictures and reaction time was measured. The type of test material (intact or fragmented pictures) was the second difference. The original fragments used by Weldon and Roediger (1987) were quite difficult ones (see Fig. 2.2) that would be considered nonrecoverable fragments in Biederman's (1987) terms. Brown et al. (1991, p. 522) suggested that word fragment completion "may be more data-driven (perceptual)" than picture naming. By extension, picture fragment naming may be more perceptual than naming of intact pictures.

In order to evaluate this idea, Srinivas (1991, Experiment 1) examined the effects of prior study of pictures or words (between subjects) on a picture fragment naming task using both recoverable and nonrecoverable fragments. The idea was to see if greater specificity of priming would be found with the harder nonrecoverable fragments (more like Weldon and Roediger's materials) than with the easier recoverable fragments (more like the Brown et al. materials).

Two groups of subjects in Srinivas' (1991) experiment saw either a set of pictures or a set of words (the names of the pictures) prior to taking an implicit picture fragment naming test. One other group was also included, in an attempt to replicate another problematic finding in the literature. This group generated words from conceptual clues. Hirshman, Snodgrass, Mindes, and Feenan (1990) reported evidence that subjects who generated words to conceptual clues showed more priming on a version of a picture fragment naming task than did subjects who simply read the words. Unfortunately, they did not include picture priming conditions within these same experiments, so it is unclear whether the priming from generated words was of the same magnitude as from pictures. The present design permits a direct comparison of priming for subjects who studied words, generated words, or studied pictures. In addition, the picture priming task used by Hirshman et al. (1990; see too Snodgrass & Feenan, 1990) involved exposure of successive fragments that contained increasing amounts of information, with the dependent measure being the number of such fragments shown prior to naming the fragment. This procedure is in contrast to our typical procedure of giving subjects a single data-limited display that they must attempt to name. Schacter, Delaney, and Merikle (1990) argued that the procedure involving the ascending method of limits may invite explicit retrieval and hence reveal conceptual processing. Therefore, we attempted to replicate their findings with our test procedures.

In short, Srinivas (1991, Experiment 1) exposed different groups of subjects to words or pictures, or had them generate the words from conceptual clues. Later, subjects received a picture fragment naming test that included both recoverable and nonrecoverable fragments. Srinivas expected to replicate past findings of sharp perceptual specificity with the nonrecoverable fragments, but to show more general transfer from words and generated words with the easier recoverable fragments (more like test items used by Brown et al., 1991, and by Hirshman et al., 1990). The results are shown in Table 2.3. Pictures produced considerable priming on both types of fragments given at test, whereas words produced small priming effects. Generating words from conceptual clues did not enhance priming on the picture fragment naming test relative to reading the word out of context; indeed, the slight trend was in the opposite direction. Despite the

TABLE 2.3
Priming on Two Types of Picture Fragments as a Function of Three Study Conditions

	Fragment Type	
Study Condition	Recoverable	Nonrecoverable
Pictures	.29*	.26*
Generated Words	.03	.02
Words	.05	.04
Nonstudied	(.37)	(.28)

Note. Scores are priming, the difference between studied and nonstudied proportions. Nonstudied baserates are given in parentheses at the bottom. An asterisk indicates significant priming. Results from Srinivas (1991, Experiment 1).

fact that type of material was manipulated between subjects, Srinivas replicated earlier findings of Weldon and Roediger (1987) and Weldon et al. (in preparation) by showing, at best, only small priming effects from prior study of words on picture fragment naming.

Srinivas (1991) failed to replicate either the general transfer reported by Brown et al. (1991) from words to pictures or the conceptual priming effect shown by Hirshman et al. (1990). Of course, we cannot say for certain why their outcomes did not occur. Obviously, the results in Table 2.3 provide no evidence for the notion that ease of recovery of the object from the fragment plays a major role, because the same pattern of results was obtained for both recoverable and nonrecoverable fragments. Another possibility is that subtle differences among implicit memory tests can have profound differences in performance. Naming intact pictures may differ considerably from trying to name degraded pictures; also, in the former case the dependent measure is the latency to respond and in the latter it is the probability of correctly naming the picture. Similarly, trying to name pictures from successive fragments may differ from getting one shot at the task, as in our procedure. Both Brown et al. (1991) and Schacter, Delaney, and Merikle (1990) have suggested that task differences such as these may underlie some of the apparent inconsistencies across experiments in the literature, and we concur for lack of a more compelling alternative. At this point, we need experiments directly comparing several nonverbal implicit tests under the same conditions, just as Rajaram and Roediger (in press) and Roediger, Weldon, Stadler, and Riegler (1992) have done with verbal implicit tests that seem perceptual in nature. At the present time, we are persuaded that the implicit test of providing subjects with single picture fragments out of context reveals the pattern of results that we have referred to as perceptual (or data-driven) priming. Other tasks such as picture naming may not reveal this pattern.

GENERALITY OF PRIMING: SIZE, REFLECTION, LOCATION

In this section we review evidence showing generality of nonverbal priming across dimensions that we have not yet considered. These include the size of objects, their reflection and rotation in space, and their location in space. In all cases, as much priming is observed when these dimensions mismatch between study and test as when they match. We review the evidence briefly and then try to account for when specific and nonspecific patterns of transfer will occur.

Biederman and Cooper (1992) showed that varying the size of the distal stimulus between study and test does not affect priming on a picture naming task. That is, the match or mismatch in size of a test object (small or large) to a studied object seen earlier (small or large) had no effect on how quickly the test picture could be named. Just as much priming occurred when the sizes mismatched between study and test as when they matched. Similar results were reported by Cooper, Schacter, Ballesteros, and Moore (1992) on an object decision task in which subjects were required to decide whether a given object could exist in a three-dimensional world. (Interestingly, in both sets of experiments the manipulations of size had robust effects on recognition memory.) Priming also does not appear to be affected by variations in the left-right orientation of the object between study and test. Thus, as much priming is obtained on a picture naming task (Biederman & Cooper, 1991b) or an object decision task (Cooper et al., 1992) when the object is presented in the same left-right orientation at study and test as when one orientation is presented at study and the reverse orientation is given at test.

The effects of rotating objects in depth on priming have not been consistent. Bartram (1974) found some evidence for specificity in priming, so that pictures that were repeated in the same view across eight blocks of practice trials yielded shorter naming times and greater practice effects than pictures that were repeated in different views. On the other hand, Biederman (1987, p. 141) "failed to obtain any effect of variation in viewing angle" in four experiments with colored slides. Priming was apparently not affected by changes in viewpoint between study and test. Biederman and Gerhardstein (1992) also found no effect of variation in viewing angle on priming, as long as the different angles did not obscure object parts or geons.

What happens when viewing angles do obscure different object parts, or show different parts of the same object? Will this stronger manipulation of visual angle affect priming? Srinivas (1991, Experiment 3) explored the effects of varying the viewing angles between study and test when different object parts appeared in the viewpoints. In this experiment, she selected one viewpoint that was a typical viewing angle for the object (the "usual" view), and another was that was an atypical viewing angle (the "unusual" view; see Fig. 2.8 for an example). Subjects studied either the usual or the unusual view of the object, and were then asked to name brief presentations of the same objects that were either in the same view or in a different view. This resulted in four study-test conditions: (a) usual view at study and usual view at test (same view), (b) unusual view at study and unusual view at test (same view), (c) usual view at study and unusual view at test (different view), and (d) unusual view at study and usual view at test (different view).

The results are presented in Table 2.4, where the amount of priming is given relative to the nonstudied baseline in parentheses at the bottom of the table. In general, greater priming was obtained when the same viewing angle was maintained between study and test than when different viewing angles were presented between study and test. However, the decrement in priming from switching viewing angles was small when subjects studied the unusual view and were then transferred to the usual view, as seen in the left column of Table 2.4. This outcome indicates that subjects were somehow reconstructing the usual view

FIG. 2.8. Usual and unusual views of objects used in Srinivas (1991,
Experiment 3). The usual view is at the bottom.

TABLE 2.4
Priming From Seeing the Same View or Different Views of an Object at Study and Test When
the Objects Are Viewed From Either Usual or Unusual Perspectives

	Test Perspective	
Study / Test Relation	Usual	Unusual
Same view	.15*	.42*
Different view	.12*	.19*
Nonstudied	(.32)	(.29)

Note. An asterisk indicates significant priming. Results from Srinivas (1991, Experiment 4).

from the unusual view of the object during study. On the other hand, much greater priming was obtained from the unusual view than the usual view when the test view was unusual (see the data in the right column). When the change in viewpoints obscures the component parts used in recognizing the objects, perceptual specificity is observed.

Finally, priming also generalizes across different fragments of the same picture, under certain conditions. Biederman and Cooper (1991a) explored the effects of presenting different fragments of the same object, with two different types of fragments. One set of fragments was created by deleting alternate lines and vertices in the picture (see the top of Fig. 2.9 for an example). The other set of fragments was created by deleting alternate convex components (or object parts) in the picture (see the bottom of Fig. 2.9). Priming was measured on a task requiring the naming of these briefly presented fragmented pictures. At test, subjects were presented with a fragment identical to the fragment presented at study (identical condition), or a complement of the studied fragmented image (complementary condition). The results indicated no effect of switching fragments on priming when the fragments were constructed by the deletion of alternate lines and vertices (top of Fig. 2.9). However, a large decrement was obtained in priming for fragments constructed by the deletion of alternate convex components, as in the bottom of Fig. 2.9.

According to Biederman and Cooper (1991a), these results suggest that priming is mediated by an abstract representation that encodes common object parts between study and test objects. When alternate lines or vertices are deleted, study and test fragments still share common parts or components (geons). Hence priming generalizes across identical and complementary conditions. When whole components of the object are deleted, study and test fragments do not share any common parts or components. Hence, specificity in priming from one fragment to another is observed. However, this explanation cannot account for Srinivas' (1991, Experiment 2) results that were discussed earlier. In her experiments, intact pictures (that presumably have all the parts presented in the fragment) were not as effective primes as the fragments themselves. Thus it appears that sim-

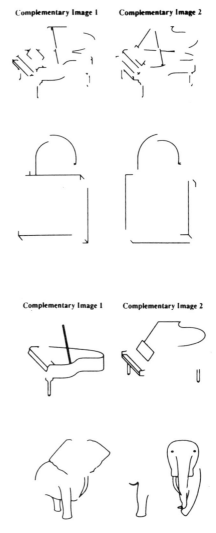

FIG. 2.9. Different types of fragments used by Biederman and Cooper (1991). Those at the top are complementary contour-deleted images; those at the bottom are complementary component-deleted images. Reprinted by permission of Academic Press.

ilarity in perceptual processes in identifying the fragments, other than (or in addition to) those used in recognizing component parts of the objects, is responsible for priming.

How are we to account for these differences in specificity of priming? Why do some manipulations produce such robust changes in priming, whereas others (size, reflection) have no effect? There is no sure answer to these questions. From a purely behavioral perspective, we suggest that the perceptual system is insensitive to features that reflect only accidental properties of objects. From this perspective, features such as size of an object (reflecting viewing distance) and left-right rotation or other simple transformations (reflecting viewing angle) ought not to matter. The perceptual system is not particularly interested in information that only informs us about such accidental data that are typically irrelevant to the task of identifying objects. It would be interesting to test the effects of size and left–right reflection in a priming paradigm when the cue functioned as an important one for recognizing the object. For example, a white ball that is 12 inches wide is unlikely to be a ping-pong ball; similarly, b and d are left-right reversals of the same object. We conjecture that if size and reflection can be made to matter for object recognition (and thereby no longer be accidental properties), they will also affect priming. However, this hypothesis must await further research.

Schacter (1992) suggests that a cognitive neuroscience perspective is also helpful in unraveling these puzzles of when manipulating visual features will produce evidence of perceptual specificity and when not. The cognitive neuroscience perspective interrelates knowledge of responding in neural systems to behavior in analyzing cognitive processes such as memory (see Polster, Nadel, & Schacter, 1991, for a history of such attempts).

For example, Schacter (1992) hypothesizes that regions of the inferior temporal cortex (IT) play a major role in computing the form and structure of visual objects (the evidence is reviewed by Plaut & Farah, 1990). If so, then predictions about the factors that affect priming may be made based on known properties of the underlying neural structures, as discovered through studies of brain-damaged patients, lesion studies in other primates, or even single-cell recordings in lower animals.

Studies using single-cell recording techniques have shown that cells in IT are little affected by changes in the size of objects on the retina; roughly the same neural activity in IT is observed when small or large versions of the same object are presented (Plaut & Farah, 1990). The same holds true when objects are reversed left to right (Schacter, 1992). Therefore, if IT underlies perceptual priming of objects, then size and left-right reversal would be expected to have little impact on priming, which is just what prior research shows for priming in picture naming (Biederman & Cooper, 1991b) and in the object decision task (Cooper et al., 1992). As Schacter (1992) points out, "If a system similar to IT plays an important role in object decision priming and if retinal size is not a relevant property for this system, then the absence of size change effects is no embarrassment to a transfer appropriate processing view . . . [H]ypotheses about the properties of a system that is involved in a particular type of priming can help to guide and refine predictions about the kinds of transfer appropriate processing effects that should be observed" (p. 564).

In short, the cognitive neuroscience perspective is also useful because it makes predictions that can be tested, just as does a more purely behavioral approach. Further, the cognitive neuroscience perspective may undergird purely behavioral accounts (by laying bare the neural mechanisms of behavior) or may suggest—as Schacter (1992) does—under what circumstances a particular behavioral outcome (such as perceptual specificity) will occur. Of course, at the moment the cognitive neuroscience approach takes us only part way in our understanding of perceptual priming phenomena. We know of no ready account that would explain why Srinivas (1991, Experiment 2) found such striking specificity effects in priming of nonverbal objects. Subjects exposed to either recoverable or nonrecoverable fragments (with the names of the relevant objects) showed more priming when tested on those same fragments, relative to prior study of the intact scene (see Fig. 2.7). Her results showing perceptual specificity in transfer from usual to unusual views of objects (Fig. 2.9 and Table 2.4) provide the same challenge. Finally, the cognitive neuroscience approach thus far does not provide an understanding of why changes in size produce large effects on recognition memory but no effects on priming (although see Biederman & Cooper, 1992, for an interesting hypothesis). These and similar puzzles may be worked out in the future as understanding of the brain proceeds. As Schacter (1990, 1992) points out, the cognitive/behavioral approach (as exemplified in the transfer appropriate processing view and others) and the cognitive neuroscience approach can provide complementary information and each can serve to guide the other.

CONCLUSIONS

This chapter has reviewed considerable evidence showing specificity in perceptual priming. Perceptual priming occurs in both verbal and nonverbal tasks. Strong dissociations are usually found between these two domains: Pictures prime the naming of picture fragments, but have little or no effect on naming of fragmented words that form the names of the relevant pictures. Correspondingly, prior exposure to words primes word fragments but not picture fragments. Specificity of priming is also generally found within both verbal and nonverbal perceptual priming paradigms. However, some perceptual manipulations produce little or no effect on priming. In verbal paradigms, typographic manipulations often have small effects or none at all, unless attention is drawn to the relevant dimension through some orienting task (Graf & Ryan, 1990). In nonverbal tasks, size and mirror reflection of objects have no effect. Following Schacter (1992), we have suggested that these differences may be partly understood through a cognitive neuroscience approach.

ACKNOWLEDGMENTS

Preparation of this chapter was supported by grant 91-0253 from the Air Force Office of Scientific Research. We appreciate the advice of James R. Pomerantz in helping to shape several of our points. The chapter also benefited from comments by Eric Eich, John Gardiner, Peter Graf, Dawn Macauley, Kathleen McDermott,

James Neely, Suparna Rajaram, Lee Ryan, Endel Tulving, and Mary Sue Weldon.

REFERENCES

Baddeley, A. D., & Warrington, E. K. (1970). Amnesia and the distinction between long- and short-term memory. *Journal of Verbal Learning and Verbal Behavior, 9,* 176–189.

Bartram, D. J. (1974). The role of visual and semantic codes in object naming. *Cognitive Psychology, 6,* 325–356.

Bartram, D. J. (1976). Levels of coding in picture-picture comparison tasks. *Memory and Cognition, 4,* 593–602.

Begg, I., & Snider, A. (1987). The generation effect: Evidence for generalized inhibition. *Journal of Experimental Psychology: Learning, Memory and Cognition, 13,* 553–563.

Biederman, I. (1987). Recognition-by-components: A theory of human image understanding. *Psychological Review, 94,* 115–147.

Biederman, I. (1990). Higher level vision. In O. Osherson, S. Kosslyn, & J. Hollenbach (Eds.), *Cognition and action: An invitation to cognitive science* (Vol. 2). Cambridge, MA: MIT Press.

Biederman, I., & Cooper, E. E. (1991a). Priming contour-deleted images: Evidence for intermediate representations in visual object recognition. *Cognitive Psychology, 23,* 393–419.

Biederman, I., & Cooper, E. E. (1991b). Evidence for complete translational and reflectional invariance in visual object priming. *Perception, 20,* 585–593.

Biederman, I., & Cooper, E. E. (1992). Scale invariance in visual object priming. *Journal of Experimental Psychology: Human Perception and Performance, 18,* 121–133.

Biederman, I., & Gerhardstein, P. C. (1992). *Recognizing depth rotated objects: Evidence for 3D viewpoint invariance.* Unpublished manuscript.

Blaxton, T. A. (1989). Investigating dissociations among memory measures: Support for a transfer-appropriate processing framework. *Journal of Experimental Psychology: Learning, Memory, and Cognition, 15,* 657–668.

Brown, A. S., Neblett, D. R., Jones, T. C., & Mitchell, D. B. (1991). Transfer of processing in repetition priming: Some inappropriate findings. *Journal of Experimental Psychology: Learning, Memory, and Cognition, 17,* 514–525.

Cohen, N. J., & Squire, L. R. (1980). Preserved learning and retention of pattern analyzing skill in amnesia: Dissociation of knowing how and knowing that. *Science, 210,* 207–209.

Cooper, L. A., Schacter, D. L., Ballesteros, S., & Moore, C. (1992). Priming and recognition of transformed three dimensional objects: Effects of size and reflectance. *Journal of Experimental Psychology: Learning, Memory and Cognition, 18,* 43–57.

Craik, F. I. M. (1991). On the specificity of procedural memory. In W. Kessen, A. Ortony, & F. I. M. Craik (Eds.), *Memories, thoughts and emotions: Essays in honor of George Mandler.* Hillsdale, NJ: Lawrence Erlbaum Associates.

Donnelly, R. E. (1988). *Priming across modality in implicit memory: Facilitation from auditory presentation to visual test of word-fragment completion.* Unpublished doctoral dissertation, University of Toronto.

Durgunoğlu, A., & Roediger, H. L. (1987). Test differences in accessing bilingual memory. *Journal of Memory and Language, 26,* 377–391.

Durso, F. T., & Johnson, M. K. (1979). Facilitation in naming and categorizing repeated pictures and words. *Journal of Experimental Psychology: Human Learning and Memory, 5,* 449–459.

Durso, F. T., & O'Sullivan, C. S. (1983). Naming and remembering common nouns and pictures. *Journal of Experimental Psychology: Learning, Memory and Cognition, 9,* 497–510.

Gardiner, J. M., Dawson, A. J., & Sutton, E. A. (1989). Specificity and generality of enhanced priming effects for self-generated study items. *American Journal of Psychology, 102,* 295–305.

Gollin, E. S. (1960). Developmental studies of visual recognition of incomplete objects. *Perceptual and Motor Skills, 11*, 289–298.

Graf, P., & Ryan, L. (1990). Transfer-appropriate processing for implicit and explicit memory. *Journal of Experimental Psychology: Learning, Memory, and Cognition, 16*, 978–992.

Graf, P., & Schacter, D. L. (1985). Implicit and explicit memory for new associations in normal and amnesic subjects. *Journal of Experimental Psychology: Learning, Memory, and Cognition, 11*, 501–518.

Graf, P., Shimamura, A. P., & Squire, L. R. (1985). Priming across modalities and priming across category levels: Extending the domain of preserved function in amnesia. *Journal of Experimental Psychology: Learning, Memory, and Cognition, 11*, 385–395.

Graf, P., Squire, L. R., & Mandler, G. (1984). The information that amnesic patients do not forget. *Journal of Experimental Psychology: Learning, Memory, and Cognition, 10*, 164–178.

Greene, R. L. (1990). Spacing effects on implicit memory tests. *Journal of Experimental Psychology: Learning, Memory, and Cognition, 16*, 1004–1011.

Hamann, S. (1990). Levels of processing effects in conceptually driven implicit tests. *Journal of Experimental Psychology: Learning, Memory, and Cognition, 16*, 970–977.

Hayman, C. A. G., & Tulving, E. (1989). Is priming in fragment completion based on a "traceless" memory system? *Journal of Experimental Psychology: Learning, Memory and Cognition, 15*, 941–956.

Hirshman, E., Snodgrass, J. G., Mindes, J., & Feenan, K. (1990). Conceptual priming in fragment completion. *Journal of Experimental Psychology: Learning, Memory and Cognition, 16*, 634–647.

Jacoby, L. L. (1983). Remembering the data: Analyzing the interactive processes in reading. *Journal of Verbal Learning and Verbal Behavior, 22*, 485–508.

Jacoby, L. L. (1991). A process dissociation framework: Separating automatic from intentional uses of memory. *Journal of Memory and Language, 30*, 513–541.

Jacoby, L. L., Baker, J. G., & Brooks, L. R. (1989). Episodic effects on picture identification: Implications for theories of concept learning and theories of memory. *Journal of Experimental Psychology: General, 110*, 306–340.

Jacoby, L. L., & Dallas, M. (1981). On the relationship between autobiographical memory and perceptual learning. *Journal of Experimental Psychology: General, 110*, 306–340.

Jacoby, L. L., & Hayman, C. A. G. (1987). Specific visual transfer in word identification. *Journal of Experimental Psychology: Learning, Memory, and Cognition, 13*, 456–463.

James, W. (1890). *Principles of psychology*. New York: Holt.

Kirsner, K., & Dunn, J. C. (1985). The perceptual record: A common factor in repetition priming and attribute retention. In M. I. Posner & O. S. M. Marin (Eds.), *Mechanisms of attention: Attention and performance, XI* (pp. 547–566). Hillsdale, NJ: Lawrence Erlbaum Associates.

Kirsner, K., Dunn, J. C., & Standen, P. (1989). Domain-specific resources in word recognition. In S. Lewandowsky, J. C. Dunn, & K. Kirsner (Eds.), *Implicit memory: Theoretical issues* (pp. 99–122). Hillsdale, NJ: Lawrence Erlbaum Associates.

Kolers, P. A. (1975). Specificity of operations in sentence recognition. *Cognitive Psychology, 7*, 289–306.

Kolers, P. A. (1979). A pattern-analyzing basis of recognition. In Cermak, L. S., & Craik, F. I. M. (Eds.), *Levels of processing in human memory* (pp. 363–386). Hillsdale, NJ: Lawrence Erlbaum Associates.

Kolers, P. A., & Roediger, H. L. (1984). Procedures of mind. *Journal of Verbal Learning and Verbal Behavior, 23*, 425–449.

Leeper, R. (1935). A study of a neglected portion of the field of learning—The development of sensory organization. *Journal of Genetic Psychology, 46*, 41–75.

Light, L. L., & Carter-Sobell, L. (1970). Effects of changed semantic context on recognition memory. *Journal of Verbal Learning and Verbal Behavior, 9*, 1–11.

MacLeod, C. M. (1989). Word context during initial exposure influences degree of priming in word fragment completion. *Journal of Experimental Psychology: Learning, Memory, and Cognition, 15,* 398–406.

Madigan, S. (1983). Picture memory. In J. C. Yuille (Ed.), *Imagery, memory, and cognition: Essays in honor of Allan Paivio* (pp. 65–89). Hillsdale, NJ: Lawrence Erlbaum Associates.

Masson, M. E. J. (1986). Identification of typographically transformed words: Instance-based skill acquisition. *Journal of Experimental Psychology: Learning, Memory, and Cognition, 12,* 479–488.

Masson, M. E. J. (1989). Fluent reprocessing as an implicit expression of memory for experience. In S. Lewandowsky, J. C. Dunn, and K. Kirsner (Eds.), *Implicit memory: Theoretical issues.* (pp. 123–138) Hillsdale, NJ: Lawrence Erlbaum Associates.

McDaniel, M. A., & Einstein, G. O. (1986). Bizarre imagery as an effective memory aid: The importance of distinctiveness. *Journal of Experimental Psychology: Learning, Memory and Cognition, 12,* 54–65.

Medin, D. L. (1989). Concepts and conceptual structure. *American Psychologist, 44,* 1469–1481.

Mitchell, D. B., & Brown, A. S. (1988). Persistent repetition priming in picture naming and its dissociation from recognition memory. *Journal of Experimental Psychology: Learning, Memory and Cognition, 14,* 213–222.

Morris, C. D., Bransford, J. D., & Franks, J. J. (1977). Levels of processing versus transfer appropriate processing. *Journal of Verbal Learning and Verbal Behavior, 16,* 519–533.

Nelson, D. L. (1979). Remembering pictures and words: Appearance, significance, and name. In L. S. Cermak & F. I. M. Craik (Eds.), *Levels of processing in human memory* (pp. 45–76). Hillsdale, NJ: Lawrence Erlbaum Associates.

Nelson, D. L., Keelean, P. D., & Negrao, M. (1989). Word-fragment cueing: The lexical search hypothesis. *Journal of Experimental Psychology: Learning, Memory, and Cognition, 15,* 388–397.

Plaut, D. C., & Farah, M. J. (1990). Visual object representation: Interpreting neurophysiological data within a cognitive neuroscience framework. *Journal of Cognitive Neuroscience, 2,* 320–343.

Polster, M. R., Nadel, L., & Schacter, D. L. (1991). Cognitive neuroscience analyses of memory: A historical perspective. *Journal of Cognitive Neuroscience, 3,* 95–116.

Poulton, E. C. (1982). Influential companions: Effects of one strategy on another in within-subjects designs of cognitive psychology. *Psychological Bulletin, 9,* 673–690.

Rajaram, S., & Roediger, H. L. (in press). Direct comparison of four implicit memory tests. *Journal of Experimental Psychology: Learning, Memory and Cognition.*

Rappold, V. A., & Hashtroudi, S. (1991). Does organization improve priming? *Journal of Experimental Psychology: Learning, Memory and Cognition, 17,* 103–114.

Richardson-Klavehn, A., & Bjork, R. A. (1988). Measures of memory. *Annual Review of Psychology, 39,* 475–543.

Roediger, H. L. (1990a). Implicit memory: A commentary. *Bulletin of the Psychonomic Society, 28,* 373–380.

Roediger, H. L. (1990b). Implicit memory: Retention without remembering. *American Psychologist, 45,* 1043–1056.

Roediger, H. L., & Adelson, B. (1980). Semantic specificity in cued recall. *Memory & Cognition, 8,* 65–74.

Roediger, H. L., & Blaxton, T. A. (1987a). Effects of varying modality, surface features, and retention interval on priming in word fragment completion. *Memory & Cognition, 15,* 379–388.

Roediger, H. L., & Blaxton, T. A. (1987b). Retrieval modes produce dissociations in memory for surface information. In D. Gorfein & R. R. Hoffman (Eds.), *Memory and learning: The Ebbinghaus Centennial Conference.* Hillsdale, NJ: Lawrence Erlbaum Associates.

Roediger, H. L., & Challis, B. H. (1992). Effects of exact repetition and conceptual repetition on free recall and primed word fragment completion. *Journal of Experimental Psychology, 18,* 3–14.

Roediger, H. L., & McDermott, K. L. (in press). Implicit memory in normal human subjects. In H. Spinnler & F. Boller (Eds.), *Handbook of Neuropsychology*, Vol. 8. Amsterdam: Elsevier.

Roediger, H. L., Rajaram, S., & Srinivas, K. (1990). Specifying criteria for postulating memory systems. In A. Diamond (Ed.), *The development and neural basis of higher cognitive function.* (pp. 572–589). New York: New York Academy of Sciences Press.

Roediger, H. L., & Weldon, M. S. (1987). Reversing the picture superiority effect. In M. A. McDaniel & M. Pressley (Eds.), *Imagery and related mnemonic processes: Theories, individual differences, and applications.* (pp. 151–174). New York: Springer Verlag.

Roediger, H. L., Weldon, M. S., & Challis, B. H. (1989). Explaining dissociations between implicit and explicit measures of retention: A processing account. In H. L. Roediger & F. I. M. Craik (Eds.), *Varieties of memory and consciousness: Essays in honour of Endel Tulving.* Hillsdale, NJ: Lawrence Erlbaum Associates.

Roediger, H. L., Weldon, M. S., Stadler, M. A., & Riegler, G. L. (1992). Direct comparison of two implicit memory tests: Word fragment and word stem completion. *Journal of Experimental Psychology: Learning, Memory, and Cognition, 18,* 1251–1269.

Scarborough, D. L., Cortese, C., & Scarborough, H. S. (1977). Frequency and repetition effects in lexical memory, *Journal of Experimental Psychology: Human Perception and Performance, 3,* 1–17.

Schacter, D. L. (1987). Implicit memory: History and current status. *Journal of Experimental Psychology: Learning, Memory and Cognition, 13,* 501–518.

Schacter, D. L. (1990). Perceptual representation systems and implicit memory: Towards a resolution of the multiple memory systems debate. In A. Diamond (Ed.), *The development and neural bases of higher cognitive functions* (pp. 545–578). New York: Annals of the New York Academy of Sciences.

Schacter, D. L. (1992). Understanding implicit memory: A cognitive neuroscience approach. *American Psychologist, 47,* 559–569.

Schacter, D. L., Bowers, J., & Booker, J. (1989). Intention, awareness, and implicit memory: The retrieval intentionality criterion. In S. Lewandowsky, J. C. Dunn, & K. Kirsner (Eds.), *Implicit memory: Theoretical issues* (pp. 47–65). Hillsdale, NJ: Lawrence Erlbaum Associates.

Schacter, D. L., Cooper, L. A., & Delaney, S. M. (1990). Implicit memory for unfamiliar objects depends on access to structural descriptions. *Journal of Experimental Psychology: General, 119,* 5–24.

Schacter, D. L., Delaney, S. M., & Merikle, E. P. (1990). Priming of nonverbal information and the nature of implicit memory. In G. H. Bower (Ed.), *The Psychology of Learning and Motivation,* Vol. 26 (pp. 83–123). New York: Academic Press.

Sherry, D. F., & Schacter, D. L. (1987). The evolution of multiple memory systems. *Psychological Review, 94,* 439–454.

Shimamura, A. P. (1986). Priming effects in amnesia: Evidence for a dissociable memory function. *Quarterly Journal of Experimental Psychology, 38A,* 619–644.

Smith, M. C. (1991). On the recruitment of semantic information for word fragment completion: Evidence from bilingual priming. *Journal of Experimental Psychology: Learning, Memory and Cognition, 17,* 234–244.

Snodgrass, J. G., & Feenan, K. (1990). Priming effects in picture fragment completion: Support for the perceptual closure hypothesis. *Journal of Experimental Psychology: General, 119,* 276–298.

Snodgrass, J. G., & Vanderwart, M. (1980). A standardized set of 260 pictures: Norms of name agreement, image agreement, familiarity and visual complexity. *Journal of Experimental Psychology: Human Learning and Memory, 6,* 174–215.

Squire, L. R. (1987). *Memory and brain.* New York: Oxford University Press.

Squire, L. R., & Zola-Morgan, S. (1991). The medial temporal lobe memory system. *Science, 253,* 1380–1386.

Srinivas, K. (1991). *Specificity of priming in nonverbal tests.* Unpublished doctoral dissertation, Rice University, Houston.

Srinivas, K. (in press). Perceptual specificity in nonverbal priming. *Journal of Experimental Psychology: Learning, Memory and Cognition, 19.*

Srinivas, K., & Roediger, H. L. (1990). Testing the nature of two implicit tests: Dissociations between conceptually-driven and data-driven processes. *Journal of Memory and Language, 28,* 389–412.

Tenpenny, P. L., & Shoben, E. J. (1992). Component processes and the utility of the conceptually-driven/data-driven distinction. *Journal of Experimental Psychology: Learning, Memory and Cognition, 18,* 25–42.

Thorndike, E. L. (1903). *Educational psychology.* New York: Lemcke & Buechner.

Tulving, E. (1972). Episodic and semantic memory. In E. Tulving & W. Donaldson (Eds.), *Organization of memory* (pp. 590–600). New York: Academic Press.

Tulving, E. (1983). *Elements of episodic memory.* New York: Oxford University Press.

Tulving, E., & Schacter, D. L. (1990). Priming and human memory systems. *Science, 247,* 301–306.

Warren, C., & Morton, J. (1982). The effects of priming on picture recognition. *British Journal of Psychology, 73,* 117–129.

Warrington, E. K., & Weiskrantz, L. (1968). New method of testing long-term retention with special reference to amnesic patients. *Nature, 217,* 972–974.

Warrington, E. K., & Weiskrantz, L. (1970). Amnesic syndrome: Consolidation or retrieval? *Nature, 228,* 629–630.

Weldon, M. S. (1991). Mechanisms underlying priming on perceptual tasks. *Journal of Experimental Psychology: Learning, Memory, and Cognition, 17,* 526–541.

Weldon, M. S., & Roediger, H. L. (1987). Altering retrieval demands reverses the picture superiority effect. *Memory & Cognition, 15,* 269–280.

Weldon, M. S., Roediger, H. L., & Beitel, D. (in preparation). *Investigating effects of repeating pictures and words on implicit and explicit memory tests.*

3 Fluent Rereading: An Implicit Indicator of Reading Skill Development

Betty Ann Levy
McMaster University

Although much of the research on implicit memory involves the study of individual words, a parallel literature has evolved in the study of text processing. Paul Kolers' work on memory for messages read in transformed typographies provided the intellectual lead. This chapter traces the development of research that followed Kolers in using transfer measures as a way to explore memorial representations. The studies investigated how prior reading of a message influenced the subsequent reading of that message. In other words, what remained in memory following a reading encounter that facilitated the rereading of that message? The procedure opens a window for exploring the ways in which practice or experiences can influence the development of reading skill.

The main measure used in these transfer studies is rereading time. As with other implicit indicators, rereading provides a transfer measure that requires "the subject to engage in some cognitive or motor activity, when the instructions refer only to the task at hand and do not make reference to the prior event" (Richardson-Klavehn & Bjork, 1988, p. 478). Memory is indicated when rereading performance is influenced by the earlier reading experience. Rereading time, like other implicit measures, shows effects of prior experience even when the reader is unable to recall the prior reading event (Cohen & Squire, 1980; Kolers, 1976).

READING TRANSFORMED TEXT

The psycholinguistic influence during the 1970s led to a strong belief that language processing was best viewed as the search for meaning that was hidden in the language signals. The signals themselves were shells that had to be processed so as to uncover the kernel meaning. After the meaning was understood and the underlying semantic propositions were encoded in memory, the surface shell could be eliminated. Long-term memory stored meaning that was divorced from the surface characteristics of the signals and from the linguistic surface structure that had transported that message (see Kintsch, 1974; Craik & Lockhart, 1972). It was against this backdrop that Kolers presented his startling evidence that memory for typography was quite good over long retention intervals.

Kolers (1975) asked subjects to read aloud a set of sentences that were typed with the letters in either their normal (N) or an inverted (I) orientation, and then to reread them in the inverted orientation. The lag between repetitions varied from 1 to 11 sentences. Other sentences were read only once in inverted script. Thus there were three basic conditions: NI where the first reading was normal but the second was inverted, II where both readings were inverted, and New I where the single reading was inverted. Kolers' interest was in the effect of the first reading on skill in reading the repetition, as indicated by improved reading times for repetitions compared with new sentences. He found that for all repetition lags, the repeated sentences were read faster than the new sentences, indicating that memory for the first reading provided a transfer benefit to the second reading. Importantly, this transfer benefit was larger when the typography was also repeated (II) compared to when it differed on the two readings (NI). These data indicated that memory for typography participated in the rereading benefit.

Kolers studied inverted typescripts because he was interested in the development of pattern recognition processes. He believed that inverted typescript produced unfamiliar graphemic displays for adults, thus confronting them with a pattern recognition problem akin to the problem faced by beginning readers who have little skill in reading normally written displays. He argued that the NI and II conditions in his experiment provided identical semantic information for transfer to rereading, so the additional benefit for the II condition must be due to the earlier experience with the specific inverted letter patterns. There was good retention of the surface characteristics of the sentences, over and above any contributions due to retention of the semantic information. Kolers argued that the message and its medium were represented together, in memory for the procedures required to analyze the printed script. He emphasized the centrality of pattern recognition processes in causing the improved reading speed for repeated sentences.

Kolers' stress on long-term memory for the visual patterns was carried further in two studies demonstrating the specificity of transfer to the exact visual patterns experienced. Kolers and Magee (1978) demonstrated that college students who had practiced reading text in inverted typescript were later able to read new texts in that inverted typescript better than students whose practice had been on reading inverted letters. Thus experience with letter combinations provided more transfer to text reading than reading letters in isolation. Also, reading isolated letters led to more facilitation in a later letter naming task than did prior reading of texts, indicating that text reading did not seem to practice individual "letter recognizers" particularly well. Again the idea was that larger orthographic units are involved in text processing and these larger units form the basis of text reading skill. This point was reinforced by the demonstration that changes in the type font, or in the spacing between letters, for the two readings of an inverted text were sufficient to disrupt the transfer of skill between repetitions (Kolers, Palef & Stelmach, 1980). Again the argument was that gains in rereading speed were mediated by improved pattern recognition and this improvement was based on analyzing visual patterns that were larger than individual letters. These patterns included the script features and the interletter spacings. An important point to be taken from Kolers' work is that transfer was largely centered at the visual pattern recognition level and not at the lexical or semantic levels of analyses. Further, Kolers argued forcefully that these pattern recognition skills can be observed even a year after initial reading and when the reader is unable to remember having seen that text before (Kolers, 1976).

Why then do readers normally appear to retain the message but forget the surface structure and visual characteristics of the print? According to Kolers (1979), skilled readers so automatically decode normal typographies that very little processing of visual details is actually required. Much more attention is paid to figuring out the message. The more extensive semantic processing leads to better retention of the message than of its shell. Kolers (1979) said, "By turning things around a bit to leave the semantic content in its usual form while making the graphemes more opaque, I have achieved the opposite result: Graphemic analysis produced a deeper and richer representation of sentences . . ." (p. 384), and later, "the graphemic is usually lost, not because it is graphemic, but because its acquisition requires little analysis, at least by the skilled reader" (p. 384). Thus Kolers argued that the extensiveness of processing produces explicit memorability. These surprising results and controversial claims spawned several lines of investigation. I next trace results indicating that Kolers' interpretation of the memorability of unusual typography is in question, but I return later to the question of whether truly fluent reading is semantically, not graphemically, based.

Several investigators have offered alternative explanations of the greater transfer to reading transformed script, from having first read that material in transformed rather than normal typography. Masson and Sala (1978) showed that inverted typography affected not only the extensiveness of the graphemic analysis but also the extensiveness of the semantic analysis of sentences. They asked subjects either to read aloud a deck of unrelated sentences, or to read them silently and provide a continuation for each sentence. The sentences in the deck were typed in either normally oriented or inverted script. They found that recognition was better for II than NI repetitions for the reading aloud task, replicating Kolers' findings. However, this typography effect disappeared in the sentence continuation task. Masson and Sala argued that in the sentence continuation task, readers had to thoroughly process the meaning, whether they were reading normal or transformed typography. Consequently the difference in the degree of semantic elaboration during oral reading of transformed versus normal typographies was eliminated in the sentence continuation task. So too was the typography effect!

Masson and Sala also demonstrated that the II superiority over NI was equally large whether the sentences read in the repetition phase were verbatim or paraphrase versions of the original sentences. If the transfer of skill resided with the pattern recognition analysers, then less transfer should occur when the wording was changed between readings. Such changes occurred for paraphrases, where the lexical analyses for the second version was different from that used in the first version. Yet, the typography benefit for II over NI was not lessened when wording changed. The results of Masson and Sala clearly indicated that more than graphemic analyses were altered in reading inverted script (see also Masson, 1984). Graf and Levy (1984) argued that semantic processes carried all of the rereading benefit observed by Kolers. They found that while II transfer was greater than NI transfer, this was equally true whether the texts were verbatim repetitions, were paraphrases, or were verbatim but typed in very different type fonts. Thus the transfer benefit for transformed scripts did not depend on word repetition (paraphrase) or visual feature repetition (typefont). They interpreted the data as offering strong support for semantic involvement, with little evidence that pattern recognition processes were involved in the rereading benefit.

Horton (1985) reported results very consistent with those of Graf and Levy (1984). In a series of studies, Horton asked subjects to read and then reread a set of sentences. During the first reading, sentences could be typed in Normal, Inverted, or Rotated typographies, but on the second reading the sentences appeared only in Inverted or in Rotated orientations. Horton found that transfer to rereading the transformed typographies was greater when a transformed rather than a normal typography had been read on the first reading. However, an important finding was that it didn't matter whether the transformed typographies matched on the two readings. That is, II and RR were not better than IR or RI. It was the act of figuring out the difficult "squiggles" that produced the better transfer, not the pattern similarities themselves. Horton credited transfer to semantic processes. He claimed that graphemic information may be encoded during reading but it was not used, or maybe could not be used, to aid rereading. In a later paper, Horton (1989) demonstrated that graphemic details of transformed text can be explicitly remembered over long intervals (48 h). Horton therefore claimed that, "When either semantic or nonsemantic features or both are usable, subjects show a strong tendency to utilize the semantic features" (p. 290). This work then supports Kolers' claim that surface features of sentences are not discarded from memory once the kernel meaning has been extracted. It also suggests, however, that the rereading transfer observed in the Kolers' studies was not mediated by these perceptual representations. Rather, transformed typographies led to enhanced encoding and use of semantic information.

We might have considered the matter settled except for a paper by Masson (1986), in which he claimed that rereading skill was instance-based and that instance use depended on the reinstatement of surface form information. Masson suggested that the skill gained with practice in reading transformed text may be *general,* in that the skill transfers to new items typed in that typography. Or, the skill may be *specific* to the trained items, with any generalization of skill based on the physical similarity between the trained and any new items. To test for general versus specific transfer, Masson trained subjects to read words written in transformed typography. Importantly, these training words were composed of only 13 letters of the alphabet. Thus subjects' pattern recognition systems were practiced on only a subset of the alphabet in that typography. During testing, three types of words (in transformed script) were used: trained words, new words formed from the 13 trained letters, and new words formed from the untrained letters of the alphabet. Masson found maximal transfer for trained words, less but significant transfer to new words in the practiced letters, but no transfer to new words whose letters had not been experienced in transformed script. He argued that the data supported instance-based transfer because it was maximal to the trained item with some generalization to similar words. There was no general skill in figuring out how to reorient the rotated letters, as indicated by the failure to find transfer to words formed from untrained inverted letters. Masson demonstrated that this pattern of results held after extensive training, and when visual patterns were maintained or changed across repetitions using case manipulations. Importantly, in his final experiment, he found that individual words were reread faster in their trained case, compared with the alternative case. These findings were interpreted as indicating that word memory maintained visual format information in instance-based representations. Masson suggested that rereading benefits were attributable to the use of these word representations, with their graphemic and semantic information. An important implication of this position is that the script repetition effect is dependent on repetition of the trained instances.

These fascinating conclusions have not gone unchallenged. Tardif and Craik (1989) argued that most of Masson's (1986) data could be explained by general skill in learning to handle the trained letters in a particular typography, rather than any word-specific skill. They based this view on the transfer of skill to new words that also used the trained typography and letters. They argued that this transfer is not instance-based, but rather is based on new general skills with the training set. They agreed, however, that the word-specific effects found in Masson's final experiment did suggest instance representations with visual specificity, but these effects were small. Tardif and Craik pointed out that in the Kolers rereading task, transfer could involve effects due to repeated typography, repeated wording, or repeated meaning. Further, the skill with the "strange" typographies could be general or it could be tied to the specific words trained.

Tardif and Craik reported an experiment in which subjects read short paragraphs in normal typography (N), or in one of two transformed forms, A and B. Rereading was tested 7 days later, and always in a transformed typography. The "old" passages could be reread in the same transformed typography as the original (AA, BB), or they could be reread in a different form (BA, AB, NA, NB). A critical innovation was the introduction during rereading of an entirely new typography, C. Thus, old passages could also be reread in an entirely new visual form. Similarly, new passages could be read in the trained typographies (A,B) or in the new typography (C). The important findings during rereading were that old passages were read faster than new passages; old typographies, A and B, were read faster than the new typography, C; but AA and BB were not reliably faster than AB and BA, replicating Horton. These findings indicate that there was transfer of the general skill in reading A and B, but the skill was not specific to rereading a specific passage in a specific typography. Further, the new passages showed as much rereading benefit as the old passages due to the familiar typographies (A,B), compared with the unfamiliar script (C). That is, the typography repetition effect was additive with the effect due to passage repetition, not dependent on passage repetition as would be expected by the instance-based position. Tardif and Craik argued against Masson's instance-based explanation of the Kolers rereading effect.

Where does that leave us? The controversy surrounding the appropriate explanation of Kolers' demonstration continues to rage furiously, and in so doing it produces important new findings. The better retention of messages read in transformed typographies, as indicated by the implicit rereading time measure, is clearly a multifaceted effect. Reading a strange typography leads to enhanced perceptual, lexical, and conceptual processing. All of these can transfer to rereading, and the remaining controversy lies in whether their contributions are additive (as Tardif and Craik suggest) or interdependent (as Masson and Kolers suggest). Although the study of transformed typography tells us how skilled readers adapt to a new perceptual challenge, I would argue that it does not provide a mirror for observing the beginning stages of reading skill development, as Kolers suggested. Adults can bring many sources of knowledge to bear on the new perceptual problem, and they have available more diverse and flexible processing skills than those available to the novice reader. However, the transfer methodology developed by Kolers and others in the pursuit of the script transformation effect has been applied in more natural reading tasks. We next explore that literature for hints about the sources of transfer in rereading.

REREADING NORMAL TEXTS

Kolers originally studied the reading of transformed typographies because he believed that fluent adult readers were so skilled in reading normal typescript that little data-driven processing could be observed during normal reading. In Kolers' view, analysis of the print had become so efficient that attention was focused almost entirely on semantic elaboration. While Kolers argued that skilled graphemic analyses were not sufficiently elaborated to allow explicit retrieval, he did not consider implicit measures as a way to observe the graphemic contribution to normal reading. One reason may have been the powerful influence of top-down reading models in that era.

Is Print Analysis Attenuated During Fluent Reading?

An issue of some interest to reading researchers is how the processes involved in reading change with experience, practice, and knowledge. This question was brought into focus by claims that skilled readers sampled rather than fully read the printed text. The top-down or conceptually driven model of reading (e.g., Goodman, 1970; Smith, 1971, 1973) made strong claims regarding the mechanisms underlying skill development. From this perspective, reading is a psycholinguistic guessing game whereby the cognitive system entertains hypotheses, based on prior text context and on general knowledge about the topic, about the likely message embedded in the text being read. The print is sampled just enough to confirm the semantic hypotheses. The more skilled the reader, the more likely the reader will generate useful hypotheses from a minimal sampling of print. The beginning or slow reader must laboriously plod through the print, leaving little processing resource for the important comprehension aspects of reading. Thus skill results from the use of knowledge and context to circumvent the need to fully analyze the printed display. That is, skill results in attenuation of visual print analyses.

What does recent research tell us about the role of contextual guessing in reading? Guessing is a slow, not a fast, cognitive act. Poor readers are less able to correctly guess words from context than good readers, and yet they are more likely to rely on such guessing during reading (Perfetti & Roth, 1981; Stanovich, 1981). Guessing from context is an unskilled, not a fluent, form of reading. Fluent readers rapidly and automatically analyze the graphemic array, making slower guessing processes unnecessary for skilled reading. This conclusion is supported by eye movement measures that indicate that fixation time and probability of fixation do not differ markedly for contextually predictable and unpredictable words (e.g., McConkie & Zola, 1981, but see also Ehrlich & Rayner, 1981). Even though the cognitive system could easily predict the next word, the eyes continue to process the visual display.

We have reached very similar conclusions based on studies of rereading. An advantage of the repeated readings paradigm is that the researcher knows exactly what the subject's prior experience with that text has been. One can then ask whether knowledge about the text leads to changes in the way the printed display is read. In our earliest studies of rereading (Levy, 1983; Levy & Begin, 1984), we addressed this issue by asking subjects to read 350-word passages as rapidly and accurately as possible. While they were reading, subjects also crossed out any misspelled words they noticed. All spelling errors were single-letter substitutions that changed a word into a nonword, so they were relatively obvious errors. Subjects read and detected misspellings for some texts that they had never seen before, and for others with which they were familiar because they had just read them several times in their error-free form. The question was whether familiarity with the text would lead to top-down reading and sampling the print, compared with the reading of unfamiliar passages. If so, then reading should be faster but with poorer error detection for familiar than for unfamiliar texts. We found that familiar passages were read faster than unfamiliar ones, and yet errors were just as well detected in familiar as in unfamiliar passages. These findings suggested that knowledge did not lead to guessing or sampling the print. The print was more rapidly, but just as thoroughly, read for familiar as for unfamiliar texts.

Was the reading speed benefit for familiar texts localized at the pattern recognition level? A study by Levy, Newell, Snyder, and Timmins (1986) suggested that rereading transfer was more complex than that. Subjects read and crossed out misspellings for four or five readings of the same text. The passage was the same on every reading but the misspelled words changed on each trial. Thus the reader had to continue to thoroughly analyze the print on each reading in order to find the misspelled words. Reading time decreased gracefully across trials, with speed gains of 25–30 sec over the repetitions. Was speed gained by not reading the printed words? No—the nonword errors were as well detected on the fifth as on the first reading. Did readers just scan for nonword errors, thus not fully reading the text for meaning, once they knew the message from prior readings? Again no— spelling errors that were real words (thus passing a lexical access check), but that made the sentence meaning go astray, were actually better detected across reading trials, indicating that readers became even more sensitive to semantic violations as they read more fluently. Nonword errors were better detected than word errors on all trials, suggesting that their detection occurred at a different level of analysis. Levy et al. argued that nonword error detection indicated the presence of perceptual processes during rapid rereading, while word errors, which could only be detected after syntactic or semantic analyses of the sentence, indicated involvement of those levels of analyses during fluent rereading.

The data from these studies suggested that Kolers' transfer paradigm, with rereading time as a measure, could be profitably used to study the effects of experience on reading fluency. The error detection studies suggested that both conceptual and perceptual processes were involved in rereading fluency. Repetition fluency resulted from more efficient processing, not from attenuation of either perceptual or conceptual processing during reading.

What Is Represented in Memory Following Text Reading?

One of the main controversies in the text rereading literature centers on the nature of the memorial representations that mediate transfer across readings. The major point of dispute is whether these representations are at an abstract word level or whether they are representations of the specific text episode. Because most of the early work on implicit transfer from memory involved individual words, much of the theorizing in this domain focused on word-level representations. Jacoby and Dallas (1981) argued that transfer from word reading to a later perceptual task involved specific word encodings because transfer reflected the perceptual characteristics of the prior processing instance. If transfer were mediated by stable abstract word representations, such as logogens or lexical modules (e.g., Morton, 1969), then one prior reading of the word should have little effect on its later perceptibility, and transfer would not reflect the particular perceptual characteristics of that single encounter. Because other chapters in this book discuss this controversy for word processing, I focus instead on how words within texts are represented and how they influence rereading transfer. My discussion focuses on context effects and on the perceptual specificity of rereading benefits.

Oliphant (1983) asked whether word repetition effects were an automatic consequence of a recent encounter with that word. He used a lexical decision task in which letter strings were judged to be words or nonwords. The critical contrasts were between words presented once as lexical decision stimuli, words presented twice as lexical decision stimuli, and words presented once as lexical decision stimuli that had just been read as part of the task instructions or as part of a questionnaire. He found the expected repetition effect within lexical decision, such that decisions were faster for repeated words than for once-presented items. Interestingly, words that had previously been read in the instructions or questionnaire, rather than as lexical decision stimuli, did not show a repetition benefit. These findings led Oliphant to conclude that repetition effects "depend on subjects noticing that some stimuli are repeated, and adopting some (as yet unknown) strategy to facilitate the recognition of repeated items" (p. 402). A recent processing occurrence per se was insufficient to produce a repetition effect.

We know, however, that awareness is not a necessary condition for repetition effects. Cohen and Squire (1980) reported repetition benefits in reading typographically transformed words for amnesic patients who could not remember the words. More recently, Musen, Shimamura, and Squire (1990) reported a text rereading benefit for amnesics who could not explicitly remember those texts. Clearly, the ability to explicitly retrieve and become aware of the repetition is not a necessary condition for implicit remembering. Fortunately, Oliphant's findings are consistent with results reported by Jacoby (1983) in a word repetition study. Jacoby varied the context in which target words were initially encountered. They were read in isolation, or they were read in the context of a semantic associate (e.g., north-south), or they were generated from the semantic associate (e.g., north ————). Jacoby suggested that these manipulations varied the degree of conceptual support offered to the word recognition process. Words read in isolation depended entirely on data-driven or perceptual processes. Words generated from associates were dependent on conceptual processing, because no perceptual "data" were available for processing. Words read in context were processed by both perceptual and conceptual processes.

The results showed an interesting dissociation of effects for memory as measured by explicit and by implicit indicators. A later explicit recognition test indicated that memory was better for words initially processed in a semantic context (i.e., generated or read with an associate). However, a later perceptual identification test led to better identification of words originally read in isolation compared with those read or generated in context. Jacoby argued that explicit remembering relied heavily on conceptual representations, while implicit remembering heavily reflected perceptual representations. He suggested that words read in context required less perceptual processing because of the top-down support offered by the context, resulting in poorer transfer to the later perceptual identification task.

In view of Jacoby's results, an alternative explanation of Oliphant's finding is that words read in task instructions or in a questionnaire, compared with words read singly, were given less perceptual processing because of the contextual support of the surrounding words, leading to loss in the repetition benefit for the later lexical decision task. This position received further support from a study by MacLeod (1989). He had subjects first read short paragraphs or lists of unrelated words and then complete a word fragment completion test, in which some of the fragments were for new words and some were for words repeated from the reading task. Fragment completion was better for repeated than for new words, and there was much more facilitation for words originally read in a word list than for words originally read in short paragraphs, replicating the results of Oliphant and Jacoby. The new and interesting twist in MacLeod's study was that while reading the short paragraphs, subjects crossed out phrases that did not make sense. Half of the target words for the fragment completion task came from these crossed out nonsensical phrases and half came from sensible phrases of the paragraphs. MacLeod found more repetition benefit for words read in the nonsense phrases than for words read in the sensible phrases. It appeared that meaningful context reduced the processing that led to transfer in the fragment completion task. MacLeod concluded that, "As a word moves from being contextually bound in meaningful discourse to being isolated in a list, its probability of priming increases" (p. 398).

These findings are consistent with the top-down view of reading, but they seem inconsistent with Kolers' view that as pattern recognition processes become skilled, they become more efficient but not necessarily abbreviated. Efficiency was gained through the formation of larger pattern recognition units. Automatic processing by these larger units speeded processing, but the patterns were not accessible to conscious retrieval. Efficient pattern processing was the essence of Kolers' view of reading skill. Similarly, our error detection studies suggested that the printed displays of familiar, rapidly read texts were still fully analyzed. How can one reconcile these discrepant findings? Should we go back to the claim that the linguistic shell is not retained in memory once the message has been abstracted? I think not. Levy and Kirsner (1989) first had subjects process target words from unrelated word displays or in the context of 525-word passages. They then reprocessed these target words, along with new words, in a perceptual identification task. Orthogonal with this contextual manipulation, Levy & Kirsner also varied the perceptual features of the words. During initial reading, the words or texts were in elite font, or in script font, or they were presented auditorily, but in the perceptual identification task they were always in elite type font. Thus the perceptual features either matched or differed on the two encounters. The logic was that if the transfer observed from reading to perceptual identification is mediated largely by perceptual processes, then transfer should be reduced when the perceptual features are different, rather than repeated, on the two processing occurrences. Levy and Kirsner found better perceptual identification for old than for new words, but only when the words were first processed in isolation. Text context eliminated transfer, replicating Oliphant (1983). Further, the transfer from isolated word reading to perceptual identification was sensitive to the modality manipulation (the script effect was there but not statistically reliable), indicating that perceptual processes were involved in the transfer.

It was tempting to conclude that words read in context lose their perceptual representations. However, in two further experiments Levy and Kirsner asked subjects to read or listen to these 525-word texts and then to reread those same texts. Again the script or modality were varied on the two encounters as already described. This time the measure was rereading time compared with original reading time. Repeated passages were reread faster than they were read on the first encounter, indicating improved fluency with practice. Importantly, the same perceptual specificity was found in text-to-text rereading transfer as was found for word-to-word transfer in the first experiment. Thus rereading transfer for texts shows the perceptual characteristics taken to indicate the involvement of data-driven processes in the single word studies (see Roediger & Blaxton, 1987). Levy and Kirsner argued that text representations are holistic, retaining information about word and perceptual processing that is embedded in the text's episodic representation. The individual words cannot be taken out of memory for the text and used in isolation. This information can only be used if the text episode itself is recruited during reprocessing. Failure of transfer from text reading to later word identification results from failure of the words to recruit the text's memorial record. The rereading paradigm solves this problem because the original and reprocessing tasks are the same, so that recruitment of the memorial representations occurs, and one then also sees evidence of perceptual contributions to rereading. This, Levy and Kirsner believed, was consistent with Kolers' original views of transfer of skill; the medium and its message form a processing package.

Alas, all was not to be so straightforward! Carr, Brown, and Charalambous (1989) presented contradictory evidence. They asked subjects to read aloud short paragraphs that were either coherent or were scrambled word arrangements of the paragraphs. Subjects then reread the same passage in either its coherent or scrambled form, so as to produce four conditions: both readings coherent, both readings scrambled, first coherent then scrambled, and finally first scrambled then coherent. Carr et al. found a repetition benefit for all conditions, but there was no differential benefit in rereading when the forms matched rather than mismatched on the two readings. This result led Carr et al. to localize rereading transfer at the word level, with no transfer due to text-level properties. Similarly, transfer was equivalent whether the scripts were the same or different on the two readings, suggesting that there was no perceptual specificity in rereading transfer either. Carr et al. suggested that rereading transfer was mediated by abstract word representations.

The Carr et al. paper evoked several responses. Whittlesea (1990) asked subjects to read a scrambled version of the text and then to read either the same or a different scrambled version. He found more transfer when the scrambled versions matched on the two readings compared to when different scramblings were read on each encounter, suggesting that contextual surround did affect transfer even for scrambled word arrays. His point was that the Carr et al. manipulations changed not only a word's context on the two processing encounters, but for scrambled to normal and normal to scramble transfer conditions there was also a mismatch in linguistic level of analysis. This confound made it difficult to draw conclusions about the role of processing context. In the scrambled to scrambled conditions studied by Whittlesea only local context varied, and then contextual specificity was found. This specificity could not be accounted for by abstract word representations.

Levy and Burns (1990) attacked the problem differently. They reported three experiments using the Carr et al. basic design, with coherence matched or mismatched on the two readings. They used silent rather than oral reading, and subjects were instructed to read for meaning, even when reading scrambled texts, so that a strong text comprehension orientation was given to the task. The main manipulation was the linguistic level of the scrambling. In the first experiment the logical order of the text's message was disrupted by scrambling the order of all paragraphs beyond the first. Thus the sentences and individual paragraphs were intact, just the logical unfolding of the message was scrambled. In the second experiment the sentence order was scrambled so that both macrostructure and paragraph structure were disrupted. Finally, in the third study the words were scrambled so that no higher order structure was maintained. If transfer is mediated by abstract word units, as Carr et al. suggested, then the magnitude of the rereading benefit should be the same in all three studies, because the words are equally repeated in all cases. The results were not consistent with the Carr et al. view. There was complete transfer across paragraph scrambling, but sentence scrambling led to less transfer to normal text reading, and word scrambling led to a complete loss of transfer to text reading. That is, transfer to rereading coherent texts decreased as more of the linguistic structure was disrupted in the original text. Levy and Burns argued that the coherent rereading passage could not easily recruit or use the information stored from a prior reading of scrambled sentences or scrambled words. Our data offered support for a role for text properties in rereading transfer.

Carr and Brown (1990) responded to Whittlesea by pointing out that the contextual specificity found with scrambled to scrambled text transfer was very variable, and seemed to depend on the stimulus set used. They reported that they also now found contextual specificity, rather than abstract word transfer, in a number of studies. In comparing their studies with those in the literature, they concluded that the important variable was the level of focal attention during reading. This idea was elaborated, with supporting data, in Carlson, Alejano, and Carr (1991), where they suggested that when the reader focused on meaningful processing, as in the Levy and Burns studies, then the text was encoded episodically, with later transfer being contextually-specific. If the reader focused attention at the individual word level, however, even though those words were part of a text, then the underlying representation that mediates transfer was at the abstract word level. Carlson et al. demonstrated that instructions to read word by word, with sanctions against any relational processing, produced rereading transfer that appeared to be mediated by word units. Transfer to reading the text was equivalent whether the first reading was of the text itself or was a scrambled word version of that text (replicating Carr et al., 1989). On the other hand, when the instructions were to read the texts for meaning, there was contextual specificity, such that transfer was greater from a prior reading of the text itself than from a prior reading of a scrambled word version of the text (replicating Levy & Burns, 1990). They concluded that abstract word units mediate rereading transfer when the reading is word by word, but transfer is mediated by episodic text representations when the passage is read for meaning.

The Carlson et al. paper offers a satisfying solution to the apparent discrepancy that existed, but I offer a word of caution in applying this solution too broadly. Specifically, under what conditions can reading be viewed as word by word? In the Carlson et al. study the instructions were very strong. Under no circumstance was the reader to relate any two words of the text. Even poor readers may not read in such an extreme fashion. It is tempting to think that any data-driven orientation to analyze the print carefully may be sufficient to produce the abstract word transfer. Such is not the case. Levy, Masson, and Zoubek (1991) reported two studies using the scrambled/normal text comparisons of Carr et al. (1989). The new twist was that for one study the reader's attention was focused on a careful analysis of the print, so as to cross out as many Greek letters in the text as possible, while for the other study the focus was on the passage's message, so the reader could later summarize the main ideas in the text. Despite clear evidence that readers adopted these very different reading orientations, transfer to rereading the coherent text was much better from a prior reading of the text than from a prior reading of the scrambled words of the text, irrespective of the reader's orientation. In a table summarizing four studies using different reading orientations, Levy et al. showed that transfer from reading words to reading the text composed of those words is essentially zero. Yet in all cases there was good text to text transfer. Levy et al. concluded that if the reader treats the text as a text, rather than an isolated word set, then transfer will be mediated by the episodic text representation irrespective of reading orientation adopted. Word representations do not transfer to text reading, any more than text reading facilitated the perceptual identification of individual words in the Levy and Kirsner study.

Although we would argue that fluent readers almost always read texts so as to yield episodic transfer, we later discuss some new work with children who are poor readers that may provide a naturalistic occurrence of the Carlson et al. word-by-word transfer. Before going to the developmental work, however, there is one more fluent reprocessing issue that is receiving attention.

Is Rereading Transfer Sensitive to Changes in Visual Features?

The transfer work in text processing began with Kolers' remarkable demonstrations of sensitivity to visual feature differences between readings. He reported that changing the typescript and spacing of letters between two readings was sufficient to disrupt the rereading benefit for transformed typographies (Kolers et al., 1980). Although with normally oriented typescript it has been possible to demonstrate more transfer from reading to rereading than from listening to rereading (i.e., modality specificity), it has been remarkably difficult to find evidence of visual feature specificity. The word recognition literature contains some reports of transfer that is sensitive to changes in visual detail (e.g., Kirsner, Dunn, & Standen, 1987; Roediger & Blaxton, 1987), but such effects are most robust when difficult or distorted scripts are used (e.g., Jacoby & Hayman, 1987; Kolers, 1975; Masson, 1986). In text reading with normal scripts, influences due to changes in typescript are small and rarely statistically reliable (e.g., Carr et al., 1989; Levy et al., 1986; Levy & Kirsner, 1989). This difficulty in finding reliable effects of visual detail on rereading transfer for normal scripts, while easily finding effects for difficult scripts that focus processing at the perceptual levels, led Masson and Freedman (1990) to suggest that perceptual information is involved only in the early stages of skill development. With sufficient practice the reader has representations with different visual features, so these features play little role in transfer for fluent readers. Masson and Freedman suggested that transfer during fluent reading is mediated by semantic processes. A similar conclusion was reached by Carlson et al. (1991), who suggested that episodic representations are at the text level, accompanied by loss of surface structure information.

One has a sense of deja vu! Was this not where Kolers started? Why do we find so little sensitivity to visual features in rereading transfer for normal typographies? Jacoby, Levy, and Steinbach (1992) offered a suggestion. They argued that fluency is a fast, automatic form of reading that is mediated by episodic representations. This form of reading is optimally observed when the reader's focus is on semantic processing, with the act of reading itself back-grounded in the service of the semantic task. When this form of automatic reading is in gear, then the rereading text automatically recruits the episodic representation of the original text, and then all aspects of that representation, including its visual features, will influence rereading transfer. In most rereading studies the act of reading itself has been foregrounded, as in oral reading where articulating words is the focus of the task. This foregrounding is a nonoptimal way to observe skilled reading. Jacoby et al. examined sensitivity to visual feature changes between repetitions for two tasks. In the oral reading task, subjects first read aloud as quickly as possible, or listened to, a set of questions. The type font varied from question to question. After this task, subjects read aloud another set of questions, always in elite type font, but where some of the questions were repeated from the first phase and some were new. The empirical issues were whether old questions would be read faster in Phase 2 than new questions, and whether the repetition effect would be greater for old questions in the same modality or in the same type font than for old questions that differed in these features on the two occasions.

The results were clear-cut. For oral reading, there was a repetition benefit for old compared with new questions, and this transfer was sensitive to changes in modality (read-read was better than listen-read), but it was insensitive to type-font changes across readings, replicating past studies. These results can be con-trasted with those for the other task studied, question answering. The questions used by Jacoby et al. asked about simple, everyday knowledge that most under-graduates can retrieve quickly from memory (e.g., "How many nickels are there in a quarter?"). So, in the question answering task, subjects pretended that they were participating in a game show. They first answered a set of questions they either read or heard, as quickly as possible. The modality and typescript varia-tions were as in the oral reading task. In the second phase the participants again answered questions (some repetitions, some new) always typed in elite font. Thus the two tasks differed only in whether the subjects read aloud or answered the questions. The measure in the question answering task was time to read and begin answering the question. Old questions were answered faster than new questions and, importantly, in three studies, the magnitude of the repetition benefit was less if either the modality or the type font were changed between processing occurrences. That is, in this semantic retrieval task where the focus was on the message, the reprocessing benefit was sensitive to visual feature changes. Jacoby et al. took these results to be consistent with notions of episodic transfer during fluent reprocessing.

In a similar vein, Levy, Di Persio, and Hollingshead (1992) used the silent rereading task described by Levy et al. (1986). Subjects read the same text four or five times, crossing out word and nonword errors as they read. In the experiments of interest, the text was always typed in elite type font for the early readings. On the final reading, 10 words in the text were unexpectedly typed in script font. This unexpected change in type font of a few words caused a loss in the rereading benefit, compared to a final repetition where all of the words were in the same script. Why were readers so sensitive to this irrelevant and minor change in the visual display? By the final reading the text was read very rapidly and fluently, yet this subtle change affected reprocessing. Would this subtle change in typescript affect reading when the text was unfamiliar and therefore read in a less fluent manner? To answer that question, a group of subjects read the texts only once, with some passages typed all in elite font and some with the 10 script words as in the final trial described above. There was absolutely no difference in reading times for these two types of passages when the subject was unfamiliar with the texts, and reading them less fluently. The sensitivity to the visual "blips" occurred only when the reader was reading in the fluent manner that we have suggested is mediated by the recruitment of episodic representations. Thus, as in the Jacoby et al. study, we again observe sensitivity to visual feature changes when the reader is operating in the fluent episodic mode, not when the reader is reading in a slow nonfluent fashion.

I offer these studies as food for thought. What is the representation that mediates this form of fast, automatic reading? I think it is a form of the episodic or instance memory that is believed to influence concept formation (Brooks, 1978), reading (Masson, 1986), social decision making (Kahneman & Miller, 1986), and other forms of remembering (e.g., Jacoby & Brooks, 1984). Logan (1988, 1990) suggested that much of the work on automaticity and repetition priming is best explained by instance (or episodic) representations, rather than by an abstract or rule-based form of representation. Much of the fluency we observe in reading may also be based on the automatic recruitment and use of knowledge stored in memory from prior reading events. This event memory may appear to have "schema-like" properties, but I suspect that further research will show that such knowledge maintains properties of specific prior occurrences, suggesting that it is based on the retrieval of quite specific memory representations. The rereading work spawned by Kolers' insightful studies of transfer continues to uncover valuable information about the nature of knowledge representations. Although I would put less stress on the centrality of pattern recognition processes than did Kolers, I concur with his notion that the message and its surface properties form a processing package that acts in a holistic fashion to mediate future fluent reading.

READING DEVELOPMENT

Although most of the rereading work in cognitive psychology has focused on the recruitment of knowledge representations to aid fluent reading, there is an emerging literature that looks at the effects of repetition or practice on the development of reading skill, particularly in children experiencing reading problems. The focus has been on the use of drill or repetition as a form of remedial training. However, the theoretical issues raised by this work are often similar to those addressed by the fluent reading studies already reviewed. I discuss some studies of single word recognition and of text rereading to highlight some of these issues.

Speeding up Word Recognition

One of the important developmental issues is the relationship between the speed with which a child can recognize printed words and his or her ability to comprehend the message conveyed by those words. A widely accepted developmental view is that word recognition processes must become fast and automatic so that the reader's attention can be devoted to higher order comprehension processes (Perfetti & Lesgold, 1977). If word recognition is slow, then a bottleneck in processing results, and word-level information arrives at a rate too slow to enable efficient meaning analyses. Consequently, not only must decoding be accurate, but it must also be fast and require little attention, so that the reader's processing resources can be devoted to message understanding. An interesting assumption here is that the speed of single-word processing reflects how those words will be read and comprehended when they are embedded in meaningful contexts.

This verbal efficiency view has been tested in a number of repetition studies that attempted to first train rapid single-word recognition and then observe the effect of this training on comprehension. The results have been mixed. Fleisher, Jenkins, and Pany (1979) trained poor readers in Grades 4 and 5, using a flash card drill, until each word could be recognized within 1 sec of presentation. These words were then embedded in short passages, and passage reading time and comprehension were measures. Although the poor readers who received training learned to read the isolated word list as rapidly as good readers of the same age, they did not match the good readers in reading time when those words were embedded in a passage. However, the trained students read both word lists and passages faster than untrained poor readers, indicating that the word drill did improve word decoding fluency, even in context. Unfortunately, this improvement in word decoding speed was not coupled with an improvement in comprehension, as indicated by question answering. Similar results were reported by Piggins and Barron (1982).

Other studies have used training tasks that combined repetition or practice with highlighting the spelling to sound regularities of printed words. Using methods that asked the child to "construct a word" by combining beginnings and endings, or to find and correct the vowel errors in words, Roth and Beck (1987) were able to substantially reduce naming times for single words in children with reading problems. Although this training on individual words did lead to better understanding of sentences composed of those words, there was no improvement in comprehension beyond the single sentence level. Lovett, Ransby, Hardwick, and Jones (1989) reported success in using repetition training to facilitate the word decoding of dyslexic readers, but again there was no transfer of this training to reading the words in context. Thus it is unclear that there is much transfer of training from the single-word level to reading those words in context, just as with fluent readers.

We have recently attempted to understand the nature of the representation that is facilitated by single word repetition drills, in order to pursue these failures in transfer of training. Lemoine, Levy, and Hutchison (in press) reported three studies examining the effects of repetition on the acquisition of rapid naming skill for poor readers in Grades 3 and 4. The important results were that naming times decreased dramatically over the first 10–15 repetitions; if repetition practice was continued well beyond the point at which naming times asymptoted (i.e., into overlearning), then retention of the trained skill was essentially perfect over a week-long retention interval. Importantly, even when the orthographic to pronunciation relationships were highlighted by blocking similar words in training (e.g., might, sight, right, fight), there was no generalization of the newly acquired rapid naming skill to untrained words that shared that orthography (light). The representations that were facilitated by repetition training appeared to be whole-word units. Repetition facilitated visual access to word units, rather than facilitating any abstract rule representations for segmenting the words into orthographic units. Lemoine et al. argued that as in early language acquisition, children may first need to acquire a substantial whole-word vocabulary that they can rapidly read, before the print to sound regularities can be understood and stored as abstract decoding rules. Poor readers may be particularly poor rule learners (Manis & Morrison, 1985), yet they can benefit from repetition training to automate their sight vocabulary. It is critical to get children reading early, by whatever means possible, in order to ensure that they will read outside of school and thus gain the benefits to exposure to print that have recently been documented by Cunningham and Stanovich (1990, 1991).

Text Rereading: What Improves with Repeated Reading?

In the single-word section I have suggested that single-word reading may facilitate visual access paths, thus aiding reading, but not through abstract decoding skills. Rather, access to whole-word representations is facilitated by repetition training. We next explore training when the emphasis is on text rereading fluency and comprehension, rather than single word recognition. What is learned through text repetition training? Dahl (1974) and Samuels (1979) reported results of a reading program that developed a "method of repeated readings." In this task, Grade 2 poor readers repeatedly read the same passage until a criterion speed was reached. Then the student chose another passage and engaged in repeated readings until that passage too was read at the criterion rate. This procedure was repeated for five passages selected by the student. Results indicated that reading rate improved with each rereading, and that this fluency was coupled with fewer reading errors. Thus poor readers showed the same improvement in reading fluency across rereadings that we discussed earlier for adult readers. The authors also claimed that passage comprehension improved with repeated readings training, but no convincing data were provided on that point.

We have recently begun some comparative studies that will allow us to more carefully evaluate the nature of rereading transfer in child readers, using procedures similar to those we have studied with fluent adult readers. The findings are preliminary but we think they are informative. In one study (Levy, Nicholls & Kohen, 1993) we asked good and poor readers in Grades 3, 4, and 5 to silently read passages four times in succession, and we measured reading time on each reading. While they read, they also crossed out misspelled words. There were 10 word and 10 nonword misspellings on each reading, and these differed on the four reading trials for each passage. This study, then, followed the design used by Levy et al. (1986), allowing us to examine how thoroughly the printed display was analyzed as the reader became more familiar with the text. Again we expected nonword error detection to provide an indication of processing at the lexical level, because these errors are detectable by a lexical access check. The word errors, however, can only be identified when the sentence meaning is calculated, because the error words are lexically acceptable but when combined with the other words of the sentence, a nonsense utterance results. Thus, detection of these two types of errors provided an on-line indication of the depth of analysis during reading. We also asked comprehension questions after each reading in order to assess the level of text comprehension.

Our main interest in this study was whether good and poor readers would benefit differentially from repeated readings. Some have suggested (e.g., Mitterer, 1982) that poor readers are inflexible and unable to share their limited processing resources between word- and text-level processes. Does this mean that improvements for poor readers, with repetition, will be localized at either the single word or the meaning level, whereas those for good readers are at both levels, as they are for adult readers? The results were quite similar for all three grades. Reading time decreased gracefully across the four readings, and the gains were greater for poor than for good readers, although poor readers' rates never reached those of good readers. For both good and poor readers, word error detection actually improved across rereading trials, indicating that their analysis of the passage's meaning became more efficient with practice. Nonword error detection was higher than word error detection, indicating that good and poor readers could detect these lexical violations at an earlier stage of processing than the syntactic/semantic errors. For both error types, detection by poor readers was lower than that by good readers.

Comparing the pattern of results for good and poor readers, one is struck by their similarity. Clearly, poor readers are approaching the reading task with the same flexibility in allocation of processing resources as good readers, and they benefit from practice in the same way. Further, comprehension, as indicated by question answering, also improved with rereadings for both good and poor readers. The only qualitative difference between reader groups was in their sensitivity to passage difficulty. Good readers in Grades 4 and 5 adjusted their reading rates to match passage difficulty, while poor readers did not. However, for both good and poor readers, question answering varied with passage diffi- culty. Thus the results suggested that rereading texts is a good remedial technique for poor readers, with both word recognition and meaning analyses becoming more efficient with practice. Further, these results suggested that, as with fluent adult readers, both data-driven and conceptually driven processes participate in fluent rereading in child readers.

Transfer Across Texts

The studies just described suggest that rereading facilitates processing of the trained text, but is there any transfer of this type of training to untrained pas- sages? There have been interesting hints in a few studies. In a replication and extension of the Dahl and Samuels work, Herman (1985) reported improvements in reading speed and accuracy, both within and across passages. However, she also measured the number of pauses made while reading. While the number of pauses during reading decreased across readings of the same passage, there was no improvement in pausing across passages. Herman argued that pausing indi- cates a reading disruption, and that the change in pausing across readings of the same text indicated that fewer reading problems were encountered while reading. The failure to see any change in pausing when a new passage was encountered suggested to Herman that any generalization of skill across passages may be mediated by more rapid reading of individual words shared in the new and trained passages, rather than by any general reading skill changes.

This emphasis on transfer across texts at the single-word level was echoed in a rereading study by Rashotte and Torgeson (1985). For poor readers in Grades 2 to 5, they compared rereading benefits for texts that shared many or only a few words with the previously trained text. In both cases the texts were conceptually unrelated. Rashotte and Torgeson found more transfer in reading speed to the texts with many overlapping words, compared with texts with only a few shared words. However, there was no benefit to comprehension for the stories with many rather than a few overlapping words. They argued that any improvements in reading speed observed across different stories can be accounted for entirely by the number of words in common between the new and trained texts. That is, repeated readings improves single-word recognition, and this improvement transfers across texts.

Heather Faulkner and I have been looking at how similar two texts must be in order to observe transfer between them. We reasoned that if text representations are established across rereadings, transfer of text-specific knowledge should vary with similarity between the new and old texts. Would individual word overlap between the stories capture all of the transfer, as suggested by the work of Rashotte and Torgesen, or do text-level properties mediate transfer as well? To examine this question, Faulkner and I first trained good and poor readers in Grade 4 to rapidly read one text. We then measured transfer of training to a standard text. The critical manipulation was in the similarity of the training text to the standard transfer text. In one condition the training story was the preceding section of the standard text. The texts therefore overlapped in theme, setting, structure, and characters. They also shared a large number of words. In another condition, the stories differed in theme, setting, structure, and characters, but they had the same word overlap as in the similar texts. If Rashotte and Torgesen's word-level hypothesis is correct, transfer should be the same in the similar and the high word overlap conditions, because their word overlap is equivalent. These two conditions were compared to a transfer condition where the texts differed in all aspects and also had little word overlap. The basic result was that for good readers there was no difference among the three conditions, probably because they were reading the texts rapidly in all conditions. However, for poor readers, a prior reading of both the similar and the high word overlap passages facilitated reading of the standard transfer text, and transfer was equivalent in the two conditions. That is, transfer was just as great from reading overlapping words in different contexts as from reading overlapping words in very similar text contexts. This result is consistent with the results of Rashotte and Torgesen, and it is reminiscent of the Carlson et al. finding for fluent readers who were instructed to read in a word by word fashion, not relating any text words. We may have here a naturalistic occurrence of Carr's claims for abstract word mediation of rereading transfer.

The developmental results are preliminary, but they raise interesting issues regarding repetition benefits. The adult research suggested that improved reading fluency with rereading was based on episodic text representations, unless the reader read in an 'unrelated' word fashion. In some recent studies of transfer across texts with adult readers (Levy, Barnes & Martin, 1993), we found no transfer for texts that shared only words, unlike the effects found by Faulkner and me for poor-reading children. There are clearly developmental changes in the benefits that accrue with practice that have to be explored. Does practice or repetition first consolidate single-word representations that only later enter into higher order text representations, where the words become contextually bound for transfer? We need a better understanding of the nature of the representations that result from different types of repetition or practice. We know that children who read early also read more, and this early reading leads to greater fluency. What kinds of representations are formed at different skill levels and how do these lead to improved reading skill? Both cognitive and educational psychology will benefit from the understanding of these fundamental learning issues.

ACKNOWLEDGMENT

Preparation of this chapter was supported by operating grants from the Natural Sciences and Engineering Research Council and the Ontario Mental Health Foundation, as well as a Senior Research Fellowship from the Ontario Mental Health Foundation.

REFERENCES

Brooks, L. R. (1978). Nonanalytic concept formation and memory for instances. In E. Rosch & B. Lloyd (Eds.), *Cognition and categorization* (pp. 169–211). Hillsdale, NJ: Lawrence Erlbaum Associates.

Carlson, L., Alejano, A., & Carr, T. H. (1991). The level of focal attention hypothesis in oral reading: Influences of strategies on the context specificity of lexical repetition effects. *Journal of Experimental Psychology: Learning, Memory, and Cognition, 17,* 924–931.

Carr, T. H., & Brown, J. S. (1990). Perceptual abstraction and interactivity in repeated oral reading: Where do things stand? *Journal of Experimental Psychology: Learning, Memory, and Cognition, 16,* 731–738.

Carr, T. H., Brown, J. S., & Charalambous, A. (1989). Repetition and reading: Perceptual encoding mechanisms are very abstract but not very interactive. *Journal of Experimental Psychology: Learning, Memory, and Cognition, 15,* 763–778.

Cohen, N. J., & Squire, L. R. (1980). Preserved learning and retention of pattern analyzing skill in amnesia: Dissociation of knowing how and knowing that. *Science, 210,* 207–209.

Craik, F. I. M., & Lockhart, R. S. (1972). Levels of processing: A framework for memory research. *Journal of Verbal Learning and Verbal Behavior, 11,* 671–684.

Cunningham, A. E., & Stanovich, K. (1990). Assessing print exposure and orthographic processing skills in children: A quick measure of reading experience. *Journal of Educational Psychology, 82,* 733–740.

Cunningham, A. E., & Stanovich, K. (1991). Tracking the unique effects of print exposure in children: Associations with vocabulary, general knowledge, and spelling. *Journal of Educational Psychology, 83,* 264–274.

Dahl, P. (1974). *An experimental program for teaching high speed word recognition and comprehension skills* (Final Rep. Prog. #3-1154). Washington, DC: National Institute for Education. (ERIC Document Reproduction Service No. ED 099812).

Ehrlich, S. F., & Rayner, K. (1981). Contextual effects on word perception and eye movements during reading. *Journal of Verbal Learning and Verbal Behavior, 20,* 641–655.

Fleisher, L. S., Jenkins, J. R., & Pany, D. (1979). Effects on poor readers' comprehension of training in rapid decoding. *Reading Research Quarterly, 15,* 30–48.

Goodman, K. S. (1970). Reading: A psycholinguistic guessing game. In H. Singer & R. B. Ruddell (Eds.), *Theoretical models and processes in reading* (pp. 257–271). Newark, DE: International Reading Association.

Graf, P., & Levy, B. A. (1984). Reading and remembering: Conceptual and perceptual processing involved in reading rotated passages. *Journal of Verbal Learning and Verbal Behavior, 23,* 405–424.

Herman, P. A. (1985). The effect of repeated readings on reading time, on reading rate, speech pauses, and word recognition accuracy. *Reading Research Quarterly, 20,* 553–565.

Horton, K. D. (1985). The role of semantic information in reading spatially transformed text. *Cognitive Psychology, 17,* 66–88.

Horton, K. D. (1989). The processing of spatially transformed text. *Memory & Cognition, 17,* 283–291.

Jacoby, L. L. (1983). Remembering the data: Analyzing interactive process in reading. *Journal of Verbal Learning and Verbal Behavior, 22,* 485–508.

Jacoby, L. L., & Brooks, L. R. (1984). Nonanalytic cognition: Memory, perception, and concept learning. In G. H. Bower (Ed.), *The psychology of learning and motivation: Advances in research and theory,* Vol. 18 (pp. 1–47). New York: Academic Press.

Jacoby, L. L., & Dallas, M. (1981). On the relationship between autobiographical memory and perceptual learning. *Journal of Experimental Psychology: General, 3,* 306–340.

Jacoby, L. L., & Hayman, C. A. G. (1987). Specific visual transfer in word identification. *Journal of Experimental Psychology: Learning, Memory, and Cognition, 13,* 456–463.

Jacoby, L. L., Levy, B. A., & Steinbach, K. (1992). Episodic transfer and automaticity: The integration of data-driven and conceptually-driven processing in rereading. *Journal of Experimental Psychology: Learning, Memory, and Cognition, 18,* 15–24.

Kahneman, D., & Miller, D. T. (1986). Norm theory: Comparing reality to its alternatives. *Psychological Review, 93*(2), 136–153.

Kintsch, W. (1974). *The representation of meaning in memory.* Hillsdale, NJ: Lawrence Erlbaum Associates.

Kirsner, K., Dunn, J. C., & Standen, P. (1987). Record-based word recognition. In M. Coltheart (Ed.), *Reading: Attention and performance* XII: *The psychology of reading* (pp. 147–167). London: Lawrence Erlbaum Associates.

Kolers, P. A. (1975). Specificity of operations in sentence recognition. *Cognitive Psychology, 1,* 283–306.

Kolers, P. A. (1976). Reading a year later. *Journal of Experimental Psychology: Human Learning and Memory, 2,* 554–565.

Kolers, P. A. (1979). A pattern-analyzing basis of recognition. In L. S. Cermak & F. I. M. Craik (Eds.), *Levels of processing in human memory* (pp. 363–384). Hillsdale, NJ: Lawrence Erlbaum Associates.

Kolers, P. A., & Magee, L. E. (1978). Specificity of pattern-analyzing skills in reading. *Canadian Journal of Psychology, 32,* 43–51.

Kolers, P. A., Palef, S. R., & Stelmach, L. B. (1990). Graphemic analysis underlying literacy. *Memory & Cognition, 8,* 322–328.

Lemoine, H., Levy, B. A., & Hutchison, A. (in press). Increasing the naming speed of poor readers: Representations formed across repetitions. *Journal of Experimental Child Psychology.*

Levy, B. A. (1983). Proofreading familiar text: Constraints on visual processing. *Memory & Cognition, 11,* 1–12.

Levy, B. A., Barnes, L., & Martin, L. (1993). Transfer of fluency across repetitions and across texts. *Canadian Journal of Psychology,* in press.

Levy, B. A., & Begin, J. (1984). Proofreading familiar text: Allocating resources to perceptual and conceptual processes. *Memory & Cognition, 12,* 621–632.

Levy, B. A., & Burns, K. I. (1990). Reprocessing text: Contributions from conceptually driven processes. *Canadian Journal of Psychology, 44*(4), 465–482.

Levy, B. A., Di Persio, R., & Hollingshead, A. (1992). Fluent rereading: Repetition, automaticity and discrepancy. *Journal of Experimental Psychology: Learning, Memory, and Cognition, 18,* 957–971.

Levy, B. A., & Kirsner, K. (1989). Reprocessing text: Indirect measures of word and message level processes. *Journal of Experimental Psychology: Learning, Memory, and Cognition, 15,* 407–417.

Levy, B. A., Masson, M. E. J., & Zoubek, M. A. (1991). Rereading text: Words and their context. *Canadian Journal of Psychology, 45,* 492–506.

Levy, B. A., Newell, S., Snyder, J., & Timmins, K. (1986). Processing changes across reading encounters. *Journal of Experimental Psychology: Learning, Memory, and Cognition, 12,* 467–478.

Levy, B. A., Nicholls, A., & Kohen, D. (1993). *Repeated readings: Process benefits for good and poor readers.* (Manuscript submitted for publication).

Logan, G. D. (1988). Toward an instance theory of automatization. *Psychological Review, 95,* 492–527.

Logan, G. D. (1990). Repetition priming and automaticity: Common underlying mechanisms? *Cognitive Psychology, 22(1),* 1–35.

Lovett, M. W., Ransby, M. J., Hardwick, N., & Jones, M. S. (1989). Can dyslexia be treated? Treatment-specific and generalized effects in dyslexic children's response to remediation. *Brain and Language, 37,* 90–121.

MacLeod, C. M. (1989). Word context during initial exposure influences degree of priming in word fragment completion. *Journal of Experimental Psychology: Learning, Memory, and Cognition, 15,* 398–406.

Manis, F. R., & Morrison, F. J. (1985). Reading disability: A deficit in rule learning? In L. S. Seigel & F. J. Morrison (Eds.), *Progress in cognitive development: Atypical children* (pp. 1–26). New York: Springer-Verlag.

Masson, M. E. J. (1984). Memory for the surface structure of sentences: Remembering with and without awareness. *Journal of Verbal Learning and Verbal Behavior, 23,* 579–592.

Masson, M. E. J. (1986). Identification of typographically transformed words: Instance-based skill acquisition. *Journal of Experimental Psychology: Learning, Memory, and Cognition, 12,* 479–488.

Masson, M. E. J., & Freedman, L. (1990). Fluent identification of repeated words. *Journal of Experimental Psychology: Learning, Memory and Cognition, 16,* 355–373.

Masson, M. E. J., & Sala, L. S. (1978). Interactive processes in sentence comprehension and recognition. *Cognitive Psychology, 10,* 244–270.

McConkie, G. W., & Zola, D. (1981). Language constraints and the functional stimulus in reading. In A. M. Lesgold & C. A. Perfetti (Eds.), *Interactive processes in reading* (pp. 155–175). Hillsdale, NJ: Lawrence Erlbaum Associates.

Mitterer, J. O. (1982). There are at least two kinds of poor readers: Whole-word poor readers and recoding poor readers. *Canadian Journal of Psychology, 36(3),* 445–461.

Morton, J. (1969). Interaction of information in word recognition. *Psychological Review, 76,* 165–178.

Musen, G., Shimamura, A. P., & Squire, L. R. (1990). Intact text-specific reading skill in amnesia. *Journal of Experimental Psychology: Learning, Memory, and Cognition, 16,* 1068–1076.

Oliphant, G. W. (1983). Repetition and recency effects in word recognition. *Australian Journal of Psychology, 35,* 393–403.

Perfetti, C. A., & Lesgold, A. M. (1977). Discourse comprehension and sources of individual differences. In M. Just & P. Carpenter (Eds.). *Cognitive processes in comprehension* (pp. 141–183). Hillsdale, NJ: Lawrence Erlbaum Associates.

Perfetti, C. A., & Roth, S. F. (1981). Some of the interactive processes in reading and their role in reading skill. In A. M. Lesgold & C. A. Perfetti (Eds.). *Interactive processes in reading* (pp. 269–297). Hillsdale, NJ: Lawrence Erlbaum Associates.

Piggins, W. R., & Barron, R. W. (1982). *Why learning to read aloud more rapidly does not improve comprehension: Testing the decoding sufficiency hypothesis.* Paper presented at a meeting of the American Educational Research Association, New York.

Rashotte, C. A., & Torgeson, J. K. (1985). Repeated reading and reading fluency in learning disabled children. *Reading Research Quarterly, 20(2),* 180–202.

Richardson-Klavehn, A., & Bjork, R. A. (1988). Measures of memory. *Annual Review of Psychology, 39,* 475–543.

Roediger, H. L., & Blaxton, T. A. (1987). Effects of varying modality, surface features, and retention interval on priming word fragment completion. *Memory & Cognition, 15,* 379–388.

Roth, S. F., & Beck, I. L. (1987). Theoretical and instructional implications of the assessment of two microcomputer word recognition programs. *Reading Research Quarterly, 22,* 197–218.

Samuels, S. J. (1979). The method of repeated readings. *Reading Teacher, 32,* 403–408.

Smith, F. (1971). *Understanding reading.* New York: Holt, Rinehart & Winston.

Smith, F. (1973). *Psycholinguistics and reading.* New York: Holt, Rinehart & Winston.

Stanovich, K. E. (1981). Attentional and automatic context effects in reading. In A. M. Lesgold & C. A. Perfetti (Eds.) *Interactive processes in reading* (pp. 241–267). Hillsdale, NJ: Lawrence Erlbaum Associates.

Tardif, T., & Craik, F. I. (1989). Reading a week later: Perceptual and conceptual factors. *Journal of Memory and Language, 28*(1), 107–125.

Whittlesea, B. W. A. (1990). Perceptual encoding mechanisms are tricky but may be very interactive. Comment on Carr, Brown, and Charalambous. *Journal of Experimental Psychology: Learning, Memory, and Cognition, 16,* 727–730.

4 Mood Dependence in Implicit and Explicit Memory

Dawn Macaulay
Lee Ryan
Eric Eich
University of British Columbia

Emotions—joy and sadness, fear and anger, passion and regret—play a pivotal role in the definition of human existence. The milestones of one's life, such as the birth of a child or the loss of a loved one, are events imbued with profound emotion. For many years, perhaps for a lifetime, the memory of such an event might rekindle in us the same emotional experience. And too, perhaps for a lifetime, experiencing a similar emotion under a completely different set of circumstances might unexpectedly revive the memory of that special event. So, sitting at a concert contemplating a beautiful melody, we may suddenly remember gazing at the sun as it set upon the ocean—an event we had perceived while experiencing a similar sense of wonder.

The link between emotional experience and memory poses many intriguing questions. How do emotion and memory influence one another? Under what circumstances does an emotion trigger the recollection of a prior event? Is emotion acting in the same manner as other environmental contexts, such as a particular scent or a distinctive sound, to remind us of prior experiences? Or is there something different, perhaps unique, about emotional memory? Perhaps emotions serve as retrieval cues that we use as part of a conscious recollection strategy. Or do emotions influence remembering in more subtle, imperceptible ways?

In recent years, memory research has highlighted the idea that a single prior experience may influence our subsequent thought processes in many ways, ways of which we are not necessarily aware. This notion has added a new perspective to the investigation of human memory and is the subject of this book, namely, implicit memory. Graf and Schacter (1985) described the distinction between explicit and implicit memory. *Explicit memory* refers to the intentional or deliber-

75

ate recollection of a specific prior event or episode. *Implicit memory* refers to the influence of prior experiences on subsequent task performance in circumstances where intentional recollection of specific episodes is not required (cf. Graf & Schacter, 1985). The role of emotion in both implicit and explicit remembering is the focus of the present chapter.

From its inception, the investigation of emotion and memory has employed, almost exclusively, explicit memory tasks such as recall and recognition. More recent work with implicit memory has added a new dimension to our understanding of emotion and memory. Taken together, the results have allowed us to identify the circumstances necessary for emotion to influence memory and, more specifically, to speculate about the mechanisms by which emotion mediates memory. In the following sections, we review some of the literature on emotion and memory and propose a general framework that accounts for the effect of emotion on both explicit and implicit memory. Within such a framework, we hope to build a theoretical bridge between the study of emotion and memory and the broader issue of contextual effects in memory.

A second bridge we hope to build is between cognitive psychology and theories concerning the nature of emotion. Exploring the very different views regarding the essence of emotion and emotional experience suggests new approaches to the investigation of emotion and cognition. Just as theories of emotion might lead to the development of promising ideas for future cognitive research, cognitive psychology may be very useful in evaluating and distinguishing between such theories. We conclude our chapter with a discussion of several theories of emotion and their implications for future research in this area.

COGNITIVE PSYCHOLOGY AND EMOTIONAL MEMORY

Early psychologists such as William James and Carl Lange were convinced of the necessity of studying emotion and cognition. They, and others after them, brought scientific methods to bear on the enterprise (see Mandler, 1984, for a historical review). However, the lack of theoretical consensus regarding the nature of emotion, together with the difficulty of measuring its presence objectively, made many psychologists uneasy. The answer for some was to exclude it, at least temporarily, from the agenda of scientific psychology. Indeed, some still do: In *The Mind's New Science*, Howard Gardner (1985, p. 6) regards emotion as a factor "which may be important for cognitive functioning but whose inclusion at this point would unnecessarily complicate the cognitive-scientific enterprise."

Other cognitive psychologists, such as George Mandler (1984), have sought to study emotion by adopting methods that have proven effective with other difficult issues such as reasoning, understanding, and memory. This approach finesses the definitional problems of emotion by focusing instead on the underlying processes that produce the collective phenomena referred to as emotional experience. It is sufficient to assert that an emotion is, first, experienced as a distinctive internal state, and second, associated with a unique *schema*. The schema refers to an emotion-specific set of interrelated information including vocabulary, semantic and conceptual knowledge, memories of prior experiences, and physiological sensations. Thus, when I am in a certain state, I recognize that I am in that state, and I can label it as, for example, sadness. I know the words (such as *blues, miserable, depression*) and the concepts (such as *tears, death, loneliness*) that are related to this state, and I may recall other times and other circumstances that have made me, or would likely make me, sad.

From this perspective two approaches to research have arisen, one of which focuses on the influence of emotional schemata. Underlying this approach is the idea that an individual experiencing a particular mood tends to interpret experiences in a manner consistent with that mood while he or she selectively attends to, elaborates upon, and learns material that is similar in affective tone. The material is presumed to be included in the schema through prior association with the emotion, and its biased processing is referred to as *mood-congruent memory*. A classic example of mood congruence comes from a study by Bower, Gilligan, and Monteiro (1981), where subjects were asked to read a story about two characters, one who is sad and one who is happy. Two groups of subjects were induced, using hypnotic suggestion, to feel either sad or happy while reading the story. Later, while in a neutral mood, the two groups differed in their interpretation and subsequent recall of the story. Subjects who had felt sad while reading the story identified more with the sad character, thought the story was about him, and recalled more details regarding him than regarding his happy counterpart. For subjects who were happy while reading the story, subjects identified with the happy character; the story was reported to be about the happy character, and they remembered more details regarding him.

An alternative research approach focuses on the memorial consequences of emotion as a distinctive state and is a natural extension of research on state-dependent learning both in animals (Overton, 1984) and in humans (Eich, 1980). The phenomenon of interest, *mood-dependent memory,* is evident when memory for a past event is enhanced by the presence of a mood that is similar to the one that was present during the original encoding of that event. Importantly, the enhanced memory should occur for all aspects of the event, regardless of the affective valence of the material itself. Thus, when subjects learn material while sad, the presence of a sad mood later on will enhance the memory for that material, regardless of whether the emotional valence of the material is happy, sad, or neutral. (For reviews of both mood congruence and mood dependence, see Blaney, 1986; Bower, 1981, 1987; Eich, 1989.)

These two approaches may reflect methodological differences rather than distinct phenomena; whereas the mood congruence approach assumes the prior association of information or experience with a specific emotion (Bower, 1981), the mood dependence approach essentially supplies the subject with a new experience to be associated with the emotion. This chapter deals mainly with mood-dependent memory, because we are chiefly concerned with the transfer of information across different emotional states and with the circumstances surrounding both event encoding and subsequent retrieval that may be necessary for emotion to influence memory performance.

MOOD-DEPENDENT MEMORY: NOW YOU SEE IT, NOW YOU DON'T

Prior to the 1970s, little empirical work had been done on mood-dependent memory. However, interest in the phenomenon blossomed after Bower, Monteiro, and Gilligan (1978) demonstrated mood dependence in an experiment in which affective states were modified via hypnotic suggestions. Reasoning that moods create distinctive contexts that might be used to influence later retrieval, these researchers had subjects learn two lists of words, one while happy and the other while sad. Subsequently, the subjects were tested for the recall of both lists while in either a happy or a sad mood. The key finding was that subjects recalled significantly more items from the list that they had learned while in the matching mood—a clear and compelling demonstration of mood-dependent memory. Other researchers reported similar effects with children (Bartlett, Burleson, & Santrock, 1982), and with different types of mood induction procedures (Mecklenbrauker & Hager, 1984; Schare, Lisman, & Spear, 1984). Mood-dependent memory appeared to be a reliable phenomenon.

Or so it seemed at the time. Over the course of the next several years, researchers reported difficulty in documenting mood dependence using similar methods (e.g., Johnson & Klinger, 1988; Wetzler, 1985). What is more, Bower and Mayer (1989) attempted to replicate and extend the results reported by Bower et al. (1978) in six additional studies. On all but one occasion they failed to find evidence of mood dependence. The stark contrast between the original, positive outcomes and the newer, negative results led Bower and Mayer (1989, pp. 153–154) to lament that:

> We have hit an impasse in our experiments on MDR [mood dependent retrieval]. We have searched in vain for some variable that we consider "significant" which would distinguish among experimental arrangements that produced positive versus negative results on MDR. One begins with the hope that the outcomes do not depend on "insignificant" irrelevancies such as the experimenter's appearance, tone of voice, exact room temperature, and so on. However, the inconsistent results in this area have caused us considerable despair. Since we cannot even identify the critical variables, it seems that we are far from understanding theoretically what is going on in such experiments. We can only hope that future research will clarify what now appears to us as a very muddled scene.

As Bower and Mayer (1989) have also remarked, the capriciousness of the phenomenon is particularly puzzling in light of the fact that virtually every theorist who considers the issue of context and memory would predict mood dependence. Indeed, Bower's (1981) semantic network model, Baddeley's (1982) conception of contextual associations, Tulving's (1983) encoding specificity principle, and Morris, Bransford, and Franks' (1977) concept of transfer appropriate processing all augur forcefully for mood dependence. In each case, reinstatement of the affective state in which an event had been encoded would be expected to enhance the subsequent retrieval of that event. This leads to the obvious question, why some times and not others? If mood dependence is not a robust phenomenon, then under what circumstances might it reliably occur?

MOOD-DEPENDENT MEMORY: EMOTION-RELEVANT PROCESSING

In order to demonstrate mood dependence, is it sufficient for a person to simply be in a mood and then learn a list of unrelated and emotionally neutral words? Or does there have to be something more? To understand the circumstances that would lead reliably to mood-dependent memory, we take as a premise the simple idea that in order for emotion to affect memory, it must have some relevance or connection to the task with which the subject is presented. The difficulty remains in defining what would constitute memory tasks that are emotion relevant. In this section, we present a theoretical framework from which to begin our search, and we go on to discuss some experiments that shed light on this issue.

In the 1970s, Morris et al. (1977) introduced the concept of transfer-appropriate processing (TAP) by proposing that memory performance is facilitated to the extent that the cognitive operations engaged during event retrieval echo those engaged during event encoding. The specific task demands determine which cognitive processes will be engaged; the experience of remembering is the increased fluency of those cognitive operations when they are reengaged (Kolers, 1973, 1975). In keeping with Tulving's principle of encoding specificity (e.g., Tulving, 1983), a TAP account assumes that only those aspects of the original event that are processed at encoding will be included in the memory representation of the target event, and hence may be available to aid its later retrieval. This simple idea has provided a powerful heuristic that encompasses many disparate findings in memory research.

Applying TAP principles in order to understand mood/memory interactions in general and mood-dependent memory in particular, it follows that it is critical to identify emotion-relevant processes or the cognitive operations that are influenced by mood, and to employ both encoding and retrieval tasks that engage such processes. By this account, mood-dependent effects would be evident to the extent that moods influence cognitive operations at encoding, and that a similar mood at retrieval influences these cognitive operations in the same manner. The question thus arises: What might constitute emotion-relevant processing?

One plausible answer, advanced by Bower (1987; Bower & Mayer, 1989), centers on the idea that mere contiguity between a mood and a set of to-be-remembered or target events is not sufficient to create the necessary connections between the mood context and the items; rather, subjects must perceive the events as causing their present mood state. In the only study in the Bower and Mayer (1989) series to show mood dependence (their Experiment 4), the materials used to induce a particular mood (16 happy or sad scenarios that subjects imagined themselves experiencing) also served as the targets of subsequent memory testing. Consequently, the targets could be seen as causing—rather than simply co-occurring with—the subjects' mood. It should be noted that a similar idea has been suggested by Fernandez and Glenberg (1985) in connection with environmental context or place-dependent memory. By their account, events experienced in a particular physical environment, such as a classroom or a playground, are unlikely to become associated with that place unless subjects conceive of the environment as causing or enabling the events to happen. Though evidence concerning the role of causal belongingness in context dependence is mixed—indeed, the positive results revealed by Bower and Mayer's (1989) fourth study were not replicated in their fifth experiment—the core idea seems sound, and it clearly merits further study.

An alternative answer to the question of what constitutes emotion-relevant processing has been proposed by Eich and Metcalfe (1989). They conjectured that events generated through internal mental operations such as reasoning, imagination, or interpretation may be more closely connected to or deeply colored by one's current mood than are events whose processing is guided by external sources. If so, then a shift in mood state between the occasions of event encoding and event retrieval should have a greater adverse impact on memory for internal than for external events. Consistent with this notion, tasks such as word association, narrative construction, and interpersonal assessment are often performed in a mood congruent manner (Bower et al., 1981; Isen, Johnson, Mertz, & Robinson, 1985; Lewinsohn, Mischel, Chaplin, & Barton, 1980). Furthermore, tests of retention, such as free recall, that rely on internally generated responses are more likely to reveal mood dependence than are tests, like cued recall or old/new recognition memory, that rely on externally provided reminders (Blaney, 1986; Schare et al., 1984). This is consistent with Eich's (1980) observation that drug-dependent memory occurs frequently in free recall but rarely in cued recall or recognition.

Eich and Metcalfe (1989) investigated these intuitions in a series of studies that involved procedures similar to those used in Slamecka and Graf's (1978) well-known research on the *generation effect* in memory. Specifically, subjects either read a target item, such as gold, that was paired with a category name and a related exemplar (e.g., *precious metals: silver–gold*), or they generated (with a very high probability) the same item when primed with its initial letter, in combination with the category name and exemplar cues (e.g., *precious metals: silver–g*). In this manner, memory for one and the same item could be assessed in relation to its source: either internal (the generate condition) or external (the read condition).

During the encoding session of the first experiment, every participant generated 16 target items and read 16 others while experiencing either a pleasant or an unpleasant mood—states that had been induced by asking the subject to contemplate pleasant or unpleasant incidents from the personal past while she or he listened to various selections of "happy" or "sad" classical music. During the retrieval session, which met 2 days after encoding, all subjects received two surprise tests of retention: first free recall, and then old/new recognition memory. Subjects undertook these tests either in the same mood in which they had generated or read the target items, or in the alternative affective state. Thus, the experiment entailed a 2 × 2 × 2 × 2 mixed design, with encoding mood (pleasant versus unpleasant) and retrieval mood (again, pleasant versus unpleasant) as between-subject factors, and item type (generate versus read) and retention test (recall versus recognition) as within-subject variables.

Four key findings emerged from the experiment. First, the probability of recall, averaged across encoding and retrieval moods, was much higher for generated than for read items—evidence indicative of the familiar generation effect (Slamecka & Graf, 1978). Second, subjects in the matched mood conditions recalled more items than subjects in mismatched moods, indicating mood dependence. Third, the advantage of matched over mismatched moods for free recall was greater for items that had been generated than for those that had been read—a finding that supports the supposition that internally generated events may be especially susceptible to mood dependence. Finally, reminiscent of earlier research (e.g., Bower, 1981), there was no sign of mood dependence in the recognition of either generated or read items.

In three subsequent studies, Eich and Metcalfe (1989) secured results that were generally, though not perfectly, compatible with those of the first. In Experiment 2, for instance, an effort was made to reduce, and perhaps even reverse, the generation effect by giving subjects three opportunities to read certain target items, but only one opportunity to generate certain others. Though the probability of recall, averaged across encoding/retrieval moods, was higher for thrice-read than for once-generated items, only the latter type of target showed significant mood dependence. In Experiment 3, however, the recall of thrice-read items showed the same degree of mood dependence as did the recall of thrice-generated targets. Finally, in Experiment 4, a reliable mood-dependent effect was evident in the recall of once- or thrice-generated items, but not in the recall of either once- or thrice-read words.

Considered collectively, these results suggest that events generated through internal mental processes are more colored by one's current mood than are events that derive from external sources, and, as a consequence, internal events are particularly apt to be forgotten following a shift in mood state. To pursue this idea further, we have recently undertaken a new series of studies employing a different kind of item generation task, one that capitalizes on the idea of internal generation. The studies entailed the same basic encoding mood/retrieval mood design as in Eich and Metcalfe (1989), with pleasant and unpleasant moods again induced using appropriate music coupled with personal contemplation. During the encoding session, subjects are asked to recollect episodes or experiences from their personal past that were called to mind by emotionally neutral probes, such as *ocean* and *gold*. After describing the recollection of each experience in detail, subjects rate the event along several dimensions, including its original emotional valence and intensity (i.e., how positive or negative the event seemed at the time it transpired). Two or 3 days later, the subjects are asked, unexpectedly, to freely recall the autobiographical events and their eliciting cues from the initial session.

Compared to the task of generating, say, *gold* in response to *precious metals: silver–g*, the task of generating a gold-related memory from one's personal past seems likely to place a greater premium on internal mental processing. Also, since the latter task allows subjects a much broader range of responses, their selection of responses may reflect their present mood state. It seems plausible to predict, then, that the recall of autobiographical memories should show strong signs of mood dependence.

This prediction has been borne out in three separate studies. Representative results, derived from the initial study in the series (Eich & Ryan, 1989), are depicted in Fig. 4.1. The illustration shows the mean proportions of positive and negative autobiographical events that were recalled in each of the four encoding mood/retrieval mood conditions. As is apparent in the figure, the recall of either type of event was considerably higher under matched than under mismatched mood conditions—a clear demonstration of the oftentimes cloudy phenomenon of mood-dependent memory.

To summarize the main points of this section, what we have advanced is essentially a TAP view of mood-dependent memory. Mood influences the remembrance of events when subjects engage in processing, at encoding as well as at retrieval, that is sensitive to mood. We suggest that emotion-relevant processing is especially likely to occur when the source of the events is internal. That is, when subjects engage in imagination, interpretation, or other forms of internal mental operations, their current mood is more likely to influence performance than when they engage in processes that are more perceptual in nature or guided by external sources. Thus, imagining oneself in emotional situations (Bower & Mayer, 1989), generating category exemplars (Eich & Metcalfe, 1989), recollecting autobiographical experiences (Eich & Ryan, 1989), or recalling events in the absence of observable cues or reminders (Eich, 1980) all constitute tasks in which subjects' responses are apt to be colored by their emotional state. To the

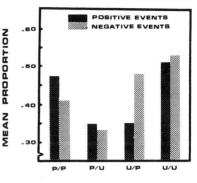

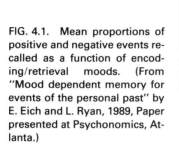

FIG. 4.1. Mean proportions of positive and negative events recalled as a function of encoding/retrieval moods. (From "Mood dependent memory for events of the personal past" by E. Eich and L. Ryan, 1989, Paper presented at Psychonomics, Atlanta.)

extent that a mood present at both encoding and retrieval promotes similar alterations in processing, memory performance will be facilitated. Concurrently, to the extent that two different moods will result in different alterations in processing, memory performance will be disrupted, perhaps even inhibited.

THE NATURE OF EMOTIONAL MEMORY: EXPLICIT OR IMPLICIT?

The discussion thus far has centered on the influence of emotion in situations where we are trying to consciously recollect prior events. A more true-to-life scenario might be one like the earlier example of being suddenly reminded of watching a sunset while listening to a beautiful melody. Importantly, such a memory seems to arise unexpectedly, when we are not trying to recollect anything. We often describe the phenomenon as a feeling of familiarity, of having experienced something similar once before, although we cannot pinpoint where or when. We then may continue to search our memory in order to fill in the details of that experience. Perhaps emotions—and for that matter other aspects of the environmental context such as fragrances, textures, sounds, or even drug-produced sensations—enhance memory for prior events more by virtue of some similarity between the past and present, rather than by any conscious effort to remember.

Graf and Schacter (1985) employed the term implicit memory to describe situations where a prior experience enhances task performance without the necessity of subjects becoming consciously aware of that prior experience. An important aspect of the implicit/explicit distinction is the intention of the subject. In explicit tasks, like recall or recognition, the subject makes a conscious effort to remember a prior episode and may use various strategies and available cues to achieve this aim. In implicit tasks, like category production or word identification, prior experiences that overlap with the present episode on relevant features are processed more fluently than are other experiences. This processing fluency will *prime* or enable these experiences to spring to mind more readily, and hence will improve task performance even though the subjects are not consciously trying to remember past events.

To date, virtually all research on mood-dependent memory has been carried out with tasks such as free recall, recognition, or cued recall, where the subject must consciously recall past events. The effect of emotion on implicit tasks is, however, of particular interest in that implicit tasks may provide clues to the mechanisms mediating mood-dependent memory. One view holds that mood encourages the elaboration of information in mood-relevant ways, thereby establishing associations between the original learning episode and the mood. These associations allow a similar mood to become a salient cue during subsequent retrieval, especially in the absence of other conceptual or perceptual cuing information. Mood might thus be employed by subjects as part of their conscious retrieval strategies. If so, one would not expect mood to influence implicit memory, because elaboration and conscious retrieval strategies typically affect performance on explicit tasks but not on implicit ones (Graf, Mandler, & Hayden, 1982).

An alternative view is that mood exerts its influence because it is incorporated along with other relevant aspects of a target event into a unitary memory representation. The later experience of a similar mood acts as a partial re-presentation of the prior event. The reprocessing of this partial information may enable the redintegration of the entire memory representation and allow matching events to come to mind more readily (Graf & Ryan, 1990; Horowitz & Prytulak, 1969; Mandler, 1980, 1988). If so, then performance on implicit tests of memory should be enhanced by the presence of similar moods.

Further, if one considers mood as a special aspect of the environmental context, then implicit tasks are of interest because they are sensitive to the manipulation of other contextual variables. For example, changes between study and test in the modality of presentation (e.g., Clarke & Morton, 1983; Roediger & Blaxton, 1987) or in the visual display of the target stimuli (e.g., Graf & Ryan, 1990; Jacoby & Dallas, 1981) decrease the size of the priming effect in various implicit tasks. Recently, several studies of place dependent memory also have shown that alterations in the environmental circumstances surrounding encoding and retrieval attenuates priming (Graf, 1988; Smith, Heath, & Vela, 1990). If mood is akin to other types of contexts (see Eich & Birnbaum, 1988), then implicit tasks should be sensitive to shifts in mood.

Several recent investigations of mood dependence in implicit memory have had mixed results. Consider the outcomes of two studies reported by Eich and Ryan (1990), the first of which investigated mood dependence within the context of an implicit test of word-stem completion. During the encoding session of this study, subjects experiencing pleasant or unpleasant moods rated neutral words for goodness of meaning, visual imageability, and associative difficulty. During the retrieval session, which occurred 2 days later, subjects experiencing matching or mismatching moods were asked to complete three-letter words stems with the first words that came to mind; half of the stems corresponded to old words (ones that had been rated during the initial session) and half corresponded to new words. The second study employed an implicit picture identification test. At encoding, slides of common objects were presented in clear focus to subjects who were asked to think about and describe aloud their last contact with each object. Two days later, subjects were asked to identify objects portrayed on blurry or out-of-focus slides; some of the objects were old (pictures that had been shown during the previous session), and others were new.

The results of both of these studies were similarly disappointing. Although there was reliable priming in all conditions—the three-letter stems elicited many more old than new words in the first study, and old objects were more often identified than new objects at comparable degrees of blurriness—there was no sign of mood dependence. That is, in neither study was priming significantly greater among subjects whose encoding and retrieval moods matched than among those whose moods mismatched.

After completing these two studies, it occurred to us that we were not following our own advice regarding the choice of potentially emotion-sensitive encoding and retrieval tasks. More to the point, neither study employed an encoding task that would encourage subjects to engage in the kinds of internal mental processing that may foster the emergence of mood-dependent effects. Moreover, by requiring the production of discrete rather than continuous responses, both word-stem completion and picture identification may enjoin subjects from engaging in internal mental processing at retrieval.

These considerations gave rise to a third attempt to demonstrate mood dependence in implicit memory. The encoding task employed in this study was identical to the one previously cited in connection with our recent research on mood dependence in autobiographical memory. Thus, subjects in pleasant or unpleasant moods generated episodes or events from their personal past in response to emotionally neutral probes, such as *flute* and *pearl*. The subjects described every event in detail, then specified its original emotional valence (either positive, neutral, or negative), its original emotional intensity, and other attributes. As noted earlier, this is a task that should place a premium on internal mental processing. During the retrieval session, held 2 days later, subjects in matched or mismatched moods completed two tests of retention of the autobiographical memory probes. A random half of the probes were tested via category production—an implicit measure of memory. For this purpose, subjects were given a category name, such as *musical instruments*, and were asked to name the first six category exemplars that came to mind. The remaining half of the probes were tested via category cued recall—an index of explicit memory. Again, subjects were given a category name, such as precious stones, but this time they were

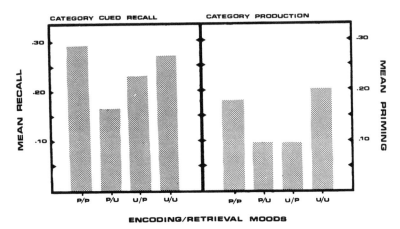

FIG. 4.2. Mean proportion of autobiographical memory probes remembered in the explicit test of category cued recall (panel A), and mean proportion of autobiographical memory probes produced above baserate in the implicit test of category production (panel B), both as a function of encoding/retrieval moods. (From "Mood dependence in implicit memory" by E. Eich and L. Ryan, 1990, Paper presented at Psychonomics, New Orleans.)

asked to use the cue as a aid in consciously recollecting a related probe from the initial session.

The results of this study are depicted in Fig. 4.2. On the category production task, priming was evidenced by the increased probability of producing the probe words in response to the category names over baserate conditions. Importantly, the pattern of results for the implicit test was similar to that shown by the explicit measure. In both category production and category cued recall, memory was mood dependent. That is, subjects in the matched mood conditions revealed more priming and recalled more probes than did their counterparts in the mismatched mood conditions.

Though interesting in their own right, these results seem especially intriguing in light of the recent research reported by Tobias, Kihlstrom, and Schacter (1990). Their first experiment—like that of Eich and Ryan (1990)—failed to find evidence of mood dependence in the performance of an implicit test of word-stem completion. In a second experiment, Tobias and her colleagues employed two memory tests, namely, free recall and its implicit analog. In the latter case, subjects were simply given a set of blank spaces and the instructions to write down the first words that came to mind. Priming in this implicit test was mood dependent—puzzlingly, however, free recall was not.

Taken together, the studies by Tobias et al. (1990) and by Eich and Ryan (1990) suggest that implicit measures of memory, like those of an explicit nature, differ in their sensitivity to the detection of mood-dependent effects. Moreover, the characteristics of a test that determine its sensitivity seem to be similar for both explicit and implicit measures. In particular, mood-dependent effects may be more readily detected via tests—such as category production, category cued recall, and free recall—that allow the subject a wide range of responses than by means of tests—such as picture identification, word-stem completion, and old/new recognition memory—that restrict the range of responses by making it necessary for subjects to match their responses to the specific physical features of the presented cues.

CONTEXT-DEPENDENT MEMORY

Contextual variables other than mood have also been shown to produce context-dependent effects in both implicit and explicit tests of memory. Recently, Graf and Ryan (1990) reported that recognition of targets and word identification priming was better for words presented in the same unusual script fonts than for words presented in different unusual script fonts. However, this was true only when the study task required subjects to attend to the physical characteristics of the words; when they attended to semantic attributes, altering the script fonts had no appreciable effect on either test. The authors argued that in order to obtain visual-format-dependent memory, both the study task and the memory tests must rely on visually relevant processing of the target words.

In a very different approach to context-dependent memory, Nissen, Ross, Willingham, Mackenzie, and Schacter (1988) investigated the transfer of information across personalities in a patient with multiple personality disorder. As a rule, these personalities are associated with different past histories and markedly different moods (Putnam, 1989). To the extent that the personalities are experienced by the patient as distinctive states, analogous to the mismatched encoding/retrieval conditions of a mood dependence study, switching personalities would be expected to interfere with memory performance. Indeed, mood-dependent memory is often cited as an explanation of transpersonality amnesia (Bliss, 1986; Bower, 1981; Putnam, 1989). Nissen et al. (1988) found that when one personality learned a list of words and an alternate personality was tested with cued recall or word identification, memory performance was as good as when the original personality had been reinstated prior to testing. However, when one personality interpreted ambiguous text passages or made pleasantness judgements of target words, and an alternate personality was asked to interpret the same ambiguous passages or to freely recall the target words, memory performance was severely impaired. Nissen and her associates concluded that regardless of the implicit or explicit nature of the retention tests, evidence of personality-dependent memory emerged to the extent that the encoding and retrieval tasks allowed for the expression of personality-specific factors.

A TAP ACCOUNT OF CONTEXT-DEPENDENT
MEMORY

It appears to us that TAP provides a general framework for understanding the circumstances under which changes in seemingly disparate aspects of experience, including induced mood, visual format, multiple personality, and other forms of context, will result in context-dependent memory. The phenomenon occurs only when the cognitive operations at both encoding and retrieval engage the relevant aspect of the context. By this view, it is essential to identify the types of tasks that will require context-relevant processing, and these will differ depending on the context of interest. Importantly, this TAP view can account for the contextual effects in both explicit and implicit memory.

Although memory research has most often highlighted the dissociations between implicit and explicit memory, the circumstances that produce context dependence are similar for implicit priming tasks and for explicit recollective tasks. Given this association, it is parsimonious to posit a single mechanism mediating all context-dependent effects, regardless of whether the memory task does or does not require conscious recollection. Contextual variables may reinstate memories via redintegrative processes that have been implicated as the basis of implicit memory (Graf & Mandler, 1984). That is, a similar context may act as a partial re-presentation of the original event, and thereby promote the redintegration of the entire memory representation. This presupposes that the contextual feature of interest was originally integrated into the memory representation by an appropriate encoding task.

Although it may seem strange to suggest that redintegration plays a pivotal role in the performance of a task such as free recall, it should be remembered that Mandler (1980, 1988) originally invoked the concepts of elaboration and integration as the two fundamental bases of recognition—a task generally considered to be explicit. He argued that when subjects have no direct retrieval routes available, they will rely on familiarity or fluency of processing to make their recognition judgments. Graf and Mandler (1984) extended this idea to account for dissociations between performance on implicit and explicit tasks. We suggest that context-dependent effect in any memory test may be mediated by the familiarity or fluency of processing of information. This familiarity or fluency of processing will act by increasing the ease with which context matching experiences come to mind. In the most extreme case, a very distinctive context, such as a particular fragrance or internal emotional state, might cause us to unexpectedly reexperience a prior event, as in the case of spontaneous recollection. In other situations, contextual features may not be sufficiently specific or distinctive to be reliable cues for conscious retrieval. However, given the right conditions, they may enhance the processing of context-matching events sufficiently to produce context-dependent effects. On implicit tests, the overlap of contextual features will boost priming by virtue of the increased fluency of processing of information necessary for the test.

MOOD AND MEMORY AND EMOTION THEORIES

As is evident in the previous discussion, cognitive psychologists have focused on emotion as a feature of the environment. Researchers studying emotion and memory have, for the most part, overlooked the difficult issue of the nature of emotion and emotional experience. With due respect to Gertrude Stein, the prevailing assumption has been that a mood is a mood is a mood. That is, any two moods experienced as distinctive states should be sufficient to result in mood-dependent memory. However, the studies of mood dependence that we have discussed all compare only two emotions, namely, happiness and sadness, and it is possible that there is something particular—perhaps peculiar—about the nature of these two emotions. Indeed, theories of emotion are as concerned with the unique aspects of various emotions as with their similarities. In this last section, we turn to three views of the nature of emotion that have unique implications for understanding the relation between emotion and cognition.

Russell's (1980) circumplex model of affect suggests that although emotions may differ in many ways, all can be categorized along two key dimensions: pleasure–displeasure and high arousal–low arousal. Although happiness and sadness clearly differ on the level of pleasure, they also tend to differ on level of arousal, and there is a moderately positive correlation between the two dimensions (see Eich & Metcalfe, 1989). Are differences on both of the basic components of emotions necessary for the production of mood-dependent effects? There has been one report of arousal-dependent memory (Clark, Milberg, & Ross, 1983), although pleasure–displeasure was not specifically measured. In our own lab, we find that subjects who show the greatest changes in both pleasure and arousal also show the strongest mood-dependent effects (Eich & Metcalfe, 1989). This observation suggests that arousal is an important variable to consider in mood and cognition experiments, and that it might have an interactive, possibly synergistic effect with pleasure–displeasure.

Russell's (1980) model leads one to consider the possibility of mood-dependent effects between two affective states that differ on only one of the two principal dimensions. Would these effects be evident when contrasting fear and sadness, which are both clearly unpleasant states but which differ substantially on level of arousal? Another interesting comparison would be between fear and anger, because both emotions are unpleasant and highly aroused states. Comparisons like these may provide information about the contribution of each basic dimension to mood-dependent memory.

A different type of emotion theory proposes a set of basic, unique emotions (see Mandler, 1984). One variant of this theory suggests that there are five basic emotions, each of a qualitatively different nature and serving a different evolutionary purpose (e.g., Johnson-Laird & Oatley, 1988). Each basic emotion is related to certain types of events. For example, happiness results from the establishment and maintenance of attachments, whereas sadness stems from the loss of such attachments. Fear, anger, and disgust are said to prepare us for escape or submission, aggression, and the rejection of a person or object, respectively. These emotions are thought to ready us for different action patterns. It follows that these action patterns may include the accentuation of various cognitive processes. So, for example, fear may encourage attention to our environment as we seek out and select information about potential danger (Mathews & Eysenck, 1987), whereas sadness may encourage attention to ourselves as we remember the attachment and reflect on our loss (Pyszczynski, Hamilton, Herring & Greenberg, 1989).

This approach forces us to consider each emotion as unique. The question of interest becomes not "How does mood influence memory?" but rather "How do distinct moods influence different cognitive processes?" This question may hold a key to understanding how emotions influence remembering. Perhaps happiness and sadness have been successfully employed in the production of mood-dependent effects through their influence on generative cognitive operations, whereas other emotions which influence other operations may require the use of different tasks to demonstrate mood dependence.

Mood-congruent effects provide some evidence about the changes in cognitive processing that may be specific to a particular mood. Subjects are biased in various ways toward material having an affective tone similar to their current mood. The types of biases, however, may be mood specific. On the one hand, there is a large and consistent literature documenting enhanced memory for negatively toned material in sad subjects (see Blaney, 1986); on the other hand, evidence from several sources suggests that sad subjects show no bias in their perception of sad stimuli (e.g., Bower, 1987; Challis & Krane, 1988; MacLeod, Tata, & Mathews, 1987). Researchers have consistently demonstrated biased perception of threatening material in fearful subjects (see Mathews & Eysenck, 1987), but the few studies investigating any enhancement of memory for such material have been inconsistent (e.g., McNally, Foa, & Donnell, 1989; Richards & Millwood, 1989). In sum, there seems to be strong evidence for mood-congruent effects of sadness—but not fear—on memorial processes, and for mood-congruent effects of fear—but not sadness—on perceptual processes.

Drawing on the mood congruence literature just cited, one might expect sadness, but not fear, to produce mood-dependent memory. In a recent investigation (Watts & Dalgleish, 1991), spider phobics studied fear-relevant and neutral words in the presence of a spider or while performing relaxation exercises. Presumably, this manipulation created two affective states—one frightening and agitating, the other pleasant and relaxing. Regardless of whether subjects attempted to recall the words under matching or mismatching mood conditions, they remembered similar amounts of information. Notwithstanding these negative results, it would seem worthwhile to continue to explore the possibility of fear-dependent memory, either by using methods that appear to work with happiness and sadness—namely, internal processing at encoding and reliance on internal cues at testing—or by identifying tasks, perhaps those that rely heavily on attentional or perceptual processes, that encourage fear-relevant processing.

Yet a third theory of emotion is centered on cognitive appraisal and arousal (Mandler, 1984; Schachter & Singer, 1962). This theory maintains that one labels the experience of physiological changes in arousal through cognitive appraisal, which depends on situational contexts. High arousal in the presence of a spider may be interpreted as fear, whereas high arousal in the presence of a stranger may be seen as sexual attraction. The assumption, then, is that a cardinal difference between moods is the contents of our thoughts. Interestingly, Perrig and Perrig (1988) observed mood-congruent effects in subjects who had been asked to simulate sadness and happiness. The Perrigs suggested that mood-relevant schemas—which include mood-specific vocabulary, conceptual information, and personal life events—are available to us without necessarily experiencing the emotion. If the cognitive component is critical in creating the distinctive context of mood, one should likewise be able to mimic mood-dependent effects through a change in cognitions alone, without the subjective experience of mood. Alternatively, if one holds that there is something special about emotion beyond its informational value, then the subjective experience of emotion should be critical in producing the cognitive effects that we have discussed. This point is of central concern to our future understanding of emotion and memory.

SUMMARY

In this chapter, our main aims were to accentuate the features of mood and memory research that may be of interest to a broad spectrum of memory investigators, and to demonstrate how the exploration of such effects is another means of revealing basic principles about memory. In the course of reviewing the conditions necessary for establishing mood-dependent effects, we developed a TAP-based view for understanding the influence of mood and, more generally, context on remembering. This view entails two tenets: (a) that both study tasks and memory tests must engage context-relevant processes, and that the specific processes will differ depending on the contextual feature of interest, and (b) that context may influence performance on both implicit and explicit tests through redintegrative processes, and that context dependence will be evident only in the absence of more specific and reliable memory cues. We then turned to theories of emotion for insights into the nature of the relationship between cognition and subjective emotional experience. This is an area that cognitive psychologists interested in emotion and memory have tended to avoid. We believe that such cross-fertilization is timely and will be fruitful for understanding both the nature of emotion and its impact on cognition.

ACKNOWLEDGMENT

Preparation of this chapter was aided by Grant 37335 from the Natural Sciences and Engineering Research Council of Canada. Our thanks to Peter Graf and Robert Lockhart for their cogent comments and criticisms, and to Ainslie Winter, Christine Beck, and Andria Sankey for their assistance in conducting the research reported here.

REFERENCES

Baddeley, A. (1982). Domains of recollection. *Psychological Review, 89*, 708–729.

Bartlett, J. C., Burleson, G., & Santrock, J. W. (1982). Emotional mood and memory in young children. *Journal of Experimental Child Psychology, 34*, 59–76.

Blaney, P. H. (1986). Affect and memory: A review. *Psychological Bulletin, 99*, 929–246.

Bliss, E. L. (1986). *Multiple personality, allied disorders and hypnosis.* New York: Oxford University Press.

Bower, G. H. (1981). Mood and memory. *American Psychologist, 36*, 129–149.

Bower, G. H. (1987). Commentary on mood and memory. *Behaviour Research and Therapy, 25*, 443–455.

Bower, G. H., Gilligan, S. G., & Monteiro, K. P. (1981). Selectivity of learning caused by affective states. *Journal of Experimental Psychology: General, 110*, 451–473.

Bower, G. H., & Mayer, J. D. (1989). In search of mood-dependent retrieval. *Journal of Social Behavior and Personality, 4*, 121–156.

Bower, G. H., Monteiro, K. P., & Gilligan, S. G. (1978). Emotional mood as a context for learning and recall. *Journal of Verbal Learning and Verbal Behavior, 17*, 573–585.

Challis, B. H., & Krane, R. V. (1988). Mood induction and the priming of semantic memory in a lexical decision task: Asymmetric effects of elation and depression. *Bulletin of the Psychonomic Society, 26*, 309–312.

Clark, M. S., Milberg, S., & Ross, J. (1983). Arousal cues arousal-related material in memory: Implications for understanding effects of mood on memory. *Journal of Verbal Learning and Verbal Behavior, 22*, 633–649.

Clarke, R., & Morton, J. (1983). Cross modality facilitation on tachistoscopic word recognition. *Quarterly Journal of Experimental Psychology, 35A*, 79–96.

Eich, E. (1980). The cue-dependent nature of state-dependent retrieval. *Memory & Cognition, 8*, 157–173.

Eich, E. (1989). Theoretical issues in state dependent memory. In H. Roediger & F. Craik (Eds.), *Varieties of memory and consciousness: Essays in honour of Endel Tulving* (pp. 331–354). Hillsdale, NJ: Lawrence Erlbaum Associates.

Eich, E., & Birnbaum, I. M. (1988). On the relationship between the dissociative and affective properties of drugs. In G. M. Davies & D. M. Thomson (Eds.), *Memory in context: Context in memory* (pp. 81–93). Chichester, England: John Wiley.

Eich, E., & Metcalfe, J. (1989). Mood dependent memory for internal versus external events. *Journal of Experimental Psychology: Learning, Memory, and Cognition, 15*, 443–455.

Eich, E., & Ryan, L. (1989, November). *Mood dependent memory for events of the personal past.* Paper presented at Psychonomics, Atlanta.

Eich, E., & Ryan, L. (1990, November). *Mood dependence in implicit memory.* Paper presented at Psychonomics, New Orleans.

Fernandez, A., & Glenberg, A. M. (1985). Changing environmental context does not reliably affect memory. *Memory & Cognition, 13,* 333–345.

Gardner, H. (1985). *The mind's new science.* New York: Basic Books.

Graf, P. (1988, November). *Implicit and explicit remembering in same and different environments.* Paper presented at Psychonomics, Chicago.

Graf, P., & Mandler, G. (1984). Activation makes words more accessible but not necessarily more retrievable. *Journal of Verbal Learning and Verbal Behavior, 23,* 553–568.

Graf, P., Mandler, G., & Haden, M. (1982). Simulating amnesic symptoms in normal subjects. *Science, 218,* 1243–1244.

Graf, P., & Ryan, L. (1990). Transfer appropriate processing for implicit and explicit memory. *Journal of Experimental Psychology: Learning, Memory, and Cognition, 16,* 978–992.

Graf, P., & Schacter, D. (1985). Implicit and explicit memory for new associations in normal and amnesic subjects. *Journal of Experimental Psychology: Learning, Memory, and Cognition, 11,* 501–518.

Horowitz, L. M., & Prytulak, L. S. (1969). Redintegrative memory. *Psychological Review, 84,* 519–531.

Isen, A. M., Johnson, M. M., Mertz, E., & Robinson, G. F. (1985). The influence of positive affect on the unusualness of word associations. *Journal of Personality and Social Psychology, 48,* 1413–1426.

Jacoby, L. L., & Dallas, M. (1981). On the relationship between autobiographical memory and perceptual learning. *Journal of Experimental Psychology: General, 110,* 306–340.

Johnson, T. L., & Klinger, E. (1988). A nonhypnotic failure to replicate mood dependent recall. *Bulletin of the Psychonomic Society, 26,* 191–194.

Johnson-Laird, P. N., & Oatley, K. (1988). Are there only two primitive emotions? A reply to Frijda. *Cognition and Emotion, 2,* 89–93.

Kolers, P. A. (1973). Remembering operations. *Memory & Cognition, 1,* 347–355.

Kolers, P. A. (1975). Memorial consequences of automatized encoding. *Journal of Experimental Psychology: Human Learning and Memory, 1,* 689–701.

Lewinsohn, P. M., Mischel, W., Chaplin, W., & Barton, R. (1980). Social competence and depression: The role of illusory self-perceptions. *Journal of Abnormal Psychology, 89,* 203–212.

MacLeod, C., Tata, P., & Mathews, A. (1987). Perception of emotionally valenced information in depression. *British Journal of Clinical Psychology, 26,* 67–68.

Mandler, G. (1980). Recognizing: The judgement of previous occurrence. *Psychological Review, 87,* 252–271.

Mandler, G. (1984). *Mind and body.* New York: Norton.

Mandler, G. (1988). Memory: Conscious and unconscious. In P. R. Solomon, G. R. Goethals, C. M. Kelley, & B. R. Stephens (Eds.), *Memory: Interdisciplinary approaches* (pp. 84–106). New York: Springer-Verlag.

Mathews, A., & Eysenck, M. (1987). Clinical anxiety and cognition. In M. J. Eysenck & I. Martin (Eds.), *Theoretical foundations of behavior therapy* (pp. 217–234). New York: Plenum Press.

McNally, R. J., Foa, E. B., & Donnell, C. D. (1989). Memory bias for anxiety information in patients with panic disorder. *Cognition and Emotion, 3,* 27–44.

Mecklenbrauker, S., & Hager, W. (1984). Effects of mood on memory: Experimental tests of mood-state-dependent retrieval hypothesis and of a mood-congruity hypothesis. *Psychological Research, 46,* 355–376.

Morris, C. D., Bransford, J. D., & Franks, J. J. (1977). Levels of processing versus transfer appropriate processing. *Journal of Verbal Learning and Verbal Behavior, 16,* 519–533.

Nissen, M., Ross, J., Willingham, D., Mackenzie, T., & Schacter, D. (1988). Memory and amnesia in a patient with multiple personality disorder. *Brain and Cognition, 8,* 117–134.

Overton, D. A. (1984). State dependent learning and drug discriminations. In L. L. Iverson, S. D. Iverson, & S. J. Snyder (Eds.), *Handbook of psychopharmacology* (Vol. 18, pp. 59–127). New York: Plenum Press.

Perrig, W. J., & Perrig, P. (1988). Mood and memory: Mood congruity effects in absence of mood. *Memory & Cognition, 16,* 102–109.

Putnam, F. (1989). *Diagnosis and treatment of multiple personality disorders.* New York: Guilford Press.

Pyszczynski, T., Hamilton, J. C., Herring, F. H., & Greenberg, J. (1989). Depression, self-focused attention, and the negative memory bias. *Journal of Personality and Social Psychology, 57,* 351–357.

Richards, A., & Millwood, B. (1989). Colour-identification of differentially valenced words in anxiety. *Cognition and Emotion, 3,* 171–176.

Roediger, H. L., & Blaxton, T. A. (1987). Effects of varying modality, surface features, and retention interval on priming in word-fragment completion. *Memory & Cognition, 15,* 379–388.

Russell, J. A. (1980). A circumplex model of affect. *Journal of Personality and Social Psychology, 39,* 1161–1178.

Schachter, S., & Singer, J. E. (1962). Cognitive, social and physiological determinants of emotional state. *Psychological Review, 69,* 379–399.

Schare, M. L., Lisman, S. A., & Spear, N. E. (1984). The effects of mood variation on state-dependent retention. *Cognitive Therapy and Research, 8,* 387–408.

Slamecka, N. J., & Graf, P. (1978). The generation effect: Delineation of a phenomenon. *Journal of Experimental Psychology: Human Learning and Memory, 4,* 592–604.

Smith, S. M., Heath, F. R., & Vela, E. (1990). Environmental context-dependent homophone spelling. *American Journal of Psychology, 103,* 229–242.

Tobias, B. A., Kihlstrom, J. F., & Schacter, D. L. (November, 1990). *Mood, emotion and implicit memory: Prospects and problems.* Paper presented at Psychonomics, New Orleans.

Tulving, E. (1983). *Elements of episodic memory.* Oxford: Oxford University Press.

Watts, R. N., & Dalgleish, T. (1991). Memory for phobia-related words in spider phobics. *Cognition and Emotion, 5,* 313–329.

Wetzler, S. (1985). Mood state-dependent retrieval: A failure to replicate. *Psychological Reports, 56,* 759–765.

5 Implicit Processes in Problem Solving

Robert S. Lockhart
A. Boyd Blackburn
University of Toronto

Experimental psychologists have traditionally been suspicious of the unconscious. However, as is clear from other chapters in this volume, there is now widespread experimental support for the claim that in the domains of perception and memory important cognitive processes occur outside the realm of conscious awareness. But what of problem solving? Perhaps more than any other area of cognitive psychology, problem solving abounds in anecdotes of unconscious processes. Solutions are reached with sudden flashes of insight or leaps of intuition that defy introspective causal analysis. Such alleged implicit processes are among the most persistently reported but least understood phenomena in cognitive psychology.

In discussing implicit processes in problem solving it is helpful to begin by making two broad distinctions. The first contrasts two dimensions; values on these dimensions can be thought of as the relative contribution of two sources of difficulty in solving a problem. Roughly, the distinction we wish to make is between *conceptual access* as a source of difficulty and the difficulty of *constructing or assembling procedures*. The second distinction is between implicit *learning* and implicit *memory,* a distinction that as Reber (1989) points out is both important and neglected. Both these distinctions require a great deal of refinement and elaboration before they will carry much theoretical weight (an exercise well beyond the scope of this chapter), but as reference points for organizing our discussion of implicit processes in problem solving the distinctions are useful and not especially controversial. The two distinctions are related: Our plan is to examine the possible role of implicit learning in the construction of procedures, and the role of implicit memory in conceptual access.

CONCEPTUAL ACCESS AND PROCEDURAL PROCESSING

This distinction is partly prompted by Greeno's (1978) useful typology of problems, and partly from contemporary computational theories of problem solving (e.g., Anderson, 1983). Greeno distinguishes problems of inducing structure (such as analogies) from problems of transformation (such as the Tower of Hanoi problem, described later) and of rearrangement (such as anagrams). For present purposes a broader distinction is appropriate with a somewhat different emphasis. We wish to distinguish aspects of a problem that can be solved through the direct application of an existing set of cognitive procedures (a production system existing in procedural memory, for example) from those that require the construction of novel procedures, or a novel structuring of existing procedures.

Conceptual Access

By conceptual access in problem solving we mean those retrieval processes that lead to the activation of existing cognitive representations that are essential to achieving a solution. Because we make frequent use of the term cognitive representations, it is important to be clear what we mean (and do not mean) by the term. We are using the term at a strictly functional level to refer to any set of procedures that serve to organize experience, and to support such cognitive functions as making inferences and answering questions. The representations may be as simple as a single concept or word meaning, or as complex as a script, frame, schema, or connectionist net. The way in which concepts can organize a simple stimulus set is well illustrated with a typical result from an experiment by Cofer (1951). Given the sequence of words *skyscraper, cathedral, temple, prayer,* subjects tend to consider *prayer* to be the odd word, but if the sequence is ordered *prayer, cathedral, temple, skyscraper* then *skyscraper* is judged to be the odd word. In these cases the different grouping of the elements is a consequence of different concepts being accessed through the cuing properties of the initial words in the sequence. We prefer to think of representations in procedural rather than in static structural terms. The important point, however, is that these representations exist in long term memory as organized procedures, so that, when confronted with a problem to which these representations are relevant, it is their activation not their acquisition or construction that is critical.

Perhaps the purest examples of problems that have conceptual access as virtually their only source of difficulty are simple riddles of the kind used by Auble, Franks, and Soraci (1979). Consider, for example, the problem posed by the following riddle: *John threw the rock far out into the lake where it rested on the surface for two months before sinking to the bottom 20 feet below.* Solutions to such simple riddles hinge on accessing a single concept (ice, frozen, or some such); once this concept is accessed, comprehension is almost immediate, giving rise to the subjective sense of insight or "aha!" Any difficulty in solving such problems is due to a failure to access the appropriate concept; indeed, riddles (and many jokes) are constructed on the principle of blocking immediate access to a key concept that, when it is accessed, provides an immediate resolution to an apparently impossible state of affairs.

Procedural Processing

At the other extreme from riddles are problems that pose little or no difficulty in terms of conceptual access but involve extensive assembling and application of procedures. Among problems studied by experimental psychologists, the Tower of Hanoi problem or cryptarithmetic would be prototypical examples. In the simplest version, the Tower of Hanoi is a problem consisting of three pegs and three different sized discs. The subject is required to move the three discs, one at a time, from their starting position on one peg to a designated goal peg, subject to the constraint that a larger disc can never be on top of a smaller one. Cryptarithmetic is a problem in which two rows of letters arithmetically sum to form a third row when the letters are replaced with the appropriate digits. With such problems there is little or no difficulty of conceptual access; they are to a large degree *conceptually transparent*. The major source of difficulty lies in the assembling of procedures (in these examples, a sequence of moves or operations), because for such problems there is no existing concept or schema that needs merely to be activated for the solution to be generated. Unlike standard arithmetic problems, which, for the person proficient in basic arithmetic, involve the execution of existing procedures, cryptarithmetic requires the construction of a novel set of procedures assembled from the set of more basic arithmetic operations. In this sense the source of difficulty in solving a problem in cryptarithmetic is not one of conceptual access but lies in the organizational complexity of the procedures. Performing tasks, such as standard arithmetic, that are both conceptually transparent and do not require the construction of novel procedures are better thought of in terms of skilled performance rather than problem solving. It follows that with repeated practice, a task such as cryptarithmetic or a specific version of the Tower of Hanoi can become decreasingly one of problem solving and increasingly a matter of exercising a skill.

The distinction between conceptual access and procedural processing readily lends itself to formulation in computational terms. Indeed, some form of the distinction is an integral part of most computational theories. For example, theories such as ACT* (Anderson, 1983) or Soar (Laird, Newell, & Rosenbloom, 1987) have architectures that contain stored representations that are activated via a working memory. In these terms the difficulty of conceptual access is a matter of establishing in working memory the conditions needed for the execution of existing conceptual representations. The representations themselves may be expressed as sets of productions, scripts, or networks. Procedural processing becomes a source of difficulty in problem solving insofar as effective conceptual representations do not exist but must be acquired or assembled from more basic elements.

Some Examples

For most problems both conceptual access and procedural processing are significant sources of difficulty. Even with heavily procedural problems such as the Tower of Hanoi or the missionaries and cannibals problem, the problem solver's assembling of the procedures that generate an optimal solution may be inhibited by a failure to access certain relevant concepts such as those required to recognize the need for a certain subgoal. In solving the Tower of Hanoi, for example, it is essential that one make use of the concept of a "holding" peg, rather than attempt to move the discs directly to the goal peg. As in other areas of cognitive psychology, and especially in the study of implicit cognition, it is dangerous to assume that a particular task is a pure embodiment of a hypothetical underlying process. In this connection it is helpful to analyze a few examples in greater detail.

Series-Completion Problems.   Consider series-completion problems such as being required to find the next number in the series

2 4 6 . . .

Solving such problems consists of (a) accessing a rule, using the given data as a cue, and (b) applying this rule as a procedure to generate the next number in the series. Each of these components is a potential source of difficulty in solving the problem. This particular example is trivially easy, at least if the correct rule is "even ascending digits." If the rule is something else, such as the simpler rule "any ascending sequence of digits," the biased cuing properties of the given digits (2 4 6), along with the subjects' strategies for hypothesis revision, render this simpler rule virtually inaccessible (Wason, 1960, 1977). The rule remains undiscovered despite its being generally familiar and thus potentially available to subjects.

Analogies.   The distinction between conceptual access and execution of procedures is, in one way or another, an integral part of most current analyses of analogical reasoning and problem solving. Analogical reasoning problems such as

shoe is to *foot* as *glove* is to _____?

require accessing a rule of relationship that applies to the first two terms (such as "is worn on") and that can be applied to the third term as a procedure to generate the missing element (Sternberg, 1977). As with number series problems, the data (the three given terms of the above analogy) serve two functions: They act as retrieval cues to access the correct relational concept, in part by constraining the set of possible rules of relationship, and they enable the rule to be used to infer the desired response.

Two problems are analogous if they can be solved by the application of a common conceptual representation. The term analogical problem solving is used to refer to a situation in which a target problem is solved by accessing and then applying the conceptual representation that was used to solve a previous analogous problem. In the studies of Gick and Holyoak (1980, 1983) the target was Duncker's radiation problem. In this problem subjects are asked to devise a method of applying intense radiation to an inoperable tumor without damaging surrounding healthy tissue. The solution is to direct low-intensity radiation simultaneously from many directions so that the rays intersect and summate only at the tumor. Prior to trying to solve this problem subjects were given the solutions to one or more analogous problems such as extinguishing an oil-well fire through the simultaneous use of many narrow-gauge hoses. Thus the problems are solved using the same conceptual representation, but their surface content is quite different. The conceptual representation is described as a convergence schema that captures the property of a number of small forces converging at a single point and summating to form a large force. For subjects uninformed of a possible relationship between the target problem and the prior analogue problem, there is very little spontaneous transfer to the target problem. On the other hand, if the experimenter points out the relevance of the prior problem, subjects have little difficulty in applying the solution concept to the target problem and reaching a correct solution. This result indicates that procedural processing—making use of the schema once it has been accessed—seems not to be a significant source of difficulty. Rather, the absence of transfer is a consequence of a failure of conceptual access. Although the relevant schema is readily cued by the semantic content of the original problem, a switch in content makes the schema inaccessible. Thus, failure of transfer can be thought of as a case of encoding specificity in which access to the schema is achieved only through the specific content of its prior activation. Note that we are not claiming that solving such problems involves no procedural processing. Rather, the claim is that in these examples procedural processing is not a major source of difficulty.

The Nine-Dot Problem.   Weisberg and Alba (1981a, 1981b) criticized the Gestalt concept of fixation and insight by examining performance on insight problems such as the nine-dot problem. In this problem nine dots are arranged in a square of three rows of three dots. Subjects are asked to connect all nine dots with just four straight lines without lifting their pen from the paper. Subjects find this task difficult because the solution requires that the lines go beyond the borders of the square implied by the dots. The grounds of Weisberg and Alba's criticism is that disabusing subjects of their fixating assumption (that their solution must remain within the square) did not yield an immediate and direct solution. One way of preserving the notion of insight as a useful concept is to identify insight with problems that have conceptual access as their only real source of difficulty. One can then argue that tasks such as the nine-dot problem do not provide a good example of insight because they have substantial sources of difficulty in addition to those attributable to conceptual access. That is, there is a strong component of procedural processing in the nine-dot problem, so that even when the major conceptual block has been overcome, considerable (procedural) problem solving remains to be done.

The Nature of Insight

Because Gestalt concepts such as insight and restructuring might be considered obvious candidates for analysis in terms of implicit processes, it is worth pursuing the foregoing analysis in relation to these terms. According to this analysis, insight is that component of problem solving involving conceptual access. Restructuring is the reorganization of the data that results from the application of the concept. Insofar as this reorganization is highly automatized and therefore leads rapidly to a perceived solution, it will generate the subjective sense of "aha!" commonly associated with so-called insight problems. Such rapid automatized reorganization is precisely what occurs in solving the simple riddles of the type described previously.

The claim that insight is to be identified with conceptual access—a memory process—may seem to be contradicted by the results from experiments by Metcalfe (1986). Metcalfe presented subjects with either insight problems or trivia questions. For those problems that subjects failed to solve, or questions they failed to answer, in the short time allowed, subjects were asked to predict whether, given more time, they would succeed. Metcalfe found that subjects could not predict their future problem-solving performance, but could predict their performance in the memory task, and concluded that insight is therefore different from memory. Apart from the fact that many of the problems are almost certainly not pure insight problems (i.e., they have procedural processing as well as conceptual access as a source of difficulty), there are a number of difficulties with this general conclusion. A simpler interpretation is that the observed dissociation reflects two very different kinds of remembering. In the case of problem solving, the target of the memory retrieval process is an abstract concept; in the case of trivia questions it is a concrete fact. Probably of greater importance is the difference between the two tasks in terms of their cue-target relationships. For trivia items (e.g., "Who was Tarzan's girlfriend?") the cue-target relationship is between a question and a previously learned answer—a straightforward retrieval from declarative memory. With insight problems the solution is achieved through the content of a problem serving as a cue to access a concept, typically in a quite novel context.

Consider by way of example the problem that requires the problem solver to place 27 animals into four pens with the restriction that each pen contains an odd number of animals. Since the sum of four odd numbers must be an even number, the problem, as with all good riddles, seems impossible at first. The solution is obtained through accessing the concept of concentric circles, a concept not readily cued by the context of the problem. Once this concept is applied to the problem, the procedural processing involved in assigning numbers of animals to pens is straightforward. Thus the major source of difficulty in solving such problems is one of conceptual access and in this sense is a memory phenomenon involving the capacity of problem content to cue the appropriate concept.

IMPLICIT LEARNING AND IMPLICIT MEMORY

We now turn to the second of our two major distinctions. By implicit learning we mean the acquisition of a novel rule or a new conceptual representation, the acquisition of which does not depend on the rule's availability to conscious introspection. Implicit learning is to be contrasted with learning that proceeds through the inductive evaluation (confirmation or disconfirmation) of an explicitly conjectured rule. In both cases learning is reflected in behavior becoming increasingly rule governed, but in the case of implicit learning acquisition proceeds without the rule being articulated. The acquisition of syntactic rules in first language learning is frequently cited as a paradigm case of implicit learning. In the laboratory, one of the earliest claims for the possibility of implicit learning, and a frequently cited example, was made by Hull (1920) in his study of concept learning. Hull's subjects were confronted with the problem of finding a rule (a common figural element) that would serve to classify sets of Chinese ideograms. Hull found that many subjects were able to classify exemplars correctly without being able to draw the defining element. He concluded that "ability to define is not necessarily a true index of the functional value of a concept" (Hull, 1920, p. 44).

Implicit memory, on the other hand, is a retrieval rather than an acquisition phenomenon. It refers to conditions under which existing knowledge is accessed rather than to conditions under which new knowledge is acquired. At an operational level implicit memory can be defined as the influence of a single prior event on a subsequent task when two conditions have been met: (a) the task instructions make no reference to the prior event, and (b) performing the task requires no conscious recollection of the prior event. For purposes of the present discussion we need to make only minimal theoretical assumptions, and we can certainly avoid the entire issue of whether implicit memory is a distinct memory system. In claiming that implicit memory is essentially a retrieval rather than an acquisition phenomenon, we mean that implicit memory is a modification of the relationship between a retrieval cue and a target that already exists in memory. Priming is the paradigm case of such a modification as when, for example, the prior presentation of a word enhances the capacity of a word fragment to cue the entire word. The purpose of describing implicit memory as a modification of a cue-target relationship is to reinforce the point that implicit memory for a word (as revealed in a primed fragment completion task) is not to be thought of as some general "strengthening" of that word in memory, because the enhanced memory for the word occurs only under highly specific cuing conditions. Rather, the memory is the enhanced capacity of the fragment to cue the whole word. In the context of problem solving, the cue consists of the current representation of the (problematic) data, and the target is the conceptual representation needed to achieve the solution to the problem. That is to say, in problem solving, implicit memory occurs when a prior event modifies the cuing properties of data and thus enhances the current accessibility of an available conceptual representation. The memory is implicit if this modification does not depend on conscious recollection of the event.

In stressing the point that implicit memory is the modification of a cue–target interaction rather than some form of memory enhancement of the target alone, we wish to align ourselves with those such as Roediger (1990) who place implicit memory processes firmly within the context of theoretical perspectives such as transfer-appropriate processing and encoding specificity. As we shall see, this alignment is particularly important in the domain of problem solving. This same alignment may, however, seem incompatible with the sharp distinction we have drawn between implicit learning and implicit memory. It might be argued that, as with explicit remembering, performance is determined by the interactive relationship between the processing involved in acquisition and that involved in retrieval. We have no wish to deny this argument; the data supporting it are overwhelming. Nevertheless, we believe it valuable to distinguish between the term implicit applied on the one hand to the conditions under which new rules might be acquired and, on the other, to the retrieval conditions that govern the accessibility of rules already available in long-term memory.

A frequently offered example of implicit memory in problem solving is from Maier's (1931) two-string problem. Subjects are confronted with two strings suspended from the ceiling and asked to tie them together. However, the strings are at such a height and separated by such a distance that both strings cannot be reached at once. The favored solution is to tie an object (e.g., a pair of pliers) to one string and swing it as a pendulum; then, while holding the other string, catch the first one as it swings by. In one condition, subjects who had been unsuccessful in solving the problem were given a hint consisting of the experimenter "accidentally" brushing one of the strings, thereby setting it in motion. This hint was effective, but for present purposes the important point is that few subjects reported having noticed the experimenter brush against the string, and most attributed their success to quite different causes.

Having described our two basic distinctions, we can set out our basic plan for the remainder of the chapter. Our assumption is that the study of implicit learning is relevant to the procedural components of problem solving, whereas the study of implicit memory is relevant to conceptual access. We therefore begin with a discussion of the role of implicit learning in the procedural processing components of problem solving. We then offer an analysis of implicit memory in relation to conceptual access.

IMPLICIT LEARNING IN PROBLEM SOLVING

The question posed in this section is: Under what conditions can implicit learning, through the implicit acquisition of novel rules, serve the needs of procedural processing in problem solving? We accept the view that implicit learning in some form or other is a genuine phenomenon (see Reber, 1989, for a general review). This claim may seem unwarranted in the light of critiques of implicit learning such as of Perruchet, Gallego, and Savy (1990), but even so trenchant a criticism as theirs does not lead to the rejection of all forms of implicit learning. Rather, the argument made by Perruchet et al. is that the learning displayed by subjects in the experiments of Lewicki, Hill, and Bizot (1988) is not good evidence for the claim that subjects had acquired implicitly the explicit rule used by the experimenters to generate the learning material. Instead, subjects appear to have learned relative frequencies. Thus the issue is not so much whether such learning exists, but rather what kinds of cognitive representations can be acquired implicitly and whether this form of learning can play a significant role in problem solving. It should be noted that our discussion is limited to problem solving as traditionally studied in experimental psychology. In particular, we do not concern ourselves with issues of implicit learning in perceptual pattern recognition or in natural language acquisition.

Work with Artificial Grammars

A finite-state grammar is defined by a set of transition rules that distinguish acceptable ("grammatical") sequences of symbols from sequences that are unacceptable ("ungrammatical"). In his early study using such artificial grammars, Reber (1967) used entirely incidental learning conditions: Subjects were not attempting to solve a problem by discovering an underlying representation (transition rules); their instructions were merely to remember the items. Nevertheless, learning was revealed in subjects' above-chance performance in a subsequent transfer test. In a later study Reber (1976) explored the role of instructional set. In this study subjects in one group were placed in a problem-solving mode by being given explicit instructions to search for the structure underlying the stimuli. The result was that these subjects performed more poorly than did incidental subjects who had been given neutral instructions. Similarly, Brooks (1978), using a paired-associate learning procedure and the same type of artificial grammar, found poorer performance for subjects who had been informed of the rule-based nature of the letter strings. Although such interfering effects of explicit instructions have been replicated in a number of studies, there are also reported cases in which instructional set has either no effect (e.g., Dulaney, Carlson, & Dewey, 1984; Danks & Gans, 1975) or, under some conditions, yields superior performance (Howard & Ballas, 1980; Reber, Kassin, Lewis, & Cantor, 1980).

Although this pattern of results suggests that the effect of instructional set on rule learning may be complex, the balance of evidence supports the view that the interference effect is a real one, at least under some conditions, and has led some writers to claim that two distinct modes of learning are involved: implicit and explicit (Hayes & Broadbent, 1988; Mathews et al., 1989; Reber, 1976). A particularly useful formulation of these two modes is that of Hayes and Broadbent (1988), who use the terms *s-mode* and *u-mode* corresponding to what we have termed respectively explicit and implicit learning. S-mode learning is selective, effortful, and reportable, whereas u-mode learning is the passive aggregation of information, is unselective, and is unavailable for verbal report. In these terms, instructional manipulations such as those of Reber (1976) serve to induce either s-mode or u-mode learning. Of course, u-mode is not literally unselective, because subjects will not attend to all features of a stimulus array. Rather, learning is unselective in the sense that the basis of selection is not controlled by conscious goal directed thought.

Although favoring a different terminology, Mathews et al. (1989) make essentially the same distinction as that made by Hayes and Broadbent; both papers provide strong evidence in support of the two types of learning. Hayes and Broadbent (1988) examined the effects of a secondary verbal task and found that it interfered with s-mode learning but actually facilitated u-mode learning. Mathews et al. (1989) explored the interactions between the two types of learning. In Experiment 3 they showed that in attempting to learn a finite-state grammar, the two types of learning are equivalent. However, in learning a simpler biconditional rule (Experiment 4) they found that implicit learning alone was poorer than explicit, but that when the two types of learning were employed sequentially (implicit followed by explicit) learning was even better. Thus, under some conditions the two forms of learning can function synergistically.

Reber (1989), Hayes and Broadbent (1988), and Mathews et al. (1989) all draw essentially the same conclusions. They may be briefly stated as follows:

1. There exists an implicit form of learning capable of acquiring patterns of covariation of features (family resemblances), contingency relations, and relative frequencies.

2. In rule-learning tasks, implicit learning can be effective if the structure of the rule can be captured or approximated by these low-level relationships. To the extent that solving a problem requires cognitive representations that cannot be approximated by these basic relations, then implicit learning will not support problem solving. Implicit learning is therefore relevant to problem solving insofar as problems are of the kind for which low-level relationships can be recruited to help achieve a solution.

3. If the formal rule is too complex to be generated as an explicit hypothesis but is well approximated by the low-level relations just described, implicit learning will be as effective as, and in many cases more effective than, explicit learning.

4. Explicit learning may be more effective than implicit learning if the rule already exists in long-term memory or is simple enough to be generated as a hypothesis, or if the relevant features on which implicit learning can be based are not salient.

It is important to understand that the implicit learning that underlies subjects' ability to solve the finite-state grammar problem (or at least perform at above-chance level) is not the implicit counterpart of the explicit formulation of the finite-state rules. Under the conditions of Reber's experiments, subjects appear unable to learn such complex rules either implicitly or explicitly. What is learned implicitly is something quite different—relative bigram frequencies, for example. Such learning constitutes a (partial) solution because this simpler representation captures certain features of (is partially isomorphic with) the more complex rule that is actually generating instances. In other cases these simpler representations may be completely isomorphic with their explicit counterparts. Examples of such are considered in the next section. Thus, there can be no general answer to the question of whether or not problem solving can be achieved through, or aided by, the processes of implicit learning. Rather, the status of implicit learning in problem solving is a matter of the degree of structural equivalence between what can be learned implicitly and the problem's formal structure.

Before leaving this discussion of implicit rule learning, a brief comment on instance theories (e.g., Brooks, 1978) is in order. Such theories claim that in tasks such as Reber's artificial grammar, no abstract rule at all is learned. Rather, test items are compared with previously presented exemplars and answered on the basis of a judged similarity relationship between the two. The first point to note is that there is strong evidence (e.g., Brooks, 1978) that such instance-based performance does occur under some conditions. However, even such exemplar-based performance cannot occur without some form of abstract learning. If a novel instance is judged as being an instance of a rule by virtue of its similarity to previous instances, then it is reasonable to ask about the kind of knowledge needed to make this judgment of similarity between the novel instance and the remembered exemplar. After all, similarity can vary along multiple dimensions so that a novel instance of a class, say dog, may be more similar to a previously experienced cat with respect to size, age, color, and a whole host of other features. What knowledge is needed to pick out and appropriately structure just those features that constitute "dog-similarity"? The point is that the basis of the similarity judgment is nothing other than the implicit abstract knowledge (such as patterns of covariation) that exemplar theory seeks to avoid. However, it does not follow from this argument that remembered instances have no role to play; what follows is that the role of instances is not to bypass the need for abstract conceptual knowledge. The role of instances would seem to be to facilitate the accessing and consequent use of such abstract knowledge through comparison of novel with previous exemplars.

Problems in Probabilistic Reasoning

Given that the major forms of implicit learning are frequency/contingency relations, it would seem that the domain of probabilistic reasoning would be a particularly fruitful one in which to observe implicit rule learning. Such is indeed the case. To begin, the history of probability theory contains many examples in which implicit learning contrasts sharply with attempts to find an explicit rule-based solution. In these cases implicit knowledge preceded an explicit or reasoned justification. For example, the appropriate rank ordering of poker hands (e.g., that a straight is more common than a flush) was known with considerable accuracy long before such an ordering could be proved explicitly through the formal apparatus of probability theory (Kendall, 1956).

Hacking (1975) describes an even more interesting example from the 17th century. It is based on a memorandum from Galileo resolving an apparent contradiction between two claims concerning the probability of certain outcomes from tossing three dice. Which is the more probable outcome, a total of 9 spots on the one hand or of 10 on the other? Attempts to provide a solution through explicit reasoning came up with the answer that they were equally likely since there are exactly six combinations of spots that yield each of these outcomes. Galileo describes the contradictory claim that "it is known from long observation that dice players consider 10 and 11 to be more advantageous than 9 and 12" (quoted by Hacking, 1975, p. 52). Galileo resolved the conflict in favor of long observation by pointing out the relevance of permutations rather than combinations. Assuming equiprobable permutations leads to the result that 10 and 11 are indeed "more advantageous" than 9 or 12.

An impressive feature of this "long observation" is that it represents the discrimination of a difference in probability of 0.009 or, more relevantly, of odds 27:25. This difference is so small that has led at least one statistician to claim that such a discrimination is impossible (see Hacking 1975, p. 53). Yet although this kind of discrimination has not been systematically studied by experimental psychologists, there is enough evidence to show that such a high level of discrimination is not at all unlikely. Results reported by Erlick (1961) and by Estes (1976) show above-chance performance in frequency discrimination tasks with small differences in relative frequency. One of Erlick's subjects, for example, was able to discriminate with 87% accuracy the difference in frequency between two symbols one of which was presented 80 times and the other 72 times randomly ordered at the rate of four symbols per second. Reber (1989) reported that in his probability learning experiments, subjects were so accurate in tracking the relative frequencies of events that they were able to use their response rates to detect small errors in the generating program!

It is important to note that this accuracy pertains only to judgments of relative frequency. It does not translate into corresponding accuracies in judgments of differences in probabilities (Estes, 1976; Whitlow & Estes, 1979). Ordinal relations between probabilities and relative frequencies coincide provided the conversion to probabilities is based on a common population size. But if frequency and probability are unconfounded by asking subjects to compare two event types drawn from populations of different sizes, subjects' responses are controlled by frequencies, not probabilities. For example, an event that is observed to occur 40 times out of a possible 100 occasions might be judged more probable than an event that has occured 30 times out of a possible 50 occasions. The first event is more frequent, but has a lower probability. This result is important in that it provides a further demonstration of the limited nature of implicit learning. Unlike relative frequencies, probabilities require the estimation of ratios; if what has been learned (relative frequencies) is isomorphic with probabilities, as often is the case, then it may seem that the more complex knowledge of probabilities has been acquired. As in the case of Reber's artificial grammar studies, it requires appropriate transfer tests to reveal that a more primitive form of learning is serving the function of something more complex.

The fact that subjects in probability learning experiments so accurately track relative frequencies may seem to be at odds with the well-documented result in probabilistic reasoning that subjects ignore base-rate information (e.g., Bar-Hillel, 1980). A reasonable account of this seeming contradiction is provided by the distinction between implicit learning and explicit learning. Our survey of the evidence indicates that in all cases in which base-rate information is ignored, the base rate is presented as an explicit probability, usually a numerical value. In cases where base-rate information is implicit it influences judgments. The converse is not true, because there are clearly conditions in which explicit base-rate information does influence judgments (e.g., Ajzen, 1977).

The general conclusion is that the value of implicit learning in problem solving is limited. If solving a problem requires the acquisition of a novel rule, implicit learning may be effective but only to the extent that the rule's structure can be captured by elementary frequency and contingency relations. In the context of traditional studies of problem solving there appears to be no evidence that more complex rules can be acquired implicitly.

The results reported by Cohen (1984) would seem to be an exception to this general conclusion. Cohen found that amnesic patients could learn to solve the Tower of Hanoi problem despite having little or no recollection of having worked on the task in prior trials. What is impressive about these results is not so much their performance on the original learning task, but their performance on a transfer task. The original learning could be interpreted in terms of procedural learning of the literal sequence of physical moves, and could be treated in the same terms as the acquisition of a motor skill. However, in one transfer test patients were asked to solve the puzzle with the middle peg as the goal rather than the rightmost peg, which had served as the goal in the initial training trials. Cohen reports that patients had no difficulty in solving this transformed version of the task, suggesting that what had been learned was something relatively abstract. Although there is some question as to the generality of these results (Butters, Wolfe, Martone, Granholm, & Cermak, 1985), such a result, if established as a replicable finding, would be evidence for a more complex form of implicit learning than has been obtained with normal subjects.

IMPLICIT MEMORY IN PROBLEM SOLVING

The question we address in this section is whether manipulations of the kind used to demonstrate implicit memory can facilitate conceptual access in problem solving. Can a single experienced event modify the accessibility of a relevant conceptual representation, without that event being consciously remembered? Although most of the priming reported in the memory literature appears to depend on a perceptual match between study and test items, there is also considerable evidence of priming at the conceptual level, the level most likely to be relevant to problem solving. An example of conceptual priming is Blaxton's (1989) finding that with implicit instructions subjects answered more general knowledge questions when the answers had been included in a long list of study items. Further, Smith (1991) demonstrated cross-lingual priming in which French words that were generated in the first phase of the experiment facilitated word-fragment completion of their English translations. Graf and Schacter's (1985) work with priming of new associations also implicates the conceptual system, although later work (Schacter & Graf, 1986) that found such priming only in normal and moderately amnesic subjects (but not severe amnesics) raises the possibility that their findings depend critically on the involvement of explicit processes.

There is also a considerable body of data from research in social perception to support the existence of conceptual priming (Bargh & Pietromanaco, 1982; Higgins, Bargh, & Lombardi, 1985; Smith & Branscombe, 1988). In these experiments the typical procedure is to present subjects with stimuli that, in a later and apparently unrelated part of the experiment, prime personality traits. For example, Higgins et al. (1985) presented subjects with four words and instructed them to use three of them to form a sentence. Some of these four word sets contained a trait adjective, either positive (e.g., brave) or negative (e.g., rash). When subsequently presented with an ambiguous description that could be categorized as either positive or negative, judgments displayed the influence of the prior incidental exposure to the trait names, although subjects were not aware that the two parts of the experiment were related. Higgens et al. manipulated the frequency and recency of particular trait names as well as the interval between the priming trials and the subsequent categorization task. They found that at brief (15 sec) intervals priming was more strongly influenced by recency than by frequency, but that after longer intervals (120 sec) this effect was reversed. Smith and Branscombe (1988) showed that having subjects generate trait words to a cue produces greater priming than having them simply read the words, a result that suggests conceptually driven processing. It would seem that social judgments can be unconsciously influenced by a prior event, a form of priming that is clearly conceptual.

Conceptual priming, then, would seem to be genuine phenomenon. However, rather than attempting to discuss the issue of conceptual priming in general, we set a more modest goal, posing our question in more operational terms and limiting our review to traditional problem-solving tasks. As noted earlier, a necessary condition in establishing operationally that implicit memory is involved is that the task instructions make no specific reference to the event. We therefore examine problem-solving situations in which subjects have been presented with a priming or training event as the first phase of an experiment, and then are given a subsequent problem to solve without being informed of the potential relevance of the first phase. We discuss three classes of problems: anagrams, simple insight problems, and problems involving analogical transfer.

Anagrams

Although anagrams are typically considered part of the problem-solving literature, they are, as Greeno (1978) noted, importantly different from other kinds of problems. In many ways anagrams have more in common with tasks such as word-fragment completion or the reading of transformed text than with problems such as the Tower of Hanoi or simple riddles. The former tasks all consist of retrieving a lexical entry on the basis of distorted text. The difference between anagrams and fragment completion lies in the particular transformation (substitution, reordering, etc.) needed to retrieve the lexical entry. Anagrams might therefore be considered to have strong perceptual as well as conceptual components. Indeed, Jacoby and Dallas (1981) reported (without data) that they obtained the same results with anagrams as they obtained with perceptual identification: a modality effect but no levels of processing effect. It is therefore difficult to interpret the evidence for repetition priming of anagrams such as that reported by Perruchet and Baveaux (1989) and by Polster and Winograd (1989), especially because there are indications that the effect is not as robust as it is for word fragment completion (Schoen, Ciofalo, & Rudow, 1989). However, results from Srinivas and Roediger (1990) enable a clearer analysis. Their findings suggest that both perceptual (data-driven) and conceptual processing is involved in anagram priming, although the former is the stronger of the two.

Although implicit memory processes in anagram solving may contain a small conceptually driven component, there is no clear evidence for conceptually based priming of anagrams other than for repetition priming. Dominowski and Ekstrand (1967) reported associative priming, but the importance of implicit processes is questionable because of the instructions they gave to subjects. Subjects who studied associates to the solution words prior to attempting the anagrams were informed at the outset that each study word was strongly associated with a forthcoming solution word. A possible strategy open to subjects would have been to generate potential solution words during the initial study phase, thereby creating a situation more like repetition priming. A more likely possibility is that the instructions encouraged conscious recollection of study words during the anagram solving phase and these words could then serve as explicit cues to help retrieve solution words. In a similar study using lower associates and incidental acquisition instructions Jablonski and Mueller (1972) found no associative priming.

Insight Problems

As outlined at the beginning of this chapter, insight problems are those that have conceptual access as their only major source of difficulty. Once accessed, the conceptual representation leads rapidly to a solution. The previously mentioned two-string problem of Maier (1931) or Duncker's box and candle problem are prototypical examples. The former depends critically on the concept of a swinging pendulum string, and the latter problem (which asks subjects to mount a candle on a wall, given only a box, matches, and thumbtacks) depends on conceiving the box as a supporting platform for the candle. For convenience we will refer to these as the solution concepts. Of course, both these problems and others similar to them are not pure insight problems in that other processing is involved in applying the solution concepts to generate a complete solution, but it seems unlikely that such additional processing would pose any difficulty in achieving a solution. In this regard such problems differ from the nine-dot problem described earlier. This difference raises an obvious but important methodological consideration. Problems that have both conceptual access and procedural processing as significant sources of difficulty are not particularly useful in attempting to evaluate the effectiveness of conceptual priming, because failure to solve the problem may coexist with successful conceptual access.

Attempts to prime the solution concepts in these insight problems have not been successful. In an early study, Judson, Cofer, and Gelfand (1956) subjects learned a list of words that included the words *rope, swing, pendulum* prior to attempting to solve Maier's two-string problem. Their general finding was that this attempt to prime the relevant concepts did not improve performance, unless subjects had access to the list while solving the problem. Essentially the same result was found by Weisberg, Dicamillo, and Phillips (1978) using Duncker's box and candle problem. Subjects who learned *candle–box* in a prior paired-associate learning task showed poor transfer to the subsequent problem unless they were informed of the relevance of this prior learning.

The fact that subjects have little difficulty in solving either of these problems once they are informed of the relevance of the prior event suggests that it is conceptual access, not procedural processing, that is the cause of the low solution rates among uninformed subjects (subjects not explicitly informed about the potential relevance of the prior event). Once accessed, the solution concept generates the solution without difficulty. It might nevertheless be argued that these problems are too complex (in the sense of involving too much additional processing) to be sensitive to such priming. However, attempts to demonstrate priming with simple riddles of the kind described at the beginning of the chapter have also yielded negative results. Perfetto, Bransford, and Franks (1983) gave subjects a set of riddles to solve after subjects had been exposed to a set of statements containing the solution concept. They found transfer only for subjects who had been informed about the relevance of these prior statements.

There is then, no evidence from the foregoing studies that implicit memory plays a role in solving simple insight problems. Simply exposing subjects to the solution concept does not increase the likelihood that the "givens" of the subsequent problem will access that concept. A possible explanation of this negative result is that the processing involved in performing this initial task is quite different from that actually needed to solve the subsequent problem (Lockhart, 1988; Lockhart, Lamon & Gick, 1988). For example, solving the rock-on-the-lake riddle given earlier requires that the word *lake* cue the concept *ice* rather than *water*. Presenting a subject with the word *ice* may serve to activate the relevant concept, but it does so in the context of cues that do not reappear with the problem. This argument exploits the principle of encoding specificity or, more generally, of transfer-appropriate processing referred to previously. The claim is that for a prime to be effective the processing of the prime must incorporate the processing needed to solve the problem. A prediction from this analysis is that if the priming condition mimics more closely the processing needed to solve the problem then "spontaneous" transfer will be obtained; that is, transfer will occur with uninformed subjects. This prediction has been confirmed in studies by Lockhart et al. (1988) and by Adams et al. (1988). In these studies the priming events that yielded spontaneous transfer consisted of presenting the solution concepts in the form of puzzles. In the rock-on-the-lake riddle, for example, a declarative prime consisting of the statement "If the water is frozen John Smith can walk on it" yields no spontaneous transfer, whereas a puzzle prime of the form "John Smith can walk on water" followed by a 5-sec pause and the word "frozen" does yield spontaneous transfer.

Although the transfer-appropriate processing account has strong empirical support, it does not provide clear evidence for any role of implicit memory. As in so many studies of implicit memory, it is difficult to rule out the mediating effects of explicit remembering. It is possible that the role of transfer-appropriate processing is to make the problem an effective reminder of the relevant priming event. Two forms of explicit remembering may be operative in these experiments. These correspond to a distinction first made by Ebbinghaus (1885/1964, p. 1): involuntary versus voluntary recollection. In the case of involuntary recollection the problem brings to mind the priming event without conscious effort. Once this involuntary reminding has occurred it can alert subjects to the relevance of the prior priming events to the experiment as a whole. Voluntary recollection or an intentional memory search for the priming events then follows because these subjects have become, in effect, no different from informed control subjects. This possibility is discussed in Lockhart et al. (1988) and has received empirical support in the work of Ross, Ryan, and Tenpenny (1989). These latter authors found transfer for uninformed subjects, but their data are best explained by the assumption that these subjects behaved as uninformed subjects only until they caught on to the relationship between the study clues and the test problems. After this critical reminding they behaved like informed subjects, engaging in an intentional memory search.

In light of this possibility, Blackburn (1990) attempted to replicate the transfer appropriate training effect found by Adams et al. (1988) and by Lockhart et al. (1988) using subjects who were informed of the relationship between the two parts of the experiment but who were discouraged from employing an intentional search by imposing time constraints on the problem-solving tasks and providing relevant study clues for only half of the problems. Under these conditions puzzle primes again facilitated problem solving more than did declarative clues. Thus there is evidence to support the claim that some form of implicit processing is involved in this transfer, even though the partial involvement of explicit processes remains a possibility. It may be that the function of the puzzle primes is to initiate a spontaneous recollection of the clue, and although such involuntary reminding might well be considered a form of implicit remembering, the conscious recollection of the clue is an essential component of achieving the solution.

Analogical Problem Solving

Studies of analogical problem solving tell much the same story as that obtained with insight problems. As argued in the introduction, experiments such as those of Gick and Holyoak (1980, 1983) illustrate a failure in conceptual access. The question is whether there are conditions under which solving one problem (the training problem) facilitates the solving of a subsequent analogous problem (the target problem) without the potential relevance of the training problem being explicitly pointed out. Can a novel target problem serve as a cue to trigger the retrieval of the solution schema used to solve the training problem? Stated more briefly, we ask whether spontaneous transfer occurs in analogical reasoning and if so whether it occurs in the absence of conscious recollection. As in studies using insight problems, transfer is spontaneous if it occurs in the absence of the experimenter making any explicit reference to the training problem.

Despite their heroic efforts, Gick and Holyoak (1980, 1983) found little evidence for spontaneous transfer. The one notable exception was when they gave subjects two analogous training problems and asked them to make a comparison between them (Gick & Holyoak, 1983, Exp. 4). However, Spencer and Weisberg (1986) showed that even this transfer fails to occur if the training problems are presented in a very different context from the target problem. These results suggest that spontaneous transfer is promoted by two factors. One is training conditions that require subjects to articulate the solution concept by making explicit comparisons of two or more training analogues; the other is the degree of contextual similarity between the training problems and the target problem. Included in the notion of contextual similarity is the degree of overlap of surface features of the problems. Evidence supporting this view is to be found in such studies as Catrambone and Holyoak (1989), Holyoak and Koh (1987), and Ross (1984).

A recent study by Needham and Begg (1991) showed that principles of transfer-appropriate training are relevant to analogical transfer as well as to transfer in simple insight problems. Their results show that spontaneous transfer is enhanced if the solution is obtained (either discovered by the subject or experimenter-provided) in the context of problem-oriented rather than memory-oriented processing. This result confirms and extends those of Adams et al. (1988) and Lockhart et al. (1988). Moreover, Needham and Begg (1991) found a dissociation between free recall of the training problem and its use in the context of solving a target problem. Lockhart et al. (1988) found a similar dissociation in showing that repetition of the training sentences increased free recall but had no effect on transfer. However, the Needham and Begg data offer a clearer picture of this dissociation by providing direct contingency data. They found that 34 (68%) subjects who engaged in problem-oriented processing and who solved the target problem failed to recall the solution from the training story. It does not follow from this result that the success of these 34 subjects can be attributed to implicit memory, although it remains a possibility. An alternative interpretation is that the dissociation is between two forms of explicit memory, rather than between implicit and explicit memory.

The conclusion to be drawn is the same as for simple insight problems. Although there are conditions that will yield spontaneous transfer, there is no clear evidence that the activation of conceptual representations such as Gick and

Holyoak's convergence schema occurs without conscious recollection of the prior training problem. What is needed is better evidence concerning the extent to which this conscious recollection plays a causal role in problem solving.

GENERAL CONCLUSIONS

Implicit learning and implicit memory are real phenomena, but at present there is little or no evidence that they play a major role in problem solving. Implicit learning can serve to capture certain structural properties of data, those involving relative frequency, covariation, and contingency. Such properties may approximate to some degree more complex conceptual representations and thereby serve to generate correct answers, but there is no evidence that the complex representations themselves are learned implicitly.

Although under certain conditions a training or priming event can facilitate the solving of a subsequent problem for uninformed subjects, there is no evidence that conceptually based transfer occurs in the absence of conscious recollection. Such spontaneous transfer seems to be driven by a combination of voluntary and involuntary recollection that depends on the degree of overlap of processing operations and the surface similarity between problems. Transfer, it would seem, typically involves explicit, although perhaps involuntary, remembering. Schacter, Bowers, and Booker (1989) discuss the claim that involuntary recollection should be considered a type of implicit memory. The grounds for such a claim is that involuntary recollection satisfies the criterion of nonintentional remembering. However, even if one is willing to consider the involuntary triggering of a past event as an implicit subcomponent of the overall recollective event, the available evidence suggests that the resulting conscious recollection is essential to the facilitation of problem solving.

Finally, it is important to stress that it would be a mistake to conclude that implicit processes play no role in problem solving. A safer conclusion is that at present the evidence suggests that its role is very limited. However, it must be emphasized that (with the possible exception of some anagram studies) none of the investigations of spontaneous transfer has set out with the purpose of studying the phenomenon of implicit memory. It may well be that current paradigms are not well suited to detect implicit processes. Even with a task as simple as word fragment completion, the difficulty of controlling extraneous factors such as explicit remembering is not negligible. With complex problem solving, the difficulty is enormous. It is probable therefore that the more satisfying answers to questions about the role of implicit processes in problem solving will require the development of new paradigms. The goal of such paradigms should be to isolate those subprocesses of problem solving that implicit processes might reasonably influence and provide some on-line measure of conscious awareness. Until such paradigms are developed and the question of implicit processes in problem solving is addressed directly, we shall have to withhold final judgment.

ACKNOWLEDGMENTS

Preparation of this manuscript was supported by a grant from the Natural Sciences and Engineering Research Council of Canada. We would like to thank H. L. Roediger and M. Masson for their generous and constructive comments on an earlier version of the manuscript.

REFERENCES

Adams, L. T., Kasserman, J. E., Yearwood, A. A., Perfetto, G. A., Bransford, J. D., & Franks, J. J. (1988). Memory access: The effects of fact-oriented versus problem-oriented acquisition. *Memory & Cognition, 16*, 167–175.

Ajzen, I. (1977). Intuitive theories of events and the effects of base-rate information on prediction. *Journal of Personality and Social Psychology, 35*, 303–314.

Anderson, J. R. (1983). *The architecture of cognition.* Cambridge, MA: Harvard University Press.

Auble, P. M., Franks, J. J., & Soraci, S. A. (1979). Effort towards comprehension: Elaboration or "aha"? *Memory & Cognition, 7*, 426–434.

Bar-Hillel, M. (1980). The base-rate fallacy in probability judgments. *Acta Psychologica, 44*, 211–233.

Bargh, J. A., & Pietromanaco, P. (1982). Automatic information processing and social perception: The influence of trait information presented outside of conscious awareness on impression formation. *Journal of Personality and Social Psychology, 43*, 437–449.

Blackburn, A. B. (1990). *Effects of processing similarity on memory access during problem solving.* Unpublished master's thesis, University of Georgia, Athens.

Blaxton, T. A. (1989). Investigating dissociations among memory measures: Support for a transfer appropriate processing framework. *Journal of Experimental Psychology: Learning, Memory, and Cognition, 15*, 657–668.

Brooks, L. R. (1978). Non-analytic concept formation and memory for instances. In E. Rosch & B. Lloyd (Eds.), *Cognition and categorization* (pp. 169–211). Hillsdale, NJ: Lawrence Erlbaum Associates.

Butters, N., Wolfe, J., Martone, M., Granholm, E., & Cermak, L. S. (1985). Memory disorder associated with Huntington's disease: Verbal recall, verbal recognition and procedural memory. *Neuropsychologia, 23*, 729–743.

Catrambone, R., & Holyoak, K. J. (1989). Overcoming contextual limitations on problem-solving transfer. *Journal of Experimental Psychology: Learning, Memory, & Cognition, 15*, 1147–1156.

Cofer, C. N. (1951). Verbal behavior in relation to reasoning and values. In H. Guetzkow (Ed.) *Groups, leadership, and men* (pp. 206–217). Pittsburgh: Carnegie Press.

Cohen, N. J. (1984). Preserved learning capacity in amnesia: evidence for multiple memory systems. In L. R. Squire & N. Butters (Eds.), *Neuropsychology of memory* (pp. 83–103). New York: Guilford Press.

Danks, J. H., & Gans, D. L. (1975). Acquisition and utilization of a rule structure. *Journal of Experimental Psychology: Learning, Memory, and Cognition, 1*, 201–208.

Dominowski, R. L., & Ekstrand, B. R. (1967). Direct and associative priming in anagram solving. *Journal of Experimental Psychology, 74*, 84–86.

Dulany, D. E., Carlson, R. A., & Dewey, G. I. (1984). A case of syntactical learning and judgment: How conscious and how abstract? *Journal of Experimental Psychology: General, 113*, 541–555.

Ebbinghaus, H. (1964). *Memory: A contribution to experimental psychology* (Trans. H. A. Ruger & C. E. Bussenius). New York: Dover. (Original work published 1885)

Erlick, D. E. (1961). Judgments of the relative frequency of a sequential series of two events. *Journal of Experimental Psychology, 62*, 105–112.

Estes, W. K. (1976). The cognitive side of probability learning. *Psychological Review, 83*, 37–64.

Gick, M. L., & Holyoak, K. J. (1980). Analogical problem solving. *Cognitive Psychology, 12*, 306–355.

Gick, M. L., & Holyoak, K. J. (1983). Schema induction and analogical reasoning. *Cognitive Psychology, 15*, 1–38.

Graf, P., & Schacter, D. A. (1985). Implicit and explicit memory for new associations in normal and amnesic subjects. *Journal of Experimental Psychology: Learning, Memory, and Cognition, 11*, 501–518.

Greeno, J. G. (1978). Natures of problem-solving abilities. In W. K. Estes (Ed.), *Handbook of learning and cognitive processes: Human information processing* (pp. 239–270). Hillsdale, NJ: Lawrence Erlbaum Associates.

Hacking, I. (1975). *The emergence of probability*. New York: Cambridge University Press.

Hayes, N. A., & Broadbent, D. E. (1988). Two modes of learning for interactive tasks. *Cognition, 28*, 249–276.

Higgins, E. T., Bargh, J. A., & Lombardi, W. (1985). Nature of priming effects in categorization. *Journal of Experimental Psychology: Learning, Memory, & Cognition, 11*, 59–69.

Holyoak, K., & Koh, K. (1987). Surface and structural similarity in analogical transfer. *Memory & Cognition, 15*, 332–340.

Howard, J. H., & Ballas, J. A. (1980). Syntactic and semantic factors in the classification of nonspeech transient patterns. *Perception and Psychophysics, 28*, 431–439.

Hull, C. L. (1920). Quantitative aspects of the evolution of concepts. *Psychological Monographs, 28* (Whole No. 128).

Jablonski, E. M., & Mueller, J. H. (1972). Anagram solution as a function of instructions, priming, and imagery. *Journal of Experimental Psychology, 94*, 84–89.

Jacoby, L. L., & Dallas, M. (1981). On the relation between autobiographical memory and perceptual learning. *Journal of Experimental Psychology: General, 110*, 306–340.

Judson, A. J., Cofer, C. N., & Gelfand, S. (1956). Reasoning as an associate process: II. "Directions" in problem solving as a function of prior reinforcement of relevant responses. *Psychological Reports, 2*, 501–507.

Kendall, M. G. (1956). The beginning of a probability calculus. *Biometrika, 43*, 1–14.

Laird, J. E., Newell, A., & Rosenbloom, P. S. (1987). Soar: An architecture for general intelligence. *Artificial Intelligence, 33*, 1–64.

Lewicki, P., Hill, T., & Bizot, E. (1988). Acquisition of procedural knowledge about a pattern of stimuli that cannot be articulated. *Cognitive Psychology, 20*, 24–37.

Lockhart, R. S. (1988). Conceptual specificity in thinking and remembering. In D. M. Thomson & G. Davis (Eds.), *Context and memory* (pp. 319–331). London: Wiley.

Lockhart, R. S., Lamon, M., & Gick, M. (1988). Conceptual transfer in simple insight problems. *Memory and Cognition, 16*, 36–44.

Maier, N. R. F. (1931). Reasoning in humans: II. The solution of a problem and its appearance in consciousness. *Journal of Comparative Psychology, 12*, 181–194.

Mathews, R. C., Buss, R. R., Stanley, W. B., Blanchard-Fields, F., Cho, J.-R., & Druhan, B. (1989). The role of implicit and explicit processes in learning from examples: A synergistic effect. *Journal of Experimental Psychology: Learning, Memory, & Cognition, 15*, 1083–1100.

Needham, D. R., & Begg, I. M. (1991). Problem-oriented training promotes spontaneous transfer: Memory-oriented training promotes memory for training. *Memory and Cognition, 19*, 543–557.

Metcalfe, J. (1986). Feeling of knowing in memory and problem solving. *Journal of Experimental Psychology: Learning, Memory, and Cognition, 12*, 288–294.

Perfetto, G. A., Bransford, J. D., & Franks, J. J. (1983). Constraints on access in a problem solving context. *Memory & Cognition, 11*, 24–31.

Perruchet, P., & Baveaux, P. (1989). Correlational analyses of explicit and implicit memory performance. *Memory and Cognition, 17*, 77–86.

Perruchet, P., Gallego, J., & Savy, I. (1990). A critical reappraisal of unconscious abstraction of deterministic rules in complex experimental situations. *Cognitive Psychology, 22,* 493–516.

Polster, M. R., & Winograd, E. (1989). No evidence of test priming between solving anagrams and completing word fragments. *Bulletin of the Psychonomic Society, 27,* 303–306.

Reber, A. S. (1967). Implicit learning of artificial grammars. *Journal of Verbal Learning and Verbal Behavior, 77,* 317–327.

Reber, A. S. (1976). Implicit learning of synthetic languages: The role of instructional set. *Journal of Experimental Psychology: Learning, Memory, and Cognition, 2,* 88–94.

Reber, A. S. (1989). Implicit learning and tacit knowledge. *Journal of Experimental Psychology: General, 118,* 219–235.

Reber, A. S., Kassin, S. M., Lewis, S., & Cantor, G. W. (1980). On the relationship between implicit and explicit modes in the learning of a complex rule structure. *Journal of Experimental Psychology: Human Learning and Memory, 6,* 492–502.

Roediger, H. L. (1990). Implicit memory: Retention without remembering. *American Psychologist, 45,* 1042–1056.

Ross, B. H. (1984). Remindings and their effects in learning a cognitive skill. *Cognitive Psychology, 16,* 371–416.

Ross, B. H., Ryan, W. J., & Tenpenny, P. L. (1989). The access of relevant information for solving problems. *Memory & Cognition, 17,* 639–651.

Schacter, D. L., Bowers, J., & Booker, J. (1989). Intention, awareness, and implicit memory: The retrieval intentionality criterion. In S. Lewandowsky, J. C. Dunn, & K. Kirsner (Eds.), *Implicit memory: Theoretical issues* (pp. 47–65). Hillsdale, NJ: Lawrence Erlbaum Associates.

Schacter, D. L., & Graf, P. (1986). Preserved learning in amnesic patients: Perspectives from research on direct priming. *Journal of Clinical and Experimental Neuropsychology, 8,* 727–743.

Schoen, L. M., Ciofalo, E., & Rudow, E. (1989). Anagram versus word-fragment solution—A comparison of implicit-memory measures. *Bulletin of the Psychonomic Society, 27,* 551–552.

Smith, E. R., & Branscombe, N. R. (1988). Category accessibility as implicit memory. *Journal of Experimental Social Psychology, 24,* 490–504.

Smith, M. C. (1991). On the recruitment of semantic information for word fragment completion: Evidence from bilingual priming. *Journal of Experimental Psychology: Human Learning and Memory, 17,* 234–244.

Spencer, R. M., & Weisberg, R. W. (1986). Context-dependent effects on analogical transfer. *Memory & Cognition, 14,* 442–449.

Srinivas, K., & Roediger, H. L. (1990). Classifying implicit memory tests: Category association and anagram solution. *Journal of Learning and Language, 29,* 389–412.

Sternberg, R. J. (1977). *Intelligence, information processing, and analogical reasoning.* Hillsdale, NJ: Lawrence Erlbaum Associates.

Wason, P. C. (1960). On the failure to eliminate hypotheses in a conceptual task. *Quarterly Journal of Experimental Psychology, 12,* 129–140.

Wason, P. C. (1977). " 'On the failure to eliminate hypotheses . . .'—a second look. In P. N. Johnson-Laird & P. C. Wason (Eds.), *Thinking: Readings in cognitive science* (pp. 307–314). New York: Cambridge University Press.

Weisberg, R. W., & Alba, J. W. (1981a). An examination of the alleged role of "fixation" in the solution of several "insight" problems. *Journal of Experimental Psychology: General, 110,* 169–192.

Weisberg, R. W., & Alba, J. W. (1981b). Gestalt theory, insight, and past experience. *Journal of Experimental Psychology: General, 110,* 199–203.

Weisberg, R., Dicamillo, M., & Phillips, D. (1978). Transferring old associations to new problems: A nonautomatic process. *Journal of Verbal Learning and Verbal Behavior, 17,* 219–228.

Whitlow, J. W., Jr., & Estes, W. K. (1979). Judgment of relative frequency in relation to shifts of event frequency: Evidence for a limited capacity model. *Journal of Experimental Psychology: Human Learning and Memory, 5,* 395–408.

6 Implicit Memory and Skill Acquisition: Is Synthesis Possible?

Kim Kirsner
Craig Speelman
Peter Schofield
University of Western Australia

Skill acquisition and implicit memory became significant growth areas in cognitive psychology during the last decade. Skill acquisition is dominated by the claim that the impact of practice on performance may be explained by reference to one process or principle over a broad, even universal set of tasks. Implicit memory has also been adopted by scientists with a broad range of interests, ranging from personality theory to advertising as well as mainstream problems concerning face, word, and object recognition. In this chapter we test the proposition that skill acquisition and implicit memory may be subsumed under a single theory or principle, thereby advancing the cause of synthesis and reduction in this otherwise expanding area.

The term *implicit memory* was coined by Graf and Schacter (1985; Schacter, 1987) to identify a family of observations and experiments that could be distinguished from more traditional aspects of memory research. The main impetus for the term, and for the idea that it should be used to identify a distinct memory form, came from two cognate lines of research. The first of these involved repetition priming and a series of papers published in 1974 (Forbach, Stanners, & Hochaus, 1974; Kirsner & Smith, 1974; Murrell & Morton, 1974), although a claim could also be made on behalf of Winnick and Daniel (1970), or, possibly, Oldfield and Wingfield (1965). The main feature of this body of papers is that performance on a variety of simple tasks is facilitated when subjects are exposed to the same stimulus at some earlier point in an experimental sequence. The effect has been observed for printed words, spoken words, and objects under data- and resource-limited treatments, for naming, lexical decision, stem completion, and letter fragment completion conditions. The critical feature in each of these tasks is that no reference is made to the earlier priming event, and subjects do not therefore have to specifically recollect information from that event. It is this feature that provides the operational distinction between implicit and explicit memory. The distinction between these putative memory systems has derived additional support from the now substantial body of research that demonstrates that performance on these task types can be dissociated experimentally (e.g., Schacter, 1987; Roediger, Weldon, & Challis, 1989; Tulving, Schacter, & Stark, 1982).

The second line of research involves evidence that repetition priming is spared in amnesics, who nevertheless show marked deficits on tests of explicit memory, in which deliberate, conscious recall or recognition is required (Warrington & Weiskrantz, 1970, 1974; Kinsbourne & Wood, 1975). Perhaps the clearest demonstration of this dissociation involved a contrast between stem completion and cued recall, where the same three-letter test stimulus was used in each treatment, and the critical difference involved the instructions: to either recall words from a study list beginning with the target stems, or produce any words beginning with the stems. The amnesics matched the control group in the latter treatment, but their deficit was exposed in the recall treatment. Evidence of this type has generally been interpreted in terms of functional dissociation, involving and perhaps defining two forms of memory.

The issue under review in this chapter does not concern the distinction between implicit and explicit memory. For the present purpose, indeed, we accept it. The issue under review here concerns a possible synthesis between skill acquisition and implicit memory. One way to conceptualize this issue treats conceptual evolution in migratory terms. According to the migratory analogy it may be suggested that implicit memory began life as an off-shoot from explicit memory. Two decades of research have demonstrated, however, that implicit memory is different in many ways from explicit memory, and that it cannot now be regarded as a branch of this knowledge domain. There is evidence, furthermore, that there are many parallels between implicit memory and yet another domain, that of skill acquisition. Indeed, the evidence that implicit memory and skill acquisition share procedures, data, and theory is so pervasive that consideration must now be given to the proposition that these two domains should be treated as one.

The approach adopted in this chapter has been governed by the importance we place on synthesis in psychological science. It is our contention that the discipline of psychological science, and cognitive psychology in particular, has been dominated by what we might refer to as the tyranny of tasks. Implicit Memory is an interesting example. Consider the following list of tasks: visual word identification under threshold conditions, fragment completion, stem completion, lexical decision, word naming latency, object naming latency, object reality judgements, and auditory word identification under threshold conditions. Repetition priming effects have been demonstrated for all of these tasks, and for some more remote variants as well. The issue is as follows. Should we focus on the similarities among these tasks, concerning the way in which they respond to exercise, variation in surface form, and so on, or should we concentrate on the dissimilarities among these tasks? The assumption adopted here is that synthesis is a necessary part of our discipline, for how else can we identify general principles? Implicit memory and skill acquisition are now ripe for such treatment.

THREE FORMS OF CONTINUITY

The main body of this chapter is organized by reference to three forms of continuity involving implicit memory and learning or, more narrowly, repetition priming and skill acquisition. The logic of our argument is as follows. First, when repetition priming is defined in operational terms, it involves a subset of a conventional skill acquisition paradigm. Second, when repetition priming is reviewed in empirical terms it is evident that it shares the hallmark of the same skill acquisition paradigm; that is, it operates under a power law in regard to: (a) experimental practice effects, (b) preexperimental practice or frequency effects, and (c) priming, when the latter is corrected for general and other practice artifacts. Third, considered together, the first and second points justify the claim that implicit memory and skill acquisition should be treated as a single domain for scientific purposes. Fourth, because repetition priming as well as skill acquisition reflects the power law, explanations of performance in the lexical area must account for this relationship as well as for other effects of more immediate experimental interest. The fourth point echoes an argument made by Logan (1988) in regard to motor skills: that models that do not provide for the power law fail the most basic test.

Operational Continuity

Skill acquisition may be defined by reference to a series of trials or tests with the following characteristics:

1. The task involves presentation of many examples of a defined type of problem, involving fault diagnosis on logic boards for example.
2. Subjects must make classification decisions about the engineering status (i.e., faultless/faulty) of each example.
3. Subjects are supplied with feedback about their response (i.e., correct/incorrect).
4. The accuracy and the speed of the response are measured.

Repetition priming is in many respects similar. It typically involves presentation of many examples of a defined type of problem, involving letter strings that may or may not be genuine English words, for example; subjects must make classification decisions about lexical status (genuine/false); and response accuracy and speed are measured.

There are some differences between the skill acquisition and repetition priming paradigms, however. The first of these involves the role of feedback. Whereas this is typically given on a trial by trial basis in skill acquisition, in repetition priming it is often supplied on a block-by-block basis, or even not at all. This difference may be important or even critical while basic knowledge about stimuli, task and response rules is being acquired, but it is probably irrelevant thereafter. Indeed, in lexical decision, for example, subjects typically know when they have made errors except where those errors stem from the use of examples that fall outside their individual vocabulary—in which case the response is not technically an error from the subject's point of view.

The second and related difference involves task novelty. Whereas skill acquisition tasks usually, although not invariably, involve problems that are novel to the subjects, repetition priming typically uses familiar items and tasks that can at least be related to everyday experience, even if they do not exactly follow normal practice in reading and listening. Thus, skill acquisition is more directly concerned with the early stages of learning, where the nature of the task and the solution are being mastered, whereas repetition priming and other implicit memory tasks are concerned with improvement in reaction time (RT) or accuracy on tasks and stimuli that are more or less familiar to the subject. The distinction is not sharp, however. For example, many recent studies of skill acquisition (e.g., Schneider & Fisk, 1984) use more than 1000 trials, a value that mimics word frequency levels of 10 per million (i.e., medium frequency), where subjects may have experienced a similar number of trials. Moreover, by including the notion of *strengthening,* Anderson's (1982) model of skill acquisition makes specific provision for performance improvement after the basic skill has been acquired.

The main implications of our analysis are as follows. First, phenomena that have been discovered and explored under repetition priming conditions should be manifest under skill acquisition conditions. Second, phenomena that have been discovered and explored under skill acquisition conditions should be manifest under repetition priming conditions. Third, the data from each domain should be tested against a common set of models, a policy that is a natural extension of Anderson's (1982) claim that he has developed a general law of learning, applicable to a wide range of skills. Finally, although this extension is not demanded by the analysis summarized already, it may be appropriate to develop a single skill acquisition model that accommodates early language experience and developmental changes in skill as well as skill acquisition and repetition priming effects.

Empirical Continuity

Consideration is given to five points. The first four involve lexical decision. The first point concerns the relationship between preexperimental practice effects and

RT or, more specifically, word frequency and RT. This should follow a power function. The second point concerns the relationship between experimental practice and RT. Following Logan (1990), RT should follow a power function for experimental practice effects. It is necessary, however, to distinguish between experimental practice effects and repetition priming effects, because the former typically include general as well as word-specific practice effects. The third point concerns the relationship between repetition priming and RT, when repetition priming has been corrected for both (a) general practice effects and (b) priming produced by earlier trials in the experiment. The fourth point concerns quantitative continuity between preexperimental and experimental practice effects. Quantitative continuity between preexperimental and experimental practice may be expected if variables such as task, context, and recency do not influence RT. The difference between the functions for preexperimental and experimental practice provides some indication of the power of these variables. The fifth point concerns the extent to which the relationship between practice and performance can be generalized to other implicit memory tasks such as word identification, object naming, fragment completion, and stem completion.

Schofield's (1990) Experiment

The second of the points just described was addressed by Logan (1990). Logan demonstrated that when words are presented repeatedly (up to 16 times in his study), RT decreases systematically as a function of practice. More specifically, he found that RT was a power function of practice, suggesting that this variable behaves in the same way as a range of other performance functions reported by Anderson (1982), Newell & Rosenbloom (1981), and others in a variety of publications dating back to the 1920s.

In an extension of Logan's work we have examined the impact of multiple repetitions on words from a range of frequency bands (Schofield, 1990). For convenience, and to highlight the functional equivalence of the lexical and skill acquisition domains, we converted *frequency* (words/million) into *practice* (number of occurrences) by assuming that our young adult subjects had experienced 25,000 words per day for 20 years, an assumption that means that a frequency value of 100/million is equal to approximately 18,000 occurrences or practice trials.

Schofield used six sessions, words from five preexperimental practice treatments, and new and old words in each session. The five preexperimental practice (i.e., word frequency) treatments involved items from bands with means at 1/million, 3/million, 10/million, 33/million, and 100/million. The first five sessions were completed in five 20-min periods on consecutive days, and the sixth, 40 days later. All of the old words and nonwords were presented once per session. Additional sets of new words and nonwords were presented in each session. A lexical decision task was used. Data from the sixth session is not reported here. Schofield tested 28 subjects.

Word Frequency and Life-Span Practice: Some Caveats.   The rule we have used to convert word frequency into life-span practice is a first approximation. However, given the illustrative nature of the experiment, it constitutes an appropriate starting point. Some of the problems that will beset scientists developing a more accurate rule are introduced next. The first problem concerns variables such as modality, morphology, and language. Do life-span practice counts accumulate across the spoken, printed, and signed forms of concepts, for example, or do each of these stimulus variants contribute to independent representations?

In brief, it is our view that accumulation occurs at a highly specialized level, where separate representations are invoked for reception and production, and for each modality (e.g., speech, print, signs, objects, and depictions of objects). Accumulation is, furthermore, specific to each lexical paradigm (e.g., *run, runs, runner, running, ran*), even if the paradigm straddles two languages (e.g., *publicity, publicidad*), although accumulation does not occur across morphologically unrelated translations (e.g., *bakery, panaderia*), or synonyms (e.g., *great, large*).

The second problem concerns changes in word frequency patterns from infancy to adulthood. Any model that equates frequency with practice will be incorrect to the extent that infant and adult frequency patterns differ. The scale of this measurement problem should not be underestimated. Consider an 18-month-old child with a vocabulary of 100 words. For convenience we assume, first, that the child receives and utters words at the same rate as an adult ($\sim$ 25,000 per day); second, that Zipf's law applies to child language as well as adult language, that is, that the number of different words found with frequency f in a large textual sample is proportional to f raised to a negative power, that is, $N = Kf^{-\alpha}$, where alpha has been estimated at 1.30 (Oldfield, 1966); and third, that these conditions apply for a period of 40 days. Given these assumptions it may be calculated that a high-frequency word (e.g., equivalent to 100 per million in adult language) will have been used 20,000 or more times in 1 month by the child. The equivalent figure for an adult for the same period would be 100.

RT and Experimental Practice (Session).   Figure 6.1 shows RT for lexical decision as a function of session for new and old words. Figure 6.1 uses a log-log graph. The results replicate Logan (1990), with RT decreasing as a function of practice from session to session. The power law offers a reasonable if less than convincing fit for the old data. In particular, it is evident that some unknown factor has led to a general increase in RT for session 5.

The RT for the new and old word treatments reflects general and specific practice effects, respectively. The extent to which the new word function departs from a slope of zero presumably reflects either increasing familiarity with the lexical decision task or, even more generally, increasing comfort with the experimental environment. There is no obvious reason why RT increases from session 4 to session 5. The difference between the functions for new and old words

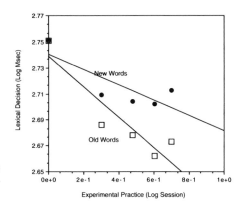

FIG. 6.1. Lexical decision as a function of experimental practice (session).

reflects the impact of experience with the particular set of words that is being repeated during each session. Scrutiny of the observations for the second, third, fourth, and fifth sessions indicates that the difference between old and new words is increasing slightly from session to session, indicating that additional priming is occurring on each block.

RT and Preexperimental Practice (Word Frequency).   Figure 6.2 shows RT as a function of preexperimental practice (i.e., a transformation of word frequency). The data in Fig. 6.2 are for new words only, for the first block of trials, and repetition and general practice effects are therefore precluded. These results are consistent with published work (e.g., Landauer, 1975), and show a systematic decrease in RT as a function of increasing preexperimental practice, or word frequency. The slope of the function relating preexperimental practice and RT is also consistent with work involving word frequency and RT, with a gain of about 50 msec/log unit of frequency or preexperimental practice.

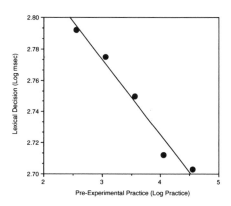

FIG. 6.2. Lexical decision as a function of preexperimental practice (word frequency).

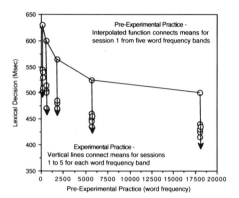

FIG. 6.3. Preexperimental (word frequency) and experimental (session) practice.

Relationship Between Preexperimental Practice (Word Frequency) and Experimental Practice (Session).   Although the fit for experimental practice is far from satisfactory, the results depicted in Figs. 6.1 and 6.2 suggest that both preexperimental practice and experimental practice may be subject to the power law. However, the slopes of the functions are quite different. Whereas a mere five sessions of experimental practice reduces RT by 0.1 log unit, it takes about 18,000 trials of preexperimental practice to achieve the same effect.

The foregoing analysis bears on the proposition that experimental practice (i.e., session effects) is a direct quantitative extension of preexperimental practice (i.e., word frequency effects). If preexperimental practice is estimated at, say, 180 from the word frequency tables,[1] words that are repeated over five consecutive days should involve the 181st, 182nd, 183rd, 184th, and 185th occurrences (ignoring extralaboratory experience), and lexical decision for these items should lie along the function for preexperimental practice. The point that may be inferred from the comparison between Figs. 6.1 and 6.2 is highlighted in Fig. 6.3, in functions that provide a direct comparison between the two forms of practice. The interpolated line indicates the expected pattern of data based on the assumption that experimental practice is a simple extension of preexperimental practice. The proposition is falsified; it is clear that experimental practice is not a continuation of the function for preexperimental practice. Indeed, when experimental practice is plotted in the same normal-normal space as preexperimental practice, RT declines so dramatically that the power law is obscured completely.

The experiment conducted by Schofield (1990) was not designed to explore those factors that selectively influence experimental practice. Several factors merit consideration, however. First, whereas preexperimental practice is spread out over years, experimental practice in this study was compressed into a few

---

[1]Given 25,000 words per day, word frequency = 1/million, and subject age = 22 years, life-span practice = 180 trials.

days. The difference could therefore be attributed to recency, even though repetition priming studies have usually found only very weak recency effects (e.g., Scarborough, Cortese, & Scarborough, 1977; Tulving et al., 1982). It should be noted that Anderson (1982) provides specifically for decay in his model.

A second factor involves practice on the task of lexical decision. Whereas most if not all preexperimental practice involved tasks other than lexical decision (e.g., reading and speaking), experimental practice involved this task in particular, and it is to be expected that specific productions (such as the production rules described in Anderson's ACT* model) would be developed and practiced to facilitate performance under these conditions. In fact, we have catered for this component in our model, by including task-specific productions that behave in the same way as stimulus-specific productions. Another and related factor involves context. As subjects become more familiar with the environment, their performance improves under all conditions.

The argument just outlined is subject to a number of qualifications of course. For example, it will only apply if all of the contexts in which a word can occur are functionally equivalent. If exposure to, say, /panoply/ has a different impact on the relevant representation when it is experienced in a book, conversation, and a lexical decision task, performance may depart radically from the preexperimental practice function.

Priming and Preexperimental Practice (Word Frequency).   Figures 6.4 and 6.5 summarize the impact of preexperimental practice (word frequency) and experimental practice (session) on repetition priming. Figure 6.4 replicates the finding originally reported by Scarborough et al. (1977), and replicated since then for a variety of paradigms (e.g., Kirsner, Milech, & Standen, 1983), that repetition priming decreases as a function of increasing preexperimental practice (word frequency). However, the pattern also appears to follow the power law, and it may be inferred that reports that repetition priming is absent with high-frequency words probably represent Type II errors, that is, conditions under

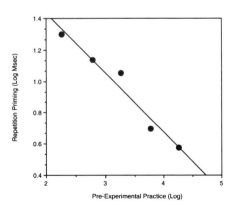

FIG. 6.4. Repetition priming as a function of preexperimental practice (word frequency).

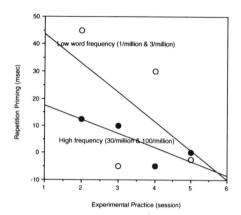

FIG. 6.5. Repetition priming as a function of preexperimental (word frequency) and experimental (session) practice.

which RT facilitation due to one additional trial is so small that it will not be detected by routine application of a Repetition Priming paradigm.

Priming and Experimental Practice (Session). The results depicted in Fig. 6.1 show RT for both new and old words as a function of experimental practice (session). The difference between the functions is of course a cumulative estimate of repetition priming, and the additional increment associated with each session is decreasing from session to session. Figure 6.5 depicts the relationship between preexperimental practice (word frequency), experimental practice (session), and priming, although the data is noisy at this level of the interaction. In fact, to provide a measure of clarity, we have pooled the results over the two high-practice data sets (word frequency bands of 30/million and 100/million) and the two low-practice data sets (word frequency bands of 1/million and 3/million). The results are as expected, with repetition priming decreasing as a function of experimental practice as well as preexperimental practice, although the fits are very poor. It should also be noted that the impact of experimental practice is greater, with stronger initial priming effects and a sharper reduction therein, for low levels of preexperimental practice, an outcome that is qualitatively consistent with the proposition that all of these functions, for preexperimental practice, experimental practice, and repetition priming, follow the power law.[2]

In summary, Schofield's (1990) findings demonstrate that experimental practice, preexperimental practice, and priming behave in ways that are qualitatively consistent with the power law of practice, although they also show that the experimental practice function is not a simple continuation of the preexperimental practice function. Of more significance for the present analysis is the fact that

---

[2]As the priming function follows subtraction of one alleged power function (i.e., old words) from another alleged power function (i.e., new words), conformity to the power law was to be expected.

preexperimental practice, experimental practice, and repetition priming follow the power law of practice, an outcome that supports our contention that a prima facie case can be made for the hypothesis that skill acquisition and repetition priming reflect the same underlying process or principle.

Generalization to Other Tasks

Lexical decision is of course just one measure of implicit memory. Do the arguments just summarized generalize to other implicit memory tasks such as word identification under degraded listening or viewing conditions, and stem and fragment completion? The following material were collected to provide some preliminary evidence about the form of the relationship between performance and preexperimental practice in other implicit memory tasks.

The following figures are based on coarse inclusion criteria. They include a mixture of unpublished and published results, and a mixture of independent and dependent data points. They have not in all cases used the same measure of central tendency for word frequency, and, depending on the aim of the research, either narrow- or broad-band frequency selection criteria may have been applied. But they do, nevertheless, provide a starting point for assessing the hypothesis. The power law has not been developed for the relationship between accuracy and preexperimental practice, but we have included accuracy-dependent tasks for comparative purposes.

Lexical Decision: Meta-Analysis. Figure 6.6 complements Schofield's study. It has been included because, when it is placed beside Schofield's study (1990), it can be used to estimate the extent to which the second meta-analysis provides a test of the hypothesis. Figure 6.6 shows the repetition priming effects from 16 studies that used a priming phase involving just one presentation of each item, a test phase involving just one presentation of each item, visual presenta-

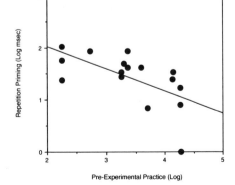

FIG. 6.6. Repetition priming (lexical decision) as a function of preexperimental practice (word frequency) for 16 experiments.

tion, and lexical decision. Consideration was restricted to experimental treatments involving physically identical priming and test stimuli. The procedure summarized earlier was used to convert word frequency into preexperimental practice. For summary statistical purposes we have assumed that all of the points are independent, although in some cases two or more points involve separate treatments from the same study. The function follows that reported in earlier discussion for Schofield (1990), although the amount of variance accounted for is substantially less in the meta-analysis ($r^2 = .61$)

Word Identification Under Degraded Viewing and Listening Conditions. Figure 6.7 shows a comparable set of data for 16 Word Identification experiments. The set includes experiments that used auditory or visual presentation of test stimuli, but the points shown in Fig. 6.7 are for the pure or intramodality conditions alone; the cross-modal results are not included here. In a typical study the auditory or visual words were presented without masking during the priming phase, but under degraded viewing or listening conditions in the test phase. For a visual test, word degradation was typically supplied by a poststimulus mask. For an auditory test, word degradation was typically supplied by mixing the test word with multispeaker babble. It should be noted that Anderson's model (e.g., Anderson, 1982) has usually been described for tasks where time is the dependent variable, and that it may not be extendable to tasks where the dependent variable is on an ordinal scale (Newell, 1991). The fit is only marginally inferior to that observed in the meta-analysis for lexical decision ($r^2 = .56$)

The results show that priming decreases systematically as a function of increasing preexperimental practice, although they do not provide a basis for discriminating between alternative accounts of the form of the relationship. The results do suggest, however, that systematic intraexperimental analysis of the relationship between repetition priming and preexperimental practice in tasks such as word identification under degraded viewing conditions may be justified,

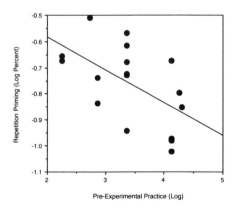

FIG. 6.7. Repetition priming in word identification as a function of preexperimental practice for 16 experiments.

despite the fact that they generally yield ordinal data. They also suggest that further consideration be given to models of skill acquisition that consider the impact of practice on accuracy, and to experimental examination of the proposition that accuracy as well as RT reflects the operation of the power law, provided that floor and ceiling effects are avoided.

Word Identification Under Fragment and Stem Completion Conditions. Consideration of the published papers using fragment and stem completion, vogue tasks in the implicit memory tradition, could not be used for even informal meta-analysis for a number of reasons. One of these is that word frequency is often unspecified. Another reason is that researchers have often used selected subsets of words from, for example, Tulving et al. (1982), without indicating which subset they have used. Yet another problem concerns selective modification of the fragments, so that the potential cohort may change from application to application.

Theoretical Continuity

It is our suspicion that a model that involves learning principles and production rules of the form described by Anderson (1982) can be refined to account for the phenomena of repetition priming as well as skill acquisition. This selection is arbitrary however. We could have developed an account based on Logan's (1988) model, using multiple representations—an approach that is much closer to our earlier use of records to explain a repetition priming phenomenon (Kirsner & Dunn, 1985; Kirsner, Dunn, & Standen, 1987, 1989)—or, possibly, connectionist principles. The critical argument that we wish to advance is that synthesis between these domains is possible, and that, on grounds of scientific parsimony, it should be attempted.

The specific model was developed from research in skill acquisition and transfer of training. A ubiquitous finding in this area is that, with practice, improvement in performance time on a task typically follows a power function of the form $T = NP^r$ (Newell & Rosenbloom, 1981). Anderson (1982) has included an account of this phenomena in his ACT* theory of skill acquisition and transfer. In this account, N represents the performance time on trial 1 and reflects the number of productions executed on this trial; P represents the amount of practice and r represents the rate at which performance improves with practice, typically in the $-1 < r < 0$ range. Our research in this area (Speelman, 1991; Speelman & Kirsner, in press), has examined how such learning functions are affected by the combination of well-practiced skills with newly acquired skills. This research demonstrated that simple power functions could not account for improvement on a task that relied on the execution of skills differing in the amount of practice they had received. Obviously, a function that involves only one parameter to describe amount of practice is not suitable for describing improvement on a task where different components have been practiced to different extents. A function consisting of several power functions, each designed to account for improvement on the separate components, provided a superior account of improvement on such a task. For example, improvement on a task that relied on execution of two sets of skills, one old and one new, could be described by equation 1:

$$T = N_o P_o^r + N_n P_n^r \tag{1}$$

where N_o represents the initial number of productions involved in performing the old components of the task, P_o represents the amount of practice a subject had with the old components, N_n represents the initial number of productions executed in performing the new components of the task, and P_n represents the amount of practice received on the new components. There are two main assumptions that underlie this combination of power functions into one omnibus equation. The first is that when skills are combined to perform a task, these skills continue to improve according to the functions that described their improvement prior to performance of this new task. The second assumption is that all new skills improve at the same rate. Thus in equation 1, r is the same value for both the old and new components. The only evidence we have to support these assumptions is the ability of functions like equation 1 to account for improvement on a task that involves old and new components. However, we are presently examining the validity of these assumptions.

Functions like equation 1 are well suited for describing implicit memory phenomena, if it is assumed that a subject's task in an implicit memory experiment involves the execution of skills with varying amounts of practice. For example, consider a typical two-phase experiment, where the first phase is a priming phase and the second a testing phase. The priming phase may involve a lexical decision task. According to the present framework, there will be at least two sets of productions involved in performing this task. One set will be associated with processing the words (and nonwords). For real words, these productions will be well practiced for adult readers. The other set of productions executed in performing this task will be associated with deciding whether each letter string is a word or not. To most adults, this will not be a well-practiced task. Certainly it can be expected that the task of lexical decision will not have been practiced to the same extent as processing words. Thus, RT in the priming phase of the experiment will be determined by the amount of practice a subject has had on each word (i.e., frequency of occurrence) and the amount of practice the subject has had with lexical decision (effectively nil at the beginning of the experiment, but increasing with each trial). If the task is also lexical decision in the testing phase of the experiment, RT to the repeated words will be predicted by adding one trial to the P_o term in equation 1 (processing words being an old skill) and adding the number of intervening trials between the first and second presentations of each repeated word to the P_n term in equation 1 (lexical decision being a new skill). The RT to new words in the testing phase will be predicted by a version of equation 1 where P_o will represent the frequency value of each new word, and P_n will represent the number of trials in the experiment up to the presentation of each new word.

This conception accounts for the two most replicated results in implicit memory research: (a) primed words are reacted to faster than unprimed words, and (b) priming facilitates low-frequency words more than high-frequency words. The first result is explained by the fact that primed words have been practiced for one more trial than unprimed words. This practice is localized to the productions responsible for processing words. The productions responsible for performing the lexical decision will, on average, have been practiced to the same extent for both primed and unprimed words during the testing phase. The second result can be understood by assuming that word frequency is an indication of how often a word has been processed by a subject (i.e., P_o in the present conception). This implies that P_o for high-frequency words is greater than for low-frequency words. An important property of power functions, and therefore learning functions, is that the amount by which performance improves with practice is reduced as practice increases. Therefore high-frequency words are further along their learning curve than low-frequency words, and so have less room for improvement. In other words, high-frequency words gain little from each lexical decision trial and so are facilitated by priming to only a small extent. In contrast, low-frequency words improve by large amounts with each trial and so priming facilitates performance to a greater extent.

The foregoing learning account of priming describes perfect transfer between processing instances of a word. That is, priming is specific to a word and will provide maximum facilitation to further processing of the same word. If functions of the form of equation 1 are to account for priming among words presented in different forms (e.g., morphological variations), modalities, and languages, then they will need to be extended in order to account for the less than perfect transfer that is typically observed in these cases. Such an extension will include additional power functions to account for improvement on more than two sets of components. The general form of such an extended function is described by equation 2:

$$T = N_{a1}P_{a1}^r + N_{a2}P_{a2}^r + \cdots + N_{b1}P_{b1}^r + N_{b2}P_{b2}^r$$
$$+ \cdots + N_{c1}P_{c1}^r + N_{c2}P_{c2}^r \tag{2}$$

where T is time; N_a, N_b, and N_c represent sets of production rules from three hypothetical stages: (a) perceptual processes, where these are required by stimulus modality (which may be speech, pictures, print or sign, etc.), (b) stimulus redescription processes required to meet task demands (i.e., for naming, which requires phonological assembly, or sign decision, which requires assembly of premotor program for a sign sequence), and (c) the decision rule per se (e.g., naming or lexical decision); P is amount of practice; and r is learning rate.

Equation 2 is designed to describe improvement in all of the processes that intervene between the presentation of a word and the execution of a response to that word. The equation is comprised of a number of power functions, where these are divided into three basic stages. The stage labeled a describes improvement in productions responsible for the initial processing of a word, where the physical stimulus is translated into some mental code. The b stage involves the execution of productions responsible for initiating appropriate responses, such as which button to press, or which articulatory muscles to use in producing a word sound. The c stage represents the execution of productions responsible for the task decision, such as deciding whether the presented letter string is a word or not.

An assumption underlying the model depicted in equation 2 is that transfer between word-processing episodes is a function of the number of common productions executed in both episodes. This assumption follows from the ACT* theory of transfer, which states that there will be transfer between two tasks to the extent that performance of these tasks relies on the same productions (Singley & Anderson, 1989). The greater the production overlap, the greater the transfer. This theory has received some empirical support in studies where transfer is predicted on the basis of an analysis of the production rules acquired during training and the production rules necessary for performance of a transfer task (Frensch, 1991; Kieras & Bovair, 1986; Singley & Anderson, 1989). Incorporating this assumption into our model leads to a number of transfer predictions. For instance, there will be perfect transfer (i.e., maximum priming) between two word-processing episodes when a subject processes the same word, presented in the same form, and makes the same decision in both episodes. Any deviation from this combination of stimulus, task, and response elements will engage different combinations of productions and so will lead to less than perfect transfer (i.e., less than maximum priming). Thus two lexical decision trials, where the stimulus is a printed word, /courage/, will engage the same productions and therefore result in maximum facilitation. In contrast, one lexical decision trial of /courage/ followed by a word identification trial of the spoken word /courageous/, will invoke fewer shared productions in the two episodes and so result in less facilitation. Of course, in this second example there will be some shared productions executed in both episodes, and so some priming will be observed in comparison with a situation where a new word is presented in place of /courageous/.

GENERALIZATION TO OTHER PROBLEMS AND DOMAINS

One way to evaluate the productivity of the account outlined above is to assess the extent to which it will generalize to other issues and findings in the repetition priming literature. Consideration is given to two such problems below. These

problems concern morphology and modality. The model offers a plausible starting point in each case.

Inflections, Derivations, and Cognates

Research involving inflections, derivations, and cognates has yielded data consistent with our model. As already noted, the critical issue concerns the extent to
which practice with specific morphological forms such as *run* changes performance in ways that imply that practice with the root form is available to inflections and derivations such as *runs, runner* and so on. The process should be
transitive, of course, so that practice with *runs* and *runner* should boost performance with *run* as well. Published work in this area indicates that RT under
repetition priming conditions is facilitated by prior exposure to inflections, derivations and cognates in both vision and audition (Cristoffanini, Kirsner, &
Milech, 1986; Downie, Milech, & Kirsner, 1986; Forbach et al., 1974; Murrell
& Morton, 1974). There is evidence, moreover, that frequency of occurrence
with root forms of words influences RT to specific surface forms that share the
same root (e.g., Bradley, 1979; Caramazza & Brones, 1979). None of these
studies provide a basis for precise quantitative evaluation, but it is evident that
practice with morphologically defined parts of words influences many if not all
surface forms that share those parts. One area of uncertainty concerns irregular
derivations, particularly where there is some change in the phonology or stress
pattern of the root (*run/ran, content/content*). The critical problem therefore
concerns the danger of circularity. A method must be developed to estimate the
extent to which two surface forms (e.g., *run, ran*) share a subset of productions,
and the extent to which they involve unique productions. It is not sufficient to
estimate this from transfer in repetition priming, order of acquisition during
language acquisition (e.g., Derwing & Baker, 1986) or transparency estimates by
adults (e.g., Derwing & Baker, 1986). These tasks simply represent alternative
ways of tapping the underlying process. They may all be strongly correlated.
However, this will not cast new light on questions about shared productions.

Modality

There is a wide body of evidence that repetition priming involves two components or stages. The basic evidence for this inference is that two repetition
priming components can generally be detected in mixed modality experiments.
The first component involves the difference between the intramodality treatment
(i.e., prime in print followed by test in print, or print–print) and the cross-
modality treatments (i.e., prime in speech followed by test in print, or speech–
print). The second component involves the difference between the cross-modality
component (defined above) and the new print treatment (i.e., test word in print
without prior exposure in any form).

TABLE 6.1
Repetition Priming as a Function of Word Frequency and Component for Word Identification

Word Frequency	Cross-Modal Component	Intramodal Component
	New Words - Picture/Print	Picture/Print - Print/Print
Low	.22	.11
High	.12	.11
	New Words - Speech/Print	Speech - Print/Print
Low	.23	.11
High	.11	.10

Notes. The cross-modality conditions involved transfer from pictures to print (Kirsner et al., 1986) and speech to print (Kirsner et al., 1983). The cross-modal component is the difference between performance (percent correct) in the new print and speech - print and picture - print treatments. The intramodal component is the difference between performance in the speech - print and picture - print treatments and the print - print treatments.

The results from typical studies involving transfer between speech and print (Kirsner et al., 1983) and pictures and print (Kirsner, Milech, & Stumpfl, 1986) are summarized in Table 6.1. The data suggest a single dissociation in which word frequency selectively influences the cross-modal component—the conventional interpretation being that the task involves two stages or processes, one of which is vulnerable to word frequency effects. The model could draw support from two-stage models involving quite different paradigms (e.g., Levelt et al., 1991), where two stages are associated with target selection and response activation, respectively, but there is a more interesting issue at stake. Let us assume that the word frequency influences information processing in both stages, and that must, after all, be one implication of the model we have outlined above, but that life-span practice on the intramodal components has been far greater than that on the cross-modal components. This would of course give us the observed interaction, with a small and nonsignificant impact of one further practice event on the intramodal component, and a larger and significant impact of one further practice event on the cross-modal component.

Is this plausible? How could the intramodal component have had more practice than the cross-modal component? The answer is in our view straightforward. Whereas the name that must be activated for the second and cross-modal stage will have a frequency count determined only by summation across its morphological relatives, subprocesses in the first or target selection stage will enjoy frequency counts associated with letters or even smaller units than letters, that is, values based on 5,000 occurrences per day (the average letter frequency given five-letter words and 25,000 words per day).

This proposition is easy to test. If a language can be identified in which the relative frequency of the subprocesses activated in the first and second stages is reversed, the pattern of the interaction should also be reversed. Fortunately, the

Japanese scripts provide us with a method of examining this question, and we have completed an appropriate experiment (although it was conducted for other reasons). The critical treatment involves Kanji. There are three scripts in Japanese. Of these, Kanji alone has several thousand characters; the others consist of just 52 characters, which stand for the syllabic units of the spoken language. For Kanji, therefore, practice is reduced substantially because it is but one of three separate scripts, and also because the perceptual information associated with each Kanji character is presented but rarely because there are several thousand other Kanjis, and there is no underlying alphabetic level over which summation can occur. We must predict, therefore, that there will be a strong frequency effect in the intramodal component in Japanese Kanji, a prediction that we have confirmed in our laboratory (Kirsner, Dunn, Kinoshita, Standen, & Hasslacher, in preparation).

CONCLUSION

The argument advanced here is that skill acquisition and repetition priming share many features. They are operationally similar; they yield similar patterns of data; and there is at least a prima facie case that they can be explained by a single model. It is therefore appropriate to evaluate the proposition that synthesis is possible, and that they may now be explained by reference to one theoretical framework. It is our tentative proposal that a model derived from Anderson's (1982) account of skill acquisition can be developed to account for the phenomena of repetition priming and skill priming, and that synthesis should now begin.

REFERENCES

Anderson, J. R. (1982). Acquisition of cognitive skill. *Psychological Review, 89*, 369–406.

Bradley, D. (1979). Lexical representations of derivational relations. In M. Aranoff & M. L. Kean (Eds.), *Juncture* (pp. 37–55). Cambridge, MA: MIT Press.

Caramazza, A., & Brones, I. (1979). Lexical access in bilinguals. *Bulletin of the Psychonomic Society, 13*, 212–214.

Cristoffanini, P. M., Kirsner, K., & Milech, D. (1986). Bilingual lexical representation: The status of Spanish-English cognates. *Quarterly Journal of Experimental Psychology, 38A*, 367–393.

Derwing, B. L., & Baker, W. J. (1986). Recent research on the acquisition of English morphology. In P. Fletcher & M. Garman (Eds.), *Language acquisition: Studies in first language development* (pp. 209–223). Cambridge: Cambridge University Press.

Downie, R., Milech, D., & Kirsner, K. (1985). Unit definition in the mental lexicon. *Australian Journal of Psychology, 37(2)*, 141–155.

Forbach, G., Stanners, R., & Hochaus, L. (1974). Repetition and practice effects in a lexical decision task. *Memory & Cognition, 2*, 337–339.

Frensch, P. A. (1991). Transfer of composed knowledge in a multi-step serial task. *Journal of Experimental Psychology: Learning, Memory & Cognition, 17(5)*, 997–1016.

Graf, P., & Schacter, D. (1985). Implicit and explicit memory for new associations in normal and amnesic subjects. *Journal of Experimental Psychology: Learning, Memory & Cognition, 11,* 501–518.

Kieras, D. E., & Bovair, S. (1986). The acquisition of procedures from text: A production system analysis of transfer of training. *Journal of Memory and Language, 25,* 507–524.

Kinsbourne, M., & Wood, F. (1975). Short-term memory processes and the amnesic syndrome. In J. A. Deutsch & D. Deutsch (Eds.), *Short-term memory* (pp. 257–291). New York: Academic Press.

Kirsner, K., & Dunn, J. C. (1985). The perceptual record: A common factor in repetition priming and attribute retention? In M. I. Posner & O. S. M. Marin (Eds.), *Mechanisms of attention: Attention and performance XI,* (pp. 547–565). Hillsdale, NJ: Lawrence Erlbaum Associates.

Kirsner, K., Dunn, J. C., Kinoshita, S., Standen, P., & Hasslacher, T. (in prep.). *Cross-modal repetition priming effects in English and Japanese: One principle; many processes.*

Kirsner, K., Dunn, J. C., & Standen, P. (1987). Record-based word recognition. In M. Coltheart (Ed.), *The psychology of reading, attention and performance XII* (pp. 147–167). London: Lawrence Erlbaum Associates.

Kirsner, K., Dunn, J. C., & Standen, P. (1989). Domain-specific resources in word recognition. In S. Lewandowsky, J. C. Dunn, & K. Kirsner (Eds.) *Implicit memory: Theoretical issues* (pp. 99–122). Hillsdale, NJ: Lawrence Erlbaum Associates.

Kirsner, K., & Smith, M. C. (1974). Modality effects in word identification. *Memory and Cognition, 2,* 637–640.

Kirsner, K., Milech, D., & Standen, P. (1983). Common and modality specific coding in the mental lexicon. *Memory and Cognition, 11,* 621–630.

Kirsner, K., Milech, D., & Stumpfel, V. (1986). Word and picture recognition: Is representational parsimony possible? *Memory and Cognition, 14(5),* 398–408.

Landauer, T. K. (1975). Memory without organization: Properties of a model with random storage and undirected retrieval. *Cognitive Psychology, 7,* 495–531.

Levelt, W. J. M., Schriefers, H., Vorberg, D., Meyer, A. S., Pechman, T., & Havinga, J. (1991). The time course of lexical access in speech production: A study of naming. *Psychological Review, 98(1),* 122–142.

Logan, G. (1988). Toward an instance theory of automaticity. *Psychological Review, 95,* 492–527.

Logan, G. (1990). Repetition priming and automaticity: Common underlying mechanisms? *Cognitive Psychology, 22,* 1–35.

Murrell, G. A., & Morton, J. (1974). Word recognition and morphemic structure. *Journal of Experimental Psychology, 102,* 963–968.

Newell, A., & Rosenbloom, P. S. (1981). Mechanisms of skill acquisition and the law of practice. In J. R. Anderson (Ed.), *Cognitive skills and their acquisition* (pp. 1–55). Hillsdale, NJ: Lawrence Erlbaum Associates.

Newell, K. M. (1991). Motor skill acquisition. *Annual Review of Psychology, 42,* 213–237.

Oldfield, R. C. (1966). Things, words and the brain. *Quarterly Journal of Experimental Psychology, 18,* 340–353.

Oldfield, R. C., & Wingfield, A. (1965). Response latencies in naming objects. *Quarterly Journal of Experimental Psychology, 17(4),* 273–281.

Roediger, H. L., Weldon, M. S., & Challis, B. H. (1989). Explaining dissociations between implicit and explicit measures of retention: A processing account. In H. L. Roediger & F. I. M. Craik (Eds.), *Varieties of memory and consciousness: Essays in honour of Endel Tulving* (pp. 3–41). Hillsdale, NJ: Lawrence Erlbaum Associates.

Scarborough, D. L., Cortese, C., & Scarborough, H. S. (1977). Frequency and repetition effects in lexical memory. *Journal of Experimental Psychology: Human Perception and Performance, 3,* 1–17.

Schacter, D. L. (1987). Implicit memory: History and current status. *Journal of Experimental Psychology: Language, Memory & Cognition, 13(3),* 501–518.

Schneider, W., & Fisk, A. D. (1984). Automatic category search and its transfer. *Journal of Experimental Psychology, Learning, Memory and Cognition, 10*, 1–15.

Schofield, P. (1990). *Word repetition and word frequency effects.* Thesis submitted to the University of Western Australia in partial fulfillment of the degree of B.A. (honours).

Singley, M. K., & Anderson, J. R. (1989). *The transfer of cognitive skill.* Cambridge, MA: Harvard University Press.

Speelman, C. (1991). *Skill acquisition: Estimating the contributions of old skills to performance on new tasks.* Unpublished Ph.D. thesis submitted to the University of Western Australia.

Speelman, C., & Kirsner, K. (in press). New goals for HCI training: How to mix 'old' and 'new' skills in the trainee. *International Journal of Human-Computer Interaction.*

Tulving, E., Schacter, D. L., & Stark, H. A. (1982). Priming effects in word-fragment completion are independent of recognition memory. *Journal of Experimental Psychology, Learning, Memory and Cognition, 8(4)*, 336–342.

Warrington, E. K., & Weiskrantz, L. (1970). Amnesic syndrome: Consolidation or retrieval? *Nature, 228*, 629–630.

Warrington, E. K., & Weiskrantz, L. (1974). The effect of prior learning on subsequent retention in amnesic patients. *Neuropsychologia, 12*, 419–428.

Winnick, W. A., & Daniel, S. A. (1970). Two kinds of response priming in tachistoscopic recognition. *Journal of Experimental Psychology, 84*, 74–81.

7

Using Artificial Neural Nets to Model Implicit and Explicit Memory Test Performance

Janet Wiles
Michael S. Humphreys
University of Queensland

Artificial neural networks provide a set of tools that can be applied to the task of modeling implicit and explicit memory test performance. These tools can be quite different from those provided by the traditional ideas about memory and cognitive processes that were based on early work with digital computers. Because of these differences, the creation of models based on artificial neural networks can provide a new way of thinking about tasks and can lead to different experimental questions. In this chapter we first review some of the tools provided by artificial neural networks and then show how these tools can be used to construct theories for implicit and explicit memory test performance.

THE COMPUTATIONAL APPROACH

Many of the computational approaches to modeling learning and memory derive from the 1960s when the computer metaphor first became widespread. The computer metaphor has been called the ultimate metaphor for the brain, and one that need never be superseded. We argue that this claim is only partly correct. Computation is the processing of information, and the same sequence of instructions can be executed by a computer, a human brain, or an "analytical engine" made out of gears, such as Babbage designed 150 years ago. Although the speed of calculating the solution may change and the effort of the programmer may be radically different, the same computational tasks can be solved. The contribution that the computer metaphor brings to the study of cognition is that it enables one to distinguish between the computational (or information processing) tasks of cognition, and the neural structures that implement such processing. This distinction allows us to talk about two levels of description, computational and implementational. The computational level is independent of any particular implementation, in the sense that there are many ways to implement the same set of processes.

There is a darker side to the computer metaphor that has entailed much more than just the understanding of computation as independent of implementation. The structures that have been proposed for human memory often presuppose many of the same properties as computer memory, and these assumptions constrain the processes that are constructed. For example, even the basic assumption that sequential search is a possible memory access mechanism relies on the unique storage of information in memory. In contrast, empirical studies of human memory have led to the development of many models that do not assume unique storage as a fundamental property of memory. Instead, the basic process of memory storage is *superposition*. The underlying notion is that there is no single trace for any memory event. Rather, memory traces are represented by distributed patterns that are alternatives over the same set of processing units. This type of representation has implications for processing, as the processing of memory can occur in a distributed manner also. Such an idea can be simulated on a traditional sequential computer, but it needs to be explicitly programmed to incorporate superpositional memories. Similarly, learning techniques can be explicitly programmed into traditional models. In neural networks, however, both superposition and learning are integral aspects of the specification of a model.

The standard argument for creating an explicit computational or mathematical model is that such a model is necessary to show that one's theoretical ideas will actually work. This rationale is an important aspect of explicit modeling but it is not the only justification. Proposers of verbal cognitive theories tend to have ideas about computations. These ideas are often implicit and they are derived from a variety of sources. Some are unacknowledged borrowings from previous theorists, others come from folk psychology, and still others come from the types of programs that ran on the early computers. Ideas about computing that derive from distributed representations are based on a different set of components, which lead to different evaluations of theoretical proposals and to new experimentation. Current models that use distributed representations are crude and inadequate in many aspects. Nevertheless, they are beginning to provide some indications as to how computing with distributed representations differs from computing with discrete representations. In this chapter we do not describe any one particular model per se, but rather first review some of the tools and techniques that are available with distributed representations and then show how these tools and techniques can be applied in theory construction.

REQUIREMENTS OF A NEURAL NETWORK MODEL

We take the view that to understand human memory, we need to understand the *function* or role of memory within the cognitive system. This role has not been formally specified, and a universally acceptable specification is probably not possible given the current state of knowledge about representation in memory (although preliminary attempts have begun for some specific memory tasks; Humphreys, Wiles, & Dennis, 1992). We first consider the structures and processes required for explicit memory modeling and then apply these components to implicit memory tasks.

In thinking about the function of implicit and explicit memory, we distinguish between *learning* and *memory*. The distinction we use is that learning involves the acquisition of information over many trials, whereas memory involves just one or a few trials. Many neural network paradigms are suitable for studying learning but not memory. This difference arises because learning in a neural network involves the formation of mappings from one set of units to another, and these mappings are created over many—sometimes thousands of—trials. There are many examples in the neural network literature in which slow learning of mappings creates a representation space in which items have systematic relations with respect to one another (von der Malsberg, 1973; Kohonen, 1984; Sejnowski & Rosenberg, 1987). In contrast to slow learning, which is suitable for the construction of representation spaces, fast learning must be focused on the items immediately at hand. Tasks in which information is stored in a single trial typically involve combining familiar items in novel ways. For example, in explicit memory tasks involving lists of words, the words themselves are familiar, and it is the occurrence of the words in a novel context (membership in the list) that constitutes the information to be remembered. We use the general term *binding* to refer to the process of combining two or more items together. An association between an item and a list context is an example of binding. In general we can view the function of explicit memory as a fast binding together of items (possibly in context). From this perspective, we can outline components of explicit memory that require neural network implementation:

1. The first step is to define a representation (or *data structure*) for items and contexts. In neural network models, representations of items are vectors, and in the next section we discuss properties of vectors and operations over vectors that make them appropriate representations.

2. Because explicit memory involves binding between items in context, we also need a representation of the binding information (another data structure). It is possible to store binding information in several ways in neural network models. In the next section we describe tensor products as one example of binding spaces that are suitable for modeling fast learning. (Another example is the convolution/correlation process of Murdock [1982].)

3. After specifying data structures for items and memory, we need storage and access processes. We view the access of information in memory as part of the memory modeling task. The choice of data structure interacts with the processes that can extract information from it. In the next section we discuss access processes for information stored in tensors.

TOOLS AND TECHNIQUES

We start with a specification of the representations, bindings, and memory access processes required for explicit memory task performance because, as we have argued elsewhere, they also suffice for implicit memory task performance (Humphreys, Wiles, & Dennis, 1992). We begin our discussion with the representation of items as vectors, and then show how bindings between vectors can be represented as tensors. We then review possible access processes on tensors, and show that different access processes are required, depending on the information available to complete the tasks (this section summarizes the results of Humphreys, Bain, & Pike [1989] and Wiles, Humphreys, Bain, & Dennis [1990, 1991]). We discuss the access problem in considerable detail as we see it as an integral part of the specification of a memory model, even though this detail is more than is strictly necessary for the applications in this chapter. In the next section we review how tensors can be applied to the development of models for explicit memory performance and then provide an example of how they can be applied to the development of models for implicit memory performance.

Representation of Items as Vectors

In neural network models of memory, items are represented as vectors. We represent an item in capital letters (e.g., X and Y) and the corresponding vector representation in small letters (i.e., **x** and **y**). A vector is a *distributed* representation of an item, in that there are many elements that all contribute to the representation of the item. In part, the utility of neural networks in terms of generalization and graceful degradation comes from the mathematical properties of vectors and operations over vectors.

Item Similarity. Vectors provide a representation of items that naturally causes similar items to be treated in similar ways, and dissimilar items not to interfere. This property allows for generalization of performance from items learned in one situation to similar, though possibly not identical, items. We measure the *similarity* between two vectors by the dot (or inner) product, denoted $\cdot$. For example, if a vector **x** is similar to another vector **y** such that $\mathbf{x} \cdot \mathbf{x} = 1.0$, $\mathbf{y} \cdot \mathbf{y} = 1.0$, and $\mathbf{x} \cdot \mathbf{y} = 0.9$, then in the memory models we will be developing, **x** is likely to behave in a similar way to **y**. Conversely, if two vectors are not very similar, or in the extreme case if they are orthogonal (i.e., $\mathbf{x} \cdot \mathbf{y} = 0$), then information learned about one item will not generalize to other items.

Item Blends. Memory tasks frequently involve combinations of items. For example, if a cue has been paired with more than one target, then accessing memory with the cue will result in some combination of the corresponding targets. Vectors provide a representation of items that naturally allows items to be combined in certain ways. One such process is the linear combination of two or more vectors, which is a superposition process that produces another vector, called a *vector bundle* (we have also used the term *blend;* Wiles et al., 1990). For example, if **x** and **y** are vectors with the same number of elements and + is linear combination, then the vector bundle $z = x + y$ is also a vector. If **x** and **y** are similar vectors, then Z will represent the prototype of X and Y. Alternatively, if **x** and **y** are dissimilar, then Z can be thought of as a combination of other items, X and Y.

In memory modeling, we take vector bundles to be the natural way in which information is represented during the intermediate stages of any processes that operate over memory (Humphreys, Wiles, & Bain, in press; Wiles et al., 1990). It is only on initial presentation and for output purposes that an item is thought of as having a unique vector representation. The following section explains some of the processes that can be explored from this perspective.

The Analogy Between Vector Bundles and Sets. One way of thinking about a vector bundle is as a set of one or more items. For example, given $z = x + y$, Z can be thought of as a set composed of the two items represented by **x** and **y**. The vectors **x** and **y** can be also considered as sets, possibly containing only themselves (i.e., single item sets). From this perspective, every vector is analogous to a set. The analogy to sets can be extended to talk about superimposed representations (using linear combination) as the *union* of component sets. The union of two sets A and B is the set of all the items that are in either A or B or both.

Problems of Decomposition. Given a method to compose sets, we also require a method to decompose them (i.e., extract the component items). Decomposition of vector bundles is not as straightforward, however, since the linear combination of vectors is *not* a reversible process in general. There are many different vectors that could be combined to form any particular vector bundle. In the foregoing example, from **z** alone there is no way to extract a unique value for **x** and **y**. To continue the analogy with sets, a vector bundle is like a set in which the component items are not individually accessible. However, decomposition is possible if constraints are placed on the possible values of **x** and **y**. This circumstance leads to some unusual properties for decomposition, and requires us to rethink what we mean by access to the information in a vector bundle. In particular, we need to consider what additional information is required and how it can be represented in memory.

The Use of Additional Information to Access Information in a Vector Bundle

The first way that we consider the use of additional information is if we know all potential vectors that could be components of a vector bundle.

Set Membership.   Given a new item, say W, it is possible to test its membership in Z using the dot product between the vector representations, $z \cdot w$. If this dot product is high, then W is similar to a component of Z or to a combination of components.

Using this test for set membership, one method of identifying the components in a vector bundle is to test all possible components individually against the vector bundle. The ones with a high match (measured by the dot product) have effectively been identified as components. If all the possible components are tested, then we will have achieved a decomposition. Note how the matching process circumvents the original decomposition problem: We provided the possible components, rather than requiring a decomposition procedure to generate them. Procedures that require us to provide specific cues we call *cue-based access*. In neural net models, all access to information is cue based. There is no search procedure for scanning items in a data structure without some knowledge of the items themselves that can be used as cues. Such additional information is typically stored in matrices embodied as weights in nonlinear networks such as the brain-state-in-a-box (Anderson, Silverstein, Ritz, & Jones, 1977) or the Hopfield net (Hopfield, 1982). How matrices can be used to retrieve components of a vector bundle is discussed later.

Selection from Sets.   In determining set membership, we viewed one vector as a vector bundle and the other as an item (or single-item set). Within our modeling framework, memory tasks such as cued recall with an extralist associate (which we discuss in the next section) require two multi-item sets. The match procedure for set membership can be applied to two vector bundles where both represent multi-item sets. If the components of both vector bundles are mutually orthogonal, the match in this case will represent the number of components that are common to both sets. If there are no common components, then the match will be zero. This procedure is analogous to counting the number of items in the *intersection* of two sets. Whereas the union of two sets A and B is the set of items in either set, the intersection of two sets is the set of items in both sets. An intersection is specified whenever two or more independent constraints must be simultaneously satisfied.

It is an interesting aspect of operations on vectors that although it is possible to calculate the number of components in the intersection of two vector bundles, there is no direct way to recover the components themselves from the vector bundles alone, because of the decomposition problem. This point is critical to our understanding of cue-based access processes in memory. What we (as memory modelers) consider to be the intersection of two vector bundles depends on what we consider the components to be.

One method of identifying the components in an intersection of two vector bundles is to provide all possible components and test each for membership in both vector bundles using the aforementioned set membership procedure. Again, note that the decomposition problem is circumvented because we provide the components to be tested. This testing process is simple and easy to understand. However, as in the method of identifying components already described, it requires individually testing each item, and therefore keeping separate representations for each of the components. It is thus an improbable way to implement an intersection process in a neural network because there is no provision for the storage of individual items, and any knowledge of the components is likely to be in superimposed form. In addition, the procedure as described is serial. As we show later, if the information about components is in the form of a tensor, the intersection can be calculated in parallel.

In summary, this section has introduced the analogy between vector bundles and sets of items, and two processes over vector bundles:

1. Combining two orthogonal vectors into a vector bundle (using the linear combination) is analogous to forming the union of two sets, where each set is represented by one of the vectors.

2. Finding the components that are common to two vector bundles is analogous to finding the intersection of two sets, where each set is represented by one of the vector bundles. Unlike the union of two vector bundles, the intersection cannot be determined from the vector bundles alone, because it is defined in terms of the components of the vector bundles and these are not uniquely determined by the vector bundles themselves.

Binding Between Vectors Can Be Represented as Tensors

For neural network research, the implication of the decomposition problem discussed in the preceding section is that care must be taken in how items and their combinations are modeled. *Linear combination* is a specific relation over vectors, one that we have identified with set membership for orthogonal vectors (a similar analogy to class membership may be made for similar vectors, though that is beyond the scope of this chapter). In memory tasks that only require information about set membership (e.g., was an item in a given list?), linear combination is a sufficient basis for modeling the memory structure. However, because there is no structure other than membership imposed on the items in a vector bundle, linear combination cannot represent other relations between items, and hence more complex combination processes are required for modeling other psychological tasks.

The Binding Issue

In the first section, we defined binding to refer to a structured combination of one or more items. In neural network models, in which items are represented by vectors, a binding is a representation of the relationship between two or more vectors. Consider the task of learning a list of pairs of items (cues and targets). The cues and targets themselves are familiar to the subject, and the list is only shown once. In this task, the subject is required to learn an association between the items, but the task does not involve any unfamiliar items. An example might be the information that A went with B, and C with D (and not vice versa). Binding involves the imposition of structure that is more than set membership, and it requires a way of combining vectors that differs from linear combination.

Representation of the Association of a Pair of Items by a Matrix

Associations between pairs of items can be represented by a matrix formed from the outer product of their corresponding vectors. If several associations are required, then the matrices can be superimposed. For example, to model a list of two items of pairs AB and CD, the memory matrix $\mathbf{M}$ is formed by $\mathbf{M} = \mathbf{a} \otimes \mathbf{b} + \mathbf{c} \otimes \mathbf{d}$ (where $\mathbf{a} \otimes \mathbf{b}$ is the outer product of $\mathbf{a}$ and $\mathbf{b}$). The combination of vectors by the outer product takes two vectors and produces a matrix that represents the association (or binding) between the two items. In the terminology introduced in the last section, a matrix can be viewed as the representation of a set of pairs of items.

To model this process in a network requires a set of input and output units, each with connections from all the input to output units. Weights on these connections correspond to the memory of the network, and can be represented by a matrix. There are several different ways to modify the weights in a network that correspond to different learning rules. For explicit memory tasks it is important to keep in mind that the binding between items is a fast process. Learning rules such as backpropagation (Rumelhart, Hinton, & Williams, 1986) that require many iterations are suited to modeling how representations are formed, rather than fast bindings between familiar items. Superposition of the outer products of pairs of items is equivalent to Hebbian learning in a pattern associator (Anderson et al., 1977; Kohonen, 1984) or a Hopfield network (Hopfield, 1982) and is more suitable for fast binding between familiar items.

Access to Information in Matrix Memories

The information stored in matrix memories can be accessed in two ways. The first is to test whether a pair of items is a member of the set specified by the matrix, by calculating the match between them. This match is calculated by pre- and postmultiplying the matrix by the cue and target vectors, resulting in a scalar match value. If the match is high, then the pair is recognized as *old* (i.e., having been learned before). This match procedure does not test the individual items, but rather whether a cue and target vector were associated together. For example, in the list given above, if a and c are orthonormal (i.e., $\mathbf{a} \cdot \mathbf{c} = 0$ and $\mathbf{a} \cdot \mathbf{a} = 1$), then $(\mathbf{a} \otimes \mathbf{b}) \cdot \mathbf{M} = 1$, but $(\mathbf{a} \otimes \mathbf{d}) \cdot \mathbf{M} = 0$. These match values mean that the pair AB would be recognized as old, but AD would not.

The second access method is *retrieval* of the target vectors that have been learned in response to a given cue. In matrix terms this process is equivalent to premultiplying the memory matrix by a cue vector. In a pattern associator network, it is equivalent to setting the activations of the input units to the cue vector. The activation from each input unit is multiplied by its corresponding weight, and summed together at each output unit. If the cues are orthogonal, then the output vector will be a bundle of target vectors learned with the cue. If the cues are not orthogonal, then the output vector bundle will include other targets weighted by the similarity of their cues to the given cue. In other models, such as the Hopfield network, the output units serve as decision elements, and more complex combinations of targets are possible (see Hertz, Krogh, & Palmer, 1991).

Binding Triples Together

A matrix can be used to represent the binding information about sets of pairs of items; however, it is insufficient to represent arbitrary sets of triples of items. As we discuss in the next section, triples are required for memory tasks that involve pairs of items in context. Pairs of items alone cannot capture information about the relation between an entire triple. A mechanism for representing higher-order relationships, such as three-way associations, is required. One such method is the use of tensors.

Tensors.   A tensor can be thought of as a generalization of a matrix. Just as a matrix can be formed from the outer product of two vectors, so a tensor of rank k can be formed from the outer product of k vectors. A vector is a special name for a tensor of rank 1, and a matrix is a tensor of rank 2. If a tensor of rank 2 is visualized as a square, then a tensor of rank 3 is analogous to a cube, because it can be formed from the outer product of three vectors. The tensor hierarchy can be generalized to arbitrarily large rank (which could be visualised as a hyper-cube). We use the symbol of multiplication with a circle around it, $\otimes$, for the outer product, and the symbol $\cdot$ for the inner product and for premultiplying a tensor by a second tensor of lower rank (specific ranks can be identified from the cue and target labels, and hence subscripts are omitted).

Just as a matrix can be viewed as a set of pairs, so a tensor of rank k can be viewed as a set of k-tuples. Tensors have been used as the basic data structure for a memory-based analogical reasoning model by Halford, Wilson, Guo, Wiles, and Stewart (in press), and tensors of increasing rank appear to form a continuum from memory tasks to reasoning tasks (Wiles et al., 1992).

Access Processes on Tensors

The access processes on tensors of arbitrary rank can be viewed as a generalization of those over matrices. Just as the outer product of two or more vectors creates a tensor of higher rank, so premultiplying a tensor by a vector creates a tensor of a lower rank. When premultiplying or calculating an inner product, the number of elements in each rank must be equal, as these processes are not defined for ranks with unequal numbers of elements. If there are as many access cues as ranks in the tensor, the process will be equivalent to a match process between the outer product of the cues, and the tensor. Note that the order of the cues will matter for this process, because a tensor binds the items in a specific configuration of the outer products, and they need to be matched in that same configuration.

If one or more cues are not available for access, there are two ways of dealing with the missing information. A fixed unit vector can be substituted for the missing cue. This procedure allows a *matching* process where items corresponding to missing ranks are approximated by the unit vector. In the second method, the available cues can be used to *retrieve* vectors corresponding to the missing items. A combination of matching and retrieval for different ranks is also possible. For further details, see Humphreys, Bain, and Pike (1989).

Intersection Tasks Using Tensors

A binding mechanism such as a rank 3 tensor is required to encode information about triples of items that have occurred together. In this section we consider tasks that involve two or more cues that have not previously been observed together. For example, find a word that is associated with rat and blue (cheese). In this example, the pairwise associations between the cues and cheese have certainly been stored; however, the higher order relationship between all three components is unlikely to have ever been explicitly encountered. In generic terms, the problem is to find a word that is associated with both A and B, where A and C, and B and C have occurred together, but A, B, and C have not. This problem requires the combination of information from memory, yet it is closer to a creative process than memory retrieval (Wiles et al. 1992). If the cue A retrieves the set of targets with which it has been associated, and the cue B does likewise, the task is to find a word that occurs in both sets. That is, it is formally equivalent to the task of finding an item in the intersection of the sets of associates of A and B.

Wiles et al. (1990, 1991) investigated various techniques for computing the intersection of sets of items represented by vector bundles. One such technique (when the possible components of a vector bundle are available as individual components) is the serial match process outlined earlier. A second method, which is more compatible with neural networks, is possible when the components are represented as self-associations in a rank 3 tensor $\mathbf{T}$. For example, if the possible components are W, X, and Y, then $\mathbf{T} = \mathbf{w} \otimes \mathbf{w} \otimes \mathbf{w} + \mathbf{x} \otimes \mathbf{x} \otimes \mathbf{x} + \mathbf{y} \otimes \mathbf{y} \otimes \mathbf{y}$. If the vectors $\mathbf{w}$, $\mathbf{x}$, and $\mathbf{y}$ are orthonormal (i.e., $\mathbf{w}$, $\mathbf{x}$ and $\mathbf{y}$ are orthogonal and $\mathbf{w} \cdot \mathbf{w} = \mathbf{x} \cdot \mathbf{x} = \mathbf{y} \cdot \mathbf{y} = 1$), then the intersection of two vector bundles, say, $\mathbf{a} = \mathbf{w} + \mathbf{x}$ and $\mathbf{b} = \mathbf{x} + \mathbf{y}$, can be calculated by $(\mathbf{a} \otimes \mathbf{b}) \cdot \mathbf{T} = \mathbf{x}$. One way of conceptualizing how this procedure works is to visualize the rank 3 tensor $\mathbf{T}$ as a cube, and the vector bundles $\mathbf{a}$ and $\mathbf{b}$ as cues to the first and second ranks. Because $\mathbf{T}$ is autoassociative, the only components retrieved on the third rank will be those that occurred on both the first and second ranks. This technique is sufficient even if the strength of the X component in both vector bundles is very weak (Wiles et al., 1990).

The process just described provides direct access to the intersection of the vector bundles. As we remarked earlier, any intersection process requires information about the possible components, or restrictions on the vectors. In this case, the information about components is stored in the form of autoassociations in the rank 3 tensor. An alternative method is to use an autoassociative rank 2 tensor and restrict the representation of items to sparse vectors (Wiles et al., 1990). The intersection can be calculated by multiplying the corresponding elements in each vector bundle, followed by a nonlinear thresholding. As we show in a simulation in the final section, the use of sparse vectors with a thresholding process can give some surprising properties as a component of an access process. A thresholding process could be implemented in a Hopfield network trained on the individual components, and cued with the element-by-element product of the two vector bundles. The noise produced by this procedure will depend on the sparseness of the vectors and the relative strengths of the components.

INCORPORATING CONTEXT IN TENSOR PRODUCT MODELS: POSSIBLE ROLES IN RECOGNITION, CUED RECALL WITH LIST ASSOCIATE, AND WITH EXTRALIST ASSOCIATE

In this section we review how the tensor product has been applied in studying the role of context in memory retrieval tasks. Suppose that a subject has studied a list of word pairs, under instructions to learn each pair so that they could recall one member of the pair if the other member was provided as a cue. Following this learning experience the subject's memory can be probed in a variety of ways. As expected by the subject, one member of the study pair can be provided as a cue for the other member (cued recall with a list associate). Alternatively, the subject can be asked to decide whether or not a target word occurred in the study list (single item recognition). Another alternative is to provide an extralist associate of one of the studied words and ask the subject to recall a word from the list that is related to the cue (cued recall with an extralist associate). A final alternative is to provide part of one of the studied words (e.g., its initial or final letters) and ask the subject to complete these letters with one of the words in the list. The approach we take in modeling these tasks is to propose a memory structure and a set of access processes that probe the structure in a variety of ways. The motivation for this approach is to show that this memory structure and a restricted set of the access processes may also serve for implicit memory tasks.

Perhaps our first decision in specifying a memory structure is whether to include context. Although many theorists (Anderson & Bower, 1973; Gillund & Shiffrin, 1984; Humphreys, Bain, & Pike 1989; Tulving, 1976) have strongly argued for a role of context in these paradigms, others (Eich, 1982; Murdock, 1982; Roediger, Weldon, & Challis, 1989) have not included context in their model or theory. Some of this reluctance to consider a role for context is understandable because it is a very slippery construct. Nevertheless, it is possible that we can get an idea about how context might work by trying to see how we might include it in an artificial neural network. It was just such an investigation as to how context might be included in the vector and tensor product memory models that provided the starting point for the theory proposed by Humphreys, Bain, and Pike (1989). The following discussion is a review of their investigation.

Suppose the study list consists of the items A, B, and C. We will represent the corresponding vectors as $\mathbf{a}$, $\mathbf{b}$, and $\mathbf{c}$ and the memory (without context) for the list as $\mathbf{V} = \mathbf{a} + \mathbf{b} + \mathbf{c}$. The match of an old item $\mathbf{a}$ and a new item $\mathbf{d}$ with the memory $\mathbf{V}$ is shown in equations 1 and 2:

$$\mathbf{a} \cdot \mathbf{V} = \mathbf{a} \cdot \mathbf{a} + \mathbf{a} \cdot \mathbf{b} + \mathbf{a} \cdot \mathbf{c} \tag{1}$$

$$\mathbf{d} \cdot \mathbf{V} = \mathbf{d} \cdot \mathbf{a} + \mathbf{d} \cdot \mathbf{b} + \mathbf{d} \cdot \mathbf{c} \tag{2}$$

We refer to the expected value of the matches in equations 1 and 2 as the matching strength of the relevant item. The matching strength for an old item is, on average, larger than the matching strength for a new item. This difference occurs because the similarity between an item and itself (the dot product of the vector representing that item with itself) is, on average, considerably larger than the similarity between two different items (the dot product between two different vectors). However, if there is a large number of preexisting memories also stored in $\mathbf{V}$ then this memory will not work without some way of isolating the list memories from preexisting memories. That is, the difference in the old and new matching strengths attributable to the match with the list memories will be overwhelmed by differences in the number of times items have been stored in the memory prior to the learning of the experimental list. The question to be addressed here is whether context can be used to isolate the list memories. The starting point is that we assume that regardless of how context is conceived (e.g., background stimuli, internal stimuli, a concept of the experimental setting, etc.), the context X can also be represented as a vector $\mathbf{x}$.

When the problem of how, in a distributed storage model, to incorporate $\mathbf{x}$

into the memory for an item is raised many people assume that one can simply append the context vector to the item vector. That is, create one long vector out of the two short vectors (we denote the appended vector **x:a**). With this assumption, $\mathbf{V} = (\mathbf{x:a}) + (\mathbf{x:b}) + (\mathbf{x:c})$ and the match of an old item **a** and a new item **d** to the memory is shown in equations 3 and 4.

$$(\mathbf{x:a})\cdot\mathbf{V} = (\mathbf{x:a})\cdot(\mathbf{x:a}) + (\mathbf{x:a})\cdot(\mathbf{x:b}) + (\mathbf{x:a})\cdot(\mathbf{x:c})$$
$$= 3(\mathbf{x\cdot x}) + \mathbf{a\cdot a} + \mathbf{a\cdot b} + \mathbf{a\cdot c} \tag{3}$$

$$(\mathbf{x:d})\cdot\mathbf{V} = (\mathbf{x:d})\cdot(\mathbf{x:a}) + (\mathbf{x:d})\cdot(\mathbf{x:b}) + (\mathbf{x:d})\cdot(\mathbf{x:c})$$
$$= 3(\mathbf{x\cdot x}) + \mathbf{d\cdot a} + \mathbf{d\cdot b} + \mathbf{d\cdot c} \tag{4}$$

The reader can easily verify that the match of two appended vectors [e.g., $(\mathbf{x:a})\cdot(\mathbf{x:b})$] is simply the sum of the separate matches (e.g., $\mathbf{x\cdot x} + \mathbf{a\cdot b}$). The result, as can be seen by comparing equations 3 and 4 with equations 1 and 2, is that adding context in this fashion does not help. The problem is that the context appended to the retrieval cue matches the stored context regardless of whether the other part of the retrieval cue is an old item or a new item. More generally, when memories are represented on the same set of units, appending two vectors does not bind them together. What is required is the storage of an association between the context and the item $(\mathbf{x}\otimes\mathbf{a})$ or an autoassociation between the combined context and item vector and itself. For example, if we represent the list memory as $\mathbf{M} = \mathbf{x}\otimes\mathbf{a} + \mathbf{x}\otimes\mathbf{b} + \mathbf{x}\otimes\mathbf{c}$ the recognition process can be thought of as using the context **x** as a retrieval cue followed by a determination of whether the output is the same as the target (equation 5 gives the matching strength for an old item and equation 6 gives the matching strength for a new item).

$$(\mathbf{x\cdot M})\cdot\mathbf{a} = (\mathbf{x\cdot x})(\mathbf{a\cdot a}) + (\mathbf{x\cdot x})(\mathbf{b\cdot a}) + (\mathbf{x\cdot x})(\mathbf{c\cdot a}) \tag{5}$$

$$(\mathbf{x\cdot M})\cdot\mathbf{d} = (\mathbf{x\cdot x})(\mathbf{a\cdot d}) + (\mathbf{x\cdot x})(\mathbf{b\cdot d}) + (\mathbf{x\cdot x})(\mathbf{c\cdot d}) \tag{6}$$

In this expression the dot product of **x** with itself can be thought of as the similarity of the context on the study and test occasions. Because the contextual similarity multiples the item similarities, the match is considerably greater when the cue was studied in the context than when it was not.

Having decided that a context-to-item association is the minimum representation required in order for context to affect single-item recognition, we can ask whether such associations are also adequate for cued recall with a list associate. Here we represent the memory for a list of pairs as associations between each cue and the corresponding target and between the context X and each target. Associations between context and cues are omitted in order to simplify the presentation. To see why this pairwise use of context will not work we turn to the *AB ABr* paradigm. In this paradigm subjects study two successive lists of word pairs, where the pairs in list 2 are rearrangements of the pairs in list 1. For example, the pairs *AB* and *CD* might be studied in list 1 and the pairs *AD* and *CB* studied in list 2. We also represent the list 1 and list 2 contexts as X_1 and X_2, respectively. With these assumptions the memory for list 1 becomes $\mathbf{M} = \mathbf{x}_1 \otimes \mathbf{b} + \mathbf{a} \otimes Bf +$ $Bf_1 \otimes \mathbf{d} + \mathbf{c} \otimes \mathbf{d}$ and the memory after learning both lists becomes $\mathbf{M} = \mathbf{x}_1 \otimes \mathbf{b} +$ $\mathbf{a} \otimes \mathbf{b} + \mathbf{x}_1 \otimes \mathbf{d} + \mathbf{c} \otimes \mathbf{d} + \mathbf{x}_2 \otimes \mathbf{d} + \mathbf{a} \otimes \mathbf{d} + \mathbf{x}_2 \otimes \mathbf{b} + \mathbf{c} \otimes \mathbf{b}$. When we cue this memory with the context X_2 and the cue A (we represent this cue as the sum of the two vectors $\mathbf{x}_2$ and $\mathbf{a}$) the composite vector that results is shown in equation 7.

$$(\mathbf{x}_2 + \mathbf{a}) \cdot \mathbf{M} = (\mathbf{x}_2 \cdot \mathbf{x}_2)\mathbf{d} + (\mathbf{a} \cdot \mathbf{a})\mathbf{d} + (\mathbf{x}_2 \cdot \mathbf{x}_1)\mathbf{d} + (\mathbf{a} \cdot \mathbf{c})\mathbf{d} + (\mathbf{x}_2 \cdot \mathbf{x}_2)\mathbf{b}$$
$$+ (\mathbf{a} \cdot \mathbf{a})\mathbf{b} + (\mathbf{x}_2 \cdot \mathbf{x}_1)\mathbf{b} + (\mathbf{a} \cdot \mathbf{c})\mathbf{b} \tag{7}$$

In the composite output vector the weight on the vector $\mathbf{d}$ (the item that was associated with A in context X_2) is exactly the same as the weight on $\mathbf{b}$ (the item that was associated with $\mathbf{a}$ in context X_1). The result is that no matter how distinctive the two contexts are, there is no benefit, in the AB ABr paradigm, to including context in this fashion. The relevance for psychological modeling lies in the constraints on the types of combination processes proposed to model this task. For example, if context is to be included in an effective fashion in the tensor product model then it is necessary to consider triples, and hence use a tensor of rank 3. That is, $\mathbf{T} = \mathbf{x}_1 \otimes \mathbf{a} \otimes \mathbf{b} + \mathbf{x}_1 \otimes \mathbf{c} \otimes \mathbf{d} + \mathbf{x}_2 \otimes \mathbf{a} \otimes \mathbf{d} + \mathbf{x}_2 \otimes \mathbf{c} \otimes \mathbf{b}$. When this memory is cued with the tensor product of the list 2 context and the cue A, the composite vector that results is shown in equation 8.

$$(\mathbf{x}_2 \otimes \mathbf{a}) \cdot \mathbf{T} = (\mathbf{x}_2 \cdot \mathbf{x}_2)(\mathbf{a} \cdot \mathbf{a})\mathbf{d} + (\mathbf{x}_2 \cdot \mathbf{x}_1)(\mathbf{a} \cdot \mathbf{c})\mathbf{d} + (\mathbf{x}_2 \cdot \mathbf{x}_1)(\mathbf{a} \cdot \mathbf{a})\mathbf{b}$$
$$+ (\mathbf{x}_2 \cdot \mathbf{x}_2)(\mathbf{a} \cdot \mathbf{c})\mathbf{b} \tag{8}$$

In this expression the contextual similarities and the item similarities also multiply just as they did in recognition. With the right parameters (e.g., the similarities between two different contexts or between two different items are approximately 1.0 and the similarity between the same context or the same item on different occasions is considerably greater than 1.0), the weight on the target that occurred with the cue A in context X_2 can be considerably greater than the weight on the target that occurred with A in context X_1.

The mathematical analysis shows that the AB ABr paradigm cannot be learned by a tensor product model of rank 2, and that the minimum rank required would be rank 3. In addition to relating the mathematical analysis to data it is also necessary to consider the generality of the mathematical analysis. If the rejection of pairwise associations only applied to a tensor product model then it would be of limited importance. This premise is not valid, however, as the analysis applies to the task itself (i.e., the AB ABr learning task), and therefore imposes requirements on every model that purports to solve it. The general requirement for any model that can learn an AB ABr paradigm in a similar fashion to the way humans learn is that the model can quickly (in a few trials) learn an XOR problem. Multilayer networks trained with backpropagation can learn to solve XOR problems but they require many trials. However, with the addition of higher order units (a multiplicative combination of the inputs) they can form a configural representation of a context and a pair of items (Sloman & Rumelhart, 1992).

The utility of a mathematical analysis does not depend on eliminating all but a few possibilities. This circumstance is fortunate, because although some models for the role of context in human learning can be eliminated by this analysis, a very large number of models remain as possibilities. The mathematical analysis can also be useful if we can compare the requirements for performing one task with the requirements for performing another task. The issue addressed here is whether the requirements for cued recall with a list associate and cued recall with an extralist associate are the same.

It is certainly possible to create a model in which the retrieval processes are essentially the same for the two cued recall tasks. For example, Freund and Underwood (1970; also see Raaijmakers & Shiffrin, 1981) suggested that subjects implicitly generate associates of the words they study. With this assumption the memory after explicitly studying a pair of words could be essentially the same as the memory that supports cued recall with an extralist associate. In the Raaijmakers and Shiffrin (1981) model the information stored is also unique to the given context and thus constitutes a binding between that context and the pair of items. Roediger and Payne (1983) proposed a theory for cued recall with an extralist associate based on the Flexser and Tulving (1978) memory model. Also basic to this idea is the assumption that memories are stored separately (which provides a binding between the context and the item) but also that the retrieval of these memories is based on similarity between the cues and the unique representation of the context and item. Thus, in this approach the extralist cue works because it is similar to the target not because it has entered into a 3-way binding with the context and target.

Both the Freund and Underwood (1970) assumption about implicit associations and the Roediger and Payne (1983) assumption that retrieval is based only on similarity could be incorporated into a neural network model. The challenge in such a task would be to demonstrate that the model could produce the differences that are found between the two forms of cued recall (Humphreys, Wiles, & Bain, in press). However, Humphreys, Wiles, and Bain (in press) explored a different alternative. They asked the question of how the computation could be performed if information about the occurrence of the cue and the target in the given context was not available. This omission would leave only pairwise information about cue-target associations and context-target associations. Their conclusion was that the computational task required under these conditions is to find the intersection between the set of targets associated with the cue and the set of targets associated with the context. In order to compute the intersection using neural networks it is necessary to represent information about list membership and cue-target associations as well as introducing a process to compute the intersection (see preceding section). In the tensor product model, if a three-way binding is employed for cued recall with a list associate then no additional memory structures are required to represent list information and cue-target associations. In discussing access processes on tensors we noted that it is possible to collapse across one or more of the ranks of a tensor by using a fixed vector as one of the input cues. Thus, a context and a fixed vector can be used to retrieve the set of items that occurred in a list, and a cue and a fixed vector can be used to retrieve the set of items that has been stored with that cue in any context.

The final task we consider in this section is cued recall with a partword cue. Because of the many similarities between cued recall with an extralist associate and cued recall with a partword cue, Humphreys, Wiles, and Bain (in press) proposed that both were intersection tasks. However, if part of an item is used to retrieve the entire item, then a self-association (an association from the item to itself) is required. There appear to be two general ways to characterize this self-association. It can be formed from representations at the same level as other memory representations (Eich, 1985), or it can be formed between a peripheral, modality-specific representation and a memory representation (Humphreys, Bain, & Pike, 1989). In the next section we explore the latter alternative as a possible means of integrating cued recall with a partword cue, semantic priming, and repetition priming.

LEARNING A MAPPING BETWEEN PERIPHERAL MODALITY-SPECIFIC REPRESENTATIONS AND MORE CENTRAL REPRESENTATIONS

To date, some of the most impressive achievements using artificial neural networks have occurred in mapping a structured set of input strings onto an arbitrary output. For example, Rumelhart and McClelland (1986) simulated the learning of English past tenses by a network that learned to map a representation of the ordered sequence of phonemes in the present tense form onto a representation of the ordered sequence of phonemes in the past tense form. Similarly, Sejnowski and Rosenberg (1987) and Seidenberg and McClelland (1989) have simulated the reading of individual words by teaching networks to map a string of graphemes onto a string of phonemes. In all of these simulations the inputs and outputs have to be represented so that at least some of the similarity structure is captured. For example, words with the same graphemes in the same positions have to be represented in a similar fashion. After a solution to the representational problem has been proposed, the network is taught to map a set of inputs onto the appropriate outputs.

The evaluation of the success of the simulation then depends on several criteria. One criterion is the extent to which the network has learned the mapping. A second is the extent to which it performs in a sensible fashion with novel inputs (automatic generalization). A final criterion is how well the network operates when provided with degraded inputs or when a portion of the network is corrupted (Hinton & Shallice, 1991). In our opinion the models that have been proposed for the learning of English past tenses and for the reading of individual words are inadequate but promising. In particular we are impressed with the potential of these networks to generalize to novel or degraded inputs. We start with the assumption that the kind of learning process exemplified by these artificial neural nets is responsible for the mapping of peripheral, modality-specific representations onto more central memory representations. We then ask whether this assumption has any implications for modeling semantic and repetition priming. However, we first need to differentiate between the kind of processes that may be responsible for semantic and repetition priming.

In the lexical decision task, wherein subjects decide whether or not strings of graphemes or phonemes are words, subjects will identify the target word *doctor* as a word more quickly if the prime (the immediately preceding word) was *nurse* than if it was *bread* (Meyer, Schvaneveldt, & Ruddy, 1975). Priming also occurs when the prime is identical to the target but these two forms of priming have somewhat dissimilar characteristics. Priming based on a semantic relationship (the prime and target are associated or have a particular semantic relationship such as synonymity) does not seem to last beyond one or two intervening words, whereas the priming produced by the repetition of a word can last for many minutes or even days (Jacoby & Dallas, 1981; Scarborough, Cortese & Scarborough, 1977; Tulving, Schacter, & Stark, 1982). Repetition but not semantic priming is also partially modality specific (Jacoby & Dallas, 1981; Kirsner & Dunn, 1986). Thus, if the study material is presented visually the repetition priming effect will be about 50% smaller if the test is auditory than if it is visual. In addition, with bilingual subjects repetition priming effects have been found with cognate translations but not with noncognate translations, but both types of translations produce semantic priming (Cristoffanini, Kirsner, & Milech, 1986).

The first step in trying to model these findings is to decide whether the prime is playing a functional or nonfunctional role in the process. Perhaps the most common assumption is that it is nonfunctional. That is, it is assumed priming is incidental to the processing of the prime and/or that the processes underlying lexical access did not evolve to utilize information derived from the prime. This assumption of a nonfunctional role appears to be incorporated in Masson's (1991) model for lexical decision. In this model there is a perceptual net and a conceptual net. The presentation of a word first activates a pattern over the perceptual net, which in turn activates a pattern over the conceptual net. The conceptual net is modeled as a Hopfield net, and the time taken to identify a word is assumed to be positively related to the number of cycles needed to converge to a stable solution. Masson assumed that when the target word was presented in a priming paradigm there would be a residual activation remaining from the prime. He was then able to demonstrate that when the prime and the target were similar (similarity was defined as the number of identical elements), fewer cycles were required for the net to reach a stable representation. In effect, the activation remaining from the prime provided a head start for the identification of the target.

The alternative assumption, namely that the prime is playing a functional role, is exemplified by the Humphreys, Wiles, and Bain (in press) interpretation of the Ratcliff and McKoon (1988) theory. The latter proposed that the global matching process that is used in several contemporary theories of pair recognition (see Humphreys, Bain, Pike, & Tehan, 1989) could be used to explain priming effects in lexical decision. In these models a compound cue is formed and "matched" against all the items or pairs in memory. If the items or pairs are stored separately as they are in SAM (Gillund & Shiffrin, 1984) and Minerva II (Hintzman, 1986), the match occurs with each memory and the separate matches are aggregated. When the items or pairs are stored in a composite memory as they are in TODAM (Murdock, 1982), in the Matrix model (Pike, 1984), and in most models based on artificial neural networks, then the match is with the composite memory. In all of these models when the elements in the compound cue have been associated a stronger match occurs than if they have not been associated. The decision about whether or not to recognize the pair is based on the strength of the match. Ratcliff and McKoon (1988) suggested that in lexical decision the compound cue would be created out of the prime and the target. They then proceeded to show how this idea could explain a wide variety of priming effects. They also produced evidence that was difficult to accommodate within standard ideas about spreading activation. What they did not do is explain why subjects should form a compound cue and use a pair recognition process in lexical decision.

However, when we think in terms of intersections, one of the clearest examples of the functional role of a prime is when a subject is asked to recognize a degraded word presented in context (a task that is closely linked to the lexical decision task discussed by Ratcliff and McKoon [1988]). In particular, assume that the prime activates its associative set and the target activates its representation plus noise. If the target is in the associative set of the prime, the intersection will be the target minus the noise. Thus, the intersection process can be used to suppress noise. In this explanation the prime is said to be playing a functional role because the process evolved to use information from the prime to aid in the identification of the target and is responsive to the information value of the prime. The same intersection process can also be used for pair recognition and lexical decision. That is, if the target is not in the prime's associative set, the intersection will be empty or will contain only noise. A decision about whether or not the target was in the prime's associative set could be based on the total amount of activation remaining in the intersection. This process is similar to the matching process used in the global matching models. When applied to lexical decision this process would correspond to the intuitive idea that a lexical decision is based on an overall measure of familiarity (see Balota & Chumbley, 1984).

The Masson (1991) and the Humphreys, Wiles, and Bain (in press) models are illustrative of the kinds of models that can be proposed for semantic priming effects using artificial neural networks. Both these models utilize a mapping between peripheral and central representation. However, neither model is extendible to repetition priming. If we assume discrete storage it may be possible that activation left over from processing the prime could persist for minutes or even longer. However, in Masson's (1991) model items are represented on the same set of units so there is almost no chance that activation could persist longer than a few intervening items. The process that produces priming in the Humphreys, Wiles, and Bain (in press) model (the use of the prime to retrieve the set of associated words) is also short lasting. It thus appears that with artificial neural networks different explanations are required for semantic and repetition priming.

Similarities between implicit and explicit tests when the same cues were used led Humphreys, Bain, and Pike (1989; also see Micco & Masson, 1991; Rueckl, 1990) to propose that changes in the weights of the network that maps peripheral modality-specific representation (the input layer) onto more central representation were responsible for repetition priming. The assumption here is that one experience at reading a well-known word such as *cold* will produce changes in the weights of a network which does this mapping. As we have already indicated, such networks tend to perform reasonably with degraded or partial inputs. Thus a single learning mechanism could conceivably explain performance changes with intact words (word naming), degraded words (perceptual identification), and partwords (stem completion). Such a mechanism could also explain why repetition priming occurs with cognate but not with noncognate translations. The basic idea here is that the effect of weight changes between the input and output layer of a network will only be observed when the same or a similar pattern is reimposed at the input layer. For example, with cognate translations we can assume that the representations are similar at both the input and output layer. Even if noncognate translations have similar central representations, no long-term repetition effect would be expected because they would have dissimilar peripheral representations. A similar explanation can be given as to why the repetition effect is reduced when the modality of the input changes. To explain why there is only a 50% reduction would, however, require additional assumptions about the nature of the pathways between the peripheral modalities and the central representation.

In evaluating the proposal that weight changes are responsible for long-term repetition effects, many cognitive psychologists have had the reaction that the weight changes could not be large enough to support the observed changes in performance. The intuition here seems to be that the reading of a familiar word such as *cold* would be so highly overlearned that no further changes would be possible. This is the kind of argument that all of us make from time to time, and it serves to illustrate that we do have implicit ideas about computation that we use in evaluating the likelihood of results and theoretical proposals. However, it is important to examine these ideas about computation very carefully for hidden assumptions. In an artificial neural network it seems self-evident that the connection strength between two units would not increase without limit. However, the connection strengths may not be on asymptote if learning a new response to a similar pattern produces unlearning. Unlearning is a feature of many artificial neural networks (McCloskey & Cohen, 1989), so opportunities to read *colt* and *bold* may prevent the connection strengths that map the graphemic representation of *cold* onto a more central representation from asymptoting. An alternative is suggested by the rank 3 tensor model, in which all learning occurs in context. Familiar words are likely to be ones that have been learned in many contexts; however, all contexts are new to some degree, and repetition may cause changes in connection strengths that are not at asymptote because of continual change in context.

In addition, in a competitive situation the relationship between a change in connection strength and a change in performance is not transparent. For example, when a subject is cued with —*old* the response can be one of cold, bold, sold, etc. If a study trial opportunity has increased the strength of the connections between the peripheral representation of cold and its central representation, the expected change in performance will depend on how the conflict between the alternative responses is resolved. If a ratio rule is used (e.g., the probability of producing *cold* is proportional to the strength of *cold* divided by the sum of the strengths of all the responses) then large changes in strength will be needed to produce large changes in performance. That is, if there are 5 alternative responses each with a strength of 1.0 then the ratio rule produces a probability of responding of .20 for every response. If the strength of one response is doubled to 2.0, the probability of responding with that item increases from .20 to .33 and for the other 4 items decreases from .20 to .17. However, if a threshold function is used (the single strongest response is always produced) then a relatively small change in strength can produce a large change in performance. This draws on similar properties of networks mentioned at the end of the second section, as one method of implementing an intersection process.

We can demonstrate this behavior by simulating the matrix memory with a threshold decision at the output, as follows: The simulation involves one cue and five targets. The cue and targets were represented as 100 dimensional vectors, c and t_1 to t_5. Vector elements were randomly assigned values 1 or 0, with 20% probability of a 1. A memory matrix $\mathbf{M}$ was formed from the outer product of the cue with each target, with the strength of the first cue-target association scaled by a parameter α as follows:

$$\mathbf{M} = \alpha\mathbf{c}\otimes\mathbf{t}_1 + \sum_{i=2}^{5} \mathbf{c}\otimes\mathbf{t}_i$$

To study the response of the memory matrix to the cue $\mathbf{c}$, the matrix was premultiplied by $\mathbf{c}$. The response was defined to be the target $\mathbf{t}_i$ that had the strongest match, $(\mathbf{c}\otimes\mathbf{t}_i)\cdot\mathbf{M}$. A run consisted of generating a set of cue and target vectors, forming a matrix memory, and determining the target recalled. A trial consisted of a series of runs using the same set of cue and target vectors, for a

TABLE 7.1
Percentage of Trials on Which Targets t_1 and t_2 Were Retrieved for Varying α and Predictions
From the Ratio Rule

α	t_1	t_2	Ratio Rule
0.5	3	23	11
1	20	20	20
1.5	51	11	27
2	76	6	33
2.5	90	2	39
3	96	1	43

range of values of α from 0.5 to 3.0. We simulated 1000 trials, and recorded the number of times each target was recalled in response to the cue, for each value of α. In trials in which k targets ($k \geq 2$) produced equally high matches, the count for each target was incremented by $1/k$.

The results for t_1 and t_2 over all trials are given in Table 7.1 (rounded to the closest decimal). The responses for targets t_3 to t_5 showed a similar pattern to t_2 (less than 2% difference). The similarity in results for t_2 to t_5 is as expected, because their associations to the recall cue were the same as t_2. The predictions of the ratio rule are shown in the last column of Table 7.1.

The results show that as α increases, t_1 is recalled an increasing percentage of the time, and the other targets are recalled fewer times. The interest in this table lies in the difference between the responses for t_1 and those predicted by the ratio rule. For $\alpha = 1.0$, both threshold and ratio rule predict that all targets have an equal chance of the highest match (20%) and hence should be recalled equally often. The difference between the two rules emerges as α differs from 1.0. In the ratio rule, if the strength of the ct_1 association is doubled, the probability of the response t_1 increases from 20 to 33%. By contrast, in the simulation, when the strength of association was doubled ($\alpha = 2.0$), the number of times t_1 is recalled increases from 20 to 76%.

In the simulation, the vectors were randomly generated, so some correlation is expected, based on the proportion of nonzero elements in each vector. The expected correlation between the targets in this simulation was 4%. This small correlation is what allows the vectors t_2 to t_5 to be recalled some of the time. If the targets were totally uncorrelated, then for $\alpha > 1.0$, t_1 would be recalled 100% of the time, and for $\alpha < 1.0$, t_1 would never be recalled.

The simulation demonstrates how a nonlinearity can enhance one item strongly above the other items even for small changes in associative strength. This behavior would also be expected in other neural networks. For example, in a Hopfield net, the relative strengths of items determine the sizes of the basins of attraction around each target. As the strength of an item increases, the size of the basin increases. Therefore, a vector bundle (i.e., the linear combination) of several uncorrelated items will lie in the largest basin and hence converge to the strongest item. If, however, the items are correlated, then there is a nonzero probability that the vector bundle will lie in a different basin and hence converge to a different item.

SUMMARY

We have described an approach to human memory that involves specifying both data structures and the access processes that operate on those structures. In applying this approach it seems that a limited number of processes may suffice for a variety of explicit and implicit memory tasks. Our approach does not establish that the same processes are necessarily involved in implicit and explicit tasks, but rather, it indicates that this possibility is worth considering and that a computational specification provides a mechanism for exploring its implications. As one example, we showed how the tensor product could bind two or more vectors together and the binding and access processes could be applied to construct theories of how context is used. There is no requirement that the tensor product must be used as the solution to any of the binding problems; however, an analysis in terms of tensor products does indicate when a solution to the binding problem is required and how many elements require binding. When we addressed issues in semantic and repetition priming, more general bindings were used.

Based on an understanding of the tasks involved in cued recall with an extralist associate and cued recall with a partword cue we proposed the use of an intersection process, ways to extract pairwise information from three-way bindings, and an additional memory structure containing bindings between peripheral, modality-specific representations and central representations. These additional access processes and the new memory structure were then used in constructing theories for semantic and repetition priming. This theory construction demonstrates that the approach of postulating memory structures and processes that operate on such structures may be a fruitful way to approach human memory. More specifically, it may be possible to construct a unified theory for these different kinds of memory out of a limited set of memory structures and the processes that act on those structures. Finally, we discussed the difference between the activation of units and the weights between units and showed how such a distinction might be helpful in understanding the differences between short-term effects in semantic priming and long-term effects in repetition priming.

ACKNOWLEDGMENTS

This research was supported by a grant from the Australian Research council. We thank Steven Young for programming the simulations and Michael Masson for helpful comments.

REFERENCES

Anderson, J. A., Silverstein, J. W., Ritz, S. A., & Jones, R. S. (1977). Distinctive features, categorical perception, and probability learning: Some applications of a neural model. *Psychological Review, 84*, 413–451.

Anderson, J. R., & Bower, G. H. (1973). *Human associative memory*. Washington, DC: Winston.

Balota, D. A., & Chumbley, J. L. (1984). Are lexical decisions a good measure of lexical access? The role of word frequency in the neglected decision stage. *Journal of Experimental Psychology: Human Perception and Performance, 5*, 252–259.

Cristoffanini, P., Kirsner, K., & Milech, D. (1986). Bilingual lexical representation: The status of Spanish-English cognates. *Quarterly Journal of Experimental Psychology, 38A*, 367–393.

Eich, J. M. (1982). A composite holographic associative recall model. *Psychological Review, 89*, 627–661.

Eich, J. M. (1985). Levels of processing, encoding specificity, elaboration and CHARM. *Psychological Review, 92*, 1–38.

Flexser, A. L., & Tulving, E. (1978). Retrieval independence in recognition and recall. *Psychological Review, 85*, 153–171.

Freund, J. S., & Underwood, B. J. (1970). Restricted associates as cues in free recall. *Journal of Verbal Learning and Verbal Behavior, 9*, 136–141.

Gillund, G., & Shiffrin, R. M. (1984). A retrieval model for both recognition and recall. *Psychological Review, 91*, 1–67.

Halford, G. S., Wilson, W. H., Guo, J., Wiles, J., & Stewart, J. E. M. (in press). Connectionist implications for processing capacity limitations in analogies. In K. J. Holyoak & J. Barnden (Eds.), *Advances in connectionist and neural computation theory, Vol. 2: Analogical connections*. Norwood, NJ: Ablex.

Hertz, J., Krogh, A., & Palmer, R. G. (1991). *Introduction to the theory of neural computation*. Redwood City, CA: Addison Wesley.

Hinton, G. E., & Shallice, T. (1991). Lesioning an attractor network: Investigations of acquired dyslexia. *Psychological Review, 98*, 74–95.

Hintzman, D. L. (1986). Schema abstraction in a multiple-trace memory model. *Psychological Review, 93*, 429–445.

Hopfield, J. J. (1982). Neural networks and physical systems with emergent collective computational abilities. *Proceedings of the National Academy of Sciences, USA, 79*, 2554–2558.

Humphreys, M. S., Bain, J. D., & Pike, R. (1989). Different ways to cue a coherent memory system: A theory for episodic, semantic, and procedural tasks. *Psychological Review, 96*, 208–233.

Humphreys, M. S., Bain, J. D., & Pike, R., & Tehan, G. (1989). Global matching: A comparison of the SAM, Minerva II, Matrix, and TODAM models. *Journal of Mathematical Psychology, 33*, 36–67.

Humphreys, M. S., Wiles, J., & Bain, J. D. (in press). Memory retrieval with two cues: Think of intersecting sets. In D. E. Meyer & S. Kornblum (Eds.), *Attention and performance XIV: Synergies in Experimental Psychology, Artificial Intelligence, and Cognitive Neuropsychology. A silver jubilee*. Cambridge, MA: MIT Press.

Humphreys, M. S., Wiles, J., & Dennis, S. (1992). *Data structures and access processes: A first approximation to a theory of human memory*. Unpublished manuscript, University of Queensland, St. Lucia.

Jacoby, L. L., & Dallas, M. (1981). On the relationship between autobiographical memory and perceptual learning. *Journal of Experimental Psychology: General, 110*, 300–340.

Kirsner, K., & Dunn, J. C. (1986). Perceptual record: A common factor in repetition priming and attribute retention. In M. L. Posner & O. S. M. Marin (Eds.), *Attention and Performance IX* (pp. 547–565). Hillsdale, NJ: Lawrence Erlbaum Associates.

Kohonen, T. (1984). *Self-organisation and associative memory*. New York: Springer-Verlag.

Masson, M. E. J. (1991). A distributed memory model of context effects in word identification. In D. Besner & G. W. Humphreys (Eds.), *Basic processes in reading: Visual word recognition* (pp. 233–263). Hillsdale, NJ: Lawrence Erlbaum Associates.

McCloskey, M., and Cohen, N. J. (1989). Catastrophic interference in connectionist networks: The sequential learning problem. *Psychology of Learning and Motivation: Advances in Research and Theory* 24:109–65.

Meyer, D. E., Schvaneveldt, R. W., & Ruddy, M. G. (1975). Loci of contextual effects on visual word recognition. In P. M. A. Rabbit & S. Dornic (Eds.), *Attention and performance V* (pp. 98–118). New York: Academic Press.

Micco, A., & Masson, M. E. J. (1991). Implicit memory for new associations: An interactive process approach. *Journal of Experimental Psychology: Learning, Memory, and Cognition, 17,* 1105–1123.

Murdock, B. B., Jr. (1982). A theory for the storage and retrieval of item and associative information. *Psychological Review, 89,* 609–626.

Pike, R. (1984). A comparison of convolution and matrix distributed memory systems. *Psychological Review, 91,* 281–294.

Raaijmakers, J. G. W., & Shiffrin, A. M. (1981). Search of associative memory. *Psychological Review, 88,* 93–134.

Ratcliff, R., & McKoon, G. (1988). A retrieval theory of priming in memory. *Psychological Review, 95,* 385–408.

Roediger, H. L., & Payne, D. G. (1983). Superiority of free recall to cued recall with "strong cues." *Psychological Research, 45,* 275–286.

Roediger, H. L., Weldon, M. S., & Challis, B. H. (1989). Explaining dissociations between explicit and implicit measures of retention: A processing account. In H. L. Roediger & F. I. M. Craik (Eds.), *Varieties of memory and consciousness: Essays in honour of Endel Tulving* (pp. 3–41). Cambridge, MA: MIT Press.

Rueckl, J. G. (1990). Similarity effects in word and pseudoword repetition priming. *Journal of Experimental Psychology: Learning, Memory, and Cognition, 16,* 374–391.

Rumelhart, D. E., Hinton, G. E., & Williams, R. J. (1986). Learning internal representations by error propagation. In D. E. Rumelhart & J. L. McClelland (Eds.), *Parallel distributed processing* (Vol. 1, pp. 318–362). Cambridge, MA: MIT Press.

Rumelhart, D. E., & McClelland, J. L. (1986). On learning the past tense of English verbs. In J. L. McClelland & D. E. Rumelhart, (Eds.), *Parallel distributed processing* (Vol. 2, pp. 216–271). Cambridge, MA: MIT Press.

Scarborough, D. L., Cortese, C., & Scarborough, H. S. (1987). Frequency and repetition effects in lexical memory. *Journal of Experimental Psychology: Human Perception and Performance, 3,* 1–17.

Seidenberg, M. S., & McClelland, J. L. (1989). A distributed developmental model word recognition and naming. *Psychological Review, 96,* 523–568.

Sejnowski, T. J., and Rosenberg, C. R. (1987). Parallel networks that learn to pronounce English text. *Complex Systems, 1,* 145–168.

Sloman, S. A., & Rumelhart, D. E. (1992). Reduced interference in distributed memory. In A. Healy (Ed.) *From learning theory to connectionist theory: Essays in honor of William K. Estes* (Vol. 1, pp. 227–248). Hillsdale, NJ: Lawrence Erlbaum Associates.

Tulving, E. (1976). Ecphoric processes in recall and recognition. In J. Brown (Ed.), *Recall and recognition* (pp. 37–73). London: Wiley.

Tulving, E., Schacter, D. L., & Stark, H. A. (1982). Priming effects in word-fragment completion are independent of recognition memory. *Journal of Experimental Psychology: Learning, Memory, and Cognition, 8,* 336–342.

von der Marlsburg, C. (1973). Self-organisation of orientation sensitive cells in the striate cortex. *Kybernetik, 14,* 85–100.

Wiles, J., Halford, G. S., Stewart, J. E. M., Humphreys, M. S., Bain, J. D., & Wilson, W. H. (1992). *Tensor models: A creative basis for memory retrieval and analogical mapping.* Department of Computer Science, University of Queensland, TR-218, January.

Wiles, J., Humphreys, M. S., Bain, J. D., & Dennis, S. (1990). *Control processes and cue combinations in a connectionist model of human memory.* Department of Computer Science, University of Queensland, TR-186, October.

Wiles, J., Humphreys, M. S., Bain, J. D., & Dennis, S. (1991). Direct memory access using two cues: Finding the intersection of sets in a connectionist model. In R. P. Lippmann, J. E. Moody, & D. Touretzky (Eds.), *Advances in neural information processing systems 3* (pp. 635–641). San Mateo, CA: Morgan Kaufmann.

II LIFESPAN DEVELOPMENT

This part includes four chapters on the development of implicit and explicit memory from the early preschool years to late adulthood. The chapters have much in common. First, they note the relatively small number of studies involving young children, compared with the large number of studies that have focused on the adult lifespan. Second, they highlight methodological problems that are peculiar to research in this area. And third, they converge on the conclusion that implicit memory is fully operational early in development and remains intact or nearly intact well into late adulthood, whereas explicit memory changes throughout the lifespan. This conclusion is based on the findings displayed in an idealized figure at the beginning of David Mitchell's chapter.

Mitchell's chapter focuses on implicit/explicit memory for pictorial materials. He points out the benefits of using pictures—as opposed to verbal materials—for memory research, especially the fact that they can be used with very young prelinguistic children, and even for comparative investigations between humans and other animals. An additional advantage may come from the fact that performance on implicit memory tests for pictures—picture identification and picture completion—is less subject to contamination by intentional recollection of the to-be-remembered materials.

Mitchell, Parkin, and Light and La Voie address the problem of intentional recollection confounding performance on implicit memory tests. This problem is especially serious in developmental/lifespan research where the focus is on subject groups that differ widely in terms of explicit memory performance, subject-controlled processing strategies, and overall metamemory abilities. To deal with this problem, Mitchell advocates using pictorial materials, based on evidence indicating that picture identification test performance does not vary with subjects' awareness of the relationship between implicit memory testing and a previously studied list of items. Parkin's chapter focuses primarily on research with verbal materials, and he shows that contamination of implicit memory test performance is a serious problem in adult lifespan studies and must be eliminated in order to obtain a pure portrait of memory changes in adulthood. Parkin discusses various methods that can be used to minimize or eliminate this problem, including the use of divided attention study tasks, and subjects' ability to make recognition decisions based on remembering (*r*) versus knowing (*k*) studied target items.

Parkin's own experimental work shows that *r* and *k* recognition decisions follow different developmental courses, producing a genuine change in the extent to which older subjects' recognition memory relies on implicit memory processes. Parkin suggests that this change is a result of age-related developments in processing that is controlled by the frontal lobes, and he then speculates about lifespan changes in implicit and explicit memory by linking these to what is known about ontogenetic and phylogenetic changes in the neuroanatomy of the brain.

Light and La Voie's chapter complements Mitchell's and Parkin's in at least two ways. First, in contrast to Mitchell, who focuses on memory for pictorial materials, Light and La Voie include all adult lifespan studies that focused on verbal materials. Second, Light and La Voie opted for a different strategy to cope with the contamination problem (i.e., the possibility that intentional recollection contaminates performance of implicit memory tests). In their chapters, Mitchell and Parkin include only those studies that could with more or less confidence be said to provide a pure index of implicit memory, or they focus on strategies that can be used to obtain such an index. By contrast, Light and La Voie begin with the assumption that these approaches involve circular reasoning and thus ought to be avoided. Consistent with this view, Light and La Voie combined the available adult lifespan studies in a meta-analysis and computed the size of effects due to age on implicit and explicit tests. The average effect sizes were larger for explicit than implicit memory tests. But more importantly, age effect sizes for implicit memory tests were clearly larger than zero, and this led Light and La Voie to a different conclusion from that reached by Mitchell and Parkin. Light and La Voie discuss the implications of their findings from various theoretical perspectives.

The chapter by Naito and Komatsu focuses primarily on the development of implicit and explicit memory in children, and it lays out the larger context within which recent work has been conducted. Naito and Komatsu do this first by giving a brief history of naturalistic and laboratory studies on the development of explicit memory, by outlining theoretical views that have guided this research, and by showing how two views in particular—Piaget's and Istomina's—provide a link between previous research and current investigations on implicit and explicit memory. Naito and Komatsu also give an overview of the findings from recent developmental work on implicit and explicit memory, and they use these findings to speculate about the role or function of implicit memory (cf. Parkin, Chapter 9, this volume) in the child's adaptation to the environment and in language acquisition, thereby highlighting the larger context in a different way.

A third way of placing recent implicit/explicit memory research in its larger context is linked to the concept of *nested structures,* the idea that every episode can be decomposed into a collection of mini-episodes and that every episode is part of one or more macro-episodes. Naito and Komatsu use the notion of nested structures to discuss various interesting findings in the literature, such as the fact that there is no priming for single words that are presented as part of continuous text (see Levy, Chapter 3, this volume). They also use this idea (a) to gain further insight into the findings on development of implicit and explicit memory in children and (b) to make predictions about the generality of these findings across various experimental conditions.

8

Implicit and Explicit Memory for Pictures: Multiple Views Across the Lifespan

David B. Mitchell
Southern Methodist University

> *One picture is worth more than ten thousand words.*
>
> —Chinese proverb

The reader who wishes to be spared the nearly 8,000 words that appear in this chapter may refer to the data pictured in Fig. 8.1. This figure summarizes data from nine studies on implicit and explicit picture memory that compared the performance of children, young adults, and older adults. Assuming that young adults are at or near peak memory performance (100%), it is clear that both children and the elderly remember less information when asked to engage in conscious recollection. In marked contrast, memory tested implicitly appears to be asymptotic and remains stable from at least age 3 to 83. For the reader who wants a close-up view of the trees that make up the forest, read on!

This chapter reviews research on implicit and explicit memory for pictures, both in children and in normal aging. Although the dissociation between implicit and explicit memory as a function of age is not unique to pictures, picture memory paradigms are useful in providing a model for procedures in which contamination of implicit memory tasks (by the intentional use of explicit memory for test information) can be diminished or eliminated. The methodological cleanup also bears on the issue of how to best interpret age-related memory dissociations. In this chapter, the findings are interpreted within a multiple memory systems framework.

WHAT'S SO SPECIAL ABOUT PICTURES?

Since there are two other chapters in this volume on developmental and aging changes in implicit and explicit memory, why do we need a separate one on the

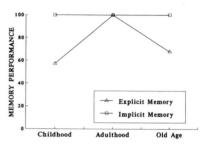

FIG. 8.1. A picture of the efficiency of picture memory performance across the life span. The data are plotted as a function of assuming that performance in young adulthood is at peak, or 100%.

same phenomena in pictures? Either there must be something special about pictures or the editors *think* there is something special about picture memory. As it turns out, there are some special things about pictures and memory, both as stimuli and in terms of empirical phenomena and theoretical accounts.

As stimuli, pictures are unique as a form of representation that is not explicitly verbal or linguistic. Thus, pictures can be used to investigate mental phenomena in prelinguistic children, animals, and language-impaired adults (Parkin, Chapter 9, this volume; Premack, 1988). Indeed, such stimuli were employed in a comparative memory study of pigeons, monkeys, and humans (Wright, Santiago, Sands, Kendrick, & Cook, 1985).

At the empirical level, there are several phenomena that are specific to pictures. For example, memory performance for pictures can be extremely high (e.g., Standing, 1973). Furthermore, memory for pictures is almost always better than memory for words, well known as the picture superiority effect (see Madigan, 1983). As another example, levels of reminiscence and hypermnesia—improved memory performance over repeated tests—are higher after studying pictures than words (Madigan & O'Hara, 1992).

At the theoretical level, picture memory phenomena have inspired Paivio's (1986) dual code theory and Nelson's (1979) sensory model, and debate about the nature of representation of pictorial information. More recently, questions about the nature of picture representation have been brought into the realm of implicit memory, with emphasis on the role of perceptual contributions to priming (Biederman & Cooper, 1991; Schacter, Delaney, & Merikle, 1990; Srinivas, 1991).

What is meant by *picture?* Pictorial stimuli can range from simple objects to complex naturalistic scenes, from simple line drawings to richly textured color photographs. Also included are human faces, kaleidoscope patterns, polygons, complex random forms, and hypothetical objects. In this chapter, I have adopted a very loose definition: Pictures are any stimuli that are nonverbal two-dimensional representations. These stimuli vary widely, of course, in the degree to which they can be verbally labeled, represented, retained, and retrieved.

Finally, there is the because-it's-not-there factor: "Most previous research on priming and aging has used verbal materials" (Schacter, Cooper, & Valdiserri,

1992, p. 300). Indeed, a quick count of 32 published implicit/explicit memory studies that included either children or elderly subjects revealed that 23 experiments (72%) employed verbal tasks.

DEVELOPMENT AND AGING AND MEMORY MECHANISMS

Just as memory pathology can provide new insights into the normal functioning of memory (see Cermak, Chapter 13; Shimamura, Chapter 12; and Bowers & Schacter, Chapter 14, all this volume), normal memory change can also teach us some things about memory mechanisms. Schacter (1992) suggested that *cross-domain hypothesis testing* can be especially fruitful: Memory models can be evaluated more rigorously in an empirical domain outside of their disciplinary home base. Thus, one cross-domain approach for assessing theoretical accounts developed within mainstream cognitive psychology (e.g., Roediger, Weldon, & Challis, 1989; Tulving, 1985) is to test them in developmental and aging contexts.

Along these lines, the multiple memory systems proposed by Tulving (1985, 1991) manifest a monohierarchical structure with strong implications for age-related memory functioning (see Mitchell, 1989). Episodic memory is responsible for conscious recollection of autobiographical experiences. In the mono-hierarchical arrangement, episodic memory is a subsystem of semantic memory, which in turn depends on procedural memory and other modular subcomponents such as perceptual representation systems (PRS) (Tulving & Schacter, 1990). As the most specialized system, episodic memory is the last to develop fully in childhood. Its unique specialization, however, may also make it the most fragile, and therefore it is the first to go in the course of normal aging. Procedural memory and PRS, on the other hand, seem to be hard-wired from the start and are very hardy in surviving the effects of aging (and trauma and disease as well): "The neural pathways that subserve episodic remembering, maturing late in childhood and deteriorating early in old age, are not necessary for priming" (Tulving, 1991, p. 16). Hereafter, I refer to procedural/priming memory phenomena as *implicit memory;* episodic memory phenomena are called *explicit memory,* in line with current usage (cf. Roediger, 1990; Schacter, 1987, 1990) and the title of this volume.

Implicit memory is measured by tasks that reveal effects of specific experience without requiring conscious recollection; explicit memory is measured by cued recall or recognition tasks, which also require concurrent subjective awareness of remembering (cf. autonoetic consciousness, Tulving, 1985, and "remember" judgments, Gardiner & Parkin, 1990). The reader should bear in mind, however, that this is an oversimplification for the sake of convenience. Both explicit memory and implicit memory systems are probably comprised of several subsystems. For example, working memory—an explicit memory system (Tulving, 1991)—is thought to have three subcomponents (Baddeley, 1992); implicit memory may be comprised of several perceptual representation subsystems and conceptual priming subsystems (Schacter, 1990; Tulving, 1991; Tulving & Schacter, 1990). We shall see that across the lifespan, memory for pictures does not behave much differently than memory for verbal stimuli, except that implicit picture memory tasks have not been plagued as much by the issue of "contamination" by explicit retrieval (Howard, 1988, 1991; Light, 1991; but see Parkin, Chapter 9, this volume).

MEMORY TASKS INVOLVING PICTURES

A substantial number of implicit picture memory paradigms have been developed, but to date only a few of these have been tested with children or older adults. Table 8.1 provides a list of these tasks. Whereas a great bulk of memory for pictures has used complex naturalistic scenes (see Loftus, 1982), almost all of the implicit memory work with pictures has relied on simple line drawings. One technique that has been used with scenes involves a measure of savings in relearning (MacLeod, 1988). The "know" versus "remember" judgments used by Gardiner and Parkin (1990) have not been used with pictures, but this should be a profitable extension.

TABLE 8.1
Implicit Memory Tasks With Pictures

A. Number of Child Development and Aging Studies

Task	Measure	Child	Aging
Category exemplar production	accuracy	1	0
Face fame judgment	accuracy	0	1
Picture fragment identification	accuracy	2	1
Object decision task	accuracy	0	2
Picture naming	latency	2	2

B. Some Tasks Not Yet Investigated Across the Lifespan

Brightness judgments of shapes (Mandler, Nakamura, & Van Zandt, 1987)
Drawing dot patterns (Musen & Treisman, 1990)
Face preference (Johnson, Kim, & Risse, 1985)
Familiar face repetition priming (Ellis, Young, & Flude, 1990)
"Know" vs. "remember" (Gardiner & Parkin, 1990)
Picture clarification (Jacoby, Baker, & Brooks, 1989)
Picture classification (Durso & Johnson, 1979)
Picture identification threshold (Warren & Morton, 1982)
Preference judgments of shapes (Kunst-Wilson & Zajonc, 1980)
Relearning savings for pictures and scenes (MacLeod, 1988)

Given the broad array of tasks available, it is important to figure out the processing requirements for each type of picture test. At one end of the continuum, a number of tasks appear to be data driven (i.e., successful priming at test requires prior processing of an identical stimulus): picture fragment completion, object decision task, picture clarification, and picture identification threshold (see Srinivas & Roediger, 1990). At the other end, many of these tasks may ultimately be classified as conceptually driven (i.e., successful priming at test can be achieved by prior processing of a related stimulus): picture naming, picture classification, and category exemplar production. The latter task is unusual in that memory for pictures can be tested implicitly with no pictorial stimuli (only the category superordinates have to be provided).

Note that some of these tasks require multiple unique responses (e.g., a different name for each picture), whereas others require only a two-choice decision (e.g., possible vs. impossible object). Whether the number of responses required is an important variable remains to be determined. Being able to specify the relative degree of data-driven and conceptually driven processing required by particular tasks will be crucial for understanding how various processes and systems interact and relate to one another (cf. Tulving, 1991), but I leave this task for a future time when we have more data.

Without calling it implicit memory, Gollin (1960) published an early study on this phenomenon in young children. Using fragmented pictures of common objects (e.g., elephant, umbrella), Gollin found that even after a 2-week retention interval, $3\frac{1}{2}$-year-old children revealed "slightly better" priming than older children (age 5) and "approached adult levels of performance" (p. 293). No measure of explicit memory was available.

STUDIES REVIEWED IN THIS CHAPTER

The criteria for studies to be included for analysis in this review were as follows. First, the study had to be developmental: that is, there had to be at least two different age groups. The modal investigation compared either two groups of children or two groups of young and older adults, and all studies were cross-sectional. There was no comparison across the entire lifespan within a single study. Second, the study had to include both implicit and explicit measures of memory. This is the critical criterion that allows us to look for dissociations of the two systems as a function of development or aging. Although there is a huge number of child development and aging studies on picture memory, almost all of these have examined explicit memory. Third, the study had to include some form of pictorial stimuli, as already defined broadly. Preferably, these stimuli were used both at study and at test. The only exception in Table 8.2 is the study by Greenbaum and Graf (1989), in which pictures were used only for study.

Research on picture memory has been prolific and has increased disproportionately in the last two decades. From 1894 to 1972, 685 picture-memory

TABLE 8.2
Memory Performance and Effect Size of Age Differences in Explicit and Implicit Picture Memory

Study	Ages	Explicit Memory				Implicit Memory			
		Task	Older	Younger	ES	Task	Older	Younger	ES
Carroll, Byrne, & Kirsner (1985)	5, 7, 10	Rec.	82%	46%	.60	Name	44 ms	53 ms	-.14*
Lorsbach & Morris (1991)	8 & 12	Rec.	80%	68%	.39	Name	90 ms	121 ms	-.19
Parkin & Streete (1988)	3, 5, 7 adult	Rec.	92%	27%	.85	Id.	37%	35%	.23*
Lorsbach & Worman (1989)	9 & 12	CR	55%	44%	.52	Id.	23%	17%	.05
Greenbaum & Graf (1989)	3, 4, 5	CR	47%	17%	.62	Gen.	17%	14%	.16
Mitchell (1989)	22 & 70	Rec.	82%	89%	.41	Name	150 ms	168 ms	.09
Mitchell, Brown, & Murphy (1990)	20 & 70	Rec.	41%	52%	.44	Name	59 ms	69 ms	.08
Schacter, Cooper, & Valdiserri (1992, Experiment 1)	18 & 69	Rec.	24%	41%	.48	OD	13%	12%	-.13*
Schacter, Cooper, & Valdiserri (1992, Experiment 2)	20 & 71	Rec.	23%	55%	.50	OD	17%	9%	-.09*

Notes. *Reported $F < 1$; assumed F-value with $p = .50$. For explicit memory tasks, Rec. = recognition, CR = cued recall. For implicit memory tasks, Name = picture naming, Id. = picture fragment completion, Gen. = category exemplar generation, OD = object decision. ES = Effect size.

studies were found by Standing, Bond, Hall, and Weller (1972). From 1973 to 1984, Kobayashi (1985) counted 703 studies, of which 579 were published in journals. A search of the PsycLIT data base from 1985 through 1991 yielded 675 studies. From this last group, 260 studies involved either children, older adults, or both. Only 14, however, met the criteria stated herein, and of those, only nine were unequivocally suitable for this chapter.

The five studies that are not summarized in Table 8.2 are worth mentioning here. Two employed picture fragment identification tasks (Heindel, Salmon, & Butters, 1990; Wippich, Mecklenbrauker, & Brausch, 1989), two measured autonomic activity during picture processing tasks (Berman, Friedman, & Cramer, 1990; Plouffe & Stelmack, 1984), and one used faces (Bartlett, Strater, & Fulton, 1991). These five studies are reviewed briefly below.

Heindel et al. (1990) compared middle-aged (mean = 55 years) to older adults (mean = 72 years). The middle-aged adults had slightly better explicit picture recognition performance than the older group (approximately 95% and 90%, respectively), but these ceiling effects obfuscated a clear view. The groups did not differ on the implicit task, both showing approximately 16% priming for naming thresholds of fragmented pictures. Another more recent aging study on picture fragment identification performance is summarized by Parkin (Chapter 9, this volume), but was not included in the current analyses because it was not yet published in a journal.

Another study compared 5-year-old and 8-year-old children on incomplete picture identification, under both implicit and explicit memory conditions (Wippich et al., 1989). (The primary source was not available until this chapter was already in press, so the results are not included in the meta-analyses that follow.) These investigators observed the typical pattern of developmental dissociation: age-related improvement on explicit memory tests (recognition: 49% vs. 75%) coupled with age invariance on implicit memory performance (picture identification priming: 18% vs. 22%, 5- and 8-year-olds, respectively).

Two studies employed measures of autonomic activity as an index of implicit memory. Because these measures are not behavioral memory measures, the data are not directly comparable with explicit memory performance. The findings, however, parallel those of the studies in Table 8.2 and conform to the general picture painted in Fig. 8.1. Berman et al. (1990) compared 9-, 15-, and 24-year-olds. They used a standard recognition task (continuous recognition) and a standard implicit task (category classification) for pictures and words, but the implicit measure used was event-related potentials (ERP). Both recognition memory and ERPs taken during recognition revealed the typical developmental memory improvement pattern (i.e., 24-year-olds better than 15-year-olds, who in turn performed better than 9-year-olds). The ERPs sampled during the implicit task, however, revealed similar repetition effects for the three age groups. Plouffe and Stelmack (1984) measured skin conductance responses (SCR) during the viewing of pictures. As usual, young adults (mean age = 20) recalled significantly more pictures than the older adults (mean age = 71). In contrast, there were no statistically significant age differences in the magnitude of SCR, presumably reflecting an absence of age effects in implicit memory functioning.

Bartlett et al. (1991) had subjects judge whether pictures of faces were famous. Dywan and Jacoby (1990) had shown that older adults reveal strong implicit memory effects when asked to judge the fame of a previously exposed (nonfamous) name. Bartlett et al. were successful in producing the false fame effect in older subjects (mean age = 72; i.e., previously presented nonfamous faces were judged more famous than new nonfamous faces), but not in young adults (mean = 28 years). Thus, their data are problematic for comparative purposes because they were unable to produce the effect in the young group. This probably occurred because the false fame effect depends on a feeling of familiarity (produced by a prior experimental exposure, i.e., implicit memory) in conjunction with a deficit in conscious recollection of the source. As Jacoby (1991) has pointed out, "conscious recollection of a name as earlier read would produce an effect opposite to that of the false fame effect" (p. 517). That is, if the face (in this case) is remembered as a nonfamous one, then it would not be (mistakenly) judged as famous. Similar to Dywan and Jacoby (1990) who failed to get a false fame effect with names in their young adults, the use of pictures by Bartlett et al. (1991) apparently produced a level of explicit source monitoring that was simply too unimpaired in their young subjects. A future replication that obtains the false fame effect for faces in young adults should simultaneously yield a relatively larger false fame effect in older adults, again because the explicit recollection mechanisms—needed to negate the implicit effects of familiarity—are relatively impaired in the latter group.

One other paradigm not reviewed in Table 8.2 deserves to be mentioned. Howard and Howard (1989) found no age differences in a serial reaction time key-pressing task. In this nonverbal, nonpictorial implicit memory task, subjects learn over many trials to anticipate a pattern of spatial locations on a computer screen. The subjects' implicit learning is manifested by their pressing of appropriately matched keys. In contrast to the absence of age differences on this task, older adults were disadvantaged on a task requiring explicit prediction of spatial locations.

ANALYSES OF PUBLISHED DATA

The studies listed in Table 8.2 met the criteria mentioned herein. The five in the top half of the table are developmental, and the four at the bottom assess aging effects. Thus, the expected direction of the older/younger means varies from top to bottom. The two means under the Older/Younger columns are for the two extreme groups when more than two age groups were included in a study. Effect size (ES) measures were calculated with a BASIC meta-analysis program

(Mullen & Rosenthal, 1987). The ES coefficients are based on r for two-group studies and on η for 3+-group studies (cf. Rosenthal & Rosnow, 1984). Eta is the square root of the proportion of variance accounted for, and its magnitude can be interpreted in the same way that r can (but without the assumption of linearity). Values of ES of .10, .30, and .50 can be considered as small, medium, and large, respectively (Cohen, 1988).

The implicit tasks used were picture naming, picture fragment completion, object decision, and category exemplar generation. In picture naming, priming is computed by subtracting median naming latencies for studied items from latencies for nonstudied items. In the other three tasks, priming is calculated by subtracting baseline rates for correctly naming, judging, or producing nonstudied items from the hit rates for the corresponding studied items. Recognition (hits minus false alarms) was the explicit memory task of choice, with the exception of two studies that used cued recall (Greenbaum & Graf, 1989; Lorsbach & Worman, 1989). Thus, seven of the studies met a criterion suggested by Schacter, Bowers, and Booker (1989): the "external cues provided to subjects on implicit and explicit tests should be the same, and only test instructions varied" (p. 53). Any differences between implicit and explicit performance in these studies cannot, therefore, be attributed to differences in environmental support (cf. Craik, 1986) or to confounds arising from differences in data-driven versus conceptually driven processes (cf. Roediger et al., 1989; Srinivas & Roediger, 1990).

The data reveal a remarkably consistent pattern: In spite of large age differences in explicit memory performance, the same subjects exhibit tiny differences in implicit memory. Note the following details. First, the mean age difference on the explicit measures was 24.6%, compared to only 0.4% on the implicit accuracy measures or -3 msec for the latency measures (the direction of the young/old difference was taken into account). Second, all of the explicit comparisons were statistically significant in the expected direction (i.e., older kids > younger kids; young adults > older adults), whereas none of the implicit comparisons even approached statistical reliability, and nearly half were in a counterintuitive direction. Third, the ES coefficients paint the same picture: large positive effects in explicit memory versus small, sometimes negative, effects in priming. In fact, there is no overlap between the two distributions of ES indices. This can be seen most clearly in Table 8.3, in a Tukey stem-and-leaf plot. (The ES indicators for the Parkin & Streete [1988] data are likely inflated because there were four age groups, and the adult group was considerably older than the oldest group of children, 7-year-olds.)

Additional meta-analyses were carried out on age effects. The weighted mean standardized difference between means (Cohen's d) was 1.10 for explicit versus only 0.001 for implicit (note that the three studies with 3+ age groups were treated as if there were only the two extreme age groups for this comparison). For the combination of the nine explicit memory experiment outcomes (total $n = 514$), $Z = 10.835$, $p < .000000001$. In an extreme case scenario in which only

TABLE 8.3
Stem-and-Leaf Plots of Effect Sizes in Nine Studies

	Memory Test	
Explicit		Implicit
	.9	
5	.8	
	.7	
2 0	.6	
2 0	.5	
8 4 1	.4	
9	.3	
	.2	3
	.1	6
	.0	5 8 9
	-.0	9
	-.1	3 4 9
	-.2	
Mean	.48	-.0006
Maximum	.85	.23
Minimum	.39	-.19

Note. Effect size indices are either r or η (eta)

statistically significant studies get published (see Mullen & Rosenthal, 1985; Rosenthal, 1984), there would have to be over 399 unpublished studies with null results stuck in file drawers in order to bring the Z down to a $p = .05$ level. In stark contrast, the combined Z for the nine implicit memory experiment outcomes (total $n = 544$) was only -0.032, $p = .487$, and the "fail-safe" number of file drawer studies would actually be negative (-9). In view of these findings, the concern about insufficient statistical power to detect age differences in implicit memory performance (cf. Hultsch, Masson, & Small, 1991) seems nugatory.

In Fig. 8.2, memory performance by younger children or older adults is plotted as a function of either older children or young adults from the same study. In other words, data from the group expected to perform better (young adults or older children) were plotted on the x axis against data from the group expected to perform more poorly (older adults or younger children) on the y axis. Explicit memory is plotted in the upper panel, and implicit memory is plotted in the lower panel (reaction time priming scores were converted to percent priming for this figure). Note that for explicit memory, all of the points in the scatterplot fall below the diagonal, again depicting the performance deficit of younger children and older adults relative to higher levels of memory in older children and young adults, respectively. In contrast, the points on the implicit memory scatterplot fall very close to the diagonal, revealing highly similar memory performance across children and adults of different ages, regardless of the relative difficulty of the

A. Explicit Memory

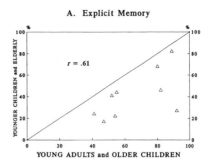

B. Implicit Memory

FIG. 8.2.   Memory performance by younger children as a
function of the memory performance of older children, and
memory performance by older
adults as a function of the memory performance of younger
adults, from the nine experiments in Table 8.2.

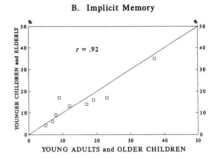

particular tasks employed. Correlation coefficients and regression equations were
calculated for the data in Fig. 8.2. For the implicit data, the correlation was very
high, $r = .92$; for the explicit data, it was relatively modest, $r = .61$. The
regression equations also differed substantially: For the implicit data, $y = 2.07 +$
$.82x$, $F = 40.79$, $p < .01$; for the explicit data, $y = -3.22 + .68x$, $F = 4.08$, p
$> .05$.

Thus, no matter how the data are viewed, the pattern that emerges is very
clear. The implicit/explicit memory dissociation is just as robust across 3-, 4-,
and 5-year-olds as it is across a 50-year difference between adults. The explicit
memory differences are of a sizable magnitude, especially considering that recognition tests, relative to cued and free recall, typically attenuate age differences.
The implicit memory differences were, in contrast, terrifically minute, and were
consistently negligible across five different tasks. How should these findings best
be accounted for? A number of theoretical alternatives are discussed.

TRANSFER-APPROPRIATE PROCESSING

Roediger and his colleagues (1989, and Chapter 2, this volume) have cham-
pioned the cause of transfer-appropriate processing (TAP) as an explanation for
many of the extant dissociation findings. Indeed, they demonstrated that a

number of early studies confounded implicit/explicit tasks with the type of processing required. They have pointed out that "most implicit tests rely heavily on the match of perceptual features between learning and test episodes, or *data-driven processing*," whereas "most explicit tests require the encoded meaning of concepts for successful recollection, or *conceptually-driven processing*" (Srinivas & Roediger, 1990, p. 390). Furthermore, they have shown that this correlation between test instructions and processing requirements can—and must—be deconfounded.

Virtually all of the studies in Table 8.2 are free of the confound between type of memory test and processing requirements. Most studies are either matched along the data-conceptual continuum or, in some cases, reversed with respect to the usual correlation between test and processing. Regardless of the combination used, the dissociation of test by age group prevailed. Thus, this pattern disconfirms an unvarnished TAP account. However, it does not rule out the possibility of TAP mechanisms operating within and across multiple memory systems (see Roediger, 1990; Schacter, 1922; Tulving & Schacter, 1990). Also, other hybrid TAP variations have been formulated, such as a greater emphasis on "the overlap in processing—not materials—between study and testing" (Graf, 1991, p. 144). Additional integration schemes are discussed further in this section, but first the various processing requirements for each study are detailed.

The studies by Schacter et al. (1992) and by Parkin and Streete (1988) required data-driven processing for both explicit and implicit tasks (recognition, picture fragment identification, object decision). Greenbaum and Graf (1989) used a conceptually driven implicit task, category exemplar generation (cf. Srinivas & Roediger, 1990). Picture naming—of intact, nondegraded pictures— used in the four remaining studies, has been classified by some as data-driven or perceptually driven (Biederman & Cooper, 1992). However, there is compelling evidence that this implicit memory task may be conceptually or at least lexically driven, somewhere along the continuum far away from the data end. First, surface alterations, such as size and mirror-image reversals, do not affect priming (Biederman & Cooper, 1992; Carroll, 1989; unpublished data from our lab). Second, we have shown that words—visually or auditorily presented, pronounced or not—can prime picture naming just as potently as a previously named identical picture (Brown, Neblett, Jones, & Mitchell, 1991). Thus, even when the explicit task is data-driven and the implicit task is conceptually driven, the age-related dissociations persist. This has also been demonstrated in the verbal realm by Light and Albertson (1989), who found that older adults were equivalent to young adults in priming on an implicit category exemplar task.

Only one study listed in Table 8.2 can be assailed on the memory test/processing requirements confound grounds: Lorsbach and Worman (1989) compared explicit cued recall with implicit picture fragment identification. The latter task is considered strongly data-driven (cf. Weldon & Roediger, 1987), whereas cued recall is relatively conceptually driven.

MULTIPLE MEMORY SYSTEMS

The dissociation of implicit and explicit memory across the life span is compatible with multiple memory systems models. As suggested earlier, the mono-hierarchical arrangement of these systems (Tulving, 1985) can predict which life-span memory patterns are possible and which are not. The pattern of findings reviewed in this chapter exemplifies the possible, in terms of episodic (explicit) memory being the only system that can undergo change without the lower implicit systems (semantic, priming) being affected. On the other hand, multiple memory classification schemes do not predict what should happen under certain conditions, as the objectives of this approach are ones of identification, specification, and delineation (Tulving, 1991).

The monohierarchical model does rule out certain patterns: A lower system cannot be impaired while simultaneously leaving a higher system intact. Thus, for instance, we would not expect to find intact episodic memory in individuals whose semantic memory was impaired. To illustrate this, we need to step outside the realm of normal aging, because semantic memory is basically unimpaired in healthy older adults (e.g., Mitchell, 1989). In the early stages of Alzheimer's disease (A.D.), patients begin to experience impairments in both episodic and semantic memory (e.g., Mitchell, Hunt, & Schmitt, 1986). Based on the arrangement of memory systems, we would not predict an individual with semantic memory difficulties to have normal episodic memory functioning, but it should be possible for memory performance mediated by priming to still be intact. We compared young adults, older adults, and older age-matched A.D. patients on three types of memory tasks (Mitchell & Schmitt, 1992). For episodic memory, subjects viewed sentences and were tested with cued recall. For semantic memory, subjects were asked to generate the names of U.S. Presidents. Priming was measured via picture naming latencies (as in Mitchell, 1989). The data, presented as percentages in Fig. 8.3, converge nicely with a monohierarchical model. Episodic memory reveals declines both in normal aging and in A.D. patients. Semantic memory is stable from young to older adults, dropping off only in the A.D. subjects. In contrast, priming is invariant across the three groups. Although the tasks used here do differ in their respective processing requirements, nonetheless the systematic pattern of three memory tasks breaking down differently across three subject groups demonstrates an outcome accommodated by a multiple memory systems approach.

The knowledge gained from the work on TAP mechanisms needs to be integrated with the systems route. "The classification approach *complements* the process-oriented approach to memory; it is not an alternative to it" (Tulving, 1991, p. 9). The recent updates and modifications (e.g., Tulving & Schacter, 1990) will continue. Use of integrative cognitive neuroscience approaches (Schacter, 1992) should allow theoretical developments that are judicious, avoiding the alarming concern that the number of memory systems will proliferate out of control (Roediger, 1990).

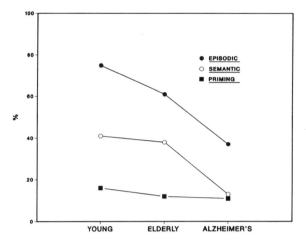

FIG. 8.3. Memory performance by young adults, normal elderly adults, and patients with Alzheimer's disease on three tasks. Cued recall served as an episodic memory task (percent correct), generation of the names of U.S. Presidents was a semantic task (percent correct), and repeated picture naming produced priming (reaction times converted to percent). *Note.* From "Multiple memory systems: Normal aging vs. Alzheimer's disease" by D. B. Mitchell and F. A. Schmitt, 1992, unpublished manuscript.

A FUNCTIONAL ACCOUNT

Craik (1986) has argued that adult age differences in memory can be understood in terms of the kinds of operations needed in a particular context. In particular, "self-initiated retrieval processes" are more difficult for older people to carry out. Thus, when environmental support is greatest, age differences should be minimized, and when such support is missing, age differences should be maximized. Craik's view accounts for a lot of findings, but the data reviewed in Table 8.2 disconfirm a strong version of this view. That is, in spite of stimulus support being equal (in eight of the studies; see preceding discussion in the section on TAP), both older adults and younger children (relative to younger adults and older children, respectively) had greater performance deficits only as a function of the type of memory processes required (i.e., implicit vs. explicit).

AUTOMATIC VS. INTENTIONAL PROCESSES

Along the lines of memory processes, another possibility recently proposed by Jacoby (1991) is that implicit memory involves automatic processes, whereas explicit memory requires consciously controlled processes (cf. Hasher & Zacks,

1979, 1988). Although Jacoby argues against equating specific memory tests with hypothetical processes, he suggests that "[s]ome special populations may have a deficit in intentional forms of processing, but preserve more automatic or unconscious forms of memory" (p. 518). Jacoby argues that automatic and controlled processes are always operating, and our task is thus to figure out the relative contributions of each on a given task performance. His "process dissociation framework" offers one way out of the test contamination issue (see next section) by pitting automatic processes of familiarity against decisions made best when explicit recollection is available. Thus, Jacoby's view can account for the memory dissociations across the lifespan. At this time, no one particular theoretical position can best account for the available findings. However, I agree with the position that "[t]he systems approach combined with appropriate processing theories seems to provide the most direct route to the future" (Tulving & Schacter, 1990, p. 305).

CONTAMINATION AND CODETERMINATION

A number of researchers have addressed the issue of contamination of implicit tasks by the use of explicit strategies (Howard, 1988, 1991; Parkin, Chapter 9, this volume; Schacter et al., 1989, 1992). In development and aging, the form this can take is that young adults or older children can make better use of explicit memory strategies (relative to older adults or younger children, respectively) in order to successfully engage in implicit memory tasks. When this happens, age differences—that may be spurious—can emerge in implicit memory performance. For instance, Light and Albertson (1989) found a nearly 5% difference in priming favoring young adults (although not statistically significant) in a category exemplar generation task. However, after eliminating the scores of subjects who reported deliberately trying to recall previously studied items in the generation task, the age difference in priming diminished to 1%.

On the average, explicit contamination in implicit memory picture tasks seems to be less of a problem (but see Parkin, Chapter 9, this volume, for an exception). The few studies where contamination was a problem employed verbal materials (see Howard, 1988, 1991). At this juncture, it is not clear if picture memory methodologies are less susceptible to contamination, or if the lower incidence is simply a function of a smaller number of studies with pictures.

Researchers have become more sensitive to this potential problem recently. One solution is the choice of the implicit task, and another is to alter the way in which implicit tasks are presented to subjects. As a measure, picture naming latency provides an optimal solution because subjects cannot use recollection of an item to affect the priming measure—this is not so in most standard implicit tasks. For example, if a target word is remembered, this information can be used to complete a word fragment or a word stem, spell a homophone in the appropriate way, solve an anagram, and in some cases identify a fragmented picture (see Parkin, Chapter 9, this volume). This is not the case with latency measures of picture naming or lexical decision. For instance, in Experiment 4 of the series in Brown et al. (1991), we blocked old and new pictures at test and gave the subjects complete memory information as to which items had been studied and which were new. The blocking and intentional memory instructions had no impact on priming: The magnitude was neither larger nor smaller than that observed in the other experiments under different conditions. Another advantage of picture naming is that explicit recognition can be tested online, that is, individually and immediately after each item is named. While the presence of the explicit task does slow down reaction times, producing somewhat larger priming scores relative to a naming-only condition, the evidence suggests that this is merely the main effect of a secondary task, not one of contamination. Specifically, we have found that the presence of an online semantic classification task boosts priming to the same degree that an online recognition task does (Radeke, 1992).

Although picture naming latencies may indeed be a relatively pure measure (see also Biederman & Cooper, 1992), a valid concern that one might raise is the old apples-and-oranges problem when we compare priming (facilitation measured in milliseconds) and recognition (accuracy measured in percentage correct). Thus, there is a good cause to employ paradigms that use accuracy measures for *both* implicit and explicit memory. What we need to do is clean up some of the implicit tasks that are susceptible to contamination from explicit recollection. One good solution is to keep the tasks, but change the way they are administered at test. For instance, we can limit the amount of time subjects are allowed to spend on each item or test trial. Weldon (1991) found, for instance, robust priming on word fragments only from visually presented words when the presentation time at test was limited to 500 msec. At a very long exposure (12 sec), even pictures and auditorily presented words produced priming, most likely because that amount of test time allowed subjects to use episodic memory to complete the fragments.

What happens if all the precautions are taken to preclude contamination and yet an age-related difference emerges on implicit memory performance? Given that all these systems and processes share the common umbrella term of memory (cf. Tulving & Schacter, 1990), it is theoretically possible that something else is going on. Tulving (1991) introduced the concept of codetermination, which says that performance on certain memory tasks may be determined by the *joint* functioning of more than one memory system. Thus, the learning of new semantic information (e.g., Dagenbach, Horst, & Carr, 1990) usually benefits from the simultaneous participation of episodic memory. This would explain why an amnesic *can* acquire and retrieve new semantic information, albeit with great difficulty (Tulving, Hayman, & Macdonald, 1991).

CONCLUSION

The principle of codetermination applied to memory phenomena in development and aging should inspire new research initiatives. The combination of processing and systems approaches holds good promise for furthering our understanding of memory. In a recent report of the National Behavioral Science Research Agenda Committee, one of the conclusions was that "recent work has uncovered new memory systems in humans, but the implications for these systems in aging are as yet unknown" (*APS Observer,* February 1992, p. 21). Our work is cut out for us, and while the picture of the future is an incomplete fragment, the 1990s are clearly an exciting and promising era for memory research.

ACKNOWLEDGMENTS

Preparation of this chapter was facilitated by a sabbatical leave granted by Dedman College, Southern Methodist University, and supported by grant AG07854 from the National Institute on Aging. I thank Endel Tulving and Peter Graf for their thoughtful comments on an earlier version of this chapter.

REFERENCES

Baddeley, A. (1992). Working memory. *Science, 255,* 556–559.

Bartlett, J. C., Strater, L., & Fulton, A. (1991). False recency and false fame of faces in young adulthood and old age. *Memory & Cognition, 19,* 177–188.

Berman, S., Friedman, D., & Cramer, M. (1990). A developmental study of event-related potentials during explicit and implicit memory. *International Journal of Psychophysiology, 10,* 191–197.

Biederman, I., & Cooper, E. E. (1991). Priming contour deleted images: Evidence for intermediate representations in visual object recognition. *Cognitive Psychology, 23,* 393–419.

Biederman, I., & Cooper, E. E. (1992). Size invariance in visual object priming. *Journal of Experimental Psychology: Human Perception and Performance, 18,* 121–133.

Brown, A. S., Neblett, D. R., Jones, T. C., & Mitchell, D. B. (1991). Transfer of processing in repetition priming: Some inappropriate findings. *Journal of Experimental Psychology: Learning, Memory, and Cognition, 17,* 514–525.

Carroll, M. (1989). Implicit memory: Compatibility between study-test operations. In S. Lewandowsky, J. C. Dunn, & K. Kirsner (Eds.), *Implicit memory: Theoretical issues* (pp. 199–212). Hillsdale, NJ: Lawrence Erlbaum Associates.

Carroll, M., Byrne, B., & Kirsner, K. (1985). Autobiographical memory and perceptual learning: A developmental study using picture recognition, naming latency, and perceptual identification. *Memory & Cognition, 13,* 273–279.

Cohen, J. (1988). *Statistical power analysis for the behavioral sciences* (2nd ed.). Hillsdale, NJ: Lawrence Erlbaum Associates.

Craik, F. I. M. (1986). A functional account of age differences in memory. In F. Klix & H. Hagendorf (Eds.), *Human memory and cognitive capabilities* (pp. 409–422). Amsterdam: Elsevier.

Dagenbach, D., Horst, S., & Carr, T. H. (1990). Adding new information to semantic memory: How much learning is enough to produce automatic priming? *Journal of Experimental Psychology: Learning, Memory, and Cognition, 16*, 581–591.

Durso, F. T., & Johnson, M. K. (1979). Facilitation in naming and categorizing repeated pictures and words. *Journal of Experimental Psychology: Human Learning and Memory, 5*, 449–459.

Dywan, J., & Jacoby, L. (1990). Effects of aging on source monitoring: Differences in susceptibility to false fame. *Psychology and Aging, 5*, 379–387.

Ellis, A. W., Young, A. W., & Flude, B. M. (1990). Repetition priming and face processing: Priming occurs within the system that responds to the identity of a face. *Quarterly Journal of Experimental Psychology, 42A*, 495–512.

Gardiner, J. M., & Parkin, A. J. (1990). Attention and recollective experience in recognition memory. *Memory & Cognition, 18*, 579–583.

Gollin, E. S. (1960). Developmental studies of visual recognition of incomplete objects. *Perceptual and Motor Skills, 11*, 289–298.

Graf, P. (1991). Implicit and explicit memory: An old model for new findings. In W. Kessen, A. Ortony, & F. Craik (Eds.), *Memories, thoughts, and emotions: Essays in honor of George Mandler* (pp. 135–147). Hillsdale, NJ: Lawrence Erlbaum Associates.

Greenbaum, J. L., & Graf, P. (1989). Preschool period development of implicit and explicit remembering. *Bulletin of the Psychonomic Society, 27*, 417–420.

Hasher, L., & Zacks, R. T. (1979). Automatic and effortful processes in memory. *Journal of Experimental Psychology: General, 108*, 356–388.

Hasher, L., & Zacks, R. T. (1988). Working memory, comprehension, and aging: A review of a new view. In G. H. Bower (Ed.), *The psychology of learning and motivation* (vol. 22, pp. 193–225). New York: Academic Press.

Heindel, W. C., Salmon, D. P., & Butters, N. (1990). Pictorial priming and cued recall in Alzheimer's and Huntington's disease. *Brain and Cognition, 13*, 282–295.

Howard, D. V. (1988). Implicit and explicit assessment of cognitive aging. In M. L. Howe & C. J. Brainerd (Eds.), *Cognitive development in adulthood: Progress in cognitive development research* (pp. 3–37). New York: Springer-Verlag.

Howard, D. V. (1991). Implicit memory: An expanding picture of cognitive aging. In K. W. Schaie (Ed.), *Annual review of gerontology and geriatrics* (vol. 11, pp. 1–22). New York: Springer.

Howard, D. V., & Howard, J. H. (1989). Age differences in learning serial patterns: Direct versus indirect measures. *Psychology and Aging, 4*, 357–364.

Hultsch, D. F., Masson, M. E. J., & Small, B. J. (1991). Adult age differences in direct and indirect tests of memory. *Journal of Gerontology: Psychological Sciences, 46*, P22–30.

Jacoby, L. L. (1991). A process dissociation framework: Separating automatic from intentional uses of memory. *Journal of Memory and Language, 30*, 513–541.

Jacoby, L. L., Baker, J. G., & Brooks, L. R. (1989). Episodic effects on picture identification: Implications for theories of concept learning and theories of memory. *Journal of Experimental Psychology: Learning, Memory, and Cognition, 15*, 275–281.

Johnson, M. K., Kim, J. K., & Risse, G. (1985). Do alcoholic Korsakoff's syndrome patients acquire affective reactions? *Journal of Experimental Psychology: Learning, Memory, and Cognition, 11*, 22–36.

Kobayashi, S. (1985). An updated bibliography of picture-memory studies. *Perceptual and Motor Skills, 61*, 91–122.

Kunst-Wilson, W. R., & Zajonc, R. B. (1980). Affective discrimination of stimuli that cannot be recognized. *Science, 120*, 557–558.

Light, L. L. (1991). Memory and aging: Four hypotheses in search of data. *Annual Review of Psychology, 42*, 333–376.

Light, L. L., & Albertson, S. A. (1989). Direct and indirect tests of memory for category exemplars in young and older adults. *Psychology and Aging, 4*, 487–492.

Loftus, G. R. (1982). Picture memory methodology. In C. R. Puff (Ed.), *Handbook of research methods in human memory and cognition* (pp. 257–285). New York: Academic Press.

Lorsbach, T. C., & Morris, A. K. (1991). Direct and indirect testing of picture memory in second and sixth grade children. *Contemporary Educational Psychology, 16*, 18–27.

Lorsbach, T. C., & Worman, L. J. (1989). The development of explicit and implicit forms of memory in learning disabled children. *Contemporary Educational Psychology, 14*, 67–76.

MacLeod, C. M. (1988). Forgotten but not gone: Savings for pictures and words in long-term memory. *Journal of Experimental Psychology: Learning, Memory, and Cognition, 14*, 195–212.

Madigan, S. (1983). Picture memory. In J. C. Yuille (Ed.), *Imagery, memory and cognition: Essays in honor of Allan Paivio* (pp. 65–89). Hillsdale, NJ: Lawrence Erlbaum Associates.

Madigan, S., & O'Hara, R. (1992). Initial recall, reminiscence, and hypermnesia. *Journal of Experimental Psychology: Learning, Memory, and Cognition, 18*, 421–425.

Mandler, G., Nakamura, Y., & Van Zandt, B. J. S. (1987). Nonspecific effects of exposure on stimuli that cannot be recognized. *Journal of Experimental Psychology: Learning, Memory, and Cognition, 13*, 646–648.

Mitchell, D. B. (1989). How many memory systems? Evidence from aging. *Journal of Experimental Psychology: Learning, Memory, and Cognition, 15*, 31–49.

Mitchell, D. B., Brown, A. S., & Murphy, D. R. (1990). Dissociations between procedural and episodic memory: Effects of time and aging. *Psychology and Aging, 5*, 264–276.

Mitchell, D. B., Hunt, R. R., & Schmitt, F. A. (1986). The generation effect and reality monitoring: Evidence from dementia and normal aging. *Journal of Gerontology, 41*, 79–84.

Mitchell, D. B., & Schmitt, F. A. (1992). *Multiple memory systems: Normal aging vs. Alzheimer's disease.* Unpublished manuscript.

Mullen, B., & Rosenthal, R. (1985). *BASIC meta-analysis: Procedures and programs.* Hillsdale, NJ: Lawrence Erlbaum Associates.

Musen, G., & Treisman, A. (1990). Implicit and explicit memory for visual patterns. *Journal of Experimental Psychology: Learning, Memory, and Cognition, 16*, 127–137.

Nelson, D. L. (1979). Remembering pictures and words: Appearance, significance, and name. In L. S. Cermak & F. I. M. Craik (Eds.), *Levels of processing in human memory* (pp. 45–76). Hillsdale, NJ: Lawrence Erlbaum Associates.

Paivio, A. (1986). *Mental representation: A dual coding approach.* New York: Oxford.

Parkin, A. J., & Streete, S. (1988). Implicit and explicit memory in young children and adults. *British Journal of Psychology, 79*, 361–369.

Plouffe, L., & Stelmack, R. M. (1984). The electrodermal orienting response and memory: An analysis of age differences in picture recall. *Psychophysiology, 21*, 191–198.

Premack, D. (1988). Minds with and without language. In L. Weiskrantz (Ed.), *Thought without language* (pp. 46–65). New York: Oxford.

Radeke, J. T. (1992). *The effects of secondary task, intersession interval, and viewing condition on repeated picture naming.* Unpublished master's thesis, Southern Methodist University, Dallas, TX.

Roediger, H. L. III. (1990). Implicit memory: Retention without remembering. *American Psychologist, 45*, 1043–1056.

Roediger, H. L., Weldon, M. S., & Challis, B. H. (1989). Explaining dissociations between implicit and explicit measures of retention: A processing account. In H. L. Roediger & F. I. M. Craik (Eds.), *Varieties of memory and consciousness: Essays in honour of Endel Tulving* (pp. 3–41). Hillsdale, NJ: Lawrence Erlbaum Associates.

Rosenthal, R. (1984). *Meta-analytic procedures for social research.* Beverly Hills, CA: Sage.

Rosenthal, R., & Rosnow, R. L. (1984). *Essentials of behavioral research: Methods and data analysis.* New York: McGraw-Hill.

Schacter, D. L. (1987). Implicit memory: History and current status. *Journal of Experimental Psychology: Learning, Memory, and Cognition, 13*, 501–518.

Schacter, D. L. (1990). Perceptual representation systems and implicit memory: Toward a resolution of the multiple memory systems debate. *Annals of the New York Academy of Sciences, 608,* 543–571.

Schacter, D. L. (1992). Understanding implicit memory: A cognitive neuroscience approach. *American Psychologist, 47,* 559–569.

Schacter, D. L., Bowers, J., & Booker, J. (1989). Intention, awareness, and implicit memory: The retrieval intentionality criterion. In S. Lewandowsky, J. C. Dunn, & K. Kirsner (Eds.), *Implicit memory: Theoretical issues* (pp. 47–65). Hillsdale, NJ: Lawrence Erlbaum Associates.

Schacter, D. L., Cooper, L. A., & Valdiserri, M. (1992). Implicit and explicit memory for novel visual objects in older and younger adults. *Psychology and Aging, 7,* 299–308.

Schacter, D. L., Delaney, S. M., & Merikle, E. P. (1990). Priming of nonverbal information and the nature of implicit memory. In G. H. Bower (Ed.), *The psychology of learning and motivation* (Vol. 26, pp. 83–123). San Diego: Academic Press.

Srinivas, K. (1991). *Specificity of priming in nonverbal tests.* Unpublished doctoral thesis, Rice University.

Srinivas, K., & Roediger, H. L. III. (1990). Classifying implicit memory tests: Category association and anagram solution. *Journal of Memory and Language, 29,* 389–412.

Standing, L. (1973). Learning 10,000 pictures. *Quarterly Journal of Experimental Psychology, 25,* 207–222.

Standing, L., Bond, B., Hall, J., & Weller, J. (1972). A bibliography of picture-memory studies. *Psychonomic Science, 29,* 405–416.

Tulving, E. (1985). How many memory systems are there? *American Psychologist, 40,* 385–398.

Tulving, E. (1991). Concepts of human memory. In L. R. Squire, N. M. Weinberger, G. Lynch, & J. L. McGaugh (Eds.), *Memory: Organization and locus of change* (pp. 3–32). New York: Oxford University Press.

Tulving, E., Hayman, C. A. G., & Macdonald, C. A. (1991). Long-lasting perceptual priming and semantic learning in amnesia: A case experiment. *Journal of Experimental Psychology: Learning, Memory, and Cognition, 17,* 595–617.

Tulving, E., & Schacter, D. L. (1990). Priming and human memory systems. *Science, 247,* 301–306.

Warren, C., & Morton, J. (1982). The effects of priming on picture recognition. *British Journal of Psychology, 73,* 117–129.

Weldon, M. S. (1991). *The time course of perceptual and conceptual contributions to priming.* Manuscript submitted for publication.

Weldon, M. S., & Roediger, H. L. (1987). Altering retrieval demands reverses the picture superiority effect. *Memory & Cognition, 15,* 269–280.

Wippich, W., Mecklenbrauker, S., & Brausch, A. (1989). Implizites und explizites Gedachtnis bein Kindern: Bleiben bei indirekten Behaltensprufungen Altersunterschiede aus? [Implicit and explicit memory in children: Absence of age differences in indirect memory tests?] *Zeitschrift-fur-Entwicklungspsychologie-und-Padagogische-Psychologie, 21,* 294–306.

Wright, A. A., Santiago, H. C., Sands, S. F., Kendrick, D. F., & Cook, R. G. (1985). Memory processing of serial lists by pigeons, monkeys, and people. *Science, 229,* 287–289.

9 Implicit Memory Across the Lifespan

Alan J. Parkin
University of Sussex, Brighton, United Kingdom

Recent research has examined how many different factors influence implicit memory performance. Of these factors, age, is perhaps the most interesting because, as well as providing insights into the mechanisms of implicit memory, studies of aging allow the concept of implicit memory to be examined from a broader developmental perspective. In this chapter I consider two basic questions:

1. Does implicit memory change with age?
2. Are there age-related changes in the contribution that implicit memory makes to overall memory performance?

IMPLICIT MEMORY AND AGING

It is a well-documented fact that normal aging produces a substantial decline in explicit memory ability (e.g., Salthouse, 1982), but studies of implicit memory present a markedly different picture. In a recent review, Graf (1990) concluded that age differences on implicit memory tasks were very small, averaging around 4%, and that interpretation of even these small differences was confounded because young and old differ in the extent to which they use explicit memory to facilitate implicit performance. This point reflects the difficulty in constructing implicit memory tasks that are purely implicit in nature, that is, tasks that, even if explicit memory of the learning episode is available, receive no benefit from that memory in task performance. Because of these confounding explicit influences, the accurate investigation of age-related changes in implicit memory is more difficult than would initially seem the case.

Several authors have reviewed in some detail age differences in implicit memory, and it is unnecessary to repeat the exercise in any detail here. Howard (1988), for example, provides an extensive account and concludes that aging effects on implicit memory are minimal except where initial acquisition conditions require a degree of cognitive effort—as is the case in paradigms examining the priming of novel associations.

The first important point to note from these reviews is that age differences in implicit memory have been almost entirely based on comparisons of young and elderly adults. There has not been much research into the equally important question of how implicit memory develops. Another feature of age-related studies is the almost total reliance on using verbal learning paradigms such as repetition priming and primed word completion tasks. A well-documented feature of aging is the relative invulnerability of language to cognitive decline. In our own research, for example, we have encountered a lady of 100 who, despite extremely poor explicit memory, can play (and win) Scrabble in three foreign languages! Moreover, formal studies showing a minimal decline in the language abilities of both normal and dementing individuals are the underlying basis for developing and using the National Adult Reading Test (NART; Nelson & O'Connell, 1976) as a means of assessing pre-morbid IQ.

The mechanisms underlying implicit memory remain largely undiscovered, but it is likely that they reflect, in part at least, domain-specific mnemonic properties of the cognitive system. By this I mean that a particular implicit memory function, such as verbal priming, is a property of the cognitive system dealing with that class of stimulus—that is, the word recognition system. Schacter and his colleagues (e.g., Schacter, 1990; Schacter, Rapcsak, Rubens, Tharan, & Laguna, 1990; Tulving & Schacter, 1990) have, on the basis of several lines of evidence, suggested that implicit memory depends on the intactness of the *perceptual representation system*. Defined briefly, this system embodies the structural representations of words and objects and enables identification of those items to be facilitated from reduced perceptual cues. Response to this facilitation, in turn, constitutes implicit memory for a given stimulus. Within this framework it can be seen that verbally based implicit memory would be critically dependent on intact language mechanisms and, given the predominant use of verbal paradigms and intactness of language in the elderly, the absence of marked age-related implicit memory deficits may be less surprising. Age differences in implicit memory therefore need to be explored across a number of domains before any firm conclusions about age-related influences can be reached. For example, are the priming effects evident for verbal material also found for pictorial material? Are there priming effects in the auditory domain?

DEVELOPMENTAL ASPECTS OF IMPLICIT MEMORY

The investigation of implicit memory from a developmental perspective has necessitated the use of nonverbal paradigms in order to include groups of pre-linguistic children. Our own study has utilized the picture completion paradigm devised by Snodgrass and her colleagues (Snodgrass, Bradford, Feenan, & Corvin, 1987). The paradigm involves presentation of an increasingly informative picture sequence until the subject can identify the depicted item. After this training phase there is a retention interval, followed by a test phase in which the original (old) sequences are represented along with new sequences. Two measures of learning can be derived from this paradigm: perceptual learning, calculated as new − old, and skill learning, calculated as train − new. Perceptual learning thus refers to the amount of learning achieved for a specific target and skill learning to general improvements on performing the task per se. Both these measures can be considered, operationally, as indices of implicit memory because the testing phase makes no overt reference to the original learning episode, although, as we will see, it is quite clear that explicit recollection can play a critical part in task performance.

Parkin and Streete (1988) used the picture completion task to examine implicit memory in children as young as three years and young adults. Using the measure of perceptual learning already described, a clear age-related increase in implicit memory was identified. However, when perceptual learning was recalculated in proportional terms (old/train) to allow for baseline differences, no age difference was found.[1] We were cautious in our interpretation of these data because of their implication that implicit memory ability shows no developmental trend and is intact by age three. However, Graf (1990) felt confident that these data were positive evidence for no age effect in implicit memory.

We have reconsidered the Parkin and Streete data in the light of Snodgrass' (1989) views concerning comparison of savings scores when groups have different baseline (training) scores. Snodgrass recommends that under these conditions perceptual learning should be calculated as new − old/new − 1. Figure 9.1 shows the Parkin and Streete data replotted using this formula, and a significant age-related improvement in perceptual learning is now clearly evident. We cannot, however, conclude that these data show an age-related improvement in implicit memory per se, because Parkin and Streete also reported age-related improvements in explicit memory as measured by subjects' ability to recognize that target sequences had been seen before. In a post hoc analysis the authors found that savings were greater for items that were recognized in all groups

---

[1]The data reported in Table 2 of Parkin and Streete (1988) were not properly explained. The values shown were calculated by the formula: second score − first score/second. The values thus show the proportion of the second score due to savings on the first score.

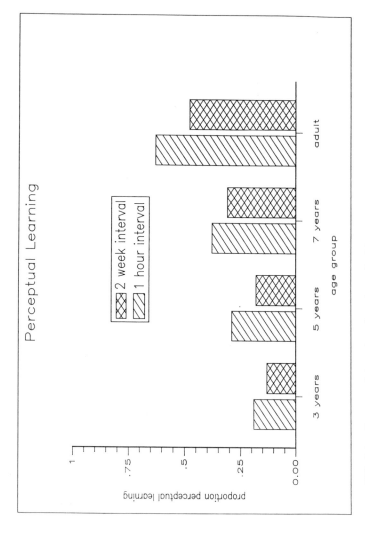

FIG. 9.1. Perceptual learning data from Parkin and Streete (1988) replotted using correction for differing baselines as a function of age.

except the very youngest, where recognition was at chance. Because of this, the age-related improvement in perceptual learning could have reflected an increasing explicit influence on picture completion—that is, recollection of targets identified in the learning phase could have provided useful cues as to the potential identity of target sequences. The Parkin and Streete data were not amenable to an analysis in which the influence of explicit memory on implicit performance could be partialed out. The conclusion from the study must be, therefore, that implicit memory appears functional when explicit memory is very poor, but the additional conclusion that implicit memory exhibits no developmental trend requires an experiment in which genuine implicit memory can be measured without the contaminating influence of explicit memory.

Two other studies do, however, appear to indicate invariant implicit memory in children of different ages. Greenbaum and Graf (1989) presented children between 3 and 5 years with pictures and tested explicit memory via free recall or implicit memory using a modified word production task. In the latter, subjects were read a story about going to a place (e.g., a zoo) and then asked to name what is typically found there. Implicit memory is measured by comparing the probability of the child producing a study item as an instance in relation to baseline. As one would expect, Greenbaum and Graf found an age-related increase in explicit remembering, but implicit memory did not change significantly. Following an earlier study by Carroll, Byrne, and Kirsner (1985), in which no age differences in verbal priming were found in children between 5 and 10 years, Naito (1990) examined repetition priming, recall, and recognition in three groups of children (6.9 years, 8.6 years, 11.7 years) and adults (22.1 years). Her results show no difference in priming with age but significant age-related improvements in recall and recognition (see Chapter 11 by Naito and Komatsu, this volume).

AGING AND NONVERBAL IMPLICIT MEMORY

Although the learning phenomena that initiated the implicit memory concept were many and varied (Parkin, 1982; Schacter, 1987), experimental research has been concentrated in the verbal learning laboratory and, as noted in the foregoing discussion, this tradition has been maintained in aging studies. However, Mitchell and his colleagues (Mitchell, Brown, & Murphy, 1990) compared young and old subjects in a picture-naming paradigm where pictures of common objects were presented on successive occasions and implicit memory was measured in terms of any reduced naming latency on the second presentation. Age differences in the magnitude of the priming effect were negligible, and the implicit nature of this effect was emphasized by showing that the priming effect was the same regardless of whether subjects explicitly remembered a given picture.

Although the task used by Mitchell et al. clearly has a perceptual component, the dependent variable is still verbally based and, as such, may serve to minimize age differences. The picture completion paradigm, described earlier, provides a better test of nonverbal implicit memory because what is primed is the subjects' ability to perform perceptual closure on an incomplete stimulus rather than the ability to name it; nonetheless, some explicit influence cannot be ruled out. Using this paradigm Russo and Parkin (in press) examined age-related differences in nonverbal implicit memory without the contaminating influence of expected explicit memory differences between young and old subjects. To achieve this it was necessary to use a paradigm in which explicit memory for the original learning episode could be reduced to similar levels in young and old prior to measuring any age-related differences in perceptual or skill learning. This was achieved using the divided attention manipulation used by Parkin and Russo (1990; see also Gardiner & Parkin, 1990; Parkin, Reid, & Russo, 1990), in which subjects undertake the initial learning phase while performing a tone-monitoring task simultaneously. Russo and Parkin found that divided attention significantly reduced young subjects' explicit memory for the training phase of the picture completion paradigm but had no effect on the degree of implicit learning exhibited. As well as supporting the differential nature of implicit and explicit memory, the study showed that implicit memory in young people could be examined under conditions where explicit memory was reduced.

In the Russo and Parkin (in press) study old subjects and three groups of young subjects undertook the training phase of picture completion. The old and one young group performed under focused attention and the two other young groups performed simultaneous tone monitoring (one version of the task was harder). Implicit memory, as measured by perceptual learning, was found to be poorer in the elderly group compared with all three young groups, despite the fact that explicit memory in the two divided attention groups did not differ significantly from the elderly (see Fig. 9.2). This finding indicated that the elderly did not show poorer perceptual learning because they had less explicit memory available compared with the young. However, it remained possible that poorer implicit memory in the elderly arose because they failed to utilize available explicit memory effectively. This possibility was supported by additional analyses showing that only the elderly failed to show greater perceptual learning for sequences that they were able to recall (see Fig. 9.3).

The Russo and Parkin (in press) study shows that, on a measure of nonverbal implicit memory, age differences are minimal when one allows for the fact that the elderly make less use of explicit memory for the learning episode to aid task performance. The next question is, why do the elderly perform in this way? The answer may lie in the growing realization that an important aspect of age-related cognitive decline is a selective deterioration of frontal lobe function (e.g., Mittenberg, Seidenberg, O'Leary, & DiGuilio, 1989). Studies of age-related memory impairment have begun to suggest that these deficits reflect particular loss of

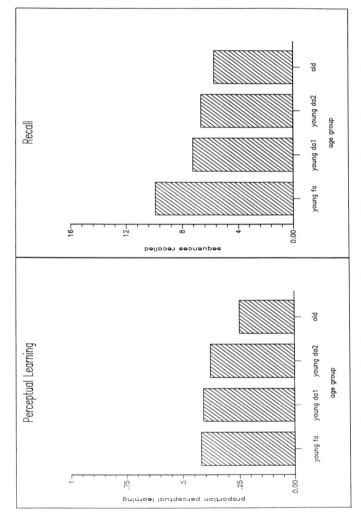

FIG. 9.2. Perceptual learning and recall data from Russo and Parkin (in press). Fa = focused attention, da1 = easy divided attention task, da2 = difficult divided attention task.

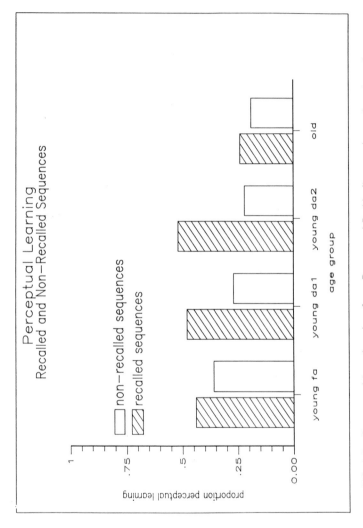

FIG. 9.3. Perceptual learning data from Russo and Parkin (in press) as a function of recall status. Key as for Fig. 9.2.

memory functions associated with the frontal lobes (Craik, Morris, Morris, & Loewen, 1990; Parkin & Walter, 1991). Among a number of memory functions attributed to the frontal lobes is the initiation of strategic retrieval operations (Moscovitch, 1989), and deterioration of this ability could be the basis of Russo and Parkin's result. It is reasonable to assume that the re-presented picture sequence acts as a retrieval cue for the training episode, which, if effective, can retrieve explicit information about target identity. It follows that, despite similar levels of available explicit memory, the selective retrieval deficit of the elderly would undermine their picture completion performance relative to young subjects because they fail use available retrieval cues to elicit information about potential target identity.

AGE-RELATED CHANGES IN THE CONTRIBUTION OF IMPLICIT AND EXPLICIT MEMORY TO OVERALL MEMORY PERFORMANCE

Although some qualifications must be raised (e.g., those of Howard, 1988), the general impression of experimental investigations is that implicit memory declines little with age. From the developmental perspective it is interesting to consider whether this state of affairs has any bearing on the nature of memory ability with advancing age. In particular, it raises the possibility that shortcomings in explicit memory might be compensated for by increased reliance on implicit memory.

On a priori grounds the memory task most sensitive to age-related decline, free recall, could not benefit from implicit compensation because, by definition, free recall has no implicit component. It is a different matter, however, with recognition, because a number of studies have now demonstrated that recognition can be based on either explicit or implicit forms of remembering. Several authors (e.g., Jacoby & Dallas; 1981; Johnston, Hawley, & Elliot, 1991) argued that, alongside explicit recollection, an item can be recognized because of perceptual fluency cues—these cues can be considered functionally equivalent to the cues arising from operation of the perceptual representation systems (PRS) described by Schacter and his colleagues.

A number of lines of evidence implicate perceptual fluency cues in the operation of recognition memory. Several studies, for example, indicate that the speed at which an item is perceptually identified can, under various conditions, act as a cue to recognition (e.g., Jacoby, 1991; Johnston, Dark, & Jacoby, 1985; Kelley, Jacoby, & Hollingshead, 1989; Mandler, 1980). In particular, perceptual fluency cues are thought to be important when explicit memory is reduced. This concept may be useful in accounting for certain phenomena in memory-impaired populations. The amnesic literature contains many instances of patients with grossly impaired recall but relatively good recognition memory. Kopelman (1985), for example, found that Korsakoff patients showed normal levels of forgetting on a recognition memory task providing they were matched with controls at acquisition. This matching was achieved by giving the Korsakoff patients far longer to study the stimuli. It might be argued that the extra study time allowed the Korsakoff patients to encode abnormal amounts of perceptual information about the targets and that this was sufficient to support apparently normal recognition memory. This explanation is supported by recent investigations in our own laboratory where we have shown that Korsakoff patients can perform well on a recognition task in which perceptual fluency cues could provide an efficient basis for responding. When task conditions are altered to remove the salience of perceptual cues, performance is very poor (Hunkin, 1991; Parkin, Leng, & Hunkin, 1990).

We have also been examining qualitative changes in recognition memory as a function of normal aging using the recognition and conscious awareness (RCA) paradigm devised initially by Tulving and developed by Gardiner and his colleagues (Gardiner, 1988; Gardiner & Java, 1990; Gardiner & Parkin, 1990). In the RCA paradigm subjects first study a series of targets and then, following a retention interval, are given a recognition test in which targets must be discriminated from novel distractors. Contingent on a recognition response, subjects are further required to classify each recognition response as either a "remember" (R) or "know" (K) response. The R responses are given for recognition associated with some specific recollection of the target's occurrence in the learning episode and the K responses for recognition based on an item merely seeming familiar.

Experimental studies of the RCA paradigm have found that orienting task manipulations, retention interval, word frequency, and divided attention all affect R responses but have no effect on K responses (Gardiner, 1988; Gardiner & Java, 1990; Gardiner & Parkin, 1990). These are all variables that also fail to have any influence on implicit memory measures such as stem and fragment completion (Parkin, Reid, & Russo, 1990; Schacter, 1987) and lead to the implication that K responses emanate from the same type of memory system as that governing other implicit phenomena.

Parkin and Walter (1992) compared old, middle old, and young subjects (mean ages 81, 67, and 21 years, respectively) on the RCA paradigm. The results are shown in Fig. 9.4. Recognition performance declines somewhat with age, but the most dramatic effect is the change in the subjective nature of recognition with age. Young subjects show approximately equal levels of R and K responses, but both older groups make significantly more K than R responses. It might be argued that this difference arises from the elderly's lower confidence in their recognition ability and a greater tendency to respond K because they are simply less sure about their memories. To examine this claim, we carried out a second experiment comparing just the old and young subjects on a similar recognition task except that, instead of requiring the R − K distinction, we asked subjects to state whether they were "sure" or "unsure" about the correctness of their re-

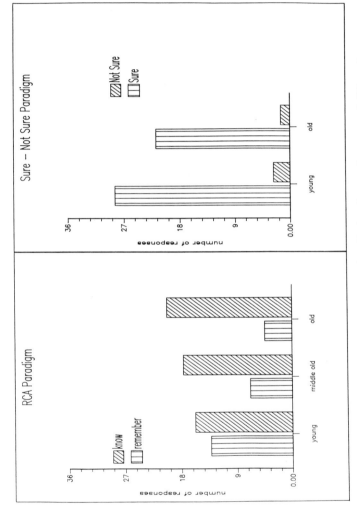

FIG. 9.4. Data from Parkin and Walter (1992) showing performance of different age groups on RCA and sure–not sure recognition tasks.

sponse. (No rating scale was used. Subjects were just told to use "sure" if they were confident about the accuracy of their response and "unsure" if not.) If K tended to be used for unsure responses and R for sure responses, we would expect this experiment to yield similar results to the first experiment, that is, significantly greater unsure responses in the older group, but, as Fig. 9.4 also shows, both young and old made substantially more sure responses.

The changing pattern of R and K responses as a function of age therefore reflects a genuine change in the nature of recognition with older subjects and, given the similarity between K responses and other implicit phenomena, we can further argue that these data indicate an age-related increase in the extent to which recognition relies on implicit memory. The value of this perspective has yet to be explored, but a number of predictions are readily apparent. Earlier, for example, we noted that the implicit contribution to recognition might be manifest via perceptual fluency cues. It follows, therefore, that variables that reduce the efficacy of perceptual fluency cues, such as perceptually overlapping distractors, should have a greater effect on the old than the young.

This hypothesis has yet to be tested directly, but there is one recent finding suggesting that it may be correct. Bartlett and Fulton (1991) compared young and old subjects on memory for unfamiliar faces. There was no age difference on hits, but the older subjects made more false positive responses. Subsequent analysis showed that these false positives arose because the older subjects were more reliant on resemblance information when making their responses, and, in a subsequent experiment, it was shown that older subjects used resemblance information more than the young in correct recognition. Given that all the faces were unfamiliar, resemblance in this study must be defined purely in terms of shared physical attributes. Increased use of resemblance in recognition could be interpreted as increased reliance on perceptual information.

On conventional tests of recognition the elderly show either no impairment (e.g., Craik & McDowd, 1987) or only mild impairments (e.g., Gordon & Clark, 1974)—findings that could be attributed to enhanced implicit responding. However, on multiple-item recognition (MIR) the elderly show quite pronounced deficits (Kausler & Kleim, 1978). In the MIR task, two or more items are exposed during learning and one is arbitrarily designated correct and the other(s) incorrect by the experimenter. On subsequent trials subjects are confronted with the item pairings and asked to identify which one is correct. Young subjects perform better overall but, more importantly, their performance is unaffected by the number of incorrect items presented concurrently. Older subjects, in contrast, perform much worse as the number of incorrect items present on a study trial is increased.

A number of explanations for age-related impairments on the MIR task have been put forward (see Kausler, 1991), but one possible explanation is that the elderly fair worse because they rely more on familiarity-based, that is, implicit, information as the basis for recognition. The MIR task requires the subject to recognize more than the item itself: Some record that "X was correct on trial Y" must also be recorded. This is tantamount to requiring some form of contextual information being recorded, and this form of memory derives purely from explicit recollection. Poor performance by the elderly, in which explicit memory is reduced and implicit memory correspondingly more dominant, would therefore accommodate the impairments shown by the elderly on MIR.

We also have to consider why explicit recognition memory deteriorates so as to allow a greater implicit contribution. Again, a plausible explanation derives from the elderly's decline in frontal lobe function. Parkin and Walter (1992) examined the relationship between the proportion of K responses made by subjects and their performance on a range of frontal lobe tests. In the oldest group it was found that subjects with poor performance on the Wisconsin Card Sorting Test also tended to place a higher proportion of their recognition responses in the K category. This correlation could reflect at least two different kinds of deficit. In order to set up a potential R response it is necessary to initiate some form of encoding, such as generation of an image, and it is possible that low numbers of R responses reflect a frontally based deficit in initiating encoding. This deficit might well be linked to the retrieval deficit we discussed earlier and be related to another memory deficit shown selectively by the elderly—impaired source memory. Stanhope (1988) has demonstrated that the locus of the elderly's source memory impairment stems from either an encoding deficit or failure to retrieve appropriate attributes of the original stimulus event at test, and Craik et al. (1990) have shown that source memory impairments in older people are related to their frontal lobe dysfunction.

IMPLICIT MEMORY: FIRST IN, LAST OUT?

Although our knowledge of how implicit memory develops is far from complete, we can assume, with some confidence, that implicit memory abilities appear before explicit ones (Parkin & Streete, 1988), remain when explicit abilities deteriorate (Howard, 1988), or are lost completely (Parkin, 1987). What, if anything, is the significance of this?

As we have seen, a prevailing view of implicit memory is that it reflects the mnemonic properties of perceptual systems. This contrasts with explicit memory, whose contents are amodal and entirely symbolic. One cannot argue, with any certainty, that any animal other than the human has explicit memory, but, given that most animals have at least some approximation to a perceptual system, there is an a priori case that animals may possess implicit memory and that this provides for some evolutionary continuity within and between phyla, extending right up to the advanced hominids.

Most animals receive little parental care, and for them learning must be initiated very early in life if survival is to be guaranteed. Young humans do not face the same challenge, but, given phylogenetic links, it should not surprise us that some implicit learning mechanisms are in place at birth or even before. Many studies, for example, have documented that young infants can learn about faces and show novelty preferences well before the age of 1. Even more remarkably there is now evidence that children can learn the characteristics of their mother's voice in the womb (e.g., DeCasper & Fifer, 1980). The new born child may therefore possess a range of implicit learning abilities that enable the development of crude classifications such as familiar-unfamiliar; furthermore, investigation of children at this point might allow an interesting comparison between the learning process of humans and other animals.

The prior appearance of implicit memory can thus be accounted for phylogenetically, and this form of explanation might also be invoked to explain the robust nature of implicit learning. Hughlings Jackson (1880) argued persuasively that the vulnerability of brain systems was inversely related to their evolutionary status. Jackson proposed that older brain mechanisms were more localized than those with more recent origin. The major implication of this was that older systems are, on average, less vulnerable to general brain insult than mechanisms that are more broadly distributed through the brain. Memory is a good case in point. On the assumption that implicit memory resides, in part at least, within a perceptual representation system-type system, we can argue that this form of memory has a high degree of localization simply because the base perceptual abilities themselves have relatively well-defined cortical sites. The more recently evolved explicit memory is far less localized in that many different brain structures (e.g., hippocampus, mamillary bodies, dorsomedial thalamic nucleus, prefrontal cortex) are critically implicated, and furthermore, these structures, especially the hippocampus, seem peculiarly sensitive to a wide range of brain insults. The greater vulnerability of explicit memory can thus be attributed to its multiple substrate nature.

CONCLUSION

In this chapter I have argued that implicit memory appears before explicit memory, and within the adult life span there appears to be little significant deterioration in implicit memory ability. I have further suggested that implicit memory may play a greater functional role with advancing age. From an evolutionary perspective implicit memory has developmental priority because it reflects phylogenetic relations with the learning abilities of other species, and its robust nature across the lifespan can be attributed to its reliance on relatively localized brain systems.

REFERENCES

Bartlett, J. C., & Fulton, A. (1991). Familiarity and recognition of faces in old age. *Memory & Cognition, 19*, 229–238.

Carroll, M., Byrne, B., & Kirsner, K. (1985). Autobiographical memory and recognition, naming latency, and perceptual identification. *Memory & Cognition, 13*, 273–279.

Craik, F. I. M., & McDowd, J. M. (1987). Age differences in recall and recognition. *Journal of Experimental Psychology: Learning, Memory & Cognition, 13*, 474–479.

Craik, F. I. M., Morris, L. W., Morris, R. G., & Loewen, E. R. (1990). Relation between source amnesia and frontal lobe functioning in a normal elderly sample. *Psychology & Aging, 5*, 148–151.

DeCasper, A. J., & Fifer, W. P. (1980). Of human bonding: Newborns prefer their mothers' voices. *Science, 208*, 1174–1176.

Gardiner, J. M. (1988). Functional aspects of recollective experience. *Memory & Cognition, 16*, 309–313.

Gardiner, J. M., & Java, R. I. (1990). Recollective experience in word and nonword recognition. *Memory & Cognition, 18*, 23–30.

Gardiner, J. M., & Parkin, A. J. (1990). Attention and recollective experience in recognition memory. *Memory & Cognition, 18*, 579–583.

Gordon, S. K., & Clark, W. C. (1974). Application of signal detection theory to prose recall and recognition in elderly and young adults. *Journal of Gerontology, 29*, 64–72.

Graf, P. (1990). Life-span changes in implicit and explicit memory. *Bulletin of the Psychonomic Society, 28*, 353–358.

Greenbaum, J. L., & Graf, P. (1989). Preschool period development of implicit and explicit remembering. *Bulletin of the Psychonomic Society, 27*, 417–420.

Howard, D. V. (1988). Implicit and explicit assessment of cognitive aging. In M. L. Howe & E. J. Brainerd, (Eds.) *Cognitive development in adulthood: Progress in cognitive development research* (pp. 3–37). New York: Springer-Verlag.

Hunkin, N. M. (1991). *Comparative study of contextual deficits in temporal lobe and diencephalic amnesia*. Unpublished D.Phil. thesis, University of Sussex.

Jacoby, L. L. (1991). A process dissociation framework: Separating automatic from intentional uses of memory. *Journal of Memory and Language, 30*, 513–541.

Jacoby, L. L., & Dallas, M. (1981). On the relationship between autobiographical memory and perceptual learning. *Journal of Experimental Psychology: General, 110*, 306–340.

Jackson, J. H. (1880). Essays on the dissolution of the nervous system. *Lancet*.

Johnston, W. A., Dark, V. J., & Jacoby, L. L. (1985). Perceptual fluency and recognition judgments. *Journal of Experimental Psychology: Learning, Memory, and Cognition, 11*, 3–11.

Johnston, W. A., Hawley, K. J., & Elliot, J. M. G. (1991). Contribution of perceptual fluency to recognition judgments. *Journal of Experimental Psychology: Learning, Memory, and Cognition, 17*, 210–223.

Kausler, D. H. (1991). *Experimental psychology, cognition, and human aging*, 2nd ed. New York: Springer-Verlag.

Kausler, D. H., & Kleim, D. M. (1978). Age differences in processing relevant versus irrelevant stimuli in multiple item recognition learning. *Journal of Gerontology, 33*, 87–93.

Kelley, C. M., Jacoby, L. L., & Hollingshead, A. (1989). Direct versus indirect tests of memory for source: Judgments of modality. *Journal of Experimental Psychology: Learning, Memory, and Cognition, 15*, 1101–1108.

Kopelman, M. D. (1985). Rates of forgetting in Alzheimer-type dementias and Korsakoff's syndrome. *Neuropsychologia, 23*, 623–638.

Mandler, G. (1980). Recognising: The judgment of previous occurrence. *Psychological Review, 87*, 252–271.

Mitchell, D. B., Brown, A. S., & Murphy, D. R. (1990). Procedural and episodic memory: Dissociations produced by time and aging. *Psychology and Aging, 5*, 264–276.

Mittenberg, W., Seidenberg, M., O'Leary, D. S., & DiGuilio, D. V. (1989). Changes in cerebral functioning associated with normal aging. *Journal of Clinical and Experimental Neuropsychology, 11*, 918–932.

Moscovitch, M. (1989). Confabulation and the frontal systems: Strategic versus associated retrieval in neuropsychological theories of memory. In H. L. Roedigger III & F. I. M. Craik (Eds.), *Varieties of memory and consciousness: Essays in honour of Endel Tulving* (pp. 133–161). Hillsdale, NJ: Lawrence Erlbaum Associates.

Naito, M. (1990). Repetition priming in children and adults: Age-related dissociation between implicit and explicit memory. *Journal of Experimental Child Psychology, 50,* 462–484.

Nelson, H. E., & O'Connell. (1976). Dementia: the estimation of premorbid intelligence levels using the New Adult Reading Test. *Cortex, 14,* 234–244.

Parkin, A. J. (1982). Residual learning capability in organic amnesia. *Cortex, 18,* 417–440.

Parkin, A. J. (1987). *Memory and amnesia: An introduction.* Oxford: Basil Blackwell.

Parkin, A. J., Leng, N. R. C., & Hunkin, N. M. (1990). Differential sensitivity to context in organic amnesia. *Cortex, 26,* 373–380.

Parkin, A. J., Reid, T., & Russo, R. (1990). On the differential nature of implicit and explicit memory. *Memory and Cognition, 18,* 507–514.

Parkin, A. J., & Russo, R. (1990). Implicit and explicit memory and the automatic effortful distinction. *European Journal of Cognitive Psychology, 2,* 71–80.

Parkin, A. J., & Streete, S. (1988). Implicit and explicit memory in young children and adults. *British Journal of Psychology, 79,* 361–369.

Parkin, A. J., & Walter, B. M. (1991). Aging, short-term memory, and frontal dysfunction. *Psychobiology, 19,* 175–179.

Parkin, A. J., & Walter, B. M. (1992). Recollective experience, normal aging, and frontal dysfunction. *Psychology and Aging, 7,* 290–298.

Russo, R., & Parkin, A. J. (in press). Age differences in implicit memory: More apparent than real. *Memory Cognition,*

Salthouse, T. A. (1982). *Adult cognition.* New York: Springer-Verlag.

Schacter, D. L. (1987). Implicit memory: History and current status. *Journal of Experimental Psychology, Learning, Memory, and Cognition, 13,* 501–518.

Schacter, D. L. (1990). Perceptual representation systems and implicit memory: Toward a resolution of the multiple memory systems debate. In A. Diamond (Ed.), *Development and neural bases of higher cognition. Annals of the New York Academy of Sciences, 608,* 543–571.

Schacter, D. L., Rapcsak, S., Rubens, A., Tharan, M., & Laguna, J. (1990). Priming effects in a letter-by-letter reader depend upon access to the word form system. *Neuropsychologia, 28,* 1079–1094.

Snodgrass, J. G. (1989). Sources of learning in the picture fragment completion task. In S. Lewandowsky, J. Dunn, & K. Kirsner (Eds.), *Implicit memory: Theoretical issues* (pp. 259–282), Hillsdale, NJ: Lawrence Erlbaum Associates.

Snodgrass, J. G., Bradford, S., Feenan, K., & Corvin, J. (1987). Fragmenting pictures on the Apple Macintosh computer for experimental and clinical applications. *Behavior Research Methods, Instruments, and Computers, 19,* 270–274.

Stanhope, N. (1988). *Source forgetting in young and elderly adults.* Unpublished D.Phil. thesis, University of Sussex.

Tulving, E., & Schacter, D. L. (1990). Priming and human memory systems. *Science, 247,* 301–306.

10 Direct and Indirect Measures of Memory in Old Age

Leah L. Light
Pitzer College

Donna La Voie
Claremont Graduate School

Older adults score lower on direct tests of memory, such as recall and recognition, which require deliberate recollection of specific episodes. In fact, Salthouse (1988) reported that the median of 22 correlations between age and memory in adult samples was $-.33$. Salthouse also assessed the magnitude of age-related memory decline by expressing the average scores of older groups in terms of the standard deviation of the younger groups to which they were being compared. He reported that for 67 comparisons, the median z score for older adults was -1.26. In other words, the average adult scored at about the tenth percentile of the young adult distribution in the studies Salthouse examined. Such results, however, should not be used as the basis for a generalization that older adults have a global memory deficit. There are many ways in which the effects of a prior experience may be expressed that do not involve deliberate recollection. When young and older adults are compared on these indirect measures of memory, age differences are generally small and unreliable, suggesting that there is a dissociation between direct and indirect measures of memory in old age (see reviews by Howard, 1988, 1991; Light, 1991).

In this chapter, we first describe the results of studies that have compared young and older adults on indirect measures of memory using verbal stimuli (for discussions of experiments using nonverbal materials see Mitchell, Chapter 8, this volume; Howard & Howard, 1989), to illustrate the type of tasks that have been used and the nature of the experimental findings. We also report the results of a meta-analysis that leads us to conclude that age differences on indirect measures of memory, while smaller than those on direct measures, may indeed be real. In the final section, we consider a number of theoretical accounts of the dissociation between direct and indirect measures of memory in old age.

INDIRECT MEASURES OF MEMORY IN OLD AGE

On indirect measures of memory, people may be asked to spell a word (Jacoby & Witherspoon, 1982), to complete the fragment of a word when given some of its letters, as in __E__D__L__M (Tulving, Schacter, & Stark, 1982), to produce a word that begins with certain letters such as ATT (Graf & Mandler, 1984), to perform a lexical decision task (Scarborough, Cortese, & Scarborough, 1977), or to read visually degraded words (Moscovitch, Winocur, & McLachlan, 1986). In these tasks, the effects of prior experience are manifested if a homophone is more likely to be spelled in accordance with a particular meaning (e.g., *grate* rather than *great*) after being presented in a context that biases that meaning, if a word fragment or word stem is more likely to be completed with a word that has been studied, if a decision that a string of letters is a word is more rapid when that string of letters has been studied before, or if identification of a visually degraded word is improved by prior presentation. The benefit accruing to old words relative to new ones is called *item priming*.

Similar tasks may also be used to assess the extent to which a new memory representation has been formed for a nonword or a new connection has been formed between unrelated words. When associative priming tasks are used, the critical question is whether performance is better when the original pairing is retained than when items are recombined. For instance, after studying the word pairs *jail-strange* and *balance-chair,* word stem completion can be tested for intact items (jail-str_____, balance-cha_____) or for re-paired items (jail-cha_____, balance-str_____); if previously studied words appear as word stem completions more often for intact than for re-paired items, association formation is inferred (Graf & Schacter, 1985). In item recognition, recognition memory for one member of a previously studied pair can be tested immediately after the other or after a word from another pair; faster responding in the first case is evidence for episodic priming. A similar line of argument is used for lexical decision tasks; faster responding for intact pairs implies new learning has taken place.

What is the typical pattern of results in studies examining performance of young and old on such indirect measures of memory? For single items, priming effects of similar magnitude for young and old have been found in fragment completion tasks (Light, Singh, & Capps, 1986), word stem completion (Dick, Kean, & Sands, 1989; Java & Gardiner, 1991; Light & Singh, 1987; Park & Shaw, 1992), identification of degraded or briefly presented words (Hashtroudi, Chrosniak, & Schwartz, 1991, Experiments 1a and 2a; Light, LaVoie, Valencia-Laver, Albertson Owens, & Mead, 1992; Light & Singh, 1987), lexical decision (Moscovitch, 1982), category judgments (Rabbitt, 1982, 1984), spelling of homophones in accordance with a previously biased meaning (Howard, 1988), word pronunciation (Light & LaVoie, 1992), anagram solution (Java, in press), and free association to a category name (Light & Albertson, 1989). In most of these studies, direct measures of memory such as free recall, cued recall, or

FIG. 10.1. The magnitude of priming in word stem completion is similar in young and old, but young adults have higher cued-recall scores than older adults. In this study, the same word stems were given as cues for word stem completion and recall. *Note:* Adapted from Experiment 2 of "Implicit and explicit memory in young and older adults" by L. L. Light and A. Singh, 1987, *Journal of Experimental Psychology: Learning, Memory, and Cognition, 13,* pp. 531–541.

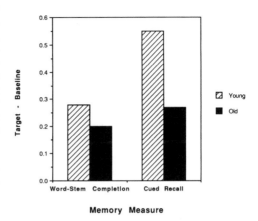

recognition were also administered. Almost invariably, performance on recall and recognition showed an advantage for the young over the old.

Figures 10.1 and 10.2 graphically illustrate this pattern of unreliable differences in priming across age coupled with better performance by the young on direct measures of memory. The data in Fig. 10.1 are taken from Light and Singh (1987, Experiment 2) and show a comparison between cued recall and word stem completion. In the word stem completion task subjects were asked to complete three-letter word stems with the first word that came to mind, whereas in the cued recall task they were asked to treat the three-letter word stems as clues to remind them of previously presented words. Young and old did not differ in the

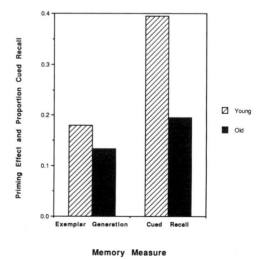

FIG. 10.2. The magnitude of priming in exemplar generation is similar in young and old, but young adults have higher cued-recall scores than older adults. The same category names were given as cues for exemplar generation and recall. *Note:* Adapted from "Direct and indirect tests of memory for category exemplars in young and older adults" by L.L. Light and S.A. Albertson, 1989, *Psychology and Aging, 4,* pp. 487–492.

extent of priming in word stem completion, but unlike the old, the young had higher levels of recall than word stem completion.

The data in Fig. 10.2 were taken from an experiment carried out by Light and Albertson (1989). In this study, generation of category members in a controlled association task was used as the indirect measure of memory and category cued recall served as the direct measure of memory. After viewing a list of words, people were asked to think of members of categories, some of which had been represented on the study list and some of which were new. Subsequent to the exemplar generation task, participants were given a cued-recall test for list members, with category names serving as retrieval cues. What Fig. 10.2 shows is that there was no reliable difference in the likelihood of generating old exemplars across age. However, younger adults recalled about twice as many words in cued recall as did older adults. As in the word stem completion study, older adults did not benefit from cued-recall instructions while young adults did.

In both Figs. 10.1 and 10.2, the age difference in item priming, while unreliable, did favor the young. Perhaps it is not surprising, then, that reliable age differences in item priming have sometimes been observed. Chiarello and Hoyer (1988), Hultsch, Masson, and Small (1991), and Davis et al. (1990) reported effects of age on word stem completion. Abbenhuis, Raaijmakers, Raaijmakers, and van Woerden (1990) found more repetition priming in word identification for young than for old. Spelling bias studies have also yielded mixed outcomes (Davis et al., 1990; Rose, Yesavage, Hill, & Bower, 1986).

The studies reviewed thus far have dealt with item priming, that is, the priming of words for which existing memory representations could be assumed. A number of studies comparing young and old have examined priming for novel stimuli or associative priming. There is a large literature demonstrating that older adults are especially impaired on direct memory tests when new connections must be formed (Burke & Light, 1981; Light & Burke, 1988). Hence, one might anticipate that unlike item priming, associative priming would always show age differences unless care were taken to equate acquisition of new connections. Should age invariance in associative priming be found when study conditions are the same across age, this would constitute evidence that formation of new associations is unaffected by aging. Age differences in recall and recognition of new associations would then signal problems in retrieval but not in acquisition.

Age-related differences in associative priming are sometimes observed (Howard, 1988; Howard, Heisey, & Shaw, 1986; Moscovitch, Winocur, & MacLachlan, 1986) but this is by no means universal (Howard et al., 1986; Howard, Fry, & Brune, 1991; Light & LaVoie, 1992; Moscovitch et al., 1986; Nilsson, Backman, & Karlsson, 1989; Rabinowitz, 1986; Whetstone, 1991). Studies of associative priming are not as numerous as those of item priming, and type of materials (word pairs, nonwords), conditions of presentation (long vs. short durations, one vs. two or more repetitions), and type of indirect memory test (word stem completion, item recognition, perceptual identification, naming) vary considerably across studies, making it hard to isolate the reasons for the discrepant findings. Howard (1988) suggested that single presentations, long study-to-test delays, less elaboration-inducing study conditions, and test order (forward vs. backward associations) may affect performance. It is also possible that different conditions must be met for priming of new associations to occur in different paradigms. Howard et al. (1991) make a strong case for the necessity of elaborative encoding of items to be associated if priming in word stem completion is to take place and present evidence that older adults show reduced priming because they are less able to engage in elaborative encoding. They found less associative priming in the old under conditions of limited, though generous (8 sec), study times for sentences containing pairs of target words for which a sentence continuation was to be generated; when study time was self-paced and people were forced to make up sentences containing the two words in a pair, no age difference was found. On the other hand, Moscovitch et al. (1986) found preserved priming for new associations in a degraded-stimulus reading task despite the fact that the study conditions were not designed to encourage elaborative encoding; here the study task was reading weakly associated word pairs out loud, and the measure of associative priming was how long it took to read pairs of words that were the same as the study pairs or that had been re-paired. Also, our own studies of naming nonwords do not use elaborative encoding orienting conditions and show preserved repetition priming.

One such study, which we conducted together with Christine Luppino (Light & LaVoie, 1992), is shown in Fig. 10.3. In this study, subjects read aloud lists of five compound nonwords (e.g., *fishdust, waygirl*) that were repeated for nine blocks of trials. The 10th block of five items consisted of either the same five compound nonwords, five compound nonwords created by swapping the first and second nouns of the compounds, or five brand new compound nonwords. Differences in reading latencies favoring the intact pairs reflect the contribution of new learning (Musen & Squire, 1991). As seen in Fig. 10.3, both young and old showed comparable effects of repetitions over the first nine blocks of trials. More critically, pronunciation latencies were faster for intact than for swapped compounds in block 10, and the magnitude of the effect was the same in young and old. The improvement in speed of naming for swapped compounds relative to new ones represents the benefit accruing to subunits from prior presentation. This effect, too, was similar in young and old. In this study, however, nonwords were repeated many times before associative learning was tested. As yet, we do not know whether, in accordance with the suggestion by Howard (1988), older adults need more repetitions for associations to be formed; had we tested after a smaller number of repetitions, age differences might have been obtained.

Thus, although our own studies have not produced reliable age differences in either item or associative priming, and although workers in other laboratories often report a similar absence of age effects, some researchers have found reliable age differences in both types of priming. Even in studies in which age

Nonword Naming Latency

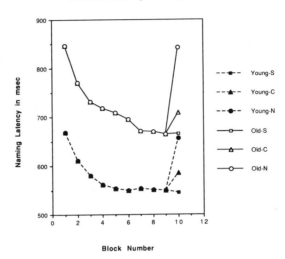

Block Number

FIG. 10.3. After reading aloud the same compound nonwords for nine blocks of trials, latencies for pronouncing new nonwords and for nonwords created by swapping the components of old nonwords are longer. The difference in naming latency between swapped nonwords and old nonwords demonstrates associative priming, whereas the difference between swapped and new nonwords reflects subunit priming. The magnitude of both effects is similar in young and old.

differences in priming are not statistically significant, they often favor young adults. Findings of small, albeit unreliable, age differences favoring the young may indicate that there are real differences in the processes underlying priming which most studies lack the power to detect. Many of the studies reviewed here used quite small Ns (see Table 10.1). Indeed, of the studies reporting reliable age differences, some had quite large samples (Davis et al., 1990; Hultsch et al., 1991). However, large sample sizes do not guarantee findings of age differences (Park & Shaw, 1992), and studies with small sample sizes sometimes find age effects in priming (Abbenhuis et al., 1990; Howard, 1988). Given the considerable variability of outcomes, we felt that combining results across studies would provide a clearer understanding of the magnitude of possible age differences in performance on a variety of indirect measures of memory. These considerations led us to undertake a meta-analysis.

THE META-ANALYSIS

Studies included in the meta-analysis met the following criteria:

1. All stimulus materials were verbal (i.e., nonpictorial) materials.

2. The indirect memory measure was a repetition priming task in that a previously presented item appeared in whole or in part on the test. For item priming studies, these tasks included homophone spelling, word stem and word fragment completion, word identification, and word pronunciation. For associative priming, the tasks included word stem completion, nonword pronunciation, lexical decision, and item recognition. This criterion led to the exclusion of studies in which the study items were not re-presented at test in whole or in part (Light & Albertson, 1989) and of conditions in which study items were generated by the subject rather than presented by the experimenter (Java & Gardiner, 1991). Moreover, because one of our goals was to determine whether the magnitude of any observed age differences in repetition priming varied as a function of task type, we included only those cases in which there were at least two experiments using a given task; this eliminated the Java (in press) study, which used anagram solution as a measure.

3. The comparison group of subjects for each study consisted of at least one group of young adults (18–40 years) and a group of healthy, community-dwelling older adults (60+ years). If a study included other comparison groups (e.g., middle-aged adults), data from these groups were not included.

Published studies rarely gave all of the information needed to carry out a meta-analysis. When information was missing, we requested it from authors of papers less than 5 years old. In the end, we had usable information from 33 separate experiments for which an effect size could be calculated. These studies included a total of 1,940 research participants, 936 young and 1,004 old. For each experiment, an effect size was calculated for the age difference in priming. In some cases the effect size could be computed directly from the reported means and standard deviations, using the formula for the standardized effect size (g) in Hedges and Olkin (1985). When the appropriate means and standard deviations were not reported, effect sizes were calculated from F, t, or r statistics (i.e., the inferential statistics for the age difference in priming), using conversion formulas given by Wolf (1986). On occasion, researchers reported priming scores for two or more different experimental conditions. In these instances, separate effect sizes were calculated for each of these conditions, and a weighted mean effect size was then calculated for the entire experiment. The effect sizes calculated according to the procedures just outlined all provide biased estimators of the true effect sizes. A correction factor (Hedges, 1984) was applied to the g values to produce unbiased estimates of effect sizes (d). For each of these d values, 95% confidence intervals were obtained (Hedges & Olkin, 1985). The unbiased effect sizes and 95% confidence intervals for each experiment are given in Table 10.1.[1]

Before pooling effect sizes from individual experiments to obtain a mean effect size for the entire collection of studies included in the meta-analysis, it was

---

[1] We would be happy to provide interested readers with a more complete rendition of the details of the meta-analysis.

TABLE 10.1
Sample Sizes, Effect Sizes, and 95% Confidence Intervals for Each Experiment
in the Meta-Analysis

Experiment	N Young	N Old	d	95% Confidence Intervals Lower Limit	Upper Limit
Item Priming					
Spelling Bias					
Davis et al. (1990, Exp. 1)[a]	45	21	.808	.272	1.344
Howard (1988b, Exp. 1)[a]	12	12	.952	.108	1.797
Howard (1988b, Exp. 1)[a,b]	24	24	.361	-.210	.931
Howard (1988b, Exp. 3)[a]	24	24	-.113	-.679	.453
Rose et al. (1986)[a]	16	16	1.175	.424	1.925
Word Stem / Fragment Completion					
Chiarello & Hoyer (1988)[b]	36	36	.657	.182	1.131
Davis et al. (1990, Exp. 2)	47	62	1.099	.693	1.505
Hultsch et al. (1991)[b]	96	203	.441	.196	.686
Java & Gardiner (1991, Exp. 1)[b]	16	16	.270	-.426	.966
Java & Gardiner (1991, Exp. 2)[b]	16	16	.188	-.506	.883
Light & Singh (1987, Exp. 1)[a,b]	32	32	.322	-.171	.815
Light & Singh (1987, Exp. 2)[a,b]	16	16	.528	-.177	1.233
Light, Singh, & Capps (1986)[a]	32	32	.308	-.184	.801
Park & Shaw (1992)[b]	51	65	.164	-.203	.531
Perceptual Identification					
Abbenhuis et al. (1990, Exp. 2)[a]	11	11	.680	-.180	1.539
Hashtroudi et al. (1991, Exp 1a)[a]	20	20	.140	-.480	.760
Hashtroudi et al (1991, Exp. 2a)[a]	30	10	.192	-.525	.909
Light & Singh (1987, Exp. 3)[a,b]	32	32	.411	-.084	.906
Light et al. (1992, Exp. 1)[a]	32	32	.476	-.021	.973
Light et al. (1992, Exp. 2)[a]	32	32	-.160	-.651	.331
Word Naming					
Light & LaVoie (1992, Exp. 1)[a]	24	24	.337	-.233	.907
Light & LaVoie (1992, Exp. 2)[a]	36	24	-.338	-.858	.182
Associative Priming					
Word Stem Completion					
Howard et al. (1991, Exp. 1)[b]	20	20	1.088	.424	1.752
Howard et al. (1991, Exp. 2)[b]	20	20	.143	-.478	.764
Howard et al. (1991, Exp. 3)[b]	24	24	.389	-.183	.960
Nonword Naming					
Light & LaVoie (1992, Exp. 1)[a]	24	24	.332	-.237	.901
Light & LaVoie (1992, Exp. 2)[a]	36	24	.133	-.384	.650
Light & LaVoie (1992, Exp. 3)[a]	24	24	.078	-.488	.644
Light & LaVoie (1992, Exp. 4)	18	18	-.047	-.701	.606
Lexical Decision					
Nilsson et al. (1989)[b]	10	10	-.453	-1.340	.435
Whetstone (1991)[b]	16	16	.693	-.020	1.406
Item Recognition					
Howard et al. (1986, Exp. 1)[a,b]	32	32	.219	-.273	.710
Howard et al. (1986, Exp. 2)[a,b]	32	32	.811	.302	1.321

Note. Negative effect sizes indicate greater priming for older adults.

[a]Effect size calculated for recognition.

[b]Effect size calculated for recall.

first necessary to determine whether the effect sizes were homogeneous, that is, whether it was reasonable to treat them as estimates of a common effect size. To do this, we used the procedures outlined in Hedges and Olkin (1985) for calculating the homogeneity of effect sizes across studies. The homogeneity statistic Q has a chi-square distribution with $k - 1$ degrees of freedom, with k equal to the number of studies included in the analysis. When using this procedure, studies can be partitioned into groups based on theoretical importance, with the between-groups estimate (Q_B) providing an index of the extent to which effect sizes differ across groups, and the within-group estimate (Q_W) providing an index of the extent to which a single effect size is representative of a group of studies. The first step in this analysis is to determine if all studies (ignoring hypothesized grouping factors) share a common effect size, by computing Q_T. If this value is significant, it can be assumed that the studies do not share a common effect size, and studies must be partitioned into groups as described in the foregoing discussion. If this partitioning reveals that the effect sizes are heterogeneous (i.e., Q_W is significant), then the studies can be further partitioned until homogeneity is achieved, and an appropriate categorical model can be fitted to the data.

We used this procedure because we believed that the effect sizes for item priming and associative priming might not be comparable. A test of the overall homogeneity statistic supported this belief, $Q_T(32) = 56.34$, $p < .05$. When we checked for homogeneity within item priming tasks, employing procedures suggested by Hedges and Olkin (1985, Chapter 12), we found that one study was an outlier (Davis et al., 1990, Experiment 2.).[2] This study was deleted from the data set and a new overall homogeneity statistic was calculated. This new $Q_T(31) = 43.58$, $.05 < p < .10$, permitting us to conclude that all the studies shared a common effect size. That is, when we eliminated the one outlier, it was not necessary to partition studies into those dealing with item priming and those dealing with associative priming.

Having determined that the effect sizes with which we were dealing were now homogeneous, we calculated an estimate of the weighted mean effect size, d_+, according to methods outlined in Hedges and Olkin (1985, p. 152). The value of d_+ was .338, with the 95% confidence interval for this effect size being .244 to .433. This confidence interval does not include zero, as it would if there were no age differences on indirect measures of memory. The obtained value of d_+ is consonant with a small to moderate effect size for age differences in repetition priming. Because we were interested in possible differences across types of priming and among specific tasks within types, we also calculated weighted mean effect sizes and confidence intervals for item and associative priming studies and for subgroupings of studies within these classes. These are given in

---

[2]The procedures for determining outliers take into account both sample size and the value of d. Hence, Davis et al. (1990), Experiment 2, was an outlier but Rose et al. (1986) with a larger d but a smaller sample size was not.

TABLE 10.2
Effect Sizes and 95% Confidence Intervals for Item and Associative Priming and for Specific Tasks
Within Type of Priming

Classification	d	95% Confidence Intervals	
		Lower Limit	Upper Limit
Item priming	.340	.229	.451
Spelling bias	.544	.265	.822
Word stem/fragment completion	.375	.222	.528
Perceptual identification	.253	.019	.487
Word naming	-.031	-.415	.353
Associative Priming	.334	.155	.512
Word stem completion	.508	.153	.863
Nonword naming	.134	-.151	.420
Lexical decision	.243	-.313	.780
Item recognition	.504	.150	.858

Note. Negative effect sizes indicate greater priming for older adults.

Table 10.2. Given the lack of heterogeneity in effect sizes and the small number of experiments in some groupings, these values should be treated as suggestive, rather than as reflecting true differences between types of priming or among classes of tasks. We nonetheless refer to these when discussing theoretical issues when we believe it would serve a heuristic purpose to do so.

Before turning to theoretical concerns, however, there are three points we need to make. First, although we obtained a small to moderate effect size for repetition priming, this finding cannot unequivocally be construed as evidence for real age differences in the processes underlying performance on indirect measures of memory. Priming tasks are subject to contamination by an intrusion of deliberate recollection. Young adults perform better than older adults on tasks requiring deliberate recollection. They may consequently be more likely to notice that they are producing or encountering previously seen list members while performing priming tasks, and having noticed this, they may be more likely to continue doing so intentionally. Tasks that require production of the target word, such as homophone spelling (Howard, 1988), word association (Light & Albertson, 1989), and word stem or word fragment completion, may be particularly susceptible to this problem. For instance, Howard (1988) found age differences on a homophone spelling task in which people frequently indicated their awareness of the relation between the studied items and the spelling test but not on a test (sentence production) that required homophone spelling without making it the focus of the task. Light and Albertson (1989) found that their small (unreliable) age difference in priming in exemplar generation pretty much disappeared altogether when only people who explicitly denied attempting to produce list members were included in the analysis. Chiarello and Hoyer (1988), who found a reliable age difference in priming in a word stem completion task, used dashes to indicate the length of the word to be produced, a procedure that seems likely to encourage subjects to treat the task as a cued-recall task. However, in two additional studies, the presence or absence of age-related differences in priming in word stem completion was unaffected by awareness (Howard et al., 1991; Park & Shaw, 1992). The role of contamination by deliberate recollection in producing age differences on indirect measures of memory is thus not yet fully understood.

Second, the effect size for our collection of indirect measures of memory was considerably smaller than that for either recognition or recall. We were able to calculate effect sizes for recognition in 17 experiments and for recall in 16 experiments (see Table 10.1). For recognition, we obtained a weighted mean effect size of .685, with a 95% confidence interval of .549 to .820. For recall, the weighted mean effect size was 1.050, with a 95% confidence interval of .920 to 1.180. Both of these are substantially larger than the weighted mean effect size of .338 for repetition priming, and the confidence intervals for the recognition and recall data do not overlap that for the priming data. Thus, the generalization that emerges from our meta-analysis is that while there may be age-related differences on indirect measures of memory, they are much smaller than those for direct measures. We are left with the task of explaining why this should be so.

Third, the mean weighted effect sizes for item and associative priming were virtually identical, .340 for item priming and .334 for associative priming. Given the small number of studies included in the meta-analysis, especially for associative priming, this result must be viewed with some caution. It is interesting that for those measures used in both item and associative priming studies, the effect sizes are rather similar—but slightly larger for associative priming. For word stem and fragment completion, the effect sizes were .375 for item priming and .508 for associative priming. For naming, the comparable values were .031 and .134 for item and associative priming, respectively. We clearly need further studies on associative priming, preferably studies in which the same young and older adults are compared on both item and associative priming.

THEORETICAL ISSUES

Why should indirect measures of memory produce smaller age differences than direct measures? Here we describe and evaluate three explanations that have been offered. These are (a) the environmental support hypothesis, (b) the multiple memory systems hypothesis, and (c) the spared activation/impaired contextual processing hypothesis.

The Environmental Support Hypothesis

Measures of memory may be either primarily data driven or primarily conceptually driven (Jacoby, 1983; Srinivas & Roediger, 1990). Performance on data-driven tests depends on the physical similarity between the materials studied and the test items and is relatively immune to the effects of orienting tasks; performance on conceptually driven tests is less affected by the physical match between study and test conditions and is sensitive to levels-of-processing effects. Most (but not all) indirect measures of memory are data driven, whereas recall and recognition are heavily (but not exclusively) conceptually driven. With regard to aging, Craik (1983) has hypothesized that sizable age-related differences in memory should be found on tasks that require self-initiated constructive operations and offer little environmental support for retrieval (e.g., free recall), whereas age-related differences should be minimal on tasks that provide substantial environmental support (e.g., perceptual identification).

One way of interpreting Craik's hypothesis is that age differences should be smaller on data driven than on conceptually driven memory tests. Indeed, there is evidence that among direct measures of memory, those that afford more retrieval support show smaller age-related differences. That is, both the results of Craik and McDowd (1987) and our own estimates of effect sizes show smaller age differences for recognition than for recall. We can also examine the results of our meta-analysis for evidence on this issue. Here we are engaged in speculation, partly because the small number of studies in each category no doubt makes the mean effect sizes and confidence intervals unstable, and partly because our assumptions about how much retrieval support a given task affords are based pretty much on intuition. Word and nonword naming tasks and lexical decision tasks would, on the face of it, appear to offer more retrieval support than word stem and word fragment completion or identification of visually degraded words. Similarly, item recognition should be pretty high in retrieval support because the entire item is presented at test. In homophone spelling tasks, the test word is presented auditorily and subjects must produce a spelling; it is harder to know how to assess the amount of retrieval support for this task, so we do not consider it further. The ordering of effect sizes for the remaining item priming tasks seems to be fairly consistent with the environmental support hypothesis in that the confidence interval for naming includes zero and the lower limit of the confidence interval for word identification is near zero, with the effect sizes for word stem completion and word fragment completion being larger. For the associative priming tasks, naming and lexical decision both have confidence intervals including zero, whereas neither item recognition nor word stem completion does. These data, incomplete as they are, are consistent with the retrieval support hypothesis.[3]

---

[3]We should also note that, with the exception of the word stem completion tasks, all of the associative priming tasks involve latency measures, whereas many of the item priming tasks involve accuracy measures. Older adults are known to be slower than young adults on many cognitive tasks. Because they are slower on baseline items, they have more opportunity to show reduced response times on repeated items than do the young who are already responding very rapidly on baseline items. Hence, it is possible that the similarity in priming shown by young and old with latency measures reflects general slowing.

Craik's (1983) statement of the environmental support hypothesis deals with two variables that we believe are best treated as separable, namely amount of environmental support for retrieval afforded by the memory task and the need for self-initiated constructive operations. In this formulation of the environmental support hypothesis, these two factors were considered to be negatively correlated—that is, memory tasks that have high demands for self-initiated constructive operations are the same as those that offer the least environmental support for retrieval. However, it is possible to hold environmental support constant across tasks while varying the processing requirements of memory tasks. As we have already seen, when the amount of retrieval support is held constant by using the same cues for both direct and indirect tests, the magnitude of the age difference on direct measures is generally much greater. The Light and Singh (1987, Experiment 2) study described earlier compared performance on word stem completion and cued recall using the same three-letter stems as cues for both tasks. Reliable age-related differences were obtained for cued recall but not for word stem completion, suggesting that the critical variable is not amount of retrieval support but intention to remember. Other studies controlling the amount of retrieval support across type of memory task reinforce this conclusion (Howard, 1991; Java & Gardiner, 1991, Experiment 1; Light & Albertson, 1989; Park & Shaw, 1992; but see Chiarello and Hoyer, 1988, for a different outcome).

It is also possible to hold intention to remember constant within a task while varying amount of retrieval support. Park and Shaw (1992) performed an experiment in which they varied the number of letters available as clues for cued recall and word stem completion from two to four. Cued recall performance was higher in the young than in the old, but the age difference in priming was not reliable. More important, although increasing the number of cues improved performance on both tasks, the benefit accruing from greater retrieval support was the same across age. If anything, increasing the number of letters in the cue was more helpful to the young than to the old, contrary to the predictions of the environmental support hypothesis and again underscoring the importance of the role of intentional remembering.

Finally, the environmental support hypothesis, in its original formulation, predicts that performance on conceptually driven indirect memory tasks should be more affected by aging than performance on data driven indirect memory tests and that performance on conceptually driven tasks should be similar for direct and indirect conceptually driven tests. There have been to date no studies explicitly comparing young and old on data driven and conceptually driven indirect memory tests within the same experiment. However, the second part of this prediction was tested in the Light and Albertson (1989) study discussed earlier, which compared performance on two conceptually driven tests, exemplar generation and cued recall. The amount of retrieval support was the same across classes of tasks but there was no re-presentation of all or part of the studied items in either. As we saw earlier, reliable age differences were found in cued recall but not in exemplar generation. Thus, appeal to notions of environmental support cannot explain why conceptual priming is relatively preserved in old age.

In sum, evidence for the environmental support hypothesis is mixed. Neither studies holding retrieval support constant across direct and indirect memory tasks nor studies holding intent to remember constant and varying amount of retrieval support provide evidence for this hypothesis. What these studies do show is that larger age differences are found on tasks that demand certain kinds of self-initiated constructive operations, namely, deliberate recollection, than on tasks that do not. They do not, however, reveal the nature of the processes that are called into play when deliberate recollection is attempted.

The Multiple Memory Systems Hypothesis

In accounting for the fact that anterograde amnesics show severe deficits in recall and recognition, but normal or near normal scores on measures of item priming (though not associative priming), Squire (1987) has hypothesized that the mechanisms supporting performance on direct and indirect memory measures are subserved by different brain systems. The view that different memory systems are differentially sensitive to aging has surfaced in at least two guises.

Tulving (1985) discussed a monohierarchical arrangement of three systems, with procedural memory containing semantic memory (knowledge needed for language use) as a specialized subsystem, and semantic memory in turn containing episodic memory (information about temporally dated episodes or events and the temporo-spatial relations among them) as a specialized subsystem. Mitchell (1989; also Chapter 8, this volume) proposed that only episodic memory is impaired in old age whereas both semantic and procedural memory are intact. In this view, repetition priming effects reflect processes occurring in procedural memory, and constancy across age in repetition priming therefore implies spared procedural memory. The evidence is not wholly consistent with this position. It is not clear that semantic memory is entirely preserved or that all aspects of episodic memory are impaired in old age (Light & Burke, 1988). For instance, word-finding difficulties are proverbial in old age (for a review see Light, 1992). And, oddly enough, preserved repetition priming can be interpreted as evidence that encoding new information in episodic memory is not a problem for the old— only retrieval. Moreover, Squire (1987) has identified several different categories of procedural learning, including cognitive skill learning, perceptual learning, motor skill learning, and classical conditioning, in addition to repetition priming. A review of the aging literature suggests that these other varieties of procedural memory are not all spared in old age (e.g., Charness, 1987; Welford, 1985; Woodruff-Pak & Thompson, 1988; for a review see Light, 1991). Thus, it is an oversimplification to argue that procedural memory is wholly spared in old age.

More recently, Tulving and Schacter (1990) have argued for the existence of a perceptual representation system (PRS) that functions at a presemantic level.

Preserved repetition priming then points to the sparing of this system in old age. Conceptual priming, on the other hand, is mediated by the semantic system and has its basis in "the modification of, or adding of new information to, semantic memory" (p. 304). Difficulties in the deliberate recollection of new information arise from impairments in episodic memory. For instance, word stem completion instructions induce a perceptual mode of cognitive operation, calling the PRS into play, whereas cued-recall instructions induce matching operations in episodic memory. It is the latter, but presumably not the former, that are impaired in old age. This view has some obvious parallels with the environmental support hypothesis—perceptual similarity between study and test items is an important determinant of repetition priming in both approaches.

According to Tulving and Schacter, one characteristic of the PRS is hyperspecificity. Any changes in the physical appearance of an item between study and test should reduce the amount of priming. Certainly it is well known that changes in modality of presentation between study and test reduce priming (see Richardson-Klavehn and Bjork, 1988, for a review), and we have recently shown that this is equally true in young and old (Light et al., 1992). However, modality change usually does not completely eliminate repetition priming in perceptual identification tasks. Residual priming (called nonspecific priming by Kirsner, Dunn, & Standen, 1989), which occurs in both young and old, must then be subserved by some other memory system and may be different in nature (i.e., conceptual). This nonspecific component of priming could be attributed to activation of nodes in semantic memory. The total priming effect then must reflect the expression of two memory systems, PRS and the semantic system, which act in concert to produce priming and which are both preserved in old age.

A further wrinkle here is that conceptual priming is said to depend on modification of or addition of new information to semantic memory. It is not clear just what these modifications might be, but to the extent that new learning is involved, we might expect the magnitude of conceptual priming to be smaller in the old than in the young. Light and Albertson (1989) found age constancy in conceptual priming, but we clearly need more information on this point. Keane, Gabrieli, Fennema, Growdon, and Corkin (1991) have shown that in early Alzheimer's disease perceptual identification is spared while priming in word stem completion is impaired. They interpret their results as evidence for the operation of two memory systems, a structural-perceptual system mediated by regions of the occipital lobe and a lexical-semantic system mediated by regions of the temporoparietal cortex. Interestingly enough, although most researchers treat word stem completion as a datadriven task because it is insensitive to manipulations of orienting task and produces a modality effect (Graf & Mandler, 1984; Graf, Shimamura, & Squire, 1985), Keane et al. class word stem completion as a lexical-semantic or conceptually driven task and note several studies in which word stem completion has shown an effect of orienting task (see also Challis and Brodbeck, 1992). The question then arises as to whether normally aging adults also show less priming in word stem completion than in perceptual identification. The results of our meta-analysis (see Table 10.2) do not shed a great deal of light on this issue. Although naming visually intact words shows the smallest age difference, with identification of degraded words showing the next smallest difference, the magnitudes of the mean weighted effect sizes for word identification (.253) and word stem and word-fragment completion (.375) are not far apart. Solid answers to questions about the dissociability of memory systems and the relative effects of aging on different priming tasks await studies that systematically compare individuals on a variety of tasks within the same experiment.

Spared Activation and Impaired Processing of Contextual Information

Many two-process theories of memory differentiate between mechanisms dependent on familiarity, activation, or perceptual fluency and mechanisms dependent on memory for new associations, either associations between events experienced together or between events and elements of the contexts in which they occur (e.g., Gillund & Shiffrin, 1984; Humphreys, Bain, & Pike, 1989; Jacoby & Dallas, 1981; Mandler, 1980). In such theories, activation, familiarity, or perceptual fluency mechanisms have been posited to underlie repetition priming phenomena, whereas context-dependent processes are thought to underlie recall and recognition (e.g., Graf & Mandler, 1984; Jacoby & Dallas, 1981). On this argument, repetition priming phenomena require only the activation of an existing representation in memory during encoding, whereas recall and recognition depend on more elaborative processing of contextual information during encoding (e.g., Graf & Mandler, 1984).

The relative sparing of repetition priming, together with impairment in recall and recognition, would then imply that activation processes are intact in old age whereas contextual information processing is not (Light et al., 1986; Light & Singh, 1987; for related views see Balota, Duchek, & Paullin, 1989; Rabinowitz, 1984). Evidence that activation is spared in old age also comes from studies of semantic priming in lexical decision and word naming, which show age constancy in the extent or breadth of priming (e.g., Balota & Duchek, 1988; Howard, McAndrews, & Lasaga, 1981; Nebes, Boller, & Holland, 1986).

There is abundant evidence that information about the contextual details of events is less available to the old than to the young. Here we are using the concept of context broadly to include all aspects of the circumstances of an experience other than its meaning. Older adults are less good at recalling whether information has been presented auditorily or visually (Kausler & Puckett, 1981a; Lehman & Mellinger, 1984; Light et al., 1992; McIntyre & Craik, 1987), in upper or lower case letters (Kausler & Puckett, 1980, 1981a), in a male or a female voice (Kausler & Puckett, 1981b), or in a particular color (Park & Puglisi, 1985). They have more trouble in remembering whether they read a word or generated it from a clue (Mitchell, Hunt, & Schmitt, 1989; Rabinowitz, 1989), in remembering whether they learned a fact in an experimental setting or knew it before (Janowsky, Shimamura, & Squire, 1989; McIntyre & Craik, 1987), in deciding whether they thought or said a word (Hashtroudi, Johnson, & Chrosniak, 1989), and in remembering which orienting task they used to encode particular words (Brigham & Pressley, 1988). Further evidence about source monitoring difficulties comes from studies showing that older adults are more susceptible to the effects of misleading information after they have witnessed a series of events (Cohen & Faulkner, 1989) and from studies showing that older adults are more likely than young adults to call a previously seen name or face "famous" when it is encountered later (Bartlett, Strater, & Fulton, 1991; Dywan & Jacoby, 1990). The latter finding suggests that perceptual fluency or activation processes are operative but source monitoring is less good in the old. Finally, Kausler (1990) has reviewed the extensive literature confirming age-related impairment in memory for spatial and temporal information.

The evidence reviewed thus far is consistent with the view that the relative preservation of repetition priming coupled with larger decrements in recognition and recall implies spared activation processes and impaired contextual information processing in old age. Because familiarity mechanisms normally play a larger role in recognition than in recall (Mandler, 1980), our finding of a smaller mean weighted effect size for recognition than for recall is not surprising. What recall usually requires, but what is more optional in recognition, and not demanded at all in repetition priming tasks, is a decision that some experience took place in a particular context, and it is this aspect of remembering that is compromised in old age. The finding that young and old show similar item priming effects, but that the difference between cued recall and word stem completion or exemplar generation is smaller for older adults, suggests that activation plays a greater role in recall for the old than for the young. Our assumption here is that cued recall involves a mix of generation processes dependent on activation and recognition processes dependent on context checking (see Jacoby and Hollingshead, 1990, for a related position). Cued-recall instructions invoke context-dependent mechanisms, which are less effective in the old, so that the relative contribution of activation processes is greater for them.

Jennings and Jacoby (in press) used an ingenious methodology to obtain separate estimates of familiarity and intentional recollection within a single paradigm. They gave young and older adults a list of nonfamous names to read. They then presented subjects with a mixed list of old and new nonfamous names together with some famous names. Subjects were first asked to indicate which names were famous and were told that all the old names on the test were really the names of famous people, so that if they remembered reading a name earlier, they could be sure it was famous. Following this test, they were told that all of the old names were in actuality nonfamous, and to avoid choosing as famous any name that they recollected reading before. These two tests, the inclusion test and the exclusion test, pit familiarity and recollection against each other. The contribution of recollection to calling a name famous was estimated by taking the difference between the probability of responding famous to old names on the two tests; the estimated value was higher for the young than the old. However, estimates of the contribution of familiarity were very similar across age, a finding consonant with the view that activation is spared in the old.

The Jennings and Jacoby result is, however, not altogether consistent with the finding of a small to moderate age effect size for indirect measures in our meta-analysis. If repetition priming tasks depend solely on activation mechanisms, we might have expected to obtain a confidence interval including zero, but we did not. Jacoby (1991) has argued that indirect memory tests are not pure measures of familiarity and that task dissociation strategies such as those used in memory and aging studies cannot isolate this process (or any other process). To the extent that performance on indirect memory measures is mediated by two or more processes, some spared and some impaired in old age, it is not surprising that age differences are observed on these tasks. As noted earlier, intrusion of deliberate recollection into indirect memory tasks would be one way in which such an outcome could be produced.

Overall, the weight of the evidence strongly favors the view that activation is relatively spared in old age whereas contextual processing is impaired. Indeed, this is the view that we believe holds the most promise for further development. There are nevertheless three reasons for caution in accepting this position uncritically. First, the concept of activation, as we have been using it, refers to activation of preexisting abstract memory representations. By itself, this approach cannot explain priming of novel stimuli (e.g., nonwords) or new associations for which there are no preexisting memory representations. Once new representations have been formed, activation mechanisms can account for priming, but additional machinery is needed to deal with the formation of the connections themselves. This issue is important here because our meta-analysis yielded similar effect sizes for item and associative priming, which were smaller than those for recall and recognition (see also Chapter 8 by Mitchell and Chapter 14 by Bowers & Schacter, this volume). Graf and Schacter (1989) have proposed that encoding processes that promote unitization of unrelated words are necessary for priming of new associations, whereas grouping operations that increase associative links between pairs (and therefore increase the number of retrieval routes linking pairs) mediate cued recall. This approach has not yet been applied to studies comparing young and older adults on direct and indirect measures of associative learning.

Second, studies in which young and older adults are interrogated about (incidental) contextual information have almost universally failed to equate young and old on memory for target information, leaving open the possibility that older adults have a generalized memory deficit. For instance, people may be asked to indicate whether particular items were presented in a male or in a female voice; if brand new items that serve as catch trials and permit an assessment of whether there are age differences in memory for the items themselves are not included on the test, it is impossible to tell whether the poorer performance of older adults is due to faulty memory for the items themselves or for the contextual detail being tested. Denney, Miller, Dew, and Levav (1991) found that memory for context is no more impaired than memory for target information, suggesting that a general memory deficit does encompass both target and context memory. If a specific deficit in contextual information processing underlies problems in recall and recognition, then equating young and old on target memory should eliminate age differences in memory for context. Schacter, Kaszniak, Kihlstrom, and Valdiserri (1991) found such an effect but it was not consistent across conditions—in some conditions, equating age groups on target recall did not eliminate age differences in source memory. This suggests that source monitoring and target memory are subserved by different memory systems altogether (cf. Craik, Morris, Morris, & Loewen, 1990). In any case, the precise relation between target and context memory is not yet fully understood.

Third, memory for contextual information in old age has been assessed almost exclusively by direct measures, that is, by asking people to recollect some particular aspect of the study experience such as its modality. Given that memory impairment is much greater for deliberate recollection of target information than for repetition priming, it is possible that age differences in memory for context would also be reduced by using an indirect test. Light et al. (1992) investigated this matter by comparing young and older adults on both direct and indirect measures of memory for the modality in which words were presented. In each of two studies, half of the words were presented auditorily and half were presented visually. The direct measure of memory for context was a recognition memory test in which subjects not only judged whether an item was old or new but also indicated the modality in which previously studied items had been presented. The indirect measure of memory for context was a perceptual identification test, with the test modality matching the study modality for half of the items and being different for the other half. For one experiment, the indirect measure of memory for context was visual identification of briefly presented words; for the other, it was ability to identify words presented auditorily in noise. Repetition priming was reduced in both studies when there was a mismatch between study and test modalities, but the magnitude of this effect was the same across age. In contrast, memory for modality as assessed on the recognition test showed an age difference favoring the young. This outcome indicates that age decrements in intentional recollection of contextual information can coexist with unimpaired utilization of contextual information in tasks such as perceptual identification that do not require deliberate recollection of that information. It also highlights the need for more careful specification of the role of context in memory. Theories that postulate context-dependent memory mechanisms generally treat that information as a type of new association without indicating how or where such information is stored in memory. Finding a dissociation between direct and indirect measures of memory for context forces us to develop models that are more precise about both the representation of contextual information and the ways in which contextual information is used in different modes of remembering.

ACKNOWLEDGMENTS

The research reported here was supported by National Institute on Aging grant R37 AG02452. We are grateful to Mark Lipsey for advice about the intricacies of meta-analysis and to Darlene Howard, Christine Chiarello, William Hoyer, John Gardiner, Hasker Davis, and Denise Park for providing us with information needed to compute effect sizes for the meta-analysis.

REFERENCES

Abbenhuis, M. A., Raaijmakers, W. G. M., Raaijmakers, J. G. W., & van Woerden, G. J. M. (1990). Episodic memory in dementia of the Alzheimer type and in normal ageing: Similar impairment in automatic processing. *Quarterly Journal of Experimental Psychology, 42A*, 569–583.

Balota, D. A., & Duchek, J. M. (1988). Age-related differences in lexical access, spreading activation, and simple pronunciation. *Psychology and Aging, 3*, 84–93.

Balota, D. A., Duchek, J. M., & Paullin, R. (1989). Age-related differences in the impact of spacing, lag, and retention interval. *Psychology and Aging, 4*, 3–9.

Bartlett, J. C., Strater, L., & Fulton, A. (1991). False recency and false fame of faces in young adulthood and old age. *Memory & Cognition, 19*, 177–188.

Brigham, M. C., & Pressley, M. (1988). Cognitive monitoring and strategy choice in younger and older adults. *Psychology and Aging, 3*, 249–257.

Burke, D. M., & Light, L. L. (1981). Memory and aging: The role of retrieval processes. *Psychological Bulletin, 90*, 513–546.

Challis, B. H., & Brodbeck, D. R. (1992). Level of processing affects priming in word fragment completion. *Journal of Experimental Psychology: Learning, Memory, and Cognition, 18*, 595–607.

Charness, N. (1987). Component processes in bridge bidding and novel problem-solving tasks. *Canadian Journal of Psychology, 41*, 223–243.

Chiarello, C., & Hoyer, W. J. (1988). Adult age differences in implicit and explicit memory: Time course and encoding effects. *Psychology and Aging, 3*, 358–366.

Cohen, G., & Faulkner, D. (1989). Age differences in source forgetting: Effects on reality monitoring and eyewitness testimony. *Psychology and Aging, 4*, 10–17.

Craik, F. I. M. (1983). On the transfer of information from temporary to permanent memory. *Philosophical Transactions of the Royal Society of London, B302*, 341–359.

Craik, F. I. M., & McDowd, J. M. (1987). Age differences in recall and recognition. *Journal of Experimental Psychology: Learning, Memory, and Cognition, 13*, 474–479.

Craik, F. I. M., Morris, L. W., Morris, R. G., & Loewen, E. R. (1990). Relations between source amnesia and frontal lobe functioning in older adults. *Psychology and Aging, 5*, 148–151.

Davis, H. P., Cohen, A., Gandy, M., Colombo, P., Van Dusseldorp, G., Simolke, N., & Romano, J. (1990). Lexical priming deficits as a function of age. *Behavioral Neuroscience, 104*, 288–297.

Denney, N. W., Miller, B. V., Dew, J. R., & Levav, A. L. (1991). An adult developmental study of contextual memory. *Journal of Gerontology: Psychological Sciences, 46,* P44–50.

Dick, M. B., Kean, M.-L., & Sands, D. (1989). Memory for internally generated words in Alzheimer-type dementia: Breakdown in encoding and semantic memory. *Brain and Cognition, 9,* 88–108.

Dywan, J., & Jacoby, L. (1990). Effects of aging on source monitoring: Differences in susceptibility to false fame. *Psychology and Aging, 5,* 379–387.

Gillund, G., & Shiffrin, R. M. (1984). A retrieval model for both recognition and recall. *Psychological Review, 91,* 1–67.

Graf, P., & Mandler, G. (1984). Activation makes words more accessible, but not necessarily more retrievable. *Journal of Verbal Learning and Verbal Behavior, 23,* 553–568.

Graf, P., & Schacter, D. S. (1985). Implicit and explicit memory for new associations in normal and amnesic subjects. *Journal of Experimental Psychology: Learning, Memory, and Cognition, 11,* 501–518.

Graf, P., & Schacter, D. L. (1989). Unitization and grouping mediate dissociations in memory for new associations. *Journal of Experimental Psychology: Learning, Memory, and Cognition, 15,* 930–940.

Graf, P., Shimamura, A. P., & Squire, L. R. (1985). Priming across modalities and priming across category levels: Extending the domain of preserved function in amnesia. *Journal of Experimental Psychology: Learning, Memory, and Cognition, 11,* 386–396.

Hashtroudi, S., Chrosniak, L. D., & Schwartz, B. L. (1991). Effects of aging on priming and skill learning. *Psychology and Aging, 6,* 605–615.

Hashtroudi, S., Johnson, M. K., & Chrosniak, L. D. (1989). Aging and source monitoring. *Psychology and Aging, 4,* 106–112.

Hedges, L. R. (1984). Advances in statistical methods for meta-analysis. In J. W. Yeaton & P. M. Wortman (Eds.), *Issues in data synthesis* (pp. 25–42). San Francisco: Jossey-Bass.

Hedges, L. R., & Olkin, I. (1985). *Statistical methods for meta-analysis.* New York: Academic Press.

Howard, D. V. (1988). Implicit and explicit assessment of cognitive aging. In M. L. Howe & C. J. Brainerd (Eds.), *Cognitive development in adulthood: Progress in cognitive development research* (pp. 3–37). New York: Springer-Verlag.

Howard, D. V. (1991). Implicit memory: An expanding picture of cognitive aging. In K. W. Schaie & M. P. Lawton (Eds.), *Annual Review of Gerontology and Geriatrics, 11,* 1–22.

Howard, D. V., Fry, A. F., & Brune, C. M. (1991). Aging and memory for new associations: Direct versus indirect measures. *Journal of Experimental Psychology: Learning, Memory, and Cognition, 17,* 779–792.

Howard, D. V., Heisey, J. G., & Shaw, R. J. (1986). Aging and the priming of newly learned associations. *Developmental Psychology, 22,* 78–85.

Howard, D. V., & Howard, J. H., Jr. (1989). Age differences in learning serial patterns. *Psychology and Aging, 4,* 357–364.

Howard, D. V., McAndrews, M. P., & Lasaga, M. I. (1981). Semantic priming of lexical decisions in young and old adults. *Journal of Gerontology, 36,* 707–714.

Hultsch, D. F. Masson, M. E. J., & Small, B. J. (1991). Adult age differences in direct and indirect tests of memory. *Journal of Gerontology: Psychological Sciences, 46,* P22–30.

Humphreys, M. S., Bain, J. D., & Pike, R. (1989). Different ways to cue a coherent memory system: A theory for episodic, semantic, and procedural tasks. *Psychological Review, 96,* 208–233.

Jacoby, L. L. (1983). Remembering the data: Analyzing interactive processes in reading. *Journal of Verbal Learning and Verbal Behavior, 22,* 485–508.

Jacoby, L. L. (1991). A process dissociation framework: Separating automatic from intentional uses of memory. *Journal of Memory and Language, 30,* 513–541.

Jacoby, L. L., & Dallas, M. (1981). On the relationship between autobiographical memory and perceptual learning. *Journal of Experimental Psychology: General, 110,* 306–340.

Jacoby, L. L., & Hollingshead, A. (1990). Toward a generate/recognize model of performance on direct and indirect tests of memory. *Journal of Memory and Language, 29,* 433–454.

Jacoby, L. L., & Witherspoon, D. (1982). Remembering without awareness. *Canadian Journal of Psychology, 36,* 300–324.

Janowsky, J. S., Shimamura, A. P., & Squire, L. R. (1989). Source memory impairment in patients with frontal lobe lesions. *Neuropsychologia, 27,* 1043–1056.

Java, R. I. (in press). Priming and aging: Evidence of preserved memory function in an anagram solution task. *American Journal of Psychology.*

Java, R. I., & Gardiner, J. M. (1991). Priming and aging: Further evidence of preserved memory function. *American Journal of Psychology, 104,* 89–100.

Jennings, J. M., & Jacoby, L. L. (in press). Automatic versus intentional uses of memory: Aging, attention, and control. *Psychology and Aging.*

Kausler, D. H. (1990). Automaticity of encoding and episodic memory processes. In E. A. Lovelace (Ed.), *Aging and cognition: Mental processes, self-awareness, and interventions* (pp. 29–67). Amsterdam: Elsevier.

Kausler, D. H., & Puckett, J. M. (1980). Adult age differences in recognition memory for a nonsemantic attribute. *Experimental Aging Research, 6,* 349–355.

Kausler, D. H., & Puckett, J. M. (1981a). Adult age differences in memory for modality attributes. *Experimental Aging Research, 7,* 117–125.

Kausler, D. H., & Puckett, J. M. (1981b). Adult age differences in memory for sex of voice. *Journal of Gerontology, 36,* 44–50.

Keane, M. M., Gabrieli, J. D. E., Fennema, A. C., Growdon, J. H., & Corkin, S. (1991). Evidence for a dissociation between perceptual and conceptual priming in Alzheimer's disease. *Behavioral Neuroscience, 105,* 326–342.

Kirsner, K., Dunn, J. C., & Standen, P. (1989). Domain-specific resources in word recognition. In S. Lewandowsky, J. C. Dunn, & K. Kirsner (Eds.), *Implicit memory: Theoretical issues* (pp. 99–122). Hillsdale, NJ: Lawrence Erlbaum Associates.

Lehman, E. B., & Mellinger, J. C. (1984). Effects of aging on memory for presentation modality. *Developmental Psychology, 20,* 1210–1217.

Light, L. L. (1991). Memory and aging: Four hypotheses in search of data. *Annual Review of Psychology, 42,* 333–376.

Light, L. L. (1992). The organization of memory in old age. In F. I. M. Craik & T. A. Salthouse (Eds.), *The handbook of aging and cognition* (pp. 111–165). Hillsdale, NJ: Lawrence Erlbaum Associates.

Light, L. L., & Albertson, S. A. (1989). Direct and indirect tests of memory for category exemplars in young and older adults. *Psychology and Aging, 4,* 487–492.

Light, L. L., & Burke, D. M. (1988). Patterns of language and memory in old age. In L. L. Light & D. M. Burke (Eds.), *Language, memory, and aging* (pp. 244–271). New York: Cambridge University Press.

Light, L. L., & LaVoie, D. (1992, April). *Repetition priming of nonwords in young and older adults: Evidence for formation of new associations?* Paper presented at the Cognitive Aging Conference, Atlanta, GA.

Light, L. L., LaVoie, D., Valencia-Laver, D., Albertson Owens, S. A., & Mead, G. (1992). Direct and indirect measures of memory for modality in young and older adults. *Journal of Experimental Psychology: Learning, Memory, and Cognition, 18,* 1284–1297.

Light, L. L., & Singh, A. (1987). Implicit and explicit memory in young and older adults. *Journal of Experimental Psychology: Learning, Memory, and Cognition, 13,* 531–541.

Light, L. L., Singh, A., & Capps, J. L. (1986). Dissociation of memory and awareness in young and older adults. *Journal of Clinical and Experimental Neuropsychology, 8,* 62–74.

Mandler, G. (1980). Recognizing: The judgment of previous occurrence. *Psychological Review, 87,* 252–271.

McIntyre, J. S., & Craik, F. I. M. (1987). Age differences in memory for item and source information. *Canadian Journal of Psychology, 41,* 175–192.

Mitchell, D. B. (1989). How many memory systems? Evidence from aging. *Journal of Experimental Psychology: Learning, Memory, and Cognition, 15,* 31–49.

Mitchell, D. B., Hunt, R. R., & Schmitt, F. A. (1986). The generation effect and reality monitoring: Evidence from dementia and normal aging. *Journal of Gerontology, 41,* 79–84.

Moscovitch, M. (1982). A neuropsychological approach to perception and memory in normal and pathological aging. In F. I. M. Craik & S. Trehub (Eds.), *Aging and cognitive processes* (pp. 55–78). New York: Plenum Press.

Moscovitch, M., Winocur, G., & McLachlan, D. (1986). Memory as assessed by recognition and reading time in normal and memory-impaired people with Alzheimer's disease and other neurological disorders. *Journal of Experimental Psychology: General, 115,* 331–347.

Musen, G., & Squire, L. R. (1991). Normal acquisition of novel verbal information in amnesia. *Journal of Experimental Psychology: Learning, Memory, and Cognition, 17,* 1095–1104.

Nebes, R. D., Boller, F., & Holland, A. (1986). Use of semantic context by patients with Alzheimer's disease. *Psychology and Aging, 1,* 261–269.

Nilsson, L.-G., Backman, L., & Karlsson, T. (1989). Priming and cued recall in elderly, alcohol intoxicated and sleep deprived subjects: A case of functionally similar memory deficits. *Psychological Medicine, 19,* 423–433.

Park, D. C., & Puglisi, J. T. (1985). Older adults' memory for the color of pictures and words. *Journal of Gerontology, 40,* 198–204.

Park, D. C., & Shaw, R. J. (1992). Effect of environmental support on implicit and explicit memory in young and old adults. *Psychology and Aging, 1,* 632–642.

Rabbitt, P. M. A. (1982). How do old people know what to do next? In F. I. M. Craik & S. Trehub (Eds.), *Aging and cognitive processes* (pp. 79–98). New York: Plenum Press.

Rabbitt, P. M. A. (1984). How old people prepare themselves for events which they expect. In H. Bouma & D. G. Bouwhuis (Eds.), *Attention and performance X: Control of language processes* (pp. 515–527). Hillsdale, NJ: Lawrence Erlbaum Associates.

Rabinowitz, J. C. (1984). Aging and recognition failure. *Journal of Gerontology, 39,* 65–71.

Rabinowitz, J. C. (1986). Priming in episodic memory. *Journal of Gerontology, 41,* 204–213.

Rabinowitz, J. C. (1989). Judgments of origin and generation effects: Comparisons between young and elderly adults. *Psychology and Aging, 4,* 259–268.

Richardson-Klavehn, A., & Bjork, R. A. (1988). Measures of memory. *Annual Review of Psychology, 39,* 475–543.

Rose, T. L., Yesavage, J. A., Hill, R. D., & Bower, G. H. (1986). Priming effects and recognition memory in young and elderly adults. *Experimental Aging Research, 12,* 31–37.

Salthouse, T. A. (1988). The role of processing resources in cognitive aging. In M. L. Howe & C. J. Brainerd (Eds.), *Cognitive development in adulthood: Progress in cognitive development research* (pp. 185–239). New York: Springer-Verlag.

Scarborough, D. L., Cortese, C., & Scarborough, H. S. (1977). Frequency and repetition effects in lexical memory. *Journal of Experimental Psychology: Learning, Memory, and Cognition, 3,* 1–17.

Schacter, D. L., Kaszniak, A. W., Kihlstrom, J. F., & Valdiserri, M. (1991). The relation between source memory and aging. *Psychology and Aging, 6,* 559–568.

Squire, L. R. (1987). *Memory and brain.* New York: Oxford University Press.

Srinivas, K., & Roediger, H. L., III. (1990). Classifying implicit memory tests: Category association and anagram solution. *Journal of Memory and Language, 29,* 389–412.

Tulving, E. (1985). How many memory systems are there? *American Psychologist, 40,* 385–398.

Tulving, E., & Schacter, D. L. (1990). Priming and human memory systems. *Science, 247,* 301–306.

Tulving, E., Schacter, D. L., & Stark, H. A. (1982). Priming effects in word-fragment completion are independent of recognition memory. *Journal of Experimental Psychology: Learning, Memory, and Cognition, 8*, 336–342.

Welford, A. T. (1985). Practice effects in relation to age: A review and a theory. *Developmental Neuropsychology, 1*, 173–190.

Whetstone, D. A. (1991). *Effects of repeated study on automatic semantic and episodic priming in young and older adults.* Unpublished doctoral dissertation, Claremont Graduate School, Claremont, CA.

Wolf, F. M. (1986). *Meta-analysis: Quantitative methods for research synthesis.* Beverly Hills, CA: Sage Publications.

Woodruff-Pak, D. S., & Thompson, R. F. (1988). Classical conditioning of the eyeblink response in the delay paradigm in adults aged 18–83 years. *Psychology and Aging, 3*, 219–229.

11 Processes Involved in Childhood Development of Implicit Memory

Mika Naito
Tokyo Metropolitan University

Shin-ichi Komatsu
Kagawa University, Japan

What stimulates research is surprise. Clear-cut dissociations between implicit and explicit memory are exactly that, and they have been producing fairly fruitful research in the adult memory literature. Less attention has been paid, however, to the developmental processes of implicit/explicit memory, as acknowledged by Schacter (1987). In this chapter, we delineate the current status of research on children's implicit memory and discuss its implications for theoretical frameworks that elucidate implicit/explicit memory. The chapter consists of three major sections. We begin with a brief review of previous studies in the developmental literature. We then compare and weigh evidence now available for revealing an age-related dissociation between implicit and explicit memory, in which children's performance is compared with that of adults using the same memory tasks. Finally, we propose a tentative framework that could link up the findings in the child memory literature with those in the adult literature.

A HISTORICAL OVERVIEW

Because there are several excellent reviews on memory development in childhood (e.g., Kail, 1990; Schneider & Pressley, 1989), we present only a brief outline of the mainstream of previous studies. Then we review a few studies that have not been duly stressed in the subsequent memory literature but now are considered to be an important precursor of the discussion on different forms of memory. Existing research on memory development falls into two major categories from a methodological viewpoint: experimental studies and ecological or naturalistic studies. Researchers in the first category have primarily explored the cause of age-related differences in performance on laboratory tasks between children and adults. In contrast, researchers in the second category have emphasized children's competence observed under more naturalistic situations including their daily activities.

Experimental Research on Memory Development

Experimental investigations have started with the fact that memory performance improves with age in terms of both its quantity and its quality. Psychologists have proposed several explanations of developmental differences in memory performance. The first explanation has been focused on capacity or resources in short-term memory. Initially, it was believed that if a task absorbs a constant amount of mental resources, memory performance improves with age because processing capacity increases with age (e.g., Pascual-Leone, 1970). The more recent version has modified the explanation so that the total processing capacity is not assumed to change with age, but that the older are the children, the more effectively they use the same amount of resources (Case, 1985). Although being fixed in total processing resources, memory processes are executed more effectively with age, thereby making it possible to allocate more resources to current processing.

The second explanation of memory development during the 1970s emphasized developmental change in the use of mnemonic strategies. It was argued that children's performance increases with age because their encoding strategies or retrieval strategies become more flexible and more effective (e.g., Kobasigawa, 1974; Moely, Olson, Halwes, & Flavell, 1969). In recent years, however, this position has been challenged by several criticisms. First, encoding and retrieval strategies cannot be dealt with separately, but they interact with each other (e.g., Ackerman, 1987). Second, the instructions given at study facilitate the use of mnemonic strategies even in the children who do not use them spontaneously (e.g., Pressley & Levin, 1978). This suggests that even young children can use memory strategies more effectively than has been thought. Finally, the use of mnemonic strategies is greatly affected by the knowledge base children gain with maturation (e.g., Ornstein & Naus, 1985).

Since the late 1970s, growing attention has been paid to the developmental processes of children's knowledge base, which includes both domain-specific factual knowledge and general world knowledge (e.g., Bjorklund, 1987; Chi & Ceci, 1987). It has been argued that developmental differences in memory performance may be attributed to the age-related change in the knowledge base (e.g., Brown, 1975; Ghatala, 1984), thus constituting a third explanation of memory development. Moreover, the usual pattern of age-related differences in memory performance can be reversed if children possess more extensive knowledge than that of adults: Chi (1978) demonstrated that 10-year-old chess experts learned meaningful chess positions better than did adult chess novices (see also

Lindberg, 1980). This indicates that the knowledge base is a crucial determinant of memory performance. Recent research is focused on how the structure of knowledge changes with age.

The fourth explanation is concerned with the issue of metamemory, which has arisen during the last decade. Metamemory involves both the ability to evaluate the contribution of variables determining task difficulty (Flavell & Wellman, 1977) and the ability to monitor what one knows and what are appropriate strategies (Brown, 1978). Recently, the notion of metaknowledge has been extended to children's theories of mind (Wellman, 1985). Research has shown clearly that both young children's monitoring and their knowledge about memory-relevant variables are less accurate than those of older children and adults (e.g., Flavell, Friedrichs, & Hoyt, 1970; Kreutzer, Leonard & Flavell, 1975), thus suggesting that metamemory develops gradually from childhood to adolescence. One problem with early work in this area is that knowledge about memory is not strongly related to memory behaviors, despite a theoretical expectation of a close relation between metamemory and actual memory performance.

In short, the research has consistently demonstrated that older children have a wide mnemonic advantage over young children, and this holds true especially when tasks require a large share of mental resources, demand sophisticated strategies or metamemory, and draw on extensive knowledge represented in an accessible and usable way.

Naturalistic Research on Memory Development

The second category of memory research came initially from Soviet psychology (see Meacham, 1977, for review). When assessing memory performance, Soviet researchers emphasized the importance of naturalistic settings in which children devoted themselves to cognitive tasks, other than memory tasks, that were embedded in their everyday activities. They also made a distinction between involuntary and voluntary memory. Involuntary memory is said to occur when children's goal is not memorizing but understanding or comprehension; the memory processes are not independent of, but integrated with, other intellectual activities. In contrast, voluntary memory occurs when the goal is to remember or recall. For instance, Istomina (1975) explored voluntary memory development by comparing preschoolers' (aged 3–7) recall in an exciting shopping-game situation with that in a typical laboratory task. Children's recall was much better in the shopping-game activity than in the laboratory task. Remembering in the game activity seems to constitute a more meaningful goal for the children, thereby inducing higher memory performance. The Soviets assumed that memory development could be characterized by a transition from involuntary memory to subject-initiated voluntary memory.

The emphasis on naturalistic situations has tended to be neglected within the tradition of experimental studies. In recent years, however, naturalistically or ecologically oriented research has been reevaluated, and some new directions have appeared (e.g., Neisser & Winograd, 1988). The most important direction for the purpose of this chapter is that by Nelson and her colleagues (see Fivush & Hudson, 1990; Nelson, 1986, 1988, for review), who have investigated children's memory for real-world events, such as baking cookies and going on a trip to a museum, that they encounter in their everyday life. In contrast to findings based on laboratory tasks, young children are highly competent on such naturalistic tasks. Fivush, Hudson, and Nelson (1984) explored 5-year-old children's memory about their visit to a museum. Memory tests after 6 weeks and after a year showed that children's general script for visiting museums changed very little, and their memory for the personal visit to a museum was astonishingly accurate even over a year. The kindergartners were able to report the stable, coherent museum script and to differentiate their specific visit from the general museum script. Thus, two aspects of children's event memory have been revealed; general event knowledge for familiar experiences, and autobiographical memory for a specific event. It has been shown that preschoolers are able to give both coherent, well-organized accounts of familiar events (e.g., Hudson, 1986) and accurate, detailed reports of novel events (e.g., Fivush, Gray, & Fromhoff, 1987).

Naturalistic research indicates that both general event knowledge and autobiographical memory are well developed even in preschoolers. Yet this does not necessarily mean that young children are as mnemonically competent as older children and adults. There are serious differences between what Nelson and her colleagues call autobiographical memory in young children and the autobiographical memory observed in older children and adults. For instance, Gopnik and Graf (1988) pointed out that full-fledged adult autobiographical memory "includes not only information about past events but also psychological information about our own experience of such events, including information about sources" (p. 1367). In their study, 3- to 5-year-olds saw, heard, or inferred from a clue the contents of a drawer, and, immediately or after a short delay, they were asked how they knew the contents. The 3-year-olds had difficulty in remembering the source after a delay, even if they had correctly identified it on the immediate test. These results suggest that 3-year-old children do not have a proficient version of autobiographical memory in that they cannot identify or retain psychological information about their experience, which is an important aspect of adult autobiographical memory.

Recently, Nelson (1990) listed distinctive characteristics of young children's specific memory. First, it is easily integrated or confused into general event knowledge. Second, despite being retained for 6–18 months, it is lost unless reactivated within this period. Third, it lacks consistency, as compared with adult autobiographical memory, in that children often rely on external cues for remembering, remember different details from those of adults, and confuse their own experience with what others have reported.

On the Distinction Between Different Forms of Memory

We have outlined the existing studies concerning developmental change in memory from childhood to adulthood. During the last decade, however, infant and adult memory research has suggested that there are two different forms of memory, only one of which has been dealt with in the child memory literature. Although this distinction has been expressed in a variety of terms, the most widely accepted is *implicit* and *explicit* memory. Explicit memory is measured by traditional memory tasks, such as recall and recognition, that require deliberate retrieval of a previously encountered episode with awareness of past occurrence. In contrast, implicit memory is measured by tasks in which retrieval with awareness of a past episode is not necessary, but detection of familiarity with the episode is sufficient. In the adult literature, a typical index of implicit memory is *repetition priming:* the facilitative processing of a studied stimulus in subsequent implicit memory tasks such as word completion, word production, and word or picture identification. With respect to the implicit/explicit memory distinction, the child memory literature has focused on the developmental processes of explicit memory, because tasks used in this research typically require children to deliberately recollect a prior episode, and thus the mnemonic goal is apparent.

A distinction similar to the implicit/explicit distinction can be found in the infant, rather than the child, memory literature. Piaget and his colleagues (Piaget, 1952; Piaget & Inhelder, 1973) distinguished between memory in the *broad* sense and memory in the *strict* sense: The former involves adaptive responses based primarily on sensorimotor schemes or procedures, whereas the latter underlies the ability to consciously recollect a specific episode in one's personal past. It was argued that memory in the broad sense developmentally precedes memory in the strict sense. In accordance with Piaget's proposal, more sophisticated formulations have been based on these two forms of memory.

Schacter and Moscovitch (1984) used the terms *early* and *late* systems to refer to two forms of memory: Whereas memory in the early system is not consciously accessible, memory in the late system entails conscious access to information or representations established by an experience of a past incident. Pointing out the similarity in memory processes between infants and amnesic patients, they argued that the early system is fully functional from birth and is preserved in amnesics, whereas the late system emerges around 8 months of age and is impaired in amnesics. Similarly, Mandler (1984, 1988) classified infants' mnemonic ability into two distinct forms: *primitive recognition* (Mandler, 1984) or *sensorimotor procedures* (Mandler, 1988) and the *ability to recall*. The terms primitive recognition and sensorimotor procedures refer to the infant's ability to recognize familiarity with a previously encountered stimulus or to detect invariance across experienced episodes. This primitive type of recognition is not accessible to consciousness but mediated by a modification of perceptual or sensorimotor operations. In contrast, the ability to recall signifies the evocation of past experiences that allows conscious access to information stored in a conceptual form. According to her formulation, infants cannot recall information unless they have conceptually represented it, but they can recognize or modify information without storing it in an accessible form.

Evidence of Familiarity Recognition

Theorists interested in familiarity base their formulation about memory classification on empirical evidence from infants. One traditional procedure widely used to explore infants' mnemonic ability involves habituation and novelty-preference paradigms that assess infants' tendency to devote more fixation time to novel stimuli than to familiar (previously seen) stimuli (e.g., Fagan, 1984). Differential preference of a novel stimulus over a familiar stimulus indicates recognition memory: Having encoded and stored information about a stimulus in memory, infants "recognize" the familiar stimulus and are less "interested" in it (but see Rovee-Collier & Hayne, 1987; Sophian, 1980). It has been reported that even 1- to 3-day-old newborns are capable of recognizing familiar stimuli that they previously saw (e.g., Friedman, 1972).

Usage of the term "recognition memory" in infancy, however, requires great caution. Although the same term, recognition, is used, the ability to recognize familiar stimuli that has been observed in infants is qualitatively different from explicit recognition memory in adults. Mandler (1984) has urged similar caution in relating the infant's ability of recognition to adult recognition memory: The adult literature assumes awareness of familiarity as a necessary aspect of recognition memory, whereas the infant literature does not. Hence, habituation and novelty preference tasks do not tap the same processes as adult recognition tasks in which awareness of a prior episode is necessary for successful performance. In contrast, familiarity recognition in infancy has a strong resemblance to implicit memory in adulthood, neither of which requires awareness of recollection of a stimulus that occurred in a past context. A similar suggestion has been made by Schacter and Moscovitch (1984). On the basis of an extensive review encompassing the infant and adult memory literature, they noted that recognition memory in infancy depends heavily on what they call the early memory system, which corresponds to implicit memory in adulthood.

Another sort of evidence of infants' ability to respond to familiarity or to detect invariance across experimental episodes comes from Rovee-Collier and her associates (for review see Rovee-Collier & Hayne, 1987), who have used conjugate reinforcement procedures in an operant conditioning paradigm: A ribbon connects a mobile to a 2- to 4-month-old infant's ankle, so that kicking moves the mobile. Conditioning was assessed by an increase in kicking over the baseline measured at the initial phase of training. As a result, reliable conditioning was confirmed for days or weeks, thereby indicating that the infant can learn and retain the contingency between kicking and the movement of a mobile.

Of great interest is what Rovee-Collier calls *reactivation* or *reinstatement*. Reactivation refers to the idea that the brief presentation of a part of a prior experience can restore conditioned actions to the level of original training even after a long interval in which forgetting would otherwise occur. Rovee-Collier, Sullivan, Enright, Lucas, and Fagen (1980) offered evidence of a striking similarity between reactivation in the conditioning paradigm with infants and repetition priming in implicit memory tasks with adults. In their experiment, following the conjugate reinforcement procedure, 3-month-olds maintained conditioned kicking to move a mobile for a week. Kicking decreased to a baseline level 13 days after original training, thereby indicating the forgetting of conditioned action. Then, subjects were reminded of their training experience: Placed in a small seat, the infant saw the mobile moving while an experimenter pulled the ribbon at the same rate at which the infant had kicked it in the original training. One day after this reactivation treatment (14 days after the original training), the infant's performance recovered to the same level as it was at original conditioning. Reactivation was highly specific to the contextual information of the original training, because the reactivation treatment was made ineffective by a change in the reminder, such as the presentation of a previously discriminated negative mobile and the novel settings of a crib (e.g., Fagen, Yengo, Rovee-Collier, & Enright, 1981).

The important point in reactivation is that a brief, single presentation of a reminder is sufficient to reinstate the stored information. It should be noted that in adult priming paradigms a single presentation of a stimulus can facilitate the subsequent processing of the same stimulus. Thus, the reactivation treatment works in the same way as does the priming stimulus, both of which make stored information available even if the information remains inaccessible to consciousness. Furthermore, the contextual specificity of infants' reinstatement is compatible with the evidence in the adult priming literature, which shows that priming effects are specific to the information of a studied stimulus (e.g., Schacter, 1990; Tulving & Schacter, 1990). A problem we have to consider here is that Rovee-Collier and her colleagues explain their results in terms of cued "retrieval and recall." With respect to this problem, however, we agree with Mandler (1984), who indicated that "conditioning experiments ignore the component of consciousness" (p. 81). That is, infants' retention of the contingency between kicking and mobile movement does not appear to be a result of conscious access to the evocation of a past training experience, but a result of selective responses to invariant features of the association between kicking and movement.

Evidence of the Ability to Recall

In contrast to the procedures illustrated in the foregoing discussion, a crucial aspect of procedures that measure the ability to recall is to require infants to bring to mind information that no longer exists in current context (Mandler, 1984,

1988; Moscovitch, 1985). One of the typical phenomena reflecting such mnemonic processes as recall is not A-not-B error in object search paradigms. The A-not-B error occurs when 8- to 10-month-old infants, having watched an object hidden at location A and successfully finding it, continue to search for it at A, after the object is hidden, in full view, at location B (Piaget, 1954). Although Piaget interpreted this phenomenon as caused by the incomplete concept of object permanence at this age, the mechanism of the A-not-B error is not yet decided; recently his position has been criticized by some researchers, who showed that infants know more about objects than has ever been thought (e.g., Baillargeon, Spelke, & Wasserman, 1985). It seems appropriate for the purpose of this chapter, however, to view the A-not-B error as evidence of a memory failure of this age.

Schacter and Moscovitch (1984) demonstrated that amnesic patients commit an A-not-B error comparable to that obtained with infants. Both amnesic and control subjects performed object search tasks: An object was hidden at invisible location A, and after a few minutes, a subject was asked to find the missing object; then, after the subject succeeded in the task (search at A) three times, the object was hidden at new invisible location B. In this case, amnesics incorrectly searched at A whereas controls successfully searched at B. Furthermore, a similar pattern of results was obtained even when the object was placed at a new visible location (C) instead of invisible location B. The amnesics' failure to find objects at B or C is obviously caused by their poor memory and not by their poorly developed object concept. Hence, the striking similarity between amnesics' and infants' performance on the same object search tasks suggests that underlying sources of the A-not-B error are the same for both groups: the failure to remember the episode of B (or C) trial or the failure to distinguish this episode from the prior repeated episodes of A trial.

Other evidence regarding recall ability in infancy derives from Meltzoff (1988), who investigated deferred imitation with 9-month-olds. Until this study, it was widely believed that deferred imitation first appears at 18–24 months of age. Using well-controlled procedures, however, Meltzoff clearly demonstrated that even 9-month-olds could imitate novel actions that they saw 24 h earlier. For the successful deferred imitation, infants must recall an absent action without now seeing it, thereby suggesting that the deferred imitation paradigm taps an ability more akin to recall than to primitive or sensorimotor recognition, and such ability is fully functional at least by the age of 9 months.

In sum, the existing studies on infant memory suggest that there are at least two different forms of memory in infancy, familiarity recognition and the ability to recall, that correspond to implicit memory and explicit memory, respectively. Although researchers differ in specifying when the ability to recall first emerges, most of them are unanimous in noting that familiarity recognition appears almost immediately after birth and that implicit familiarity recognition developmentally precedes ability in explicit recall (e.g., Schacter & Moscovitch, 1984; but see

Mandler, 1988). As described in the preceding section, the child memory literature reveals that explicit recall and recognition memory improves with age depending on developmental differences in resource allocation, mnemonic strategy use, knowledge bases, and metamemory including the concept of self. Hence, a developmental scheme from infancy to adulthood can be proposed: Implicit memory precedes explicit memory and is fully functional even in early infancy, whereas explicit memory shows a marked developmental change from infancy to adulthood.

There is serious difficulty, however, in identifying a direct correspondence between infant memory and adult memory because of a difference in experimental procedures: Memory in adults is usually measured by verbal tasks, whereas infant memory is assessed by nonverbal or sensorimotor tasks, such as conditioning and object search paradigms. Hence, empirical data on children's memory, obtained under experimental conditions comparable to those used with adults, are needed to permit us to integrate the findings of both infant and adult memory studies into a consistent theoretical framework. In the next section, we examine several studies that compare children's implicit memory with their explicit memory.

CURRENT STATUS OF RESEARCH ON IMPLICIT MEMORY DEVELOPMENT AND ITS IMPLICATIONS

With regard to the implicit/explicit distinction, despite a large number of studies in the adult memory literature, there are only a few that made children the subjects of experiments. We review and discuss four experimental studies with children as subjects that compared implicit memory performance with explicit performance. These four studies differed from one another with respect to the subjects' age range (from 3-year-olds to 12-year-olds, and adults), materials used (pictorial or verbal), and indices of memory performance (recall or recognition for explicit memory and savings in relearning or priming effects for implicit memory); some studies examined effects of other experimental variables, such as encoding tasks and retention intervals. We take them up according to the age range.

Implicit Memory in Early Childhood

Using explicit recall and implicit word production tests, Greenbaum and Graf (1989) conducted an experiment with the youngest population: 3-, 4-, and 5-year-olds. Materials were composed of a set of line-drawing pictures of familiar objects typically seen in one of the place categories such as a zoo, restaurant, kitchen, or park. Children were presented the pictures and asked to name and memorize them. Immediately after this study, they were told a brief story about going to one of the four places and then were asked what was typically found there, which constituted implicit word-production tests. Priming effects were examined by comparing the primed condition in which the corresponding pictures had been presented in the study phase with the baseline condition in which the pictures had not been presented. Then the children were tested for explicit recall of the studied pictures. The results demonstrated that although there was an age-related increase in the total number of items produced, reliable priming effects were obtained, and, more importantly, the amounts of priming were similar across age groups (14%, 10%, and 17% for 3-, 4-, and 5-year-olds, respectively). In contrast, recall performance clearly increased with age (17%, 32%, and 47% for 3-, 4-, and 5-year-olds, respectively).

The Greenbaum and Graf experiment provided strong evidence that even 3-year-olds have proficient implicit memory despite the difficulty in explicit remembering, and implicit memory performance does not change during preschool years. These findings are especially important because the experiment measured priming effects in the word production task, which has been regarded as a relatively pure measure of implicit memory and has been extensively used in the adult memory literature (e.g., Graf, Shimamura, & Squire, 1985). In both preschoolers and adults, implicit memory as reflected by priming is dissociable from explicit memory; thus, reliable priming observed in preschoolers may be functionally equivalent to that in adults. Because of the lack of an adult sample, however, the Greenbaum and Graf study is inconclusive with respect to possible equivalence between children and adults.

In a study using both preschool children and adults, Parkin and Streete (1988) made a direct comparison of memory performance across age groups. In their experiment, 3-, 5-, and 7-year-olds and adults were tested for explicit memory with recognition and for implicit memory with a fragmented-picture identification test in which subjects attempted to identify a picture presented in an incomplete form. In an initial trial, the subjects were presented the most degraded version of the picture among eight stages of fragmentation (the eighth version was the complete picture), and if they could not identify it, the next stage was shown; this procedure was continued until the subjects correctly named a picture. A complete picture was then presented. The index of implicit memory was savings: the improvement in identification of a less informative version of a picture relative to the initial trial. In addition to the subjects' age, retention intervals were manipulated from 1 hr to 2 wk after the initial trial: Subjects returned to receive both the picture identification test for degraded pictures and the succeeding recognition test for complete pictures.

The results showed that although overall savings increased with age, the age-related increase in savings disappeared when differences in baseline performance were taken into account by calculating each subjects' savings score as a proportion of his or her initial score (see Table 11.1). In addition, the proportional savings scores were greater in 1-hr tests than in 2-week tests. Recognition scores,

TABLE 11.1
Proportions of Savings as a Function of Age and Retention Interval

	Retention Interval	
Age of Subjects	1 Hour	2 Weeks
3-year-olds	.39	.35
5-year-olds	.42	.39
7-year-olds	.46	.38
Adults	.38	.37

Note. From "Implicit and explicit memory in young children and adults" by A. J. Parkin and S. Streete, 1988, *British Journal of Psychology, 79,* p. 365. Copyright (1988) by the British Psychological Society. Reprinted by permission.

analyzed only in the 2-week delay condition because of ceiling effects in the 1-hr condition, showed a reliable increase with age. Parkin and Streete also computed a correlational analysis of implicit savings and explicit recognition. There was no significant correlation between savings and recognition accuracy. These results suggest that even 3-year-olds have a fully developed implicit memory function, whereas their explicit memory is not yet fully functional. Moreover, a tentative hypothesis about the developmental processes of implicit/explicit memory can be built up on the basis of the findings from the direct comparison between pre-schoolers and adults under the same experimental conditions: Implicit memory measured by savings is insensitive to developmental changes from early childhood to adulthood, whereas explicit memory measured by recognition is sensitive to such changes.

One may argue, however, that the savings procedure as an index of implicit memory is likely to be contaminated by explicit remembering. The savings procedure has been used primarily for amnesic patients severely deficient in explicit remembering. Actually, the 5- and 7-year-olds in the Parkin and Streete study revealed better savings scores on recognized items than those on unrecognized items, whereas the 3-year-olds' savings scores did not differ between them. This pattern implies that implicit memory performance may have been affected by explicit memory that improves with age. Nevertheless, it should be noted that the 3-year-olds showed full-fledged implicit memory comparable to that of adults, even though their explicit memory is not fully functional and thus explicit remembering seems to have had little influence on the fragmented-picture test. Such findings provide encouraging evidence that implicit memory develops earlier than explicit memory, as Parkin and Streete advocated.

Another issue lies in the effects of retention intervals on implicit savings scores: Savings scores were greater in the 1-hr retention condition than in the 2-week condition, a pattern similar to that of recognition memory. In the adult memory literature, the relationship of retention intervals to implicit memory performance remains controversial. Some studies have shown little reduction in implicit memory performance over a delay of days or weeks (e.g., Komatsu & Naito, 1985; Tulving, Schacter, & Stark, 1982), whereas others have found considerable decrease (e.g., Sloman, Hayman, Ohta, Law, & Tulving, 1988). Thus the effects of retention interval on implicit memory in children deserve further attention.

Implicit Memory in Middle Childhood

Carroll, Byrne, and Kirsner (1985) investigated implicit and explicit memory with somewhat older children (aged 5, 7, and 10) and adults. Explicit memory was measured by recognition of a tachistoscopically presented picture; implicit memory was assessed by its naming latency. Priming effects here were indexed by a decrease in naming latencies for previously presented old items relative to new items. Encoding condition at study was also manipulated: In the shallow condition subjects searched for a cross marked on a picture; in the deep condition subjects judged the weight of an object depicted in a picture. In the Carroll et al. study, memory in adults (Experiment 2) and in children (Experiment 3) was examined separately, thereby making it difficult to trace directly from children to adults the relationship between age and task performance, but this was possible within the three groups of children. After studying a list of pictures under the two encoding conditions, the subjects were tested with both recognition and naming of old and new pictures.

As seen in Table 11.2, recognition improved with children's age from 5 to 10 years old. As for the effect of encoding condition on recognition, the same pattern of results was obtained in children as in adults: Picture recognition was better in the deep condition than in the shallow condition. In contrast, the results

TABLE 11.2
Proportions of Correct Recognition in Children (Experiment 3) and Adults (Experiment 2) as a Function of Encoding Task

	Depth of Encoding				
	Shallow			*Deep*	
Age of Subjects	*Old*	*New*		*Old*	*New*
5-year-olds	.28	.96		.76	.93
7-year-olds	.60	.98		.97	.99
10-year-olds	.66	.98		.99	1.00
Adults	.56	—		.91	—

Note. From "Autobiographical memory and perceptual learning: A developmental study using picture recognition, naming latency, and perceptual identification" by A. Carroll, B. Byrne, and K. Kirsner, 1985, *Memory & Cognition, 13,* p. 276. Copyright (1985) by the Psychonomic Society Inc. Reprinted by permission.

TABLE 11.3
Median Naming Latencies (Milliseconds) in Children (Experiment 3) and Adults (Experiment 2) as
a Function of Encoding Task

	Depth of Encoding					
	Shallow			Deep		
Age of Subjects	Old	New		Old	New	
5-year-olds	1170	1203	(33)	1220	1293	(73)
7-year-olds	970	998	(28)	950	1020	(70)
10-year-olds	845	875	(30)	797	854	(57)
Adults	783	833	(50)	789	822	(33)

Note. Priming effects (subtracting latencies of old items from those of new items) are in parentheses.
From "Autobiographical memory and perceptual learning: A developmental study using picture
recognition, naming latency, and perceptual identification" by A. Carroll, B. Byrne, and K. Kirsner, 1985,
Memory & Cognition, 13, p. 277. Copyright (1985) by the Psychonomic Society Inc. Reprinted by
permission.

of naming showed that although overall latencies were lower among older children, there was no interaction between age and prior exposure of items, thereby indicating that the priming effect in naming latency was the same across the age groups (see Table 11.3). The effects of encoding conditions on priming in children differed from those in adults: Whereas adults' priming in naming latencies was not affected by the encoding conditions, children's priming was greater for deep stimuli (67 msec) than for shallow (30 msec). In order to solve this incongruity, Carroll et al. conducted Experiment 4 with 7-year-olds. The index of implicit memory here was picture identification accuracy, in lieu of naming latency, and demonstrated significant priming effects, but no effect of encoding condition.

The first suggestion from the Carroll et al. study is that implicit memory is developmentally stable during childhood, whereas explicit memory is sensitive to developmental change. Second, manipulating encoding conditions does not affect implicit memory in children or adults, although it has an effect on explicit memory in both age groups. These suggestions seem to be controversial, however, on two points. First, the relationship between age and implicit memory was not determined by using one and the same experimental design with both children and adults, which hinders attempts to extend to adulthood the findings on developmental stability in childhood. Second, the null effect of encoding condition was confirmed in implicit memory, but was demonstrated when children and adults were given different tests, and was not obtained with children when a latency measure was used.

Naito (1990) carried out a series of experiments with schoolchildren (first to sixth graders) and adults. She used a word-fragment completion task with words

TABLE 11.4
Proportion of Correct Word Completion (Experiment 1) and Free Recall (Experiment 2) as a
Function of Age and Type of Items

Subject	Type of Items		
	Physical	Categorical	New
	Word Completion (Experiment 1)		
Grade 1	.42	.42	.20
Grade 3	.43	.45	.25
Grade 6	.49	.46	.25
College	.62	.63	.40
	Free Recall (Experiment 2)		
Grade 1	.05	.05	
Grade 3	.09	.20	
Grade 6	.08	.21	
College	.14	.31	

Note. Data from Naito (1990).

in the vocabulary of first graders to assess implicit memory. Children's performance on both implicit and explicit (recall or recognition) tasks was compared with that of adults. In addition, encoding condition and retention interval were manipulated because their effects on implicit and explicit memory performance were not clearly determined in previous studies.

Experiments 1 and 2 involved both subjects' age and encoding conditions. In the study phase, first, third, and sixth graders (aged 6, 8, and 11, respectively) and adults answered two types of encoding questions about a target word: a physical letter question in which subjects judged whether the target contained a letter, or an elaborative category question in which subjects decided the category name to which the target belonged. After the encoding phase, subjects were given a word completion test containing old items presented in the study phase and new items presented only on the test (Experiment 1), or a free recall test (Experiment 2). Results are shown in Table 11.4. Regardless of age, word completion performance on both physically and categorically encoded old items was better than that on new items, thereby showing reliable priming in all age groups. More important, although overall performance on word completion increased with age, the amounts of priming did not differ across age or across encoding conditions. In contrast, recall performance revealed a clear interaction between age and encoding conditions: Recall increased with age, and this held especially true when encoding involved category questions.

Experiment 3 included both age and retention intervals as independent variables. First and sixth graders (aged 7 and 12) and adults studied a list of words, and then they were tested with either word completion or recognition 7 min or 6

TABLE 11.5
Proportions of Correct Word Completion as a Function of Age and Retention Interval

| | Retention Interval | | | |
| | 7 Minutes | | 6 Days | |
Subject	Old	New	Old	New
Grade 1	.48	.26	.45	.32
Grade 6	.60	.36	.63	.44
College	.63	.43	.65	.48

Note. Data from Naito (1990, Experiment 3).

days after list presentation. Results are summarized in Table 11.5 for word completion and in Table 11.6 for recognition. Table 11.5 shows that, despite an increase in overall performance with age, the amounts of priming effects were virtually the same across age. Furthermore, priming effects in word completion did not change over the 6-day interval. In contrast, Table 11.6 reveals that recognition scores, both hits and true negatives, increased with age, except that hits in the 6-day condition were lower in adults than in schoolchildren. It was argued that the low hit rates for adults in the 6-day test may have reflected familiarity effects in recognition: Adults show some difficulty in recognizing highly familiar words, such as used in the Naito study, as having been previously presented (for discussion see Gregg, 1976; Naito, 1990). In addition, both recognition measures declined considerably over 6 days. These observations were confirmed by the d' values calculated from hits and false alarms: The d' values of adults were higher than those of children in the 7-min test, whereas there was no difference between any two age groups in the 6-day test; the d' values in all age groups markedly decreased over the 6-day interval.

TABLE 11.6
Proportions of Correct Recognition Scores (Hits and True Negatives) and d' Values as a Function of Age and Retention Interval

| | Retention Interval | | | | | |
| | 7 Minutes | | | 6 Days | | |
Subject	Hit	True Negative	d'	Hit	True Negative	d'
Grade 1	.79	.85	2.06	.68	.68	1.05
Grade 6	.77	.93	2.19	.68	.76	1.22
College	.88	.94	2.65	.57	.83	1.13

Note. Data from Naito (1990, Experiment 3).

The results indicated that priming in word completion is not sensitive to the age difference from middle childhood to adulthood, although there is sensitivity to such age differences in recall and recognition. Furthermore, recall and recognition performance are markedly affected by experimentally manipulated variables, including encoding condition and retention interval, although such variables exert little influence on priming. These findings constitute conclusive evidence that implicit memory in schoolchildren is functionally equivalent to that in adults.

Implications of the Existing Research on Implicit Memory Development

Despite the differences in age populations, experimental procedures, and materials, the four studies illustrated here permit us to delineate the developmental processes of implicit and explicit memory from childhood to adulthood: Whereas explicit memory improves with age, implicit memory remains stable from 3-year-olds to adults. Several investigators have noted a similarity between implicit memory in adulthood and the primitive type of memory in infancy, such as recognition (Mandler, 1984) and early memory (Schacter & Moscovitch, 1984), in that neither requires awareness of the past but both involve perceptual or procedural processing. In contrast, explicit memory has a strong resemblance to the ability to recall (Mandler, 1984) or late memory (Schacter & Moscovitch, 1984) in that both entail the evocation of a specific incident from the past and both require awareness of recollection. It has been suggested that the primitive type of recognition in infancy emerges from birth and precedes the ability to recall. Although differences in experimental methods have created a gap between studies of infant and adult memory, this gap can be bridged by assuming that the primitive memory in infancy corresponds to implicit memory in childhood. Implicit memory develops ontogenetically earlier than explicit memory, functions even in neonates, and remains with little change throughout childhood; explicit memory appears later in infancy and follows a developmental change from infancy to adulthood. The issue of this developmental scheme of memory is further discussed in the next section.

THEORETICAL IMPLICATIONS

We have reviewed consistent evidence of developmental dissociations between implicit and explicit memory. Implicit/explicit dissociations have also been found in the adult memory literature: There exists considerable evidence of clear and stable dissociations under a wide variety of experimental manipulations (Richardson-Klavehn & Bjork, 1988; Schacter, 1987). Theoretically, two different families of approaches have been proposed to explain experimental dissociations between implicit and explicit memory: processing views and multiple-system views. Processing views regard the dissociations as due to differences in processing operations within a unitary memory system and emphasize a general principle, *transfer-appropriate processing*, that may be applicable to all sorts of memory phenomena. In contrast, multiple-system views argue that human memory is not unitary but composed of functionally different multiple systems, each of which differentially determines memory performance, thus resulting in performance dissociations. Although it is a crucial issue for students of memory as to whether human memory is unitary or multiple, it might be possible to argue that the two approaches emphasize different aspects of the same phenomena and, de facto, hold similar views concerning the nature of implicit memory.

In this section, we examine the functions of implicit and explicit memory from a developmental perspective that encompasses both ontogenetic and phylogenetic origins. Sherry and Schacter (1987) proposed the idea of *functional incompatibility*, which can serve as an important criterion for distinguishing between memory systems: A new memory system evolves only when functional incompatibility arises between the properties of an existing memory system and the demands posed by an environmental problem. Adopting this evolutionary criterion, we present a tentative framework that can accommodate not only findings from developmental studies but some contradictory findings remaining unresolved in the adult implicit memory literature.

Functionally Distinct Memory Systems

From an evolutionary viewpoint, Nelson (1990) argued that the most basic function of memory is to provide guidance for action, which enables organisms to support action in the present and to predict what will happen. The most efficient way for such adaptation to work is to pick up and preserve frequently repeated, thus familiar, events. The detection and preservation of invariance across episodes constitute the central mechanism for gradual and incremental learning of habits and skills. It leads to smooth and automatic execution without conscious recollection. Implicit memory, dissociated from explicit memory, seems to correspond to such unconscious expressions of procedural memory (e.g., Squire, 1987). This system has been referred to as the early system (Schacter & Moscovitch, 1984), memory in the broad sense (Piaget & Inhelder, 1973), or sensorimotor procedures (Mandler, 1988) in the developmental literature, which commonly suggests that a system for the unconscious preservation of invariance emerges almost immediately from birth.

Besides being preserved unconsciously in a procedural form, invariant properties across episodes are closely related to knowledge representations in a declarative form. Naturalistic studies of very young children's memory have shown clearly that 2- or 3-year-olds possess generalized event knowledge of their everyday life in a declarative, conceptual form (e.g., Fivush & Hudson, 1990; Nelson,

1986). The memory system that preserves invariance in a declarative form has been described as a script (Schank & Abelson, 1977) or schema (Bartlett, 1932). Children's event representations are fairly abstract and serve as a prerequisite for development of autobiographical memory (e.g., Hudson, 1986). Thus, it seems likely that this system corresponds to semantic or generic memory distinguished from procedural and episodic memory under multiple-system views in the adult memory literature (Tulving, 1985).

A growing interest has been taken in the developmental processes of auto-biographical memory (e.g., Rubin, 1986) and adults' inability to recall early childhood (referred to as *childhood amnesia*). Recent research has revealed that conscious recollection is available to 6-month-old (Mandler, 1988) or 8-month-old infants (Schacter & Moscovitch, 1984), and this ability may reflect the emergence of episodic or autobiographical memory. It should be noted, however, that the infants' ability to preserve episodically variant properties differs from full-fledged autobiographical memory of adults with respect to experiential awareness (Perner, 1990), remembering past psychological states (Gopnik & Graf, 1988), and its relation to the concept of self (Brewer, 1986; Neisser, 1988). From an evolutionary viewpoint, to retain the detailed information that uniquely specifies an episode is of little value for guiding action and predicting the future. Thus, the adaptive value of preservation of variance is called to account. Point-ing out the close correspondence in onset age between autobiographical memory and learning to engage in talking about memory, Nelson (1990) proposed that the function of episodic, autobiographical memory is to talk with others about expe-riences, which affords a sociocultural significance of memory. In accordance with the concept of functional incompatibility, autobiographical memory devel-ops as a distinct memory system to cope with the sociocultural demands and thus constitutes a specific property of human memory.

The Functional Role of Repetition Priming

Repetition priming has been considered to be a typical phenomenon of implicit memory. Nevertheless, the relationship of repetition priming to functionally different memory systems remains unclear. Sherry and Schacter (1987) have pointed out that priming is not easily captured by the System I (procedural) and System II (episodic) distinction: Priming does not fit in with procedural memory in that the acquisitive processes of habits and skills are incremental and gradual, which contrasts with one-trial processes for the occurrence of priming; the un-conscious processes of repetition priming are not consistent with conscious recol-lection of episodic memory. Tulving and Schacter (1990) proposed that priming is an expression of a *perceptual representation system* (PRS) that should be distinguished from procedural, semantic, and episodic memory (see also Schacter, 1990). Developmentally, the PRS is a specialized subsystem of pro-cedural memory, and it contains semantic memory as its single subsystem in a monohierarchical scheme (Tulving, 1985). The PRS operates at a presemantic or structural level without any kind of stored memory traces.

Viewing repetition priming as an expression of a distinct memory system, we further examine the function of repetition priming from a developmental perspective. In discussing the relation of implicit memory to the acquisition of language, Durkin (1989) suggested that implicit memory may contribute to language acquisition processes as a preliminary stage of data treatment that enables children to maintain a peripheral, unanalyzed level of information. It seems plausible that the central function of repetition priming lies in the preservation of novel information in some unanalyzed form. Considering its prominent role in language acquisition, we think that such a capacity can be deemed a prerequisite for more global processes of cognitive development. Repetition priming has its own function as a preliminary stage of data treatment and thus should be distinguished from other memory systems in light of the functional incompatibility.

Throughout all phases of cognitive development, children must continuously cope with novelty. As suggested by Rheingold (1985), development can be viewed as children becoming increasingly familiar with novel events. Studies using novelty-preference tasks have revealed that the ability to deal with novelty emerges from birth and remains stable over development (Fagan, 1984). Furthermore, the ability to deal with novelty is regarded as one of the key components of intelligence (Berg & Sternberg, 1985). Hence, an important question arises as to how children's memory systems change when they are confronted with novel information inconsistent with their current structures (Brown, 1979): It becomes a matter of great concern for developmental researchers to elucidate the accommodation processes by which existing structures are modified in conformity with a novel event, as well as the process of assimilating a novel event into existing structures.

When faced with a great deal of continuous input, no one can decide whether each piece of information has adaptive value. Nelson (1990) assumed a trigger mechanism to process information when its value is not yet determined: "If repeated within x amount of time (days, weeks), file for future use; if not, drop" (p. 308). Similarly, Rovee-Collier and Hayne (1987) propounded the concept of reactivation: A single encounter with a reminder of an experience can hinder forgetting and restore memory performance to its original level. The surplus preservation of novel information at some unanalyzed level seems to be an optimal strategy to deal with novelty, thereby permitting its comparison with succeeding input and discovery of its adaptive value.

Although our approach relies on multiple-system views in which priming is deemed a functionally distinct system, processing views of implicit memory allow us to specify the detailed nature of processing operations in repetition priming. It is argued that repetition priming is mediated mainly by data-driven processing but not by conceptually driven processing, and thus a change in peripheral, surface features of stimuli between study and test considerably reduces the amount of priming (e.g., Jacoby, 1983a; Roediger & Blaxton, 1987). Similar distinctions in processing operations have been made by other researchers in the adult memory literature: integration versus elaboration (Mandler, 1979; Graf & Mandler, 1984; Graf & Ryan, 1990), unitization versus grouping (Graf & Schacter, 1989), and item-specific versus relational (Hunt & Einstein, 1981). In the developmental literature, Naus and Halasz (1979) proposed that there are two types of developmentally dissociable processing: Deliberate processing emerges over a period of years and matures by age 11 or 12, which is contrasted with automatic processing with no developmental trends (see also Hasher & Zacks, 1979; Parkin, 1989). Similarly, Muir-Broaddus and Bjorklund (1990) called these two types of processing within-item effects and between-item effects. Mandler (1988) distinguished perceptual processing from perceptual analysis: Perceptual processing is an unconscious process resulting in a modification of the perceptual apparatus itself, whereas perceptual analysis constitutes a simultaneous or sequential comparison that forms the basis of accessible concepts. Despite the variety of its labels, the proposed nature of processing in repetition priming is fairly consistent across them. Repetition priming seems to involve within-item processing to which between-item or relational information has little pertinence.

Nesting Structures of Episodes

We have discussed the function of repetition priming in the context of existing theories in the developmental literature, as well as in the context of the adult implicit memory literature encompassing both multiple-system and processing views. On attempting further developmental and ecological analysis, however, we encounter a puzzling problem, concerning the phenomenon of repetition priming, that often has been dismissed in the adult memory literature.

The problem lies in a possibility of constraints on the priming system. According to the monohierarchical arrangement of multiple memory systems, the memory system mediating repetition priming develops as a specialized subsystem of procedural memory and precedes declarative semantic and autobiographical memory. Thus, the priming system initially can work independently of explicit memory systems. Once semantic and autobiographical memory systems develop and become fully functional, however, there is the possibility that the priming system may be constrained by such higher-order systems. Developmental research has extensively demonstrated that existing semantic knowledge is a crucial factor in accounting for age-related differences in explicit memory performance (e.g., Bjorklund, 1987; Chi, 1978; Chi & Ceci, 1987). Brown (1979) used the term *headfitting* to refer to congruence between what children can understand at any point and their preexisting cognitive structures. It appears that explicit memory performance is critically determined by what is already known. We further assume that such constraints may be applicable to phenomena associated with repetition priming. That is, existing knowledge structures seem to determine the processing operations not only in the explicit memory systems but also in the priming system.

This possibility is seemingly incompatible with the widespread views of repetition priming that emphasize that the priming system operates solely at a perceptual or structural level. From a multiple-system view, Tulving and Schacter (1990) distinguished between a perceptual mode and a conceptual mode, the former of which operates unconsciously at a presemantic level and mediates repetition priming. A similar emphasis has been found in processing views: Conceptually driven or semantic processing bears little relationship to the occurrence of repetition priming. In the developmental literature, Mandler (1988) also argued that implicit perceptual processing merely sensitizes the perceptual input system, and it is the results of explicit perceptual analysis that are stored in the conceptual knowledge system. In line with these views, we have also suggested that the function of the priming system is the surplus preservation of information at a little-analyzed level. The preservation with little analysis in the priming system seems to be an optimal strategy to deal with novelty, because the adaptive value of an input stimulus is not yet determined. In that sense, the priming system has a unique function and thus seems to operate independently of higher-order memory systems. When discussing the functional role of the priming system, however, we did not define precisely what is novel and what level of information the priming system preserves. The same was true of the description of processing operations in the priming system. It has been argued that the priming system is involved primarily with unitization or within-item processing. In making this suggestion, however, we did not make it clear what constitutes a unit or item.

We would like to disentangle this puzzling problem by making a further analysis of the level at which priming units are defined. From an ecological standpoint, Neisser (1986) described complex structures of episodes as *nesting:* An episode cannot be determined at only one level of analysis; episodes defined at one level are comprised in a larger episode, and each is comprised of smaller episodes. Similarly, Mandler (1979) referred to them as *structural elaboration:* Structures vary in the degree to which they connect with other structures that may be subordinate, coordinate, or superordinate. Because an input stimulus exhibits complex nesting structures, it is impossible to describe it at only one level. There exist simultaneously different levels of information within one and the same input: Some are congruent with existing knowledge structures and thus can be incorporated into them, while others are beyond them. What is novel varies according to the developmental states of existing knowledge structures (see also Durkin, 1989). For this reason, we assume that the level at which priming units are defined may also be constrained by the developmental states of explicit declarative memory systems. Originally the priming system works to hold perceptual or structural information as it stands without any analysis. Once explicit memory systems attain their full development, they interact with the priming system in such a way that they determine what is novel at any point. What the priming system preserves at a superficially analyzed level is the novel information that is beyond current structures and thus is difficult for them to deal with. What constitutes a unit that is to be primed is not prescribed but may vary according to the developmental states of existing explicit systems.

In the preceding section, we reviewed consistent evidence that no developmental difference is found in priming experiments: Children show a reliable amount of repetition priming, comparable to that of adults. It should be noted, however, that the materials used in these priming experiments were carefully controlled, so that the children could easily identify each item with high familiarity. This implies that children did not differ from adults in preexisting explicit knowledge about the experimental materials. We assume that, owing to the developmental constraints in explicit declarative memory, an age-related difference may be found even in repetition priming. Our proposal is just a speculation without any empirical evidence. Nevertheless, this seems to provide a possible framework to resolve problems raised in the previous priming studies with adult subjects.

A Tentative Framework for Future Research

It has been pointed out that multiple memory systems interact with one another, yet the exact manner of the interactions remains unclear. From a developmental perspective, we have suggested the possibility that the priming system may be constrained by explicit declarative memory systems: The developmental states of explicit memory may define the level at which, and the unit for which, repetition priming occurs. In order to accommodate findings that contradict existing frameworks in the implicit memory literature, we further assume that to-be-primed units may be determined by environmental task demands as well as by developmental constraints. There exist three kinds of such contradictory findings. We briefly review them in turn and account for them within our tentative framework.

The first problem that both multiple-system and processing views have had difficulty accommodating is list-wide effects on repetition priming. Manipulating the proportions of study items in a test list, Jacoby (1983b) found that repetition priming is greater when study items constitute 90% of the test list than when they constitute 10% of the test list. The list-wide effects have been interpreted as the involvement of episodic components in implicit memory. Multiple-system views cannot be reconciled with these findings, because episodic memory is functionally distinct from the priming system. Processing views acknowledge within-item processing as the critical determinant of repetition priming, which bears little relationship to other items in a list, thus encountering difficulty similar to that of multiple-system views in explaining the apparent between-item processing involved in list-wide effects.

The second problem lies in the findings of null priming when target words are embedded in larger units, such as sentences and texts, during encoding (Levy & Kirsner, 1989; MacLeod, 1989; Oliphant, 1983). As with the list-wide effects, these findings can be regarded as evidence of episodic involvement in implicit memory performance. Furthermore, it is suggested that there are multiple levels of information in language materials, only one of which has been taken up in most of implicit memory research.

The third is concerned with effects of prior generation on implicit memory tasks. Clear experimental dissociations have been demonstrated between implicit and explicit memory with respect to such effects (Jacoby, 1983a): Generating a word from its antonym led to better explicit recognition than did reading a word, whereas prior reading produced greater priming in implicit identification than did prior generation. These dissociations have been considered to be a crucial criterion to distinguish data-driven processing from conceptually driven processing (see also Roediger & Blaxton, 1987). Recent research has shown, however, that generating a target from a semantic cue does induce reliable priming (termed *conceptual priming*) comparable to that in the prior reading condition. This result has not been reconciled with existing theoretical frameworks. One way to explain the phenomenon of conceptual priming within the existing frameworks is to attribute it to the use of imaging strategies during the encoding phase. This idea seems unlikely. Using foreign loan words as experimental materials, Komatsu and Naito (1992) obtained reliable amounts of conceptual priming even when the imaging strategies did not work properly during encoding. In modern Japanese writing, foreign loan words are normally written in Katakana script, although it is possible to write them in the other Kana script, Hiragana, if necessary. It was shown that generating a foreign loan word from its definition facilitated performance on subsequent completion of its fragment written in Hiragana, as well as written in Katakana, despite the fact that the writing of that word in Hiragana was orthographically unfamiliar and hence would never have been imaged during prior generation.

Some researchers have attempted to interpret these three phenomena within existing frameworks. The first interpretation calls upon the use of explicit memory strategies in implicit priming tasks. Bowers and Schacter (1989) demonstrated that the use of explicit memory strategies may bring about greater amounts of repetition priming, especially for semantically encoded words (see also Schacter, Bowers, & Booker, 1989, for discussion of similar results). Recent research has reported, however, that conceptual priming occurs reliably while being dissociated from explicit memory performance (Hirshman, Snodgrass, Mindes, & Feenan, 1990; Komatsu & Naito, 1992; Masson & MacLeod, 1992; Naito & Komatsu, 1989). The second interpretation is based on the episodic view of implicit memory in which human memory is thought to be a unitary system and composed of episodic memory traces. Allen and Jacoby (1990) replicated the results of list-wide effects on repetition priming reported by Jacoby (1983b), even under the conditions where performance on implicit perceptual identification is dissociated from performance on explicit recognition, thereby ruling out an explanation based on intentional use of explicit memory strategies. According to the episodic view, the list-wide effects are considered to result from the unconscious involvement of memory for prior episodes: Increasing proportion of overlap between study and test items makes it more likely that memory for the earlier processing of a word will be reinstated.

We have assumed that a primed unit may vary in its level according to task demands and according to developmental states of explicit memory. In implicit memory research with adult subjects, most experiments have employed a list of unrelated words as materials, and briefly exposed or fragmented words have been presented to measure the amount of priming; thus, little attention has been paid to the nesting structures of materials. We suggest that, even in an experimental situation using a list of unrelated words as test items, there exist simultaneously multiple levels at which episodes are defined: Each target word constitutes an episode at a word level; when embedded in a sentence during encoding, a target, together with a sentence cue, constitutes an episode at a sentence level; when generated from an antonym, a target integrated with its generation cue constitutes an episode beyond a word level; a set of targets constitutes an episode at a list level; and so forth. It seems likely that the level at which repetition priming occurs is determined by experimental task demands and developmental states of explicit knowledge structures. Our explanation is most directly applicable to the results of null priming when a target is embedded in a larger unit: The primed unit did not correspond to the target itself because of task demands for encoding. Moreover, priming may occur not only at a word level but also at a list level. Increasing the proportion of study items in a test list seems to enhance priming at a list level: Superior performance when a test list contains a high proportion of studied items may be attributable to both list-level and word-level priming, whereas only word-level priming is available in a list consisting of a lower proportion of studied items. With respect to conceptual priming, Masson and MacLeod (1992) made a similar suggestion. They proposed that the null effect of conceptual priming may have been due to some exceptional generation procedures, such as generating a target from its antonym or from an idiom, in which the target became highly integrated with its context during encoding.

Those working within existing frameworks have argued that priming operates at a perceptual or structural level and that data-driven or within-item processing is the crucial determinant of repetition priming. This view permits us to elucidate the phenomena of priming, as contrasted with those of explicit memory. From a developmental perspective, we have assumed that what constitutes a primed unit is not prescribed but may rely on task demands and developmental constraints. Although grounded in multiple-system views, our framework is similar to the episodic view proposed by Jacoby (1983b) in that reinstating study context is allotted a crucial role in the occurrence of repetition priming. Masson and Mac-

Leod (1992) referred to these context-dependent processes as *interpretive* encoding operations, which construct the initial interpretation of a stimulus in terms of its surrounding context. The interpretive operations are assumed to be optionally followed by *elaborative* operations that are conscious or reflective encoding processes. The distinction between interpretive and elaborative operations is noteworthy, because, assuming that the interpretive encoding contributes to repetition priming and the elaborative encoding is the major determinant of explicit memory performance, this framework can explicate the episodic involvement in repetition priming, with which neither the multiple-system and nor the processing view has been reconciled, and the widespread dissociations between implicit and explicit memory, for which the episodic view has not easily accounted. We have attempted a structural analysis of episodes in which repetition priming takes place; little analysis has been made as to encoding operations from which priming arises. By adopting the distinction between interpretive and elaborative operations, our tentative framework, based on a developmental perspective, may be of help in further elucidation of the phenomena of repetition priming, particularly with respect to the exact manner in which the priming system closely interacts with other memory systems.

CONCLUSIONS

We have discussed the developmental processes of implicit and explicit memory. In the first section, we outlined previous studies in the developmental literature. Studies of child memory have revealed a variety of age-related differences in performance between children and adults; thus, ascertaining the real cause of such differences has constituted a primary concern of researchers. Studies of infant memory, in contrast, suggested a similarity between the memory already available to newborns and implicit memory observed in adults, yet the equivalence between the two lacks confirmation because of the difference in memory tasks. In the second section, we examined recent developmental research in which implicit and explicit memory in children was directly compared with that in adults using the same tasks. It was shown that children's implicit memory was clearly dissociated from their explicit memory and was comparable to that in adults. These findings have afforded further evidence of the implicit/explicit distinction in that implicit memory is developmentally dissociable from explicit memory. Putting together the existent findings, we can characterize the marked difference in developmental processes between implicit and explicit memory. Implicit memory precedes explicit memory developmentally: It emerges almost immediately from birth and remains unchanged throughout childhood; explicit memory arises later in infancy and conspicuously develops from infancy to adulthood. In the last section, we discussed the theoretical implications of developmental research on memory, focusing on a typical phenomenon of implicit memory, namely, repetition priming. Viewing a priming effect as an expression of a distinct memory system, we suggested that the priming system closely interacts with other memory systems. It functions to preserve implicit information in superficially analyzed states, thus constituting the preliminary stage for the later analysis that leads to elaboration of existing memory structures and development of new structures. The priming system may also be affected by higher-order systems in a manner that permits the level at which priming units are defined to vary according to the developmental states of explicit memory and to environmental task demands. Despite a lack of empirical evidence, our tentative framework may shed light on the interactive processes of implicit and explicit memory development.

ACKNOWLEDGMENTS

We are grateful to Peter Graf, Michael Masson, and Alan Parkin for their insightful comments on the first draft of this article. Also, special thanks to Michael Masson, whose generosity with his time in correcting our English has been invaluable.

REFERENCES

Ackerman, B. P. (1987). Descriptions: A model of nonstrategic memory development. In H. W. Reese (Ed.), *Advances in child development and behavior* (pp. 143–183). Orlando, FL: Academic Press.

Allen, S. W., & Jacoby, L. L. (1990). Reinstating study context produces unconscious influences of memory. *Memory & Cognition, 18,* 270–278.

Baillargeon, R., Spelke, E. S., & Wasserman, S. (1985). Object permanence in five-month-old infants. *Cognition, 20,* 191–208.

Bartlett, F. C. (1932). *Remembering.* Cambridge: Cambridge University Press.

Berg, C. A., & Sternberg, R. J. (1985). Response to novelty: Continuity versus discontinuity in the developmental course of intelligence. In H. W. Reese & L. P. Lipsitt (Eds.), *Advances in child development and behavior* (pp. 1–47). New York: Academic Press.

Bjorklund, D. F. (1987). How age changes in knowledge base contribute to the development of children's memory: An interpretive review. *Developmental Review, 7,* 93–130.

Bowers, J. S., & Schacter, D. L. (1990). Implicit memory and test awareness. *Journal of Experimental Psychology: Learning, Memory, and Cognition, 16,* 404–416.

Brewer, W. F. (1986). What is autobiographical memory? In D. C. Rubin (Ed.), *Autobiographical memory* (pp. 25–49). New York: Cambridge University Press.

Brown, A. L. (1975). The development of memory: Knowing, knowing about knowing, and knowing how to know. In H. W. Reese (Ed.), *Advances in child development and behavior* (pp. 103–152). New York: Academic Press.

Brown, A. L. (1978). Knowing when, where, and how to remember: A problem of metacognition. In R. Glaser (Ed.), *Advances in instructional psychology* (pp. 77–165). Hillsdale, NJ: Lawrence Erlbaum Associates.

Brown, A. L. (1979). Theories of memory and the problems of development: Activity, growth, and knowledge. In L. S. Cermak & F. I. M. Craik (Eds.), *Levels of processing in human memory* (pp. 225–258). Hillsdale, NJ: Lawrence Erlbaum Associates.

Carroll, M., Byrne, B., & Kirsner, K. (1985). Autobiographical memory and perceptual learning: A developmental study using picture recognition, naming latency, and perceptual identification. *Memory & Cognition, 13,* 273–279.

Case, R. (1985). *Intellectual development: Birth to adulthood.* Orlando, FL: Academic Press.

Chi, M. T. H. (1978). Knowledge structures and memory development. In R. Siegler (Ed.), *Children's thinking: What develops?* (pp. 73–96). Hillsdale, NJ: Lawrence Erlbaum Associates.

Chi, M. T. H., & Ceci, S. J. (1987). Content knowledge: Its role, representation and restructuring in memory development. In H. W. Reese (Ed.), *Advances in child development and behavior* (pp. 91–141). Orlando, FL: Academic Press.

Durkin, K. (1989). Implicit memory and language acquisition. In S. Lewandowsky, J. C. Dunn, & K. Kirsner (Eds.), *Implicit memory: Theoretical issues* (pp. 241–257). Hillsdale, NJ: Lawrence Erlbaum Associates.

Fagan, J. F. (1984). Infant memory: History, current trends, relations to cognitive psychology. In M. Moscovitch (Ed.), *Infant memory: Its relation to normal and pathological memory in humans and other animals* (pp. 1–27). New York: Plenum.

Fagen, J. W., Yengo, L. A., Rovee-Collier, C. K., & Enright, M. K. (1981). Reactivation of a visual discrimination in early infancy. *Developmental Psychology, 17,* 226–274.

Fivush, R., Gray, J. T., & Fromhoff, F. A. (1987). Two-year-olds talk about the past. *Cognitive Development, 2,* 393–409.

Fivush, R., Hudson, J., & Nelson, K. (1984). Children's long-term memory for a novel event: An exploratory study. *Merrill-Palmer Quarterly, 30,* 303–316.

Fivush, R., & Hudson, J. A. (Eds.). (1990). *Knowing and remembering in young children.* New York: Cambridge University Press.

Flavell, J. H., Friedrichs, A. G., & Hoyt, J. D. (1970). Developmental changes in memorization processes. *Cognitive Psychology, 1,* 324–340.

Flavell, J. H., & Wellman, H. M. (1977). Metamemory. In R. V. Kail & J. W. Hagen (Eds.), *Perspectives on the development of memory and cognition* (pp. 3–33). Hillsdale, NJ: Lawrence Erlbaum Associates.

Friedman, S. (1972). Habituation and recovery of visual response in the alert human newborn. *Journal of Experimental Child Psychology, 13,* 339–349.

Ghatala, E. S. (1984). Developmental changes in incidental memory as a function of meaningfulness and encoding condition. *Developmental Psychology, 20,* 208–211.

Gopnik, A., & Graf, P. (1988). Knowing how you know: Children's understanding of the sources of their beliefs. *Child Development, 59,* 1366–1371.

Graf, P., & Mandler, G. (1984). Activation makes words more accessible but not necessarily more retrievable. *Journal of Verbal Learning and Verbal Behavior, 23,* 553–568.

Graf, P., & Ryan, L. (1990). Transfer-appropriate processing for implicit and explicit memory. *Journal of Experimental Psychology: Learning, Memory, and Cognition, 16,* 978–992.

Graf, P., & Schacter, D. L. (1989). Unitization and grouping mediate dissociations in memory for new associations. *Journal of Experimental Psychology: Learning, Memory, and Cognition, 15,* 930–940.

Graf, P., Shimamura, A. P., & Squire, L. R. (1985). Priming across modalities and priming across category levels: Extending the domain of preserved function in amnesia. *Journal of Experimental Psychology: Learning, Memory, and Cognition, 11,* 386–396.

Greenbaum, J. L., & Graf. P. (1989). Preschool period development of implicit and explicit remembering. *Bulletin of the Psychonomic Society, 27,* 417–420.

Gregg, V. (1976). Word frequency, recognition and recall. In J. Brown (Ed.), *Recall and recognition* (pp. 183–216). London: Wiley.

Hasher, L., & Zacks, R. T. (1979). Automatic and effortful processes in memory. *Journal of Experimental Psychology: General, 108,* 356–388.

Hirshman, E., Snodgrass, J. G., Mindes, J., & Feenan, K. (1990). Conceptual priming in fragment completion. *Journal of Experimental Psychology: Learning, Memory, and Cognition, 16,* 634–647.

Hudson, J. A. (1986). Memories are made of this: General event knowledge and development of autobiographical memory. In K. Nelson (Ed.), *Event knowledge: Structure and function in development* (pp. 97–118). Hillsdale, NJ: Lawrence Erlbaum Associates.

Hunt, R. R., & Einstein, G. O. (1981). Relational and item-specific information in memory. *Journal of Verbal Learning and Verbal Behavior, 20,* 497–514.

Istomina, Z. M. (1975). The development of voluntary memory in preschool-age children. *Soviet Psychology, 13,* 5–64.

Jacoby, L. L. (1983a). Remembering the data: Analyzing interactive processes in reading. *Journal of Verbal Learning and Verbal Behavior, 17,* 649–667.

Jacoby, L. L. (1983b). Perceptual enhancement: Persistent effects of an experience. *Journal of Experimental Psychology: Learning, Memory, and Cognition, 9,* 21–38.

Kail, R. V. (1990). *The development of memory in children* (3rd ed.). New York: W. H. Freeman.

Kobasigawa, A. (1974). Utilization of retrieval cues by children in recall. *Child Development, 45,* 127–134.

Komatsu, S., & Naito, M. (1985). Priming effects in the perceptual identification task after a long-term retention interval: In comparison with recognition memory. *Japanese Journal of Psychology, 55,* 362–365.

Komatsu, S., & Naito, M. (1992). Repetition priming with Japanese Kana scripts in word-fragment completion. *Memory & Cognition, 20,* 160–170.

Kreutzer, M. A., Leonard, C., & Flavell, J. H. (1975). An interview study of children's knowledge about memory. *Monographs of the Society for Research in Child Development, 40* (1, Serial No. 159), 1–58.

Levy, B. A., & Kirsner, K. (1989). Reprocessing text: Indirect measures of word and message level processes. *Journal of Experimental Psychology: Learning, Memory, and Cognition, 15,* 407–417.

Lindberg, M. A. (1980). Is knowledge base development a necessary and sufficient condition for memory development? *Journal of Experimental Child Psychology, 30,* 401–410.

MacLeod, C. M. (1989). Word context during initial exposure influences degree of priming in word fragment completion. *Journal of Experimental Psychology: Learning, Memory, and Cognition, 15,* 398–406.

Mandler, G. (1979). Organization and repetition: Organizational principles with special reference to rote learning. In L.-G. Nilsson (Ed.), *Perspectives on memory research: Essays in honor of Uppsala University's 500th anniversary* (pp. 293–327). Hillsdale, NJ: Lawrence Erlbaum Associates.

Mandler, J. M. (1984). Representation and recall in infancy. In M. Moscovitch (Ed.), *Infant memory: Its relation to normal and pathological memory in humans and other animals* (pp. 75–101). New York: Plenum.

Mandler, J. M. (1988). How to build a baby: On the development of an accessible representational system. *Cognitive Development, 3,* 113–136.

Masson, M. E. J., & MacLeod, C. M. (1992). Re-enacting the route to interpretation: Enhanced perceptual identification without prior perception. *Journal of Experimental Psychology: General, 121,* 145–176.

Meacham, J. A. (1977). Soviet investigations of memory development. In R. V. Kail & J. W. Hagen (Eds.), *Perspectives on the development of memory and cognition* (pp. 273–295). Hillsdale, NJ: Lawrence Erlbaum Associates.

Meltzoff, A. N. (1988). Infant imitation and memory: Nine-month-olds in immediate and deferred tests. *Child Development, 59,* 217–225.

Moely, B. E., Olson, F. A., Halwes, T. G., & Flavell, J. H. (1969). Production deficiency in young children's clustered recall. *Developmental Psychology, 1,* 26–34.

Moscovitch, M. (1985). Memory from infancy to old age: Implications for theories of normal and pathological memory. *Annals of the New York Academy of Sciences, 444*, 78–96.

Muir-Broaddus, J. E., & Bjorklund, D. F. (1990). Developmental and individual differences in children's memory strategies: The role of knowledge. In W. Schneider & F. E. Weinert (Eds.), *Interactions among aptitudes, strategies, and knowledge in cognitive performance* (pp. 99–116). New York: Springer-Verlag.

Naito, M. (1990). Repetition priming in children and adults: Age-related dissociation between implicit and explicit memory. *Journal of Experimental Child Psychology, 50*, 462–484.

Naito, M., & Komatsu, S. (1989). Effects of conceptually driven processing on perceptual identification. *Japanese Psychological Research, 31*, 45–56.

Naus, M. J., & Halasz, F. G. (1979). Developmental perspectives on cognitive processing and semantic memory structure. In L. S. Cermak & F. I. M. Craik (Eds.), *Levels of processing in human memory* (pp. 259–288). Hillsdale, NJ: Lawrence Erlbaum Associates.

Neisser, U. (1986). Nested structure in autobiographical memory. In D. C. Rubin (Ed.), *Autobiographical memory* (pp. 71–81). New York: Cambridge University Press.

Neisser, U. (1988). Five kinds of self-knowledge. *Philosophical Psychology, 1*, 35–59.

Neisser, U., & Winograd, E. (Eds.). (1988). *Remembering reconsidered: Ecological and traditional approaches to the study of memory*. New York: Cambridge University Press.

Nelson, K. (Ed.). (1986). *Event knowledge: Structure and function in development*. Hillsdale, NJ: Lawrence Erlbaum Associates.

Nelson, K. (1988). The ontogeny of memory for real events. In U. Neisser & E. Winograd (Eds.), *Remembering reconsidered: Ecological and traditional approaches to the study of memory* (pp. 244–276). New York: Cambridge University Press.

Nelson, K. (1990). Remembering, forgetting, and childhood amnesia. In R. Fivush & J. A. Hudson (Eds.), *Knowing and remembering in young children*. (pp. 301–316). New York: Cambridge University Press.

Oliphant, G. W. (1983). Repetition and recency effects in word recognition. *Australian Journal of Psychology, 35*, 393–403.

Ornstein, P. A., & Naus, M. J. (1985). Effects of the knowledge base on children's memory strategies. In H. W. Reese (Ed.), *Advances in child development and behavior* (pp. 113–148). Orlando, FL: Academic Press.

Parkin, A. J. (1989). The development and nature of implicit memory. In S. Lewandowsky, J. C. Dunn, & K. Kirsner (Eds.), *Implicit memory: Theoretical issues* (pp. 231–240). Hillsdale, NJ: Lawrence Erlbaum Associates.

Parkin, A. J., & Streete, S. (1988). Implicit and explicit memory in young children and adults. *British Journal of Psychology, 79*, 361–369.

Pascual-Leone, J. (1970). A mathematical model for the transition rule in Piaget's developmental stages. *Acta Psychologica, 32*, 301–345.

Perner, J. (1990). Experiential awareness and children's episodic memory. In W. Schneider & F. E. Weinert (Eds.), *Interactions among aptitudes, strategies, and knowledge in cognitive performance* (pp. 3–11). New York: Springer-Verlag.

Piaget, J. (1952). *The origins of intelligence in children*. New York: International Universities Press.

Piaget, J. (1954). *The construction of reality in the child*. New York: Basic Books.

Piaget, J., & Inhelder, B. (1973). *Memory and intelligence*. New York: Basic Books.

Pressley, M., & Levin, J. R. (1978). Developmental constraints associated with children's use of the keyword method of foreign language vocabulary learning. *Journal of Experimental Child Psychology, 26*, 359–372.

Rheingold, H. L. (1985). Development as the acquisition of familiarity. *Annual Review of Psychology, 36*, 1–17.

Richardson-Klavehn, A., & Bjork, R. A. (1988). Measures of memory. *Annual Review of Psychology, 39*, 475–543.

Roediger, H. L., & Blaxton, T. A. (1987). Retrieval modes produce dissociations in memory for surface information. In D. S. Gorfein & R. R. Hoffman (Eds.), *The Ebbinghaus Centennial Conference* (pp. 349–379). Hillsdale, NJ: Lawrence Erlbaum Associates.

Rovee-Collier, C., & Hayne, H. (1987). Reactivation of infant memory: Implications for cognitive development. In H. W. Reese (Ed.), *Advances in child development and behavior* (pp. 185–238). Orlando, FL: Academic Press.

Rovee-Collier, C. K., Sullivan, M. W., Enright, M., Lucas, D., & Fagen, J. W. (1980). Reactivation of infant memory. *Science, 208,* 1159–1161.

Rubin, D. C. (Ed.). (1986). *Autobiographical memory.* New York: Cambridge University Press.

Schacter, D. L. (1987). Implicit memory: History and current status. *Journal of Experimental Psychology: Learning, Memory, and Cognition, 13,* 501–518.

Schacter, D. L. (1990). Perceptual representation systems and implicit memory: Toward a resolution of the multiple memory systems debate. *Annals of the New York Academy of Sciences, 608,* 543–572.

Schacter, D. L., Bowers, J., & Booker, J. (1989). Intention, awareness, and implicit memory: The retrieval intentionality criterion. In S. Lewandowsky, J. C. Dunn, & K. Kirsner (Eds.), *Implicit memory: Theoretical issues* (pp. 47–65). Hillsdale, NJ: Lawrence Erlbaum Associates.

Schacter, D. L., & Moscovitch, M. (1984). Infants, amnesics, and dissociable memory systems. In M. Moscovitch (Ed.), *Infant memory: Its relation to normal and pathological memory in humans and other animals* (pp. 173–216). New York: Plenum.

Schank, R. C., & Abelson, R. P. (1977). *Scripts, plans, goals and understanding.* Hillsdale, NJ: Lawrence Erlbaum Associates.

Schneider, W., & Pressley, M. (1989). *Memory development between 2 and 20.* New York: Springer-Verlag.

Sherry, D. F., & Schacter, D. L. (1987). The evolution of multiple memory systems. *Psychological Review, 94,* 439–454.

Sloman, S. A., Hayman, C. A. G., Ohta, N., Law, J., & Tulving, E. (1988). Forgetting in primed fragment completion. *Journal of Experimental Psychology: Learning, Memory, and Cognition, 14,* 223–239.

Sophian, C. (1980). Habituation is not enough: Novelty preferences, search, and memory in infancy. *Merrill-Palmer Quarterly, 26,* 239–257.

Squire, L. R. (1987). *Memory and brain.* New York: Oxford University Press.

Tulving, E. (1985). How many memory systems are there? *American Psychologist, 40,* 385–398.

Tulving, E., & Schacter, D. L. (1990). Priming and human memory systems. *Science, 247,* 301–396.

Tulving, E., Schacter, D. L., & Stark, H. A. (1982). Priming effects in word-fragment completion are independent of recognition memory. *Journal of Experimental Psychology: Learning, Memory, & Cognition, 8,* 336–342.

Wellman, H. M. (1985). The child's theory of mind: The development of conceptions of cognition. In S. R. Yussen (Ed.), *The growth of reflection* (pp. 169–206). New York: Academic Press.

III NEUROPSYCHOLOGY

Neuropsychology is concerned with the relationship between brain structures and brain functions. The contributions to this part of the book examine what has been learned about this relationship from investigations of implicit and explicit memory in amnesic patients. Researchers in this area have combined methodological and conceptual tools from various disciplines, especially from cognition and neuroscience, and the following chapters highlight some of the benefits that result from such an interdisciplinary approach.

The chapter by Shimamura provides a historical overview of neuropsychological studies of amnesic patients, in which the landmark event has been the discovery of preserved memory functions in amnesia. He traces the evolution of a sequence of theories regarding preserved memory functions, with an emphasis on whether implicit memory for novel information is preserved in amnesia. A review of evidence concerning the brain structures that are required for learning and remembering leads Shimamura to conclude that different aspects of implicit memory (i.e., skill learning and priming) may be mediated by different brain struc-tures. This conclusion is consistent with evidence of performance dissociations among different kinds of implicit memory tasks. Finally, Shimamura as well as other contributors to this book argue (cf. Roediger & Srinivas, Chapter 2; Parkin, Chapter 9; Bowers & Schacter, Chapter 14) that systems and processing explanations of memory performance dissociations are not mutually exclusive—they provide different but complementary perspectives.

Cermak and his colleagues have been investigating the memory abilities of amnesic patients for over two decades, and the chapter outlines the kinds of questions that motivated his lab's research throughout this period and the empirical and theoretical insights that have emerged. By contrast with other investigators in neuropsychology who address questions about impaired memory systems, Cermak was heavily influenced by Craik and Lockhart's levels of processing framework in the 1970s and began asking questions about what kinds of processing operations are impaired or spared in amnesia. Today, Cermak's research on implicit and explicit memory is directed by the hypothesis that the memory impairments of amnesic patients are associated with deficits in consciously controlled processing. The chapter points out the importance of exploring the parallel between the controlled/automatic processing distinction that he has pursued and the perceptual/conceptual processing distinction that has influenced many other research programs.

Bowers and Schacter trace the theoretical and empirical history of research on implicit memory for novel information in amnesic patients (cf. Shimamura, Chapter 12, this volume). Whether or not amnesic patients can demonstrate implicit memory for novel stimuli has important implications for theories of amnesia, because until recently the predominant view in neuropsychology was that the memory functions that are preserved in amnesics rely on preexisting knowledge. Bowers and Schacter begin by examining what is meant by novel, and then they summarize convincing evidence that implicit memory for novel stimuli (e.g., nonwords, new associations between words, and novel objects) is preserved in amnesic patients, at least under some conditions. This evidence can be accommodated by a framework (that Schacter has developed in several previous papers) that posits a perceptual representation system that can operate independently of other memory functions.

In the final chapter, Ostergaard and Jernigan consider several concerns about the evidence that is often cited to support the view that implicit and explicit memory are mediated by different brain structures. One type of evidence is the finding of stochastic independence between implicit and explicit test performance. Ostergaard and Jernigan point out that contingency analyses may fail to detect dependence between tests because only a small proportion of performance variance is due to episodic memory processing. A second concern involves demonstrations of preserved priming in amnesic patients, or, more specifically, the power of experiments to detect deficits on implicit tests. Ostergaard and Jernigan's analysis of the power of several representative studies is disturbing and calls for caution when interpreting null effects. This chapter also reports a new study with normal subjects and patients with various brain lesions. In contrast to widely held views in neuropsychology, the findings from this study suggest that performance on both implicit and explicit memory tests may be mediated by the limbic system and that a priming deficit in amnesics may be masked by damage to other areas that impairs perceptual processing and thereby inflates priming effects.

12

Neuropsychological Analyses of Implicit Memory: History, Methodology and Theoretical Interpretations

Arthur P. Shimamura
University of California, Berkeley

Over the past 20 years, neuropsychological investigations of brain-injured patients have provided important clues to the understanding of normal cognitive function. Indeed, there has been growing interest in the relationship between cognitive and brain processes, as exemplified by new terms such as *cognitive neuroscience* and *cognitive neuropsychology* (for review, see Broadbent & Weiskrantz, 1982; Lister & Weingartner, 1991; McCarthy & Warrington, 1990; Shallice, 1988; Squire, 1987). Of course, neurobehavioral approaches have been advocated by scientists in the past (Hebb, 1949; Lashley, 1950; Luria, 1973; Tolman, 1948), and thus this research endeavor is not entirely original. Yet recent interest is significant in that it has brought a new level of interaction between cognitive scientists and neuroscientists. In memory research, this approach has been fruitful in identifying reliable associations between memory impairment and the locus of brain injury. In addition, this approach has delineated dissociations of functions—that is, circumscribed brain lesions can affect certain functions but leave others entirely intact.

Studies of organic amnesia have been a central focus in neurocognitive investigations of memory. Organic amnesia is the severe and rather selective impairment of new learning capacity, which often occurs after damage to the medial temporal region (e.g., hippocampal formation) or to the diencephalic midline (e.g., midline thalamic nuclei) (for review, see Mayes, 1988; Shimamura, 1989; Squire, 1987). In this neurological disorder, severe memory impairment occurs, despite intact intellectual, language, and social skills. Bilateral damage to these brain regions impairs the ability to learn new information received from any sensory modality, thereby affecting both verbal and nonverbal memory. Impairment can be observed on a variety of measures, including free recall, cued recall, recognition memory, and paired-associate learning.

The distinction between explicit and implicit memory was largely developed from findings of amnesic patients. The central finding was that amnesic patients exhibit intact performance on certain tests of memory, despite severe impairment on other tests (see Schacter, 1987; Shimamura, 1986; Squire, 1987). The term *implicit memory* was coined by Graf and Schacter (1985) to characterize the quality of memories that is preserved. In all cases, memory was demonstrated indirectly or implicitly—as indicated by improved skill learning, facilitation of response latency, or response biases (e.g., priming effects). Other terms, such as procedural memory, habit, and memory without awareness, have been used to characterize the same form of memory (see Jacoby & Witherspoon, 1982; Mishkin, Malamut, & Bachevalier, 1984; Squire, 1987; Squire & Zola-Morgan, 1988). The kind of memory that is impaired in amnesia has been characterized as *explicit,* declarative, or conscious. The striking distinction between impaired and preserved forms of memory in amnesia led Crowder to write: "The study of amnesic patients led the way to our growing recognition that some distinction, similar to that between procedural and declarative memory, is likely to be indispensable for any general theory of memory" (Crowder, 1985, p. 433).

Thus, unlike previous neuropsychological investigations, which typically involved the rather mundane exercise of administering standard cognitive paradigms to brain-injured patients, the study of implicit (procedural) memory was actually developed by neuropsychological researchers and has provided important information for theoretical interpretations of normal memory functions. This chapter reviews some of the major neuropsychological findings concerning implicit memory, describes methodological issues in interpreting the findings, and outlines some theoretical conceptualizations of the phenomenon.

HISTORICAL PERSPECTIVE

Clues regarding a neuropsychological distinction between implicit and explicit memory arose as early as the turn of the century in clinical observations of preserved learning in amnesic patients. Claparède (1911/1951), in an interview with an amnesic patient, observed a form of implicit memory for emotional information. He hid a pin in his fingers and surreptitiously pricked the patient's hand. Later, he again reached for the patient's hand, but the patient quickly withdrew. The patient had no conscious recollection of the previous incident but stated that "sometimes pins are hidden in people's hands." It was not until the 1960s that researchers developed experimental paradigms for the analysis of preserved memory functions in amnesia. Since the 1960s, neuropsychological research has been concerned with three primary interests: (a) to identify the existence of preserved implicit memory in amnesic patients, (b) to characterize the boundary conditions under which implicit memory is observed, and (c) to understand the biological basis of implicit memory functions. These three research interests are briefly reviewed in this section.

The Identification of Preserved Memory Functions in Amnesia

During the 1960s, evidence for preserved memory in amnesia occurred in studies of skill learning (for review see Parkin, 1982; Shimamura, 1989). For example, considerable retention of perceptual-motor skills was observed in amnesic patients on pursuit-rotor or mirror tracing tasks (Brooks and Baddeley, 1976; Corkin, 1968). These tasks required on-line hand-eye coordination, and skill learning was exhibited in the form of improved performance across training trials. Amnesic patients retained these skills for weeks, though some did not have any conscious recollection of having previously performed the task. That is, learning was demonstrated in performance, not in any verbal acknowledgement that learning had taken place.

Following these initial findings, investigators observed that the domain of preserved memory functions in amnesia is even broader. Weiskrantz and Warrington (1979) tested amnesic patients in an eyeblink classical conditioning paradigm in which a tone precedes an air puff to the eye. The conditioned response (eyeblink in response to the tone) was retained in amnesic patients for as long as 24 hr, even though they did not recollect having previously seen the test apparatus (see also, Daum, Channon, & Canavan, 1989). Cohen and Squire (1980) showed that amnesic patients could exhibit intact learning of a reading skill (i.e., reading mirror-reversed words). Amnesic patients exhibited normal learning and retention of the mirror-reading skill even when they were tested 1 month after learning. Such findings of preserved skill learning and classical conditioning suggested that amnesic patients could perform tasks involving the tuning or modification of stimulus-response associations, perceptual-motor coordination, or cognitive processes.

Amnesic patients were also reported to exhibit intact memory for item-specific information. These studies involved the memory phenomenon known as *priming* (see Schacter, 1987; Shimamura, 1986). Priming is a facilitation or bias in performance as a result of recently encountered information. The impetus for analyses of priming effects in amnesia came from studies by Warrington and Weiskrantz (1968, 1970). In these studies, amnesic patients were shown words or pictures in a fragmented form and asked to identify the stimuli. Less degraded versions of the each stimulus were shown until identification was successful. In these studies, performance by amnesic patients was facilitated when the same word or picture was repeated on a subsequent trial. This priming effect occurred despite failure to discriminate previously presented stimuli from new ones in a recognition memory test.

Graf, Squire, and Mandler (1984) identified an important variable that was necessary for the observation of intact priming in amnesic patients. They used a word-stem completion test in which words (e.g., MOTEL) are presented to subjects and later cued by three-letter word beginnings or *stems* (e.g., MOT). During the completion test, subjects were asked simply to say the first word that came to mind for each word stem. On this test, amnesic patients and control subjects performed equivalently. That is, they tended to use previously presented words in the word completion test two or three times as often as they would if they had not previously seen the word. In this test, words appear to pop into mind. However, when subjects were asked to use the same word stems as aids to recollect explicitly words from the study session (cued recall), the control subjects performed better than the amnesic patients. Various paradigms have been used to assess priming effects in amnesic patients (Cermak, Talbot, Chandler, & Wolbarst, 1985; Graf, Shimamura, & Squire, 1985; Jacoby & Witherspoon, 1982; Schacter, 1985; for review see Richardson-Klavehn & Bjork, 1988; Schacter, 1987; Shimamura, 1986). In all of these paradigms, preserved performance was observed only if memory was assessed indirectly or without conscious awareness that memory was being tested.

The Boundary Conditions of Implicit Memory in Amnesia

Extensive investigations concerning the boundary conditions of preserved priming in amnesia occurred during the 1980s. Graf et al. (1985) showed that amnesic patients exhibited normal word completion priming across sensory modalities (see Fig. 12.1). Specifically, priming was intact when words were presented auditorily and the word stems in the completion test were presented visually. Other studies showed that priming in amnesia could cross semantic boundaries (Graf et al., 1985; Schacter, 1985; Shimamura & Squire, 1984; see also Gardner, Boller, Moreines, & Butters, 1973). For example, Shimamura and Squire (1984) presented words (e.g., BABY) and later asked subjects to "free associate" to related words (e.g., CHILD). These findings indicated that intact priming occurs for semantic associates and is not restricted to sensory or perceptual cues. Many of these priming effects appeared to be short-lasting. In studies of the time course of priming effects, the effects appeared to decay to baseline levels in both amnesic patients and control subjects after a 2-hr retention interval (Graf et al., 1984; Shimamura & Squire, 1984; Squire, Shimamura, & Graf, 1987). In situations in which priming effects were long-lasting in control subjects (e.g., Tulving, Schacter, & Stark, 1982), amnesic patients still exhibited only short-lasting priming effects (Squire et al., 1987).

Findings of preserved priming effects in amnesia appeared to depend on the activation of preexisting information, such as words, pictures, or semantic associates. Indeed, early studies failed to observe implicit memory for novel verbal

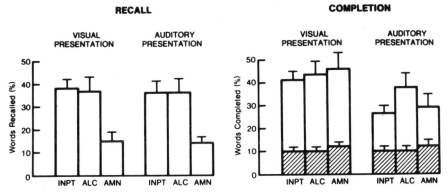

FIG. 12.1.   Free recall (left) and word completion (right) performance by amnesic patients (AMN), inpatient control subjects (INPT), and alcoholic controls (ALC). Visual presentations involved visual presentation of both study words and test cues. Auditory presentations involved auditory presentation of study words and visual presentation of test cues. The shaded area of bars shows baseline completion performance. *Note.* From "Priming across modalities and priming across category levels: Extending the domain of preserved function in amnesia," *Journal of Experimental Psychology: Learning, Memory and Cognition, 11,* pp. 386–396.

stimuli, such as pseudowords (i.e., pronounceable nonwords), as measured by performance on tests of stem completion (Diamond & Rozin, 1985) and word identification (Cermak et al., 1985). More recently, however, two studies have reported that pseudowords can be primed to some extent on the lexical decision task, a task in which subjects determine whether a stimulus is a word or nonword (Gordon, 1988; Smith & Oscar-Berman, 1990). For example, Smith and Oscar-Berman (1990) showed that patients with Korsakoff's syndrome exhibited less accurate classifications of repeated pseudowords compared to initial presentations, suggesting that the initial presentation produced a familiarity effect, thus making repeated pseudowords more wordlike. In terms of standard reaction time measures of lexical decision, the patients did not exhibit facilitation of reaction times for repeated pseudowords, whereas control subject did benefit from repetition.

Some investigations have reported preserved implicit memory for novel information. Johnson, Kim, and Risse (1985) demonstrated priming effects in amnesia for repeated but unfamiliar melodies. In that study, subjects exhibited a preference bias for repeated Korean melodies compared to new melodies. However, in the same investigation, normal preference biases were not observed in amnesic patients for faces that were associated with positive affect (Johnson et al., 1985, Experiment 2). Nissen and Bullemer (1987) reported priming (i.e., facilitation) of response latency in a four-choice reaction time task which involved a repeated sequence of trials within a block of 10 trials. Patients with Korsakoff's syndrome benefited from the repeated sequence as indicated by faster response times across four blocks of trials. Unfortunately, performance by patients with Korsakoff's syndrome was not entirely normal, because they exhibited overall slower response times than control subjects.

Intact nonverbal priming was observed in patient H. M. in a task involving implicit memory for abstract line drawings (Gabrieli, Milberg, Keane, & Corkin, 1990). Patient H. M. and control subjects copied patterns of lines that were each based on five dots. Following a short delay, the subjects were shown only the dots and were asked to draw any figure that connected the dots. H. M. tended to use previously presented patterns in this task at the same frequency as control subjects. Similar findings were reported for a group of amnesic patients in a similar test of nonverbal priming (Musen & Squire, in press). Also, Schacter and colleagues have provided considerable evidence concerning implicit memory for abstract objects (see Bowers and Schacter, Chapter 14, this volume; Schacter, Cooper & Delaney, 1990).

Evidence for priming of novel information has extended the boundary conditions of preserved implicit memory in amnesia. It suggests that priming effects extend beyond the limits of preexisting lexical or semantic representations. Another paradigm that has been used to evaluate the boundary conditions of preserved implicit memory is the finding of implicit memory for associations between previously unrelated information (Graf and Schacter, 1985). Subjects study unrelated words pairs (e.g., WINDOW-REASON) and are tested by word completion in which the first word is presented with the three-letter beginning of the second word (e.g., WINDOW-REA). This condition was compared to trials in which a recombined set was used such that the stem and cue word came from different pairs (e.g., BREAD-REA). It was initially reported that amnesic patients exhibited stronger priming effects on trials in which stems were paired with the same word used during study than on trials in which stems were recombined with other words (Graf & Schacter, 1985). However, further assessment of the effect showed that only mildly amnesic patients exhibited priming of new associations, whereas severely amnesic patient did not (Schacter & Graf, 1986). Recent studies have shown that other amnesic patients generally fail to exhibit priming of new associations in this paradigm and in related paradigms (Cermak, Bleich, & Blackford, 1988; Mayes & Gooding, 1989; Paller & Mayes, 1991; Shimamura & Squire, 1989). For example, on two testing occasions amnesic patients failed to show reliable priming effects for new associations (Shimamura & Squire, 1989), though in other studies these same patients exhibited entirely normal word completion and free association priming effects for words and word associates.

Moscovitch, Winocur, and McLachlan (1986) provided some evidence for implicit memory of new associations. They asked subjects to study word pairs and then tested reading speed for the same word pairs and for word pairs that

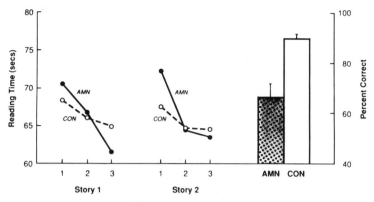

FIG. 12.2.   Time required to read aloud two different stores, each pre-sented three times in succession. Amnesic patients (AMN) exhibited normal reading speeds compared to control subjects (CON), despite impaired recognition memory for the story content (right bar graphs). *Note.* From "Intact text-specific reading skills in amnesia," *Journal of Experimental Psychology: Learning, Memory, and Cognition, 16,* 1068–1076.

contained recombined words from different sets of pairs. A group of memory-impaired patients with mixed etiologies (Alzheimer's disease, anoxic patient, head injury) exhibited faster reading speeds for previously presented word pairs compared to recombined pairs. Similar findings were also observed for intact sentences compared with recombined sentences (Moscovitch et al., 1986). Mu-sen, Shimamura, and Squire (1990) provided similar findings in a study of reading speed for a short paragraph. Amnesic patients and control subjects read the same paragraph three times and reading speed was measured. Reading speed was facilitated for both amnesic patients and control subjects across the three trials. This priming effect appeared to be item-specific, because reading speed of a different paragraph produced times comparable to the first reading of the initial paragraph (see Fig. 12.2). In the Musen et al. (1990) study, the priming effect was transient in both amnesic patients and control subjects, such that reading speed was not different from initial reading speed when a final reading trial occurred 2 hr after the initial three readings.

Future studies will undoubtedly extend and clarify the boundary conditions of preserved implicit memory in amnesia. Presently, there appears to be some limit concerning the scope of preserved memory. For example, the time course of many forms of implicit memory (e.g., priming effects) appears to be rather short-lasting in both amnesic patients and control subjects. When control subjects do exhibit long-lasting priming effects (e.g., Tulving et al., 1982), amnesic patients do not exhibit any long-lasting priming effects or their priming effects are not as strong as those observed in control subjects. Implicit memory, however, is not restricted to preexisting lexical or semantic information. Priming of nonverbal information can occur in amnesic patients. Yet there may be limits to the extent of nonverbal priming. There may also be limits to the extent of priming of new verbal associations, when the paradigm involves the linking of two unrelated words. These limits in priming new nonverbal patterns or new verbal associations may be determined by the degree to which stimuli can be unitized or chunked. One possibility is that priming depends on some form of preexisting information—presumably at a level more primitive than lexical or pictorial information (e.g., phonemes, regularity of familiar lines or edges) (for further discussion, see Bowers & Schacter, Chapter 14, this volume). One hypothesis of this interpretation is that priming effects will decrease when stimuli conform to more distant approximations to preexisting lexical, semantic, or pictorial information.

The Biological Bases of Implicit Memory Functions

What are the neutral substrates that underlie implicit memory functions? Squire (1987) suggested that implicit or procedural memory is not a single entity but instead is composed of many information processing systems, each of which can be tuned or modified by experience. Thus, no single brain structure is responsible for all forms of implicit memory. Instead, the tuning or modification of cognitive processes is specific to the processes that are activated. For implicit memory, many neural systems may contribute to its behavioral expression. For example, certain skills may depend on the coordination and integration of many perceptual and motor processes. On the other hand, forms of implicit memory may be distinct, such that some forms may depend on certain neural systems, whereas others depend on different neural systems. That is, though it is unlikely that all implicit memory functions will have same neural basis, it may be that there is some localization of implicit memory functions.

Based on the view that different forms of implicit memory will have different neural bases, it is likely, if not demanded, that dissociations of function will occur between forms of implicit memory. Indeed, double dissociations between priming and skill learning have been observed in studies of Alzheimer's disease—a cortical degenerative disease—and Huntington's disease—primarily a subcortical disease that causes cell loss in the neostriatum. Patients with Alzheimer's disease exhibit substantial impairment on tests of word-stem completion and free association priming (Heindel, Salmon, Shults, Walicke, & Butters, 1989; Keane, Gabrieli, Fennema, Growdon, & Corkin, 1991; Salmon, Shimamura, Butters, & Smith, 1988; Shimamura, Salmon, Squire, & Butters, 1987). Yet these patients exhibit preserved skill learning on the pursuit-rotor task (Heindel, Butters, & Salmon, 1988; Heindel et al., 1989). Conversely, patients with Huntington's disease exhibit intact word-stem and free association priming but are impaired on the pursuit-rotor task (Heindel et al., 1989, 1988; Salmon et al., 1988; Shimamura et al., 1987). These findings suggest that the neocortical areas damaged in Alzheimer's disease, such as association cortex, may be critical for word priming. Indeed, these areas may themselves be the storehouse of lexical and semantic representations. Neostriatal areas, such as the basal ganglia, may be critical for perceptual-motor skill learning.

Other studies have further delineated the cortical areas that contribute to priming effects. Keane et al. (1991) observed impaired word-stem completion priming in patients with Alzheimer's disease but also demonstrated preserved "perceptual" priming on tests of perceptual identification. Keane et al. (1991) suggest that the preserved priming ability is mediated by perceptual processes that involve the occipital lobe, a brain region that is not grossly affected by Alzheimer's disease. Word-stem completion is presumed to depend on conceptual or lexical processes, perhaps involving associational areas in parietal and temporal lobe. Evidence corroborating these neuropsychological findings has been provided by studies of positron emission tomography (PET) involving normal subjects. Petersen, Fox, Posner, Mintun, and Raichle (1988) have identified a region in left extrastriate occipital cortex where activity appears to be attributable to the coding of the visual form of words. Moreover, analyses of PET activation during word-stem completion testing indicate cortical activity in posterior cortex (Squire et al., 1991).

Schacter has suggested that priming effects critically involve perceptual representation systems, which code the visual representation of words and objects (Schacter, 1990; Tulving & Schacter, 1990). Drawing on neuropsychological research involving patients with acquired dyslexia and object agnosias (e.g., Humphreys & Riddoch, 1987; Coltheart, Patterson, & Marshall, 1980), Schacter suggests that implicit memory is mediated primarily by cortical areas that are used to construct and represent visual forms. Presumably these areas include the region of the occipital-temporal-parietal junction (e.g., angular gyrus) and perhaps extrastriate areas, which are known to be damaged in patients with certain forms of acquired dyslexia and visual agnosias. Interestingly, Schacter, Rapscak, Rubens, Tharan, and Laguna (1990) reported a case study of a letter-by-letter dyslexic patient with primarily extrastriate damage who exhibited good performance on a perceptual identification priming task. Based on the findings of Keane et al. (1991), one might suppose that priming in a perceptual identification paradigm would be impaired in this patient as a result of occipital lobe damage. However, Schacter et al. (1990) suggested that the word form system was not compromised in this patient, presumably because temporal-parietal areas were not severely damaged.

Studies of the biological basis of implicit memory suggests that posterior cortical areas may be important for priming effects, whereas the basal ganglia may be important for skill learning. It is likely that lexical and semantic representations are distributed rather widely in posterior association cortex. Therefore, deficits in priming ability may require widespread disruption of cortical activity in these areas, such as seen in Alzheimer's disease. Interestingly, the role of the frontal lobes has not been well characterized in terms of implicit memory functions. There is some suggestion that the frontal lobes may play a role in motor skill learning (Heindel et al., 1989). In terms of priming effects, recent findings indicate that word-stem completion performance is intact in patients with lesions involving the dorsolateral prefrontal cortex (Shimamura, Gershberg, Jurica, Mangels, & Knight, 1992).

METHODOLOGICAL CONCERNS AND
THEORETICAL INTERPRETATIONS

What do neuropsychological findings offer to theories of normal memory functions? Clearly, one advantage of the neuropsychological approach is that it may be possible to identify brain structures critical for specific memory functions. Converging evidence from both cognitive and biological investigations could significantly benefit our understanding of memory and brain mechanisms. Evidence from amnesic patients indicates that performance on certain measures of implicit memory can occur despite damage to the medial temporal region or diencephalic midline. Theoretical views have been developed to characterize this distinction in terms of multiple memory systems. Various dichotomies have been developed, such as implicit versus explicit memory (Graf & Schacter, 1985; Schacter, 1987), procedural versus declarative memory (Cohen & Squire, 1980; Squire, 1987), habit versus memory (Mishkin et al., 1984), and semantic memory versus cognitive mediation (Warrington & Weiskrantz, 1982). Recently, cognitive psychologists have emphasized the importance of the difference in mental processes that operate during implicit and explicit memory tasks (Roediger, 1990: Roediger, Weldon, & Challis, 1989).

The ways in which neuropsychological findings have been interpreted depend critically on assumptions one has about methodological techniques. In particular, techniques of analyzing dissociations and associations of mental processes in both neuropsychological and cognitive research have played a crucial role in theoretical interpretations. In the field of neuropsychology, mental operations have been dissociated on the basis of the selectivity of cognitive dysfunction following brain injury. Neuropsychological dissociations, such as those observed between implicit and explicit memory, indicate that certain brain regions contribute significantly to some mental processes yet only minimally or not at all to others. In cognitive psychology, behavioral dissociations have been used to argue that certain mental processes operate independently from others (see Baddeley, 1986; Posner, 1978; Sternberg, 1969). Indeed, some of the most elegant findings in the field of cognitive psychology have come from analyses of functional dissociations between mental operations.

Despite rather impressive findings of neuropsychological and functional dissociations, it is important to clarify some methodological assumptions concern-

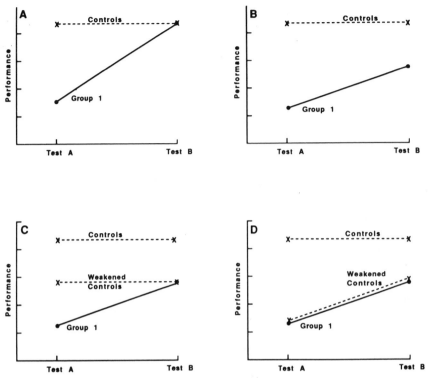

FIG. 12.3. Idealized data sets involving a control group and neuropsychological group (Group 1), and weakened controls in which performance is matched to Group 1 on a dependent measure. (A) Single
dissociation, (B) partial dissociation, (C) true partial dissociation, and
(D) spurious partial dissociation. *Note.* Adapted from *Brain Organization and Memory: Cells, Systems, and Circuits* (pp. 159–173) by J. L.
McGaugh, N. M. Weinberger, and G. Lynch, New York: Guilford Press.

ing dissociations (for further discussion of these and related issues, see Loftus,
1978; Robertson, Knight, Rafal, & Shimamura, in press; Shimamura, 1985,
1990). In memory research, dissociations imply a separation of qualitatively
different classifications or forms of memory. An idealized graph of a neuropsychological dissociation between two performance measures is shown in Fig.
12.3A. In this graph, a *single dissociation* is portrayed—a patient group (Group
1) is severely impaired compared to a control group on one task (Task A) but
performs as well as a control group on another task (Task B). Comparisons of
explicit and implicit memory in amnesic patients and control subjects conform to
this pattern. The finding of entirely normal performance on one task is essential,
because it assures that the brain area damaged in a patient group does not
contribute to performance on that task in any measurable way.

One concern with findings of single dissociations is that they are based on the failure to observe a statistical difference between patient and control groups (i.e., accepting the null hypothesis). A failure to observe a difference between groups may be attributed simply to statistical artifacts, such as ceiling effects, floor effects, or excessive within-group variability. To bolster confidence in single dissociations, it is necessary to assure that measures are sensitive and reliable. Power analyses can provide information concerning the degree to which statistical analyses are sensitive enough to locate differences, and thus they can be used effectively to strengthen claims about single dissociations. Another way to perform checks of sensitivity is to observe intact performance across different measures or across several levels of an independent variable. In this manner, it is possible to argue that the measure is sensitive to task manipulations and that preserved performance in a patient group is immune to these manipulations. For example, Graf et al. (1984) observed intact priming by amnesic patients following three different retention intervals.

It is difficult to explain single dissociations with quantitative interpretations, which would argue that amnesia simply affects implicit memory less than it affects explicit memory. By a quantitative view, one should observe in amnesic patients at least some reliable impairment on sensitive tests of implicit memory. In some investigations, a quantitative interpretation cannot be discounted because entirely normal performance is not observed on the implicit task. In such analyses, patients perform disproportionately better on an implicit test compared to an explicit test. That is, a statistical interaction between two measures is observed, yet performance is still impaired on both measures. In such cases, both quantitative and qualitative models can be used to account for the data. Graphically, such data would produce a noncrossover interaction or *partial dissociation,* such as that portrayed in Fig. 12.3B.

Partial dissociations may reflect a qualitative distinction if it is assumed that the slight but significant impairment on one task is a result of extraneous, additive effects, such as general cognitive slowness by patient groups. To test this assumption, it is necessary to add a second group of control subjects in which performance is weakened or reduced to the level of amnesic patients on one measure. Performance can be weakened in control subjects by various means, such as degrading the stimulus presentation, reducing exposure time of stimuli, or increasing the retention interval. The critical question is whether this weakened control group will exhibit the pattern of a single dissociation when performance is matched on one of the measures (see Fig. 12.3C). If so, then the findings provide a better argument for a true qualitative dissociation. If, as a result of weakening a control group, comparable performance on both measures is observed, then a quantitative model can easily explain the data (see Fig. 12.3D). Specifically, by a quantitative model the disproportionate deficit observed in the partial dissociation is spurious and can be explained simply by scaling artifacts. For example, by nature of the measurement scales used, a 10% drop in performance by amnesic patients on an implicit tasks translates to a 40%

drop in performance on an explicit task. Such problems in interpreting interactions occur for both cognitive and neuropsychological data (see Loftus, 1978, for examples in the cognitive domain).

Based on this analysis of dissociations, it is apparent that entirely normal performance by amnesic patients on implicit tests (i.e., single dissociations) provides good evidence for a qualitative distinction between the tasks. Partial dissociations may suggest a quantitative distinction, but it is necessary to include control conditions (e.g., weakened control group) that will test whether the findings are the result of a true disproportionate deficit or simply the result of scaling artifacts. Of course, double dissociations (i.e., crossover interactions) can provide even stronger evidence for memory dissociations. In this case, one patient group exhibits impairment on one task and normal performance on another task, whereas a different patient group exhibits the opposite pattern of performance. To date, reliable double dissociations between explicit and implicit memory have not been observed. That is, it has not been shown conclusively that a patient group exhibits entirely normal explicit memory for material that cannot be elicited using implicit procedures.

Other more elaborate methods have been developed to provide better confirmation of dissociations. Two related techniques are the method of reversed associations (Dunn & Kirsner, 1988) and the method of state-trait analyses (Bamber, 1979). In both cases, performance on two measures (e.g., explicit vs. implicit measures) is compared by analyzing x-y plots in which performance on one measure is plotted against performance on the other. In these analyses it is necessary to observed multiple levels of performance for both measures. For example, performance can be observed across several levels of exposure duration or retention interval in both amnesic and control subjects. When performance is plotted in this manner, nonmonotonic patterns (i.e., reversed associations) suggest a qualitative difference in performance between the two measures. That is, it can be argued that a variable (e.g., exposure duration, retention interval) affects one measure differently than it affects the other. Based on such plots, specific models can be used to characterized the effects (Bamber, 1979). None of the methodological tools mentioned above are foolproof, but they provide increasing levels of confidence about the dissociation of cognitive function.

Statistical analyses of stochastic independence also have been used to argue that one measure is dissociable from another (see Jacoby and Witherspoon, 1982; Tulving et al., 1982). In these analyses, two measures are assessed using the same stimulus items. For example, in a study by Tulving et al. (1982), subjects were first tested on an explicit measure of memory (e.g., two-alternative, forced-choice recognition memory) and then were administered a test of implicit memory for the same words (e.g., word-fragment completion). Analyses of stochastic independence indicated that the proportion of words completed in the implicit memory test was not affected by prior performance on the recognition memory test. That is, fragment completion performance for words previously recognized was no better than fragment completion performance for words not recognized.

Because it appeared that recognition memory had no bearing on whether a word was completed or not, it was argued that recognition memory operates independently of fragment completion.

Problems in interpreting findings of stochastic independence occur because the statistical analysis depends on multiple measures of the same items (for further detail, see Hintzman, 1980; Shimamura, 1985). For example, performance on the second test could be affected by performing the first test. Indeed, in a recognition memory test, one sees a study word again and determines whether that word was presented earlier. Thus, the recognition test can act as a second study trial, regardless of whether the word was recognized or not. This additional exposure of study words, independent of recognition decisions, affects the stochastic independence measure by biasing it toward independence. That is, as a result of performing in the recognition test, words not recognized receive an extra study trial, and thus this artifactually increases the probability of words completed but not recognized. These interest biases can be quite substantial, such that stochastic independence could be interpreted when in fact a correlation between measures is the true state (Shimamura, 1985).

Recently, the analysis of stochastic independence has been benefited by more sophisticated techniques. For example, Ostergaard (1992) offers a useful method in which standard measures of stochastic independence can be performed more conservatively by estimating the maximum possible level of dependence. This method, however, is not immune to the interest biases just described. In addition, memory measures have been analyzed by pairwise relationships of three measures, as in the triangulation method proposed by Hayman and Tulving (1989). It is important to note, however, that the triangulation method is only beneficial for analyzing the relative dependence between measures—that is, to indicate which of two measures is more associated with a third measure. Thus, the method does not offer a solution to the identification of qualitatively independent mental processes.

With an improved arsenal of methodological tools, such as those just described, it may be possible to provide more detailed analyses of the relationship between memory measures. Tools such as analyses of partial dissociations, pairwise relationships among several measures, and state-trait or reversed association plots involve more extensive empirical analyses than standard methods. However, the additional labor involved in the use of these tools will substantially improve the level of confidence concerning the dissociation of memory and other cognitive processes.

Forms of Memory: Multiple Systems and Processing Views

At present, reliable double dissociations have not been observed between explicit and implicit memory. For example, there have not been observations of a patient group with severely impaired implicit memory for the same material that is

FIG. 12.4. Theoretical explanation of neuropsychological findings. Each memory form represents the brain structures/ processes (identified as circles) that contribute to a measure of memory (e.g, recall, recognition, word completion). The right set represents the effects of a lesion in one brain structure/process represented by circle B, which could be the hippocampus and would presumed to disrupt declarative or explicit memory processes. *Note.* Adapted from *Brain Organization and Memory: Cells, Systems, and Circuits* (pp. 159–173) by J. L. McGaugh, N. M. Weinberger, and G. Lynch, New York: Guilford Press.

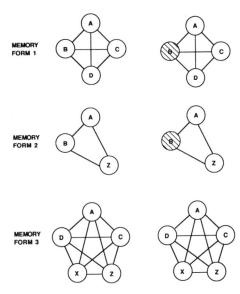

entirely intact on tests of explicit memory (e.g., impaired word-stem completion and intact word recall). Thus, it may be argued that explicit and implicit memory depend on some of the same brain/cognitive processes. It should be noted that single dissociations between implicit and explicit memory, such as those observed in amnesic patients, do not imply that two memory measures tap entirely different memory processes. In fact, studies that demonstrate a single dissociation merely indicate that at least one component or process is not shared by the two measures. Figure 12.4 illustrates in simple terms how one might interpret neuropsychological dissociations. The figure shows what might be called three *forms* of memory. Each form involves the participation of a number of cognitive processes or brain components (identified by circles), which interact and cooperate to produce behavior. Each form could be viewed as the brain structures or processes that contribute to a behavioral measure, such as recall, recognition, or word-stem completion.

It is important to note that although each form is different, there is some overlap in the components that make up the three forms of memory. For example, in Fig. 12.4, component A is shared by all three forms of memory. This component may refer to the cortical representations that store lexical and semantic information, and thus all three forms of memory may depend on this information. Suppose component B in the figure represents the hippocampus (or the processes that are mediated by the hippocampus). For example, memory forms 1 and 2 may be examples of explicit memory, such as recall and recognition memory, respectively. Disruption of component B, as indicated by the shaded circles on the right half of Fig. 12.4, would produce single dissociations because patients with hippocampal lesions would be impaired on measures of memory forms 1 and 2 but would not be impaired on measures of memory form 3. Thus, single dissociations can occur simply because one measure does not require the participation of a process that is necessary for another measure.

Based on this portrayal of memory forms or representations, it is clear that neuropsychological dissociations cannot be interpreted as providing evidence that two measures of memory involve completely independent or nonoverlapping processes. Dissociations only indicate that at least one process is not shared by the measures. It may seem that this view trivializes the contribution of neuropsychological dissociations for theoretical interpretations. It is true that any two measures of memory could potentially produce a dissociation of function, because no two measures are exactly the same. Indeed, the future of cognitive neuropsychology may be limited if subsequent findings simply added further and further memory dissociations, ad infinitum. However, it is generally the case that memory measures correlate with one another. For example, findings from neuropsychological research indicate that the areas damaged in amnesia are involved in a class of memory measures that include various forms of explicit memory, such as recall, recognition, and paired-associate learning. Subsequently, it is quite difficult to observe clear cases of single dissociations in which neurological injury severely affects one measure but does not at all influence another measure. In the case of implicit and explicit memory, neuropsychological dissociations can be quite dramatic.

This characterization of memory representations can address one debate that has been associated with theoretical interpretations of explicit and implicit memory. The multiple systems view of memory (Mishkin et al., 1984; Schacter, 1990; Squire, 1987; Weiskrantz, 1987) suggests that some brain structures are necessary for explicit memory but not for implicit memory. Based on this view, a taxonomy of memory can be established that classifies measures that depend on this system and those that do not. This method of taxonomic classification is the first step in understanding the functional significance of the brain areas that contribute to different forms of memory. Others have argued that the multiple systems view is wrong and should be replaced by views that stress the memory processes that are appropriate for different memory tasks (see Roediger et al., 1989). Transfer-appropriate processing views suggest that the data should not be used to derive different, and presumably separable, systems of memory but should instead be used to identify the underlying processes or mechanisms that operate during specific tasks.

Arguments against a multiple systems view of memory may be attributed in part to the erroneous view that neuropsychological dissociations between measures imply two independent and nonoverlapping memory systems. As noted in the description above, such dissociations cannot be interpreted in this manner. Thus, the system that provides explicit memory may depend in part on the cortical representations that are used in the implicit memory system. Thus, the multiple systems view is perhaps best viewed as a multiple subsystems or components view, in which numerous brain processes and structure are necessary for memory performance and one of these components (i.e., the hippocampus) is necessary for the expression of explicit memory. Other components will be necessary for the expression of other forms of memory. Thus, there is no need to argue for complete independence between the systems that are necessary for explicit and implicit memory.

The argument for a processing view—in contrast to a systems or structural view—is often a matter of emphasis or heuristics. In many cases, a transfer-appropriate processing view does not preclude a systems or componential view of memory (for related discussions, see also Schacter, 1990; Shimamura, 1989). Processing views attempt to identify the cognitive activity necessary for performance. However, a processing theory becomes a structural one when it attempts to identify the neural circuitry that is necessary for a process to occur. Conversely, a systems view attempts to identify the biological substrate of cognitive performance, often by demonstrating neuropsychological dissociations. However, a systems theory becomes a transfer-appropriate processing one when it attempts to identify the process or mechanism that is served by some neural circuitry.

Simply stated, the debate between transfer-appropriate processing and multiple systems views appears to be the result of scientists working from two different perspectives. Processing interpretations are tested by manipulations of variables that are associated with encoding, storage, and retrieval of information. These variables are the tools of cognitive psychology. Memory systems interpretations have been tested by human neuropsychological and animal lesion studies in which memory impairment is associated with damage to specific neural circuits or systems. These variables are the tools of behavioral neuroscience. The two perspectives emphasize different features of the mechanisms involved in memory performance, but they do not necessarily conflict with one another. Indeed, together these two perspectives may help delineate more precisely both the structures and the functions that contribute to memory performance.

ACKNOWLEDGMENTS

This work was supported by a grant from the National Institute on Aging (AG09055). I thank Laird Cermak, Felicia Gershberg, Gail Musen, and Larry Squire for helpful comments on earlier drafts of this chapter.

REFERENCES

Baddeley, A. (1986). *Working memory*. Oxford, UK: Oxford University Press.

Bamber, D. (1979). State-trace analysis: A method of testing simple theories of causation. *Journal of Mathematical Psychology, 19*, 137–181.

Broadbent, D. E., & Weiskrantz, L. (Eds.). (1982). *The neuropsychology of cognitive function.* London: Royal Society.

Brooks, D. N., & Baddeley, A. D. (1976). What can amnesic patients learn? *Neuropsychologia, 14*, 111–122.

Cermak, L. S., Bleich, R. P., & Blackford, S. P. (1988). Deficits in the implicit retention of new associations by alcoholic Korsakoff patients. *Brain and Cognition, 7*, 312–323.

Cermak, L. S., Talbot, N., Chandler, K., & Wolbarst, L. R. (1985). The perceptual priming phenomenon in amnesia. *Neuropsychologia, 23*, 615–622.

Claparède, E. (1911). Reconnaissance et moiite. *Archives de Psychologie, 11*, 79–90 [Recognitive and "me-ness." Translation in D. Rapaport (Ed.), *Organization and pathology of thought* (pp. 58–75). New York: Columbia University Press, 1951]

Cohen, N. J., & Squire, L. R. (1980). Preserved learning and retention of pattern analyzing skill in amnesia: Association of knowing how and knowing that. *Science, 210*, 207–209.

Coltheart, M., Patterson, K., & Marshall, J. (1980). *Deep dyslexia.* London: Routledge and Kegan Paul.

Corkin, S. (1968). Acquisition of motor skill after bilateral medial temporal lobe excision. *Neuropsychologia, 6*, 225–265.

Crowder, R. G. (1985). On access and the forms of memory. In N. M. Weinberger, J. L. McGaugh, & G. Lynch (Eds.), *Memory systems of the brain* (pp. 433–441). New York: Guilford Press.

Daum, I., Channon, S., & Canavan, A. G. M. (1989). Classical conditioning in patients with severe memory problems. *Journal of Neurology, Neurosurgery, and Psychiatry, 52*, 47–51.

Diamond, R., & Rozin, P. (1984). Activation of existing memories in the amnesic syndromes. *Journal of Abnormal Psychology, 93*, 98–105.

Dunn, J. C., & Kirsner, K. (1988). Discovering functionally independent mental processes: The principle of reversed association. *Psychological Review, 95*, 91–101.

Gabrieli, J. D. E., Milberg, W., Keane, M. M., & Corkin, S. (1990). Intact priming of patterns despite impaired memory. *Neuropsychologia, 28*, 417–427.

Gardner, H., Boller, F., Moreines, J., & Butters, N. (1973). Retrieving information from Korsakoff patients: Effects of categorical cues and reference to the task. *Cortex, 9*, 165–175.

Gordon, B. (1988). Preserved learning of novel information in amnesia: Evidence for multiple memory systems. *Brain and Cognition, 7*, 257–282.

Graf, P., & Schacter, D. L. (1985). Implicit and explicit memory for new associations in normal and amnesic subjects. *Journal of Experimental Psychology: Learning Memory and Cognition, 11*, 501–518.

Graf, P., Shimamura, A. P., & Squire, L. R. (1985). Priming across modalities and priming across category levels: Extending the domain of preserved function in amnesia. *Journal of Experimental Psychology: Learning, Memory and Cognition, 11*, 386–396.

Graf, P., Squire, L. R., & Mandler, G. (1984). The information that amnesic patients do not forget. *Journal of Experimental Psychology: Learning Memory and Cognition, 10*, 164–178.

Hayman, C. A. G., & Tulving, E. (1989). Contingent dissociation between recognition and fragment completion: The method of triangulation. *Journal of Experimental Psychology: Learning, Memory, and Cognition, 15*, 228–240.

Hebb, D. O. (1949). *Organization of behavior.* New York: John Wiley & Sons.

Heindel, W. C., Butters, N., & Salmon, D. P. (1988). Impaired learning of a motor skill in patients with Huntington's disease. *Behavioral Neuroscience, 102*, 141–147.

Heindel, W. C., Salmon, D. P., Shults, C. W., Walicke, P. A., & Butters, N. (1989). Neuropsychological evidence for multiple implicit memory systems: A comparison of Alzheimer's, Huntington's, and Parkinson's disease patients. *Journal of Neuroscience, 9*, 582–587.

Hintzman, D. L. (1980). Simpson's paradox and the analysis of memory retrieval. *Psychological Review, 87*, 398–410.

Humphreys, G. W., & Riddoch, M. J. (1987). *Visual object processing: A cognitive neuropsychological approach.* London: Lawrence Erlbaum Associates.

Jacoby, L. L., & Witherspoon, D. (1982). Remembering without awareness. *Canadian Journal of Psychology, 32,* 300–324.

Johnson, M. K., Kim, J. K., & Risse, G. (1985). Do alcoholic Korsakoff's syndrome patients acquire affective reactions? *Journal of Experimental Psychology: Learning Memory and Cognition, 11,* 22–36.

Keane, M. M., Gabrieli, J. D. E., Fennema, A. C., Growdon, J. H., & Corkin, S. (1991). Evidence for a dissociation between perceptual and conceptual priming in Alzheimer's disease. *Behavioral Neuroscience, 105,* 326–342.

Lashley, K. S. (1950). In search of the engram. *Society of Experimental Biology Symposium: Physiological Mechanisms in Animal Behavior, 4,* 454–482.

Lister, R. G., & Weingartner, H. J. (Eds.). (1991). *Perspectives on cognitive neuroscience.* New York: Oxford University Press.

Loftus, G. R. (1978). On interpretation of interactions. *Memory and Cognition, 6,* 312–319.

Luria, A. R. (1973). *The working brain.* New York: Basic Books.

Mayes, A. R. (1988). *Human organic memory disorders.* Cambridge, UK: Cambridge University Press.

Mayes, A. R., & Gooding, P. (1989). Enhancement of word completion priming in amnesics by cueing with previously novel associates. *Neuropsychologia, 27,* 1057–1072.

McCarthy, R. A., & Warrington, E. K. (1990). *Cognitive neuropsychology.* San Diego, CA: Academic Press.

Mishkin, M., Malamut, B., & Bachevalier, J. (1984). Memories and habits: Two neural systems. In J. L. McGaugh, N. M. Weinberger, & G. Lynch (Eds.), *Neurobiology of learning and memory.* (pp. 65–77). New York: Guilford Press.

Moscovitch, M., Winocur, G., & McLachlan, D. (1986). Memory as assessed by recognition and reading time in normal and memory impaired people with Alzheimer's disease and other neurological disorders. *Journal of Experimental Psychology: General, 115,* 331–347.

Musen, G., Shimamura, A. P., & Squire, L. R. (1990). Intact text-specific reading skill in amnesia. *Journal of Experimental Psychology: Learning, Memory, and Cognition, 16,* 1068–1076.

Musen, G., & Squire, L. R. (in press). Nonverbal priming in amnesia. *Journal of Experimental Psychology: Learning, Memory, and Cognition.*

Nissen, M. J., & Bullemer, P. (1987). Attentional requirements of learning: Evidence from performance measures. *Cognitive Psychology, 19,* 1–32.

Ostergaard, A. L. (1992). A method for judging measures of stochastic dependence: Further comments on the current controversy. *Journal of Experimental Psychology: Learning, Memory, and Cognition, 18,* 413–420.

Paller, K. A., & Mayes, A. R. (1991). New-association priming of word identification in normal and amnesic subjects. *Journal of Clinical and Experimental Neuropsychology, 14,* 104.

Parkin, A. J. (1982). Residual learning capability in organic amnesia. *Cortex, 18,* 417–440.

Petersen, S. E., Fox, P. T., Posner, M. I., Mintun, M., & Raichle, M. E. (1988). Positron emission tomographic studies of the cortical anatomy of single-word processing. *Nature, 331,* 585–589.

Posner, M. I. (1978). *Chronometric explorations of mind.* Hillsdale, NJ: Lawrence Erlbaum Associates.

Richardson-Klavehn, A., & Bjork, R. A. (1988). Measures of memory. *Annual Review of Psychology, 39,* 475–543.

Robertson, L. C., Knight, R. T., Rafal, R., & Shimamura, A. P. (in press). Cognitive neuropsychology is more than single case studies. *Journal of Experimental Psychology: Learning Memory and Cognition.*

Roediger, H. L. (1990). Implicit memory: Retention without remembering. *American Psychologist, 45,* 1043–1056.

Roediger, H. L., Weldon, M. S., & Challis, B. H. (1989). Explaining dissociations between implicit and explicit measures of retention: A processing account. In H. L. Roediger & F. I. M.

Craik (Eds.), *Varieties of memory and consciousness: Essays in honour of Endel Tulving* (pp. 3–41). Hillsdale, NJ: Lawrence Erlbaum Associates.

Salmon, D. P., Shimamura, A. P., Butters, N., & Smith, S. (1988). Lexical and semantic priming deficits in patients with Alzheimer's disease. *Journal of Clinical and Experimental Neuropsychology, 10,* 477–494.

Schacter, D. L. (1985). Priming of old and new knowledge in amnesic patients and normal subjects. *Annals of the New York Academy of Sciences, 444,* 41–53.

Schacter, D. L. (1987). Implicit memory: History and current status. *Journal of Experimental Psychology: Learning Memory and Cognition, 13,* 501–518.

Schacter, D. L. (1990). Perceptual representation systems and implicit memory: Toward a resolution of the multiple systems debate. In A. Diamond (Eds.), *Development and neural bases of higher cognitive function* (pp. 543–571). New York: Annals of the New York Academy of Science.

Schacter, D. L., Cooper, L. A., & Delaney, S. M. (1990). Implicit memory for unfamiliar objects depends on access to structural descriptions. *Journal of Experimental Psychology: General, 119,* 5–24.

Schacter, D. L., & Graf, P. (1986). Preserved learning in amnesic patients: Perspectives from research on direct priming. *Journal of Clinical and Experimental Neuropsychology, 6,* 727–743.

Schacter, D. L., Rapscak, S. Z., Rubens, A. B., Tharan, M., & Laguna, J. (1990). Priming effects in a letter-by-letter reader depend upon access to the word form system. *Neuropsychologia, 28,* 1079–1094.

Shallice, T. (1988). *From neuropsychology to mental structure.* Cambridge, U.K.: Cambridge University Press.

Shimamura, A. P. (1985). Problems with the finding of stochastic independence as evidence for independent cognitive processes. *Bulletin of the Psychonomic Society, 23,* 506–508.

Shimamura, A. P. (1986). Priming in amnesia: Evidence for a dissociable memory function. *Quarterly Journal of Experimental Psychology, 38*(A), 619–644.

Shimamura, A. P. (1989). Disorders of memory: The cognitive science perspective. In F. Boller, & J. Grafman (Eds.), *Handbook of neuropsychology* (pp. 35–73). Amsterdam: Elsevier Science.

Shimamura, A. P. (1990). Forms of memory: Issues and directions. In J. L. McGaugh, N. M. Weinberger, & G. Lynch (Eds.), *Brain organization and memory: Cells, systems, and circuits* (pp. 159–173). New York: Guilford Press.

Shimamura, A. P., Gershberg, F. B., Jurica, P. J., Mangels, J. A., & Knight, R. T. (1992). *Intact implicit memory in patients with frontal lobe lesions. Neuropsychologia, 30,* 931–937.

Shimamura, A. P., Janowsky, J. S., & Squire, L. R. (1990a). Memory for the temporal order of events in patients with frontal lobe lesions and amnesic patients. *Neuropsychologia, 28,* 803–813.

Shimamura, A. P., Janowsky, J. S., & Squire, L. R. (1990b). What is the role of frontal lobe damage in amnesic disorders? In H. S. Levin, H. M. Eisenberg, & A. L. Benton (Eds.), *Frontal lobe function and injury* (pp. 173–195). New York: Oxford University Press.

Shimamura, A. P., Salmon, D. P., Squire, L. R., & Butters, N. (1987). Memory dysfunction and word priming in dementia and amnesia. *Behavioral Neuroscience, 101,* 347–351.

Shimamura, A. P., & Squire, L. R. (1984). Paired-associate learning and priming effects in amnesia: A neuropsychological study. *Journal of Experimental Psychology: General, 113,* 556–570.

Shimamura, A. P., & Squire, L. R. (1989). Impaired priming of new associations in amnesia. *Journal of Experimental Psychology: Learning, Memory and Cognition, 15,* 721–728.

Smith, M. E., & Oscar-Berman, M. (1990). Repetition priming of words and pseudowords in divided attention and in amnesia. *Journal of Experimental Psychology: Learning, Memory, and Cognition, 16,* 1033–1042.

Squire, L. R. (1987). *Memory and brain.* New York: Oxford University Press.

Squire, L. R., Ojemann, J., Miezin, F., Petersen, S., Videen, T., & Raichle, M. (1992). Activation of the hippocampus in normal humans: A functional anatomical study of memory. *Proceedings of the National Academy of Sciences, USA, 89,* 1837–1841.

Squire, L. R., Shimamura, A. P., & Graf, P. (1987). Strength and duration of priming effects in normal subjects and amnesic patients. *Neuropsychologia, 25,* 195–210.

Squire, L. R., & Zola-Morgan, S. (1988). Memory: Brain systems and behavior. *Trends in Neuroscience, 22,* 170–175.

Sternberg, S. (1969). The discovery of processing stages: Extensions of Donder's method. *Acta Psychologica, 30,* 276–315.

Tolman, E. C. (1948). Cognitive maps in rats and men. *Psychological Review, 55,* 189–208.

Tulving, E. (1983). *Elements of episodic memory.* Oxford, UK: Clarendon Press.

Tulving, E. (1985). How many memory systems are there? *American Psychologist, 40,* 385–398.

Tulving, E., & Schacter, D. L. (1990). Priming and human memory systems. *Science, 247,* 301–306.

Tulving, E., Schacter, D. L., & Stark, H. A. (1982). Priming effects in word-fragment completion are independent of recognition memory. *Journal of Experimental Psychology: Learning Memory and Cognition, 8,* 352–373.

Warrington, E. K., & Weiskrantz, L. (1970). The amnesic syndrome: Consolidation or retrieval? *Nature, 228,* 628–630.

Warrington, E. K., & Weiskrantz, L. (1968). New method of testing long-term retention with special reference to amnesic patients. *Nature, 217,* 972–974.

Warrington, E. K., & Weiskrantz, L. (1982). Amnesia: A disconnection syndrome? *Neuropsychologia, 20,* 233–248.

Weiskrantz, L. (1987). Neuroanatomy of memory and amnesia; A case for multiple memory systems. *Human Neurobiology, 6,* 93–105.

Weiskrantz, L., & Warrington, E. K. (1979). Conditioning in amnesic patients. *Neuropsychologia, 17,* 187–194.

13

Automatic Versus Controlled Processing and the Implicit Task Performance of Amnesic Patients

Laird S. Cermak
Boston University School of Medicine, and Department of Veterans Affairs Medical Center, Boston

Successful priming of amnesics' performance on a wide variety of implicit memory tasks has been a source of fascination for investigators of memory for nearly a decade (Graf & Schacter, 1985; Graf, Squire, & Mandler, 1984; Jacoby, Toth, Lindsay, & Debner, 1992; Roediger, 1990; Schacter, 1987; Squire, 1987). These researchers have incorporated the finding that amnesic patients perform as well as normal controls on implicit tasks into their theories, relying on the phenomenon as independent neurological evidence for the existence of the dichotomy of memory systems. This interest has produced an outpouring of research on memory disorders unparalleled within other decades of psychological research. Despite this abundance of interest, data, and methodology, the payoff for a further understanding of amnesia itself, from an information processing point of view, has been disproportionately small. This is largely because, by the very nature of the investigation, what is being studied is not amnesia. Instead it entails determining what it is that amnesics can do without directing any further attention toward exploring the underlying processes that contribute to those memory tasks they cannot do. Being discovered as a viable avenue of proof has entailed a certain amount of patience on the part of memory disorders researchers who are eager to get back to studies of deficits. It is probably similar to the situation that occurs when the public discovers a particular artist, who then finds it difficult to return to her studio because of the parties she is obligated to attend. But now it is time to return to the exploration of amnesics' memory disorder, and it is the purpose of this chapter to suggest a way back that is not necessarily an abrupt change but rather a transition from the pure study of implicit memory to an investigation of processing disturbances experienced by amnesics even during the course of their apparently normal implicit performance.

Most of the work in this chapter reflects the changes in thinking that have taken place within the Memory Disorders Research Center at Boston University School of Medicine. We have certainly played a role in the ongoing investigation of amnesics' implicit memory, but we have also gradually come to the realization that all is not normal in the performance of these patients on implicit tasks. It has become apparent that some of the same processing deficits exposed while studying amnesics' explicit memory abilities also play a role in their implicit performance. We have, for instance, begun to note that amnesics' normal implicit performance is not always a consequence of normal processing. We are now keenly aware that a normal level of performance does not necessarily indicate that the underlying contributors to that performance are also normal.

The possibility that more than one type of processing could underlie implicit performance was recently suggested by Blaxton (1989) and Roediger (1990), who proposed that implicit performance can be mediated by at least two types of processing. They identified those as data-driven processes involving perceptual analysis, and conceptually driven, subject-initiated, processes. Because these processes have been shown to be involved in supporting implicit performance in normals, it has generally been assumed that they must be normal in amnesics. However, it is the contention of this chapter that acceptance of this assumption might be premature and that direct tests of amnesics' processing abilities during implicit performance are still needed. It is entirely possible that amnesic patients' processing is not normal on implicit memory tasks, even though their performance is normal and even though they can be shown capable of performing perceptual and conceptual processes. They still could differ from normals in the extent to which they rely on one or more of these independent processes during implicit task performance. Reliance on a specific feature has been demonstrated in explicit memory and formed the basis for much of the theory of impaired processing that emerged from our laboratory during the decade of the 1970s (see Butters & Cermak, 1980, for a review). Consequently, our recent emphasis while studying amnesics' implicit memory has been on those processes underlying performance on implicit tasks. Our investigations have focused on process rather than structure and on the belief that successful performance by amnesics need not indicate normal structure if different processing routes can attain the same outcome. The necessity for our approach was elegantly outlined in a chapter by Dunn and Kirsner (1989), who pointed out that while it is entirely possible to distinguish between two types of task, or two types of process, they need not necessarily map onto one another. We felt that amnesia research had focused too much on task differentiation when studying the implicit-explicit distinction, with little to no focus on process distinctions or on process deficits. Before proceeding directly to these recent studies, however, it would be helpful to review the theorizing and empirical data that brought us to our current formulations. This can be accomplished by exploring the anthology of memory system dichotomies that have been proposed to incorporate the results of amnesics' normal implicit performance.

PROCEDURAL-DECLARATIVE DICHOTOMY

One of the best known memory system dichotomies applied to amnesia research has been the procedural-declarative distinction. This dichotomy divides memory into one system that permits learning and retention of how to perform a task and one system that retains the knowledge that the specific task has been learned. Based on the oft-described clinical phenomenon that amnesic patients can learn to perform a particular act yet deny ever having performed the act (Talland, 1965), Cohen and Squire (1980) proposed that amnesics learn and retain the procedures needed to perform a task but do not acquire declarative knowledge of this act. Subsequently, Cohen (1984) enlarged the province of procedural memory to include performance on implicit verbal memory tasks that require that certain perceptual operations or procedures be repeated within the paradigm. When the same operations have to be performed again they seem to occur more easily and rapidly. Thus, the patient improves on an implicit task as a consequence of more rapidly performed perceptual procedures. When precisely the same stimuli are re-presented to the patient, the same stimulus-bound procedures reoccur even though the patient could never state, declaratively, that they had occurred before. As more and more cognitive priming tasks emerged (see conceptual tasks later in this chapter), the emphasis on the term *procedural memory* diminished because it became clear that some subject-initiated processing beyond the bounds of the pure perceptual characteristics of the stimulus could contribute to implicit performance. Rather than call this subject-driven, procedural learning, these theorists have recently chosen to substitute the term *nondeclarative* for procedural (e.g., Musen, Shimamura, & Squire, 1990). This term itself emphasizes the complexity of implicit task performance but, to date, has not received further definition. Instead, these theorists have simply pointed out that whatever nondeclarative memory encompasses, amnesic patients perform it in a normal manner. Because it is the contention in this chapter that all implicit tasks are not performed alike, and may depend on different processes, the possibility that amnesics may, or may not, successfully perform a specific type of processing has to be considered. Thus, nondeclarative as an umbrella term is probably too inclusive and ill defined for the reason that task performance and processing ability need not map onto one another.

EPISODIC-SEMANTIC DISTINCTION

An alternative to the procedural-declarative dichotomy that has frequently been used to explain amnesic patients' normal implicit performance was initially described by Tulving (1972, 1983), who called it the episodic/semantic distinction. Tulving proposed that the ability to retrieve an episode depends on recalling an item within the context in which it was presented, whereas the ability to remember a general or semantic fact does not require contextual recall. Because both types of recall require that a patient realize "that" he knows a particular item of information, it has been suggested that the two systems constitute different aspects of declarative memory and therefore should not be seen as synonymous with the procedural/declarative distinction (Cermak, Talbot, Chandler, & Wolbarst, 1985; Tulving, 1985). It has further been suggested (Cermak, 1984; Kinsbourne and Wood, 1975) that amnesics have relatively normal semantic retrieval but below normal episodic retrieval. By this model, impaired explicit task performance is seen as occurring when the patient is asked to provide an item in context ("Was this item on the list?") and contextual information is not available to the amnesic. Amnesics' normal implicit memory performance is explained as occurring via a form of noncontextual semantic memory activation. The initial stimulus presentation activates, or primes, semantic memory, thus increasing the probability of the item being more readily produced on subsequent repetitions or partial repetitions (Diamond and Rozin, 1984).

Evidence substantiating the notion that it may be necessary for a stimulus item to contact semantic knowledge in order to produce normal implicit memory in amnesics was provided by demonstrating that priming of pseudoword stimuli such as "brote" did not enhance identification of these stimuli on a perceptual identification task in a normal manner (Cermak et al., 1985). In this experiment, patients were shown either 10 real words or 10 pseudowords and asked to try to remember them for later retrieval. Before a recognition test, however, they were given a different task, which involved identifying very briefly presented words (or pseudowords). When the patient could not identify a given item, the same item was again presented at a somewhat longer (10 msec) duration. This continued until identification occurred. As can be seen from Table 13.1, amnesic (Korsakoff) patients identified real words nearly as rapidly as controls and primed for repeated (target) words as well as normals. When pseudowords were used, these same patients' identification was again nearly normal for novel (filler) items but not for the repeated items, because on these trials they required substantially more time than controls to identify target items. From this it was concluded that in order for priming to occur normally, an item first needed to be in semantic memory in order to be activated.

TABLE 13.1
Average Number of Milliseconds Necessary for Identification of Target and Filler Words or Pseudowords

Group	Words		Pseudowords	
	Target	Filler	Target	Filler
Korsakoff	53	63	140	158
Alcoholic	39	45	69	124

This theory that an intact semantic network needed to be activated to achieve normal implicit task performance in amnesics clearly suggested that new implicit learning might not be possible for amnesics just as new explicit learning was not possible. However, an unexpected result by Graf and Schacter (1985) demonstrated that new learning could actually produce primed word-stem completion performance in some amnesics. In their task, a novel association between two words (e.g., window-reason) that was clearly not in semantic memory prior to the task seemed to be able to acquire enough strength to result in what they called *contextual* word-completion performance by amnesics. In their task, completion of the word-stem for "rea-" was significantly higher in the presence of its learned associate "window" than when it was presented alone or with another stimulus. This meant that activation of already acquired associative information was not necessarily essential for amnesics' implicit task performance. There seemed to be a direct effect of the episode on the patients' performance. This implied that the patient's conceptual (associative) processing during item presentation might actually be able to play a role in their implicit task performance.

Attempts to replicate the Graf and Schacter result for all amnesics have fallen short (later scrutiny revealed that their most-impaired patients even failed the task), but the outcome opened the possibility that subject-initiated analysis during item presentation (i.e., the episode) could potentially have an effect on subsequent implicit performance. The study provided the impetus for many later investigations of processing in implicit memory. For instance, Moscovitch, Winocur, and McLachlan (1986) found that patients could read unrelated word pairs presented in a degraded, but identifiable, format faster on second presentation than on first. Schacter, Harbluk, and McLachlan (1984) showed acquisition of novel facts such as "Bob Hope's father was a fireman" by amnesics even though the patients couldn't remember where they learned it. Johnson, Kim, and Risse (1985) found amnesics acquired "preferences" for melodies they had already heard during the experimental session. Crovitz, Harvey, and McClanahan (1979) reported enhanced ability to spot hidden figures in pictures, and several reports of faster solution times to puzzles, riddles, and even problems such as the "fox and geese" dilemma have occurred. All these reports of amnesic abilities to profit from prior experience suggest the impact of a new learning experience on subsequent behavior. Not all these tasks necessarily involve just implicit memory by normals, and amnesics may not profit as rapidly or completely as normals on all the tasks, but each does show the effect of an episode on performance. Such outcomes led to the next dichotomy that emerged in the field of amnesia, namely, a dichotomy based on the notion that there can be more than one effect produced by processing during an episode: one effect of which a normal is aware, and another that does not result in awareness. The unaware effect is the one that produces preferences, enhancements, and faster solution times in amnesics.

AWARE-UNAWARE DISTINCTION

Mandler (1980) and Jacoby (1984) were among the first to suggest that two forms of processing might exist during episodic memory, and Jacoby has proposed that at least one could possibly support amnesics' implicit performance. Because an individual is aware of one of these types of processing but not the other, it is possible that the unaware component is the one that might be retained by amnesics. Unaware processing is defined as being largely automatic and probably perceptually based. Aware processing is seen as being more strategic and conceptual, producing a level of awareness that includes knowledge of the existence of the episode. Amnesics may be able to perform purely automatic processing, which may be sufficient to support their implicit performance. Strategic or conceptual processing, necessary for aware levels of retention, may not be available to amnesics, and consequently their explicit performance is impaired. Clearly, it became important for us to investigate amnesic patients' automatic perceptual and strategic conceptual processing during implicit task performance. So that is the analysis to which we next turned.

PERCEPTUAL VERSUS CONCEPTUAL PRIMING BY AMNESICS

The next series of studies of amnesics' processing abilities that we performed was based on Jacoby's notions of perceptual (possibly automatic) and conceptual (controlled) analysis of incoming information. We again used our perceptual identification task because it had already shown that pseudowords did not produce normal priming for amnesics and we wondered whether this reflected poor conceptual processing. Remember that our original interpretation of this below-normal priming for novel material (Cermak et al., 1985) had been based on the fact that pseudowords lack semantic representation. However, we realized that another important difference between pseudowords and real words is that pseudowords also have unfamiliar orthography and phonology. To determine whether deficits in analyzing these perceptual features could also account for the difference between amnesics' real word and pseudoword priming, two further perceptual identification experiments (Cermak, Verfaellie, Milberg, Letourneau, & Blackford, 1991) were performed. These studies used as stimuli pseudohomonyms that do not have an existing orthographic representation but that do share their phonology with real words (e.g, "phaire") and could in this way contact a real word's semantic representation. We found in this experiment that amnesics do show priming for pseudohomonyms and do so at a level comparable to that obtained for real words. We also found in this experiment some pseudoword priming for our amnesics, albeit still well below normal. As in our initial report

(Cermak et al., 1985), priming for pseudowords was overshadowed by the fact that control subjects showed a dramatically larger repetition effect for pseudowords, but priming for pseudohomonyms was nearly normal. It occurred to us that one reason why control subjects may demonstrate larger repetition effects of pseudowords could be because they used explicit memory. For control subjects, memory of the specific stimuli presented on the study list might be used to support their performance on the identification task. This would most likely occur for pseudowords, as opposed to real words, because these stimuli are hard to identify initially and thus might demand more initial processing. Amnesics, less capable of this initial processing, would have to rely only on implicit retention. However, this still left us with the task of explaining why they evidenced normal pseudohomonym priming.

Initially, we felt that an appropriate explanation of the normal pseudo-homonym priming by amnesics was that they automatically used the semantic connotation of a pseudohomonym to mediate priming via semantic activation. This was tested in the next experiment, which presented pseudowords, pseudohomonyms, and real words within one study list (i.e., a mixed-list design). We felt that if mediated activation occurred automatically, then the mixed list design should produce the same pattern of results as that for the unmixed design. However, we found that priming for pseudohomonyms now became considerably less than normal; in fact, it was nearly nonexistent. In other words, when pseudohomonyms were mixed within the same list as pseudowords, amnesic Korsakoff patients' priming for pseudohomonyms was nonsignificant. The fact that pseudohomonyms have a familiar auditory word form appeared to be concealed by the unfamiliar orthography of all stimuli on the list. Consequently, pseudohomonyms lost their semantic salience and simply looked like pseudowords. When pseudohomonyms were mixed with real words, Korsakoff patients' priming for pseudohomonyms also became significantly lower than was the case for the alcoholic controls. Clearly, the semantic processing of pseudohomonyms did not occur automatically simply because of their auditory correspondence with real words. Instead, such processing seemed critically to depend on the patients' realization that the orthographically unfamiliar stimuli in the study list corresponded phonemically to real words. This only occurred when all the stimuli shared this characteristic and not when stimulus types were mixed within a list. For real words, access to meaning could occur automatically, resulting in normal priming effects irrespective of task manipulations. However, for pseudohomonyms, the presence and magnitude of priming effects were affected by contextual variables, which influenced the manner in which information is processed. Left to their own devices, amnesic patients did not appear to perform the conceptual processing required for priming in this paradigm. Only when conditions acted to produce such processing did priming occur. This means that when automatic processing is sufficient to support implicit performance, amnesics are normal, but when conceptual processing is required, amnesics are not spontaneously capable of such controlled processing and will not demonstrate normal implicit performance.

Actually this proposal is identical to the one we have espoused when discussing explicit memory and its ultimate dependence on semantic analysis. Specifically, Nelson Butters and I have shown that while amnesic Korsakoff patients are capable of semantic analysis, left to their own devices they do not perform much analysis (Butters & Cermak, 1980). Consequently, they have little or no ability to reconstruct the verbal information they were explicitly asked to retain. Now, in this implicit perceptual identification task, it again appears that when all the stimuli are directed toward one form of conceptual analysis, the patients can use this feature to improve their performance. But such analysis has to be controlled for the patient, as it does not seem to occur automatically as indicated by their subpar mixed-list performance. Amnesics appear to be capable of perceptual processing because it is always automatic but are not capable of conceptual processing because it involves control beyond the automatic level. This finding supported the possibility that even when amnesics and controls perform equivalently on any given memory task, their performance may be mediated differently. To test this assumption further, it became important to try to separate the effects of such automatic processes and controlled processes within the same task so as to isolate the contribution of each to the performance of amnesics and control subjects.

OPPOSITIONAL TASK PERFORMANCE BY AMNESICS

Following Jacoby and Kelley (1991), we recently sought to separate the effect of automatic from controlled processing by creating a situation in which the effects of familiarity (felt to be an automatic perceptual process) and conscious recollection (a controlled conceptual process) are directly opposed to one another (Cermak, Verfaellie, Sweeney, & Jacoby, 1992). In the paradigm we chose, patients participated in a word-stem completion task in which they were told *not* to use the words that had just been presented to them on a study list to complete the word stems. This task we referred to as an exclusion task, because it required subjects to exclude stimuli on the basis of conscious recollection of the study list. Under these instructions, amnesic patients completed more word stems with list items than did the alcoholic controls. In fact, comparing performance on this exclusion task with that on a standard word completion task demonstrated that the exclusion instruction had very little effect on the performance of amnesics, whereas it sharply decreased the number of study words used as list completions for the alcoholic controls. It could, of course, be the case that amnesics forgot the instructions, but this is unlikely as they were reminded from time to time of the instructions. Instead, it appeared that they were unable to attribute the source of the fluency that caused them to think first of a particular word to complete a stem to its recent presentation. Subsequent research has supported this hypothesis, but before proceeding, one other finding that also emerged from this word-stem completion study must be mentioned.

The other finding of interest was that even on the standard word completion task, amnesics provided more study list completions than did the alcoholic controls. This was by no means the first time that such an occurrence has been observed. In another study (Cermak, Verfaillie, Sweeney, & Jacoby, 1992) where we presented lists of either high- or low-frequency words followed by a word-stem completion task, amnesics and controls showed equal priming when low-frequency words were used, but when high-frequency words were used, primed stem completion performance of amnesics far exceeded that of controls. This was due to the fact that alcoholic controls, having more conscious control over their performance, sometimes chose to complete stems with words other than those on the study list. The amnesics seemed more bound than the controls to respond to the fluency produced by an item's recent presentation. In a condition in which five presentation trials were given prior to word completion, controls also became more drawn to this fluency and increased the number of their inclusion responses up to the amnesics' level.

In a supporting experiment (Cermak, Verfaellie, Butler, & Jacoby, 1993), which was also designed to oppose fluency and recollection, names were randomly selected from a phone book and presented to patients. Initially, the patients were just asked to pronounce each name as it was presented. This was followed by a fame judgment task in which the previously presented nonfamous names were intermixed with new nonfamous names and with names that were indeed famous although not to the point of being immediately identifiable (e.g., Simon Bolivar, Henry Thoreau). The patients were first assured that the names they had just read were not famous, because they were randomly drawn from a phone book, and they were told that they should respond "no" if one appeared. This task was considered to be an exclusion task because patients were instructed to exclude names that had just been presented. As in the word-stem completion task, the results showed that amnesic patients were much more likely to endorse an old, compared to a new, nonfamous name as being famous. Controls did not show this effect because their conscious recollection of the names presented on the study list allowed them to exclude them. Thus, we had to conclude that amnesics are not able to use conscious processes to oppose the automatic effects of memory. The fluency generated by the initial processing of a name and reflected during its subsequent processing was apparently misattributed (to use Jacoby's term) to the supposed fame of the name rather than to its true source. Controls, however, could attribute this feeling to the correct source precisely because they could consciously remember its prior presentation.

We next asked the other side of the question, that being whether amnesics would fail to use conscious processes to enhance the effects of automatically generated fluency by testing for the effects of conscious recollection and fluency when they were not opposed. In this "inclusion" task, patients were told that names just presented on the study list were indeed famous (but obscure), and ought now to be responded to positively in the fame judgment task. In contrast to previous experiments, alcoholic patients now endorsed significantly more old nonfamous names that did the amnesics. The amnesics' performance on the inclusion task was no higher than it had been on the exclusion task, whereas the alcoholics showed a striking and highly significant effect of task instructions.

This entire series of investigations with amnesics suggests that implicit priming for amnesics generally seems to be solely a product of the familiarity produced by fluency automatically generated by the repetition of processing itself, except possibly for those instances where nonautomatic processing may be induced. Amnesics respond to fluency by producing the most easily processed word even when that word should have been explicitly excluded. They simply do not know how to attribute fluency to its source. In situations in which fluency of processing produces the correct response the patient appears to be primed—not simply because the processing has been repeated but because the repeated processing gives the amnesic the feeling of being correct. When this feeling is oppositional to the correct performance, it results in errors. It occurred to us that it was possible that those same processing skills and disabilities could underlie the diverse outcomes reported for amnesics' performance on explicit recognition tasks. There also, instructions seemed to determine whether performance would be normal or below normal. We turned, therefore, to an analysis of amnesics' explicit recognition memory performance.

EXPLICIT (RECOGNITION) MEMORY IN AMNESIA

For some time a controversy has existed concerning the normalcy of amnesic patients' recognition memory. Huppert and Piercy (1976) and Hirst and Volpe (1982) report normal recognition abilities in amnesic patients even when free recall is impaired, while Shimamura and Squire (1988) and Haist, Shimamura and Squire (1992) feel recognition memory is as impaired as free recall. One possible way to reconcile these two views is to explore recognition memory in terms of the underlying processing demanded by the task in a manner that parallels the style of investigation we have made of implicit memory. Both Mandler (1980) and Jacoby (1983) showed that recognition can be supported by two qualitatively different types of processing, which can act independently or in concert. Subjects can base their recognition response either on an intentional act of reconstruction (conceptual processing) or simply on the more automatic effect of the fluency produced by the repetition of processing during the recognition task. Clearly, recognition tasks can vary in the extent to which reliance on reconstruction or fluency affects task performance. Given the knowledge that amnesics may rely almost exclusively on fluency to achieve normal performance on implicit tasks, it stands to reason that they may also rely on fluency to perform recognition tasks. This being the case, when the task demands reliance on this automatic processing component, then amnesics' performance may be normal. When it relies on reconstruction, it may be impaired.

Evidence to support this conclusion has been provided by Verfaellie and Treadwell (1993), who examined amnesics' recognition performance under several conditions within an oppositional strategy paradigm. In the first phase of their experiment, patients read words or solved anagrams. In a second phase, they were asked to try to remember a list of words that was presented to them auditorily. This was then followed by a recognition test that included items from both Phases I and II. In an inclusion condition, patients were told to respond "old" to all previous items. In an exclusion condition they were told to respond "old" only to words presented during Phase II. Verfaellie and Treadwell found that normal controls endorsed more items in the inclusion than in the exclusion condition from Phase I of the experiment, whereas amnesics did not differ in the number of responses they gave under these two conditions. In other words, amnesics could not use conscious reconstruction as a basis for their recognition, but rather relied almost exclusively on the fluency produced by prior processing. Applying the formulas for separating these two contributors to recognition developed by Jacoby (1991) to this set of data revealed that amnesics' level of fluency was actually identical to that seen for normals, but their reconstructive ability was totally impaired. Consequently, all the patient could rely on was the intact fluency generated by his own processing in order to recognize a prior item. The patient simply attributed his sensation of fluency to the possibility that it may have been produced by a prior presentation of the word and not to any reconstructive ability to actually place that word in the context of the experiment. The same process underlying successful implicit task performance can thus be seen to underlie successful performance on this explicit task. This negates any possible interpretation that results on the two types of tasks support a distinction between two different types of memory.

An interesting secondary finding in the Verfaellie and Treadwell study was that normal controls tended to act more like the amnesics when the words were read in Phase I then when they were solved. When normals did not perform conceptual processing during item presentation, they too had to rely more on fluency during recognition than was the case when they performed conceptual processing during initial item analysis. It could be, as we have often stated, that amnesics cannot profit from conceptual processing even when instructed on how it ought to be performed, whereas normals can. But under conditions where normals are forced by instructions, or divided attention, to process on a lower level of analysis, their performance mimics that of memory impaired patients.

FUTURE DIRECTIONS FOR AMNESIA
RESEARCH AND THEORY

What still needs to be investigated is the extent to which amnesics' automatic and controlled processing abilities on implicit memory tasks parallel their use of perceptual and conceptual processing abilities. It seems that amnesics' implicit perceptual processing abilities are intact, leading to their normal implicit performance because this processing occurs automatically and results in greater fluency of processing upon repetition. However, a great deal of research in normal memory suggests the existence of a conceptual processing component in normal implicit memory, and this creates a dilemma for investigators of amnesics' processing. If it were simply the case that implicit memory was based on perceptual processes and explicit on conceptual, then it would follow that amnesics can perform perceptual (automatic) but not conceptual (controlled) processes. However, if implicit can be based on perceptual and/or conceptual memory, then the abilities of amnesics are not so easily dichotomized, particularly if conceptual processing demands some control.

Perhaps Roediger (1990) has provided a way to study this concern. He proposed that processing abilities cut across memory systems and produce different outcomes within memory systems depending on which type of processing is utilized. The processing dimensions that he considers to cut across the explicit-implicit dimension have been discussed previously in this chapter, namely, data-driven and conceptually driven. Data-driven processes are those that occur automatically as soon as the stimuli are presented and include such processes as perceptual, phonemic, or auditory. Conceptual processes are controlled by the subject and include such processing as semantic, reflective, and organizational. These processing abilities Roediger feels to be orthogonal to explicit-implicit memory systems inasmuch as they each exist within each component. The mistake investigators have been making (according to Roediger) is that they have only been exploring two cells of this two-by-two contingency table, namely, the data-driven/implicit cell and the conceptually driven/explicit cell. He suggests that we should devise tasks to look at data-driven/explicit performance and conceptually-driven/implicit performance. If we did, we might find that amnesic patients are impaired not along the explicit/implicit dimensions, but rather along the data-driven/conceptually driven dimension. The hard part, of course, is to come up with creative paradigms that test these particular cells, but Roediger believes that this is possible and he suggests two: a sound-alike cue given during recall as a data-driven explicit task, and a trivia-like question delivered during a priming portion of an experiment as a conceptually driven implicit task.

It remains to determine the results of this new analysis with amnesic patients, but the outcome that we have presented in this chapter showing the difference between the effects of fluency and reconstruction on amnesics' task performance seems to be based on their differential abilities to perform perceptual versus conceptual processing. We have suggested here that these perceptual processes are usually automatic, and hence preserved in amnesia, whereas the conceptual processes are more controlled and are impaired in amnesics. The terminology is not identical, but the meaning is the same as that proposed by Roediger. It appears that a processing ability dimension might be cutting across memory systems, with amnesics capable of one type of processing (automatic) but not the other (controlled). It remains, however, to pit the expectations of systems theories against those of processing theories in the performance of amnesics on tests that directly assess those cells of the two-by-two matrix proposed by Roediger. This will enable us, in the future, to determine if it is the difference between systems of memory that accounts for the behavior of amnesics, or whether it might be the ability (or inability) to perform specific types of processing regardless of the memory task.

ACKNOWLEDGMENTS

Much of the research reported in this chapter was performed at the Memory Disorders Research Center and was supported by an NINDS program project grant (NS26985) or an NIAAA grant (AA000187) to Boston University School of Medicine and by the Medical Research Service of the Department of Veterans Affairs. This chapter was written while the author was a Fulbright Fellow in the Psychology Department at the Hebrew University of Jerusalem.

REFERENCES

Blaxton, T. A. (1989). Investigating dissociations among memory measures: Support for a transfer-appropriate processing framework. *Journal of Experimental Psychology: Learning, Memory and Cognition, 15,* 657–668.

Butters, N., & Cermak, L. S. (1980). *Alcoholic Korsakoff's syndrome: An information processing approach to amnesia.* New York: Academic Press.

Cermak, L. S. (1984). The episodic/semantic distinction in amnesia. In L. R. Squire & N. Butters (Eds.), *Neuropsychology of memory* (pp. 55–62). New York: Guilford Press.

Cermak, L. S., Talbot, N., Chandler, K., & Wolbarst, L. R. (1985). The perceptual priming phenomenon in amnesia. *Neuropsychologia, 23,* 615–622.

Cermak, L. S., Verfaellie, M., Milberg, W. P., Letourneau, L. L., & Blackford, S. P. (1991). A further analysis of perceptual identification priming in alcoholic Korsakoff patients. *Neuropsychologia, 29,* 725–736.

Cermak, L. S., Verfaellie, M., Butler, T., & Jacoby, L. L. (1993). *Fluency vs. recollection during fame judgement performance of amnesic patients. Neuropsychology,* in press.

Cermak, L. S., Verfaellie, M., Sweeney, M., & Jacoby, L. L. (1992). Fluency vs. conscious recollection in the word completion performance of amnesic patients. *Brain and Cognition, 20,* 367–377.

Cohen, N. J. (1984). Preserved learning capacity in amnesia: Evidence for multiple memory systems. In L. R. Squire & N. Butters (Eds.), *Neuropsychology of memory* (pp. 83–103). New York: Guilford Press.

Cohen, N. J., & Squire, L. R. (1980). Preserved learning and retention of pattern-analyzing skill in amnesia: Dissociation of knowing how and knowing that. *Science, 10*, 207–210.

Crovitz, H. F., Harvey, M. T., & McClanahan, S. (1979). Hidden memory: A rapid method for the study of amnesia using perceptual learning. *Cortex, 17*, 273–278.

Diamond, R., & Rozin, P. (1984). Activation of existing memories in the amnesic syndromes. *Journal of Abnormal Psychology, 93*, 98–105.

Dunn, J. C., & Kirsner, K. (1989). Implicit memory: Task or process? In S. Lewandowsky, J. C. Dunn, & K. Kirsner (Ed.), *Implicit memory: Theoretical issues* (pp. 17–32). Hillsdale, NJ: Lawrence Erlbaum Associates.

Graf, P., & Schacter, D. L. (1985). Implicit and explicit memory for new associations in normal and amnesic subjects. *Journal of Experimental Psychology: Learning, Memory and Cognition, 11*, 501–518.

Graf, P., Squire, L. R., & Mandler, G. (1984). The information that amnesic patients do not forget. *Journal of Experimental Psychology: Learning, Memory, and Cognition, 10*, 164–178.

Haist, F., Shimamura, A. P., & Squire, L. R. (1992). On the relationship between recall and recognition memory. *Journal of Experimental Psychology: Learning, Memory and Cognition, 18*, 691–702.

Hirst, W., & Volpe, B. (1982). Temporal order judgments with amnesia. *Brain and Cognition, 1*, 293–306.

Huppert, F., & Piercy, M. (1976). Recognition memory in amnesic patients: Effect of temporal context and familiarity of material. *Cortex, 12*, 3–20.

Jacoby, L. L. (1983). Remembering the data: Analyzing interactive processes in reading. *Journal of Verbal Learning and Verbal Behavior, 22*, 485–508.

Jacoby, L. L. (1984). Incidental versus intentional retrieval: Remembering and awareness as separate issues. In L. R. Squire & N. Butters (Eds.), *Neuropsychology of memory* (pp. 145–156). New York: Guilford Press.

Jacoby, L. L. (1991). A process dissociation framework: Separating automatic from intentional uses of memory. *Journal of Memory and Language, 30*, 513–541.

Jacoby, L. L., & Kelley, C. (1991). Unconscious influences of memory: Dissociations and automaticity. In D. Milner & M. Rugg (Eds.), *Consciousness and cognition: Neuropsychological perspectives* (pp. 201–234). New York: Academic Press.

Jacoby, L. L., Toth, J. P., Lindsay, D. S., & Debner, J. A. (1992). Lectures for a layperson: Methods for revealing unconscious processes. In R. Bornstein & T. Pitman (Eds.), *Perception without awareness*. New York: Guilford Press.

Johnson, M. K., Kim, J. K., & Risse, G. (1985). Do alcoholic Korsakoff's syndrome patients acquire affective reactions? *Journal of Experimental Psychology: Learning, Memory and Cognition, 11*, 27–36.

Kinsbourne, M., & Wood, F. (1975). Short term memory processes and the amnesic syndrome. In D. D. Deutsch & J. A. Deutsch (Ed.), *Short-term memory*, (pp. 257–291). New York: Academic Press.

Mandler, G. (1980). Recognizing: The judgement of previous occurrence. *Psychological Review, 87*, 252–271.

Moscovitch, M., Winocur, G., & McLachlan, D. (1986). Memory as assessed by recognition and reading time in normal and memory-impaired people with Alzheimer's disease and other neurological disorders. *Journal of Experimental Psychology: General, 115*, 331–347.

Musen, G., Shimamura, A. P., & Squire, L. R. (1990). Intact text-specific reading skill in amnesia. *Journal of Experimental Psychology: Learning, Memory and Cognition, 16*, 1068–1076.

Roediger, H. L. (1990). Implicit memory: Retention without remembering. *American Psychologist, 45*, 1043–1056.

Schacter, D. L., Harbluk, J. L., & McLachlan, D. R. (1984). Retrieval without recollection: An experimental analysis of source amnesia. *Journal of Verbal Learning and Verbal Behavior, 23*, 593–611.

Schacter, D. L. (1987). Implicit memory; History and current status. *Journal of Experimental Psychology: Learning, Memory and Cognition, 13,* 501–518.

Shimamura, A. P., & Squire, L. R. (1988). Long-term memory in amnesia: Cued recall, recognition memory and confidence ratings. *Journal of Experimental Psychology: Learning, Memory and Cognition, 14,* 763–770.

Squire, L. R. (1987). *Memory and brain.* New York: Oxford University Press.

Talland, G. A. (1965). *Deranged memory.* New York: Academic Press.

Tulving, E. (1972). Episodic and semantic memory: Different retrieval mechanisms. In E. Tulving & W. Donaldson (Ed.), *Organization of memory* (pp. 381–403). New York: Academic Press.

Tulving, E. (1983). *Elements of episodic memory.* Oxford: Oxford University Press.

Tulving, E. (1985). How many memory systems are there? *American Psychologist, 40,* 385–398.

Verfaellie, M., & Treadwell, J. (1993). *The status of recognition memory in amnesia. Neuropsychology, 1,* 5–13.

14 Priming of Novel Information in Amnesic Patients: Issues and Data

Jeffrey Bowers
University of Arizona

Daniel L. Schacter
Harvard University

Dissociations between implicit and explicit memory have been observed across a wide variety of tasks and conditions, as documented by recent review articles (cf. Richardson-Klavehn & Bjork, 1988; Roediger, 1990; Schacter, 1987) and by other chapters in this volume. Despite the apparent ubiquity of such dissociations, it is probably safe to say that the most striking separation between implicit and explicit memory is observed in the amnesic syndrome: Densely amnesic patients perform poorly on explicit tests of memory, but they perform remarkably well, and frequently normally, on numerous implicit tests (e.g., Cohen & Squire, 1980; Graf, Squire, & Mandler, 1984; Milner, Corkin, & Teuber, 1968; Moscovitch, 1982; Schacter, 1985; Shimamura & Squire, 1984; Warrington & Weiskrantz, 1974). In addition to providing some of the strongest empirical grounds for distinguishing between implicit and explicit memory, these dissociations can provide potentially important insights for both cognitive and neurobiological theories of mnemonic processes. On the one hand, observations of preserved implicit memory in amnesia provide important constraints for cognitive theories: If a theory does not speak to or cannot accommodate the amnesia data, then it fails to explain a critical aspect of implicit memory. On the other hand, data concerning implicit memory in amnesic patients can aid neurobiological formulations by providing insights into the function of the hippocampus and related limbic structures that are typically damaged in amnesia (e.g., Milner et al., 1968; O'Keefe & Nadel, 1978; Squire, 1992), and can also be informative regarding the cortical structures that are typically preserved in amnesia (cf. Schacter, 1990, 1992a; Squire, 1992). Indeed, attempts to fully characterize the computations that these structures perform should be informed by, and must be consistent with, the known implicit memory abilities of amnesic patients.

In the present chapter, we focus on one particular type of implicit memory: the phenomenon of *priming,* or facilitated identification of words and objects from reduced cues as a consequence of recent exposure to them (e.g., Tulving & Schacter, 1990). More specifically, we consider the question of whether amnesic patients show intact priming of newly acquired or novel information. When we use the terms *implicit memory for novel information* or *priming of novel information,* we refer to memory for various kinds of materials that are not represented as a unit in memory prior to an experimental encounter with them—unrelated paired associates, nonwords, unfamiliar objects, novel dot patterns, and the like. Novel materials of this kind can be contrasted with familiar materials that are represented as a unit in memory prior to the experiment, such as real words or pictures of common objects. Although we have more to say later about conceptualizing the notion of novel information, the key point to note for introductory purposes is that a number of important cognitive and neurobiological issues turn on the question of whether amnesic patients show normal priming of novel information in various experimental paradigms.

The chapter is divided into four main sections. In the first, several neuropsychological and cognitive theories of implicit and explicit memory are briefly reviewed in order to set the stage for thinking about priming of novel information. This review highlights the idea that different theories can be divided into two groups: those that predict that priming should be limited to materials with preexisting memory representations, and those that predict that priming should extend to novel materials without preexisting memory representations. The second section considers conceptual issues surrounding the question of what constitutes novel information. Although the meaning of the phrase *novel information* has often been treated as self-evident in memory research, the matter is complex and we make use of recent discussions in the psycholinguistic literature to illuminate it. In the third section, we review priming of novel information in both amnesic patients and normal subjects. The fourth and final section evaluates theories of implicit memory in light of previous discussions.

COGNITIVE AND NEUROPSYCHOLOGICAL THEORIES
OF AMNESIA AND IMPLICIT MEMORY

Early reports that amnesic patients show some preservation of what we would now call implicit memory can be traced to late 19th and early 20th century observations (cf. Parkin, 1982; Schacter, 1987). However, the critical data for contemporary researchers were reported in two influential sets of experiments dating to the 1960s. The first were studies by Milner and colleagues showing that the famous patient H. M., who became amnesic following bilateral medial temporal lobe resection (Scoville & Milner, 1957), could acquire new motor skills despite lack of recollection for the episodes in which the skills were acquired (e.g., Milner et al., 1968). Thus, although it had been known for years that H. M. possesses intact immediate or short-term memory (Scoville & Milner, 1957), the data on motor skill acquisition suggested that some aspects of H. M.'s long-term memory are spared.

The second set of crucial experiments, which are more directly relevant to priming, were reported by Warrington and Weiskrantz (1968, 1970, 1974). These investigators demonstrated that densely amnesic patients can show relatively intact retention of information acquired from a single study episode, but only when memory is assessed with specific types of tests—perceptual fragments of words or pictures (see also Milner et al., 1968). For example, when amnesic patients viewed fragments of previously studied pictures, or viewed fragments of recently studied words, they often responded to the cues by providing the previously studied items—even though they could not explicitly remember the items on standard free recall or recognition tests. Although various interpretations of the initial Warrington and Weiskrantz data were considered, subsequent research established that amnesic patients exhibit normal memory performance with fragment cues only when they are given implicit memory instructions to respond with the first word that comes to mind; when given the same fragment cues together with instructions to try to remember study list items, impaired performance is observed (Graf et al., 1984). A number of other studies have shown normal priming and impaired explicit memory in amnesic patients under conditions in which test cues are held constant and only retrieval instructions are varied (e.g., Cermak, Talbot, Chandler, & Wolbarst, 1985; Graf, Shimamura, & Squire, 1985; Schacter, 1985; Shimamura & Squire, 1984).

In the foregoing studies, intact priming was observed for familiar materials, such as common words or highly related associates, that have preexisting memory representations. To understand the theoretical importance of the distinction between priming of familiar versus novel materials, it is useful to consider the data on spared priming in relation to ideas that have been put forward regarding other spared memory abilities in amnesic patients. For instance, the early observations on preserved short-term memory and motor skill learning in H. M. and other amnesic patients have typically been explained by appealing to impaired consolidation processes (for a historical overview, see Polster, Nadel, & Schacter, 1991). The specific nature of these consolidation processes is not well understood, but the idea that amnesia impairs processes that convert short- into long-term memories is consistent with data on spared short-term memory in amnesia and has been accepted by many neuropsychologists (Squire, Cohen, & Nadel, 1984) and connectionist modelers (cf. McClelland & Rumelhart, 1986; Carpenter & Grossberg, 1987; Wolters & Phaf, 1990). Similarly, the preserved motor learning skills of amnesic patients have also been interpreted in terms of consolidation theory. The basic idea is that long-term memory, as expressed on standard recall or recognition tests, and motor learning, as expressed on pursuit rotor and similar tasks, are mediated by separate systems: Impaired long-term recall and recognition is thought to reflect defective consolidation in a system involving the hippocampus and related structures, whereas spared motor learning is thought to depend on a separate system involving basal ganglia and related structures (e.g., Milner et al., 1968; Mishkin & Petri, 1984; O'Keefe & Nadel, 1978; Squire, 1987).

Although many if not all amnesia researchers would agree with this general approach to explaining preserved short-term memory and motor learning, attempts to apply consolidation theory to priming phenomena in amnesic patients are less clear-cut. Two different approaches to the issue can be distinguished. One approach holds that amnesia is attributable to a consolidation failure that impairs the acquisition of all new memory representations that are usually acquired in a single episode. Accordingly, it is argued that priming effects do not reflect the establishment of new memory traces within a long-term memory system, but instead are the result of spared activation processes that act on preexisting memory traces (e.g., Diamond & Rozin, 1984; Rozin, 1976; Wicklegren, 1979). For example, when a subject studies the word WINDOW, the preexisting representation for WINDOW is assumed to be activated automatically as a consequence of encountering the word, and to remain activated beyond the span of short-term memory. This activated representation is thought to be more readily accessible to the subject than is a nonactivated representation and hence provides the basis for priming on various implicit memory tests. A related idea was advanced by Graf and Mandler (1984; Mandler, 1980), who distinguished between an *integration* process that strengthens the code of preexisting memory representations and an *elaboration* process that constructs new memory representations by building novel connections among previously unrelated representations. Integration promotes the accessibility of preexisting representations, supports priming, and is spared in amnesic patients; elaboration establishes new episodic memories, supports explicit retrieval, and is impaired in amnesic patients (e.g., Graf et al., 1984).

A distinction between processes that activate or strengthen preexisting memories, and processes that establish novel memory representations is also found in various connectionist theories (cf., Carpenter & Grossberg, 1987; Wolters & Phaf, 1990). In these theories, amnesia can be modeled by selectively impairing the processes that mediate the establishment of new memories in the network.

A second general class of theories assumes that priming phenomena are mediated by memory systems that operate independently of the episodic or declarative system that depends on the hippocampus and related structures. Although these theories often assume that amnesic patients' explicit memory deficit is attributable to consolidation failure within the episodic/declarative system, they do not necessarily imply that consolidation of *all* new representations is blocked. For example, Cohen (1984) and Squire (1987) suggested that priming effects are mediated by a procedural memory system that becomes more efficient at processing information as a consequence of past experience. The system depends on cortical structures and is spared in amnesic patients (see Squire, 1992, for a revised and expanded version of this idea). According to this view, reading the word WINDOW on a study list produces a direct on-line change to the system responsible for processing words, and as a consequence of this change, the system may process the word WINDOW more effectively on subsequent exposures, or may require less information to identify this word than a nonstudied word on a subsequent test. A related idea is that many priming effects depend on a perceptual representation system (PRS) that is spared in amnesic patients (Schacter, 1990, 1992a, 1992b; Tulving & Schacter, 1990; see also Gabrieli, Milberg, Keane, & Corkin, 1990). According to this theory, priming effects are mediated by various cortical regions that represent the form and structure, but not the meaning and associative properties, of words and objects. Processing a word or object on a study list produces a perceptual representation of relevant form/structure information, and this representation provides the basis for facilitated performance—priming—on identification, completion, and similar implicit tests.

Although this thumbnail sketch of theoretical views touches on only a few main points, its main purpose is to highlight a key contrast between the two general approaches that were considered. According to activation/integration views, new memories are not consolidated normally in amnesic patients, and priming depends on activation of preexisting memory representations; hence, priming should not be observed for novel materials that require the establishment of new memory traces. According to the memory systems accounts, only certain kinds of new memories—those that depend on an episodic or declarative memory system—are subject to consolidation failure in amnesic patients. Priming depends on a separate, spared memory system and hence should be observed for both familiar and novel information: if a memory system is truly spared by amnesia, then it should operate normally.

One further account of priming, espoused by Jacoby (1983), Masson (1989), and Roediger and colleagues (e.g., Roediger & Blaxton, 1987; Roediger, Weldon, & Challis, 1989; see also, Roediger & Srinivas, Chapter 2, this volume), should be noted briefly before proceeding further. These authors have argued that a single memory system mediates both implicit and explicit memory. Implicit/explicit dissociations are thought to reflect differences in retrieval operations that are required by implicit and explicit tasks and, in conformity with the principle of transfer-appropriate processing, depend on the degree of match between such retrieval operations and the processing activities engaged during a study task. Proponents of this general viewpoint have focused on explaining various implicit/explicit dissociations that have been observed in studies of normal subjects. Unlike the theories discussed earlier, the processing approach has not been systematically related to the amnesia literature; indeed, key proponents of this view concede that the theory does not provide a straightforward explanation of intact priming effects in amnesia (Roediger et al., 1989). Nevertheless, the processing approach would appear to predict that priming should occur for both familiar and novel information. According to this view, all implicit memory effects are mediated by an episodic memory system that can store new information from a single episode.

DEFINING "NOVEL" INFORMATION

Studies that purport to assess priming of novel information have generally used nonwords, unrelated paired associates, and unfamiliar objects as target materials, and have examined whether study-list exposure to these materials produces priming on a subsequent implicit test. The general assumption has been that because nonwords, unrelated paired associates, and unfamiliar objects do not have preexisting representations as units in memory (in the sense that words, highly related associates, and familiar objects do), we are justified in assuming that they constitute "novel" materials that enter memory for the first time during a study episode. Although these stimuli may in fact be examples of novel information, further consideration suggests that the distinction between a novel and a preexisting representation is not entirely straightforward.

The complexity of the issue is highlighted by a recent debate in psycholinguistic research concerning the representational format of words. On the one hand, a number of theorists have adopted a lexical stance. According to these authors, separate and discrete representations exist for each word in our vocabulary (e.g., Forster, 1976; Morton, 1979), and the first stage of word recognition is to gain access to the appropriate lexical entry. These lexical entries are thought to specify the meaning, pronunciation, and other relevant features of previously encountered words. The critical point for our discussion, however, is that this approach assumes that words have preexisting representations and nonwords do not. By contrast, various connectionist theorists have argued that word recognition processes proceed in the absence of any lexical representations (e.g., Seidenberg & McClelland, 1989; Van Orden et al., 1990). On this view, a connectionist network can learn to associate orthographic features of words with phonological and semantic features. These associations are thought to be acquired at a *sublexical* level—that is, representations of words do not exist as discrete memory traces, but instead are emergent properties of associations between subword representations.

An important consequence of the connectionist approach is that words and nonwords have a similar representational status: The network processes information on the basis subword features, and both words and (pronounceable) nonwords possess similar subcomponents. As a simple (and perhaps simplistic) example, the items *numby* and *number* share many orthographic features in common (i.e., the letters n, u, m, and b), so they are processed similarly by the network. The critical difference between words and nonwords is *not* that words have preexisting lexical representations and nonwords do not; rather, the orthographic processes that are invoked by words access semantic codes, whereas the orthographic processes that are invoked by nonwords do not. In support of this general framework, various empirical results suggest that words and nonwords are processed similarly (e.g., Glushko, 1979; Rosson, 1985). Furthermore, several models of word recognition and naming can explain a variety of linguistic data without including lexical units in the model (e.g., Seidenberg & McClelland, 1989).

The debate regarding the nature of lexical representation is far from settled. For example, some data do suggest the need for discrete lexical entries (e.g., Besner, Twilley, McCann, & Seergobin, 1990). The reason for taking note of this debate is that its resolution has implications for theories of priming in amnesia. For example, if one adopts an activation account, and assumes that priming in amnesia is restricted to preexisting representations, then predictions regarding nonword priming effects depend on whether a lexical or sublexical view of word recognition processes is adopted. On the lexical view, words have preexisting memory representations and nonwords do not; accordingly, amnesic patients should show intact priming effects for words only. On the sublexical view, however, words and pronounceable nonwords share the same representational status in the orthographic domain. Consequently, the observation of spared nonword priming in amnesia might be consistent with some form of nonlexical activation theory—that is, rather than necessarily indicating the formation of a novel lexical representation, intact priming of nonwords in amnesics might simply reflect activation of preexisting sublexical units.

Similar issues may be raised in the domain of nonverbal or visual object priming. The question here is whether discrete visual representations exist for each object that are analogous to lexical entries for words, or whether object representations are the emergent property of what we might call "subobject" codes—primitive parts such as *geons* (e.g., Biederman, 1987)—that are active at the same time. If we adopt a position analogous to the lexical view of word representation, where each object is represented by a discrete entry, we would conclude that novel objects (e.g., unfamiliar shapes or patterns) do not have preexisting memory representations. Thus, if priming in amnesia involves only activation of preexisting representations, intact priming of unfamiliar objects should not be observed. If on the other hand, we adopt a position analogous to the sublexical account of word representation, then we might well conclude that unfamiliar objects are represented similarly to familiar objects—that is, in terms of relations among shape primitives. By this view, exposure to an unfamiliar object on a study list would produce activation of the preexisting shape primitives and, hence, even an activation account would predict intact priming in amnesic patients.

It seems clear that this lexical/sublexical debate complicates the task of using data on priming of novel information to distinguish between theories of implicit memory in amnesia. If we assume that words and objects are represented in the manner indicated by the lexical account, then an activation theory can be falsified by observing intact priming of nonword or nonobject in amnesia. Conversely, the idea that priming phenomena are mediated by novel representations in a system that is separate from episodic memory can be falsified if implicit memory effects in amnesics are restricted to familiar information that has a preexisting memory representation. However, if we adopt the sublexical approach, and thus assume that legal nonwords and unfamiliar objects do have preexisting orthographic or shape representations, respectively, then virtually all theories can accommodate nonword and nonobject priming effects in amnesia. Thus, an activation theory that assumes sublexical representations mediate priming effects may be difficult to distinguish from alternative theories that assume that novel representations mediate priming phenomena. We return to this general issue after considering pertinent data.

PRIMING OF NOVEL INFORMATION: A REVIEW

In this section of the chapter, experiments that assess priming of novel information in amnesic patients are reviewed; also, we consider briefly pertinent studies on priming of novel information in normal subjects. In light of the foregoing discussion, it is important to note that when we use the phrase "novel information," we do not make any assumptions about an item's representational status; rather, we use the term in an atheoretical sense to indicate that a nonword or nonobject is subjectively unfamiliar to the subject. Indeed, we will use the phrases novel information and unfamiliar information interchangeably.

Priming of Novel Verbal Information

Experiments concerning priming of novel verbal information have focused on two main types of materials: nonwords and unrelated paired associates. We consider in turn studies that have made use of each type of novel material.

Nonword Priming. The question of whether priming effects can be observed for nonwords was addressed in some of the earliest studies of priming in normal subjects (e.g., Forbach, Stanners, & Hochhaus, 1974). Taken as a whole, however, the literature on nonword priming in normal subjects is rather mixed. Studies that have employed lexical decision as a priming task have generally failed to observe nonword repetition effects (e.g., Forbach et al., 1974; Fowler, Napps, & Feldman, 1985; Bentin & Moscovitch, 1988), whereas studies using identification or a naming latency tasks have yielded evidence of significant priming (Carr, Brown, & Charalambous, 1989; Feustel, Shiffrin, & Salasoo, 1983; Kirsner & Smith, 1974; Rueckl, 1990; Salasoo, Shiffrin, & Feustel, 1985; Whittlesea & Cantwell, 1987). Note, however, that questions have been raised regarding the suitability of the lexical decision task for assessing nonword priming effects (Feustel et al., 1983), and if these results are set aside, then priming of nonwords is consistently observed in normal subjects. Nevertheless, theoretical interpretation of these results with respect to the implicit/explicit memory distinction is not straightforward, because studies that reported significant effects with normal subjects have not dissociated priming from explicit memory. Consequently, it is possible that the observed priming effects were mediated partly or perhaps entirely by explicit memory strategies (see Schacter, Bowers, & Booker, 1989, for general discussion).

In view of the uncertain status of nonword priming effects in normal subjects, it is perhaps not surprising that the data from amnesic patients are also rather mixed, with both positive and negative results reported (cf. Cermak et al., 1985; Diamond & Rozin, 1984; Gabrieli & Keane, 1988; Haist, Musen, & Squire, 1991; Musen & Squire, 1991a; Smith & Oscar-Berman, 1990). We now consider each of these studies individually.

The first study to provide evidence on nonword priming in amnesia was described by Rozin (1976; see Diamond & Rozin, 1984, for a full report). Six memory-disordered patients of varied etiologies and six control subjects were tested in two separate sessions; within each session, subjects studied a list of six words and six nonwords. Each of the lists was studied six times, and following each study trial, subjects were asked to complete a short distractor task and perform a free recall test. In addition, subjects were presented on several trials with the first few letters of the target item, and they were asked to complete the cues with studied items. Subjects were encouraged to guess on this cued-recall test when they did not remember the study items, so performance could be mediated in part by an implicit form of memory.

The first key result of the experiment was that although the amnesic patients showed little evidence of memory on the free recall test, they showed robust facilitation on the cued-recall test, thus replicating the earlier results of Warrington and Weiskrantz (1970). The second key result was that the patients were quite impaired on the cued-recall test for nonwords; indeed, they did not show any facilitation in cued recall relative to free recall. Thus, these results suggest that for amnesic patients, priming effects require preexisting memory representations of words. However, there are three aspects of this study that limit the force of this conclusion. First, the normal subjects did not show any facilitation for nonwords in cued recall relative to free recall, because both cued and free recall of nonwords were at or near the ceiling. Thus, it is difficult to interpret the absence of nonword facilitation in the patient group. Second, as noted earlier, Diamond and Rozin used explicit rather than implicit memory instructions, so it is not clear whether these data bear directly on priming in amnesic patients.

Third, a number of the patients in this study exhibited dementia in addition to amnesia.

In a later study, Cermak et al. (1985) used a perceptual identification task to assess implicit memory for words and nonwords in Korsakoff amnesics. In Experiment 1, amnesic patients and control subjects studied a series of lists, each composed of 10 words; following each study list, subjects completed an identification and a recognition task. For the identification task, subjects were given as much exposure time as required to identify an item; if they failed to identify an item at one exposure rate, additional, longer exposures were given until identification was achieved. Priming on this task is indicated when less time is required to identify previously studied items relative to nonstudied items. For familiar words, normal subjects and amnesic patients demonstrated priming effects of 17 msec and 10 msec, respectively. Statistical analysis revealed a main effect of prior exposure on perceptual identification performance (i.e., priming), together with a nonsignificant interaction between prior exposure and subject group (i.e., amnesics vs. controls). On the basis of these analyses, it was concluded that amnesic patients showed intact word priming effects. In Experiment 2, amnesic patients and control subjects studied a series of lists, each composed of 10 nonwords, and following each study list, they performed an identification and a recognition task. On the identification test, normal subjects and amnesic patients demonstrated 55-msec and 18-msec priming effects, respectively. Statistical analysis revealed a significant interaction between prior exposure and subject group, thus indicating that the amnesic patients showed impaired nonword priming relative to controls. The existence of the prior exposure × subject group interaction for nonwords, together with the lack of such an interaction for words, led the authors to conclude that priming in amnesic patients, but not normal subjects, requires the existence of preexisting memory representations. However, the data from the amnesic patients are rather ambiguous: the 10-msec priming effect for words was actually smaller than the 18-msec effect for nonwords, and the authors did not report simple tests for the significance of either of these effects. The fact that normal subjects showed much greater facilitation than amnesic patients for nonwords could be attributable to the use of explicit memory by normal subjects to aid nonword identification; the use of multiple trials on the identification task could well promote the use of intentional retrieval strategies by intact subjects (cf. Haist et al., 1991; Schacter et al., 1989; Schacter, Delaney, & Merikle, 1990).

In a later study using a similar paradigm, Cermak, Blackford, O'Connor, & Bleich, (1988) reported significant nonword priming in S. S., a patient with dense amnesia attributable to encephalitis. In this study, S. S. and control subjects studied a series of words and nonwords; following each list, they were tested on an identification and a recognition task. In the nonword condition, S. S. and control subjects demonstrated priming effects of 39 msec and 59 msec, respectively. Their corresponding recognition scores were 73% and 86% correct, respectively. As Cermak et al. point out, these results indicate that S. S. showed significant nonword priming effects. However, it must be noted that there is no dissociation between implicit and explicit memory in this experiment—larger priming scores in the control subjects were paralleled by higher levels of recognition performance, perhaps because of the use of explicit strategies by control subjects.

Gordon (1988) reported evidence for significant nonword priming effects in a group of amnesic patients. In this study, amnesic patients of various etiologies made lexical decisions about words and nonwords, and following 10–15 intervening items, words and nonwords were repeated. With words, amnesic patients demonstrated a 151-msec priming effect compared to a 122-msec effect for normal subjects. With nonwords, however, normal subjects showed a 73-msec priming effect and the amnesic patients showed an nonsignificant 9-msec effect. Although this result seems to suggest a lack of nonword priming in amnesic patients, Gordon reported that nonwords that were responded to especially slowly during the first presentation were responded to significantly more quickly by amnesics during the second presentation. On the basis of this latter observation, Gordon concluded that certain nonwords can be primed in amnesic patients. By the standard criterion of priming, however, amnesic patients failed to show a significant effect.

Smith and Oscar-Berman (1990) reported some evidence of nonword priming in amnesic patients. Eight Korsakoff patients completed a lexical decision task in which words and nonwords were repeated after an average lag of 15 items. Under these conditions, control subjects demonstrated a 56-msec priming effect for words and a 50-msec priming effect for nonwords. The amnesic subjects, however, demonstrated a 131-msec priming effects for words and a nonsignificant 26-msec priming effect for nonwords. These reaction time measures clearly suggest that nonword priming is not normal in amnesic patients. However, when the accuracy of the lexical decisions was measured, the authors reported data suggesting robust priming of nonwords in amnesics. In this analysis, control subjects were equally accurate in judging items as words and nonwords on the first and second exposures, probably because of ceiling effects. Amnesic subjects, however, improved their lexical decision accuracy by 14.1% for words on the second trial relative to the first, whereas their performance for nonwords was 8.9% less accurate for second exposures relative to first exposures. According to the authors, this lowered accuracy on the repeated nonwords implies that some information about nonwords was acquired on the first lexical decision trial, information that made the lexical decision more difficult on the second trial. More specifically, the authors argued that the nonwords became more familiar to the subjects as a consequence of exposure on the first trial; this feeling of familiarity biased the patients to provide more frequent "word" responses to nonwords on the second trial than on the first, thus increasing their error rate. Once again, however, it is important to note that although these data do provide some evidence of nonword priming in amnesic patients, the amnesic patients failed to show intact nonword priming by a standard measure.

Several other studies, however, provide rather more convincing evidence of normal nonword priming effects in amnesic patients. In a briefly described study, Gabrieli and Keane (1988) reported evidence of normal nonword priming on a perceptual identification task in patient H. M., despite near-chance levels of recognition memory. Musen and Squire (1991) reported repetition effects for nonwords on a reading task with a group of amnesic patients. In Experiment 1, control subjects and amnesic patients of various etiologies read lists of 100 items that were composed in four different ways: (a) 100 unique words, (b) 5 words repeated 20 times, with an average of 4 intervening items between repetitions, (c) 100 unique nonwords, and (d) 5 nonwords repeated 20 times each. The dependent measure was reading time, and this measure was obtained following each 10-item sequence. The key result was that amnesic subjects performed similarly to the control subjects: Reading times improved as a consequence of repetition, and the nonword reading times showed more improvement than did the words for both groups. In addition, it was found that the amnesic patients were significantly impaired on a recognition task relative to the control subjects, a result that suggests that performance of the reading task was not mediated by explicit memory. Experiment 2 was essentially a replication of Experiment 1, except that the target lists were reexposed 10 min after the first presentation, so priming could be assessed with a 10-min delay. Once again, amnesic subjects showed a normal facilitation of reading time for nonwords.

Although the Musen and Squire (1991) study used numerous repetitions of target items, evidence of intact implicit memory for nonwords in a more standard priming paradigm has been reported by Haist et al. (1991), who modified the perceptual identification task that had been used previously by Cermak et al. (1985). In the Haist et al. study, exposure duration on the perceptual identification task was calibrated individually for each patient so that baseline identification accuracy was approximately 50% correct for words and for nonwords. Subjects were then given four sets of study-test blocks; they made liking judgments about words and nonwords during the study phase and were then given perceptual identification and recognition tests. Amnesic patients showed normal priming for both words and nonwords. Haist et al. also assessed whether the observed priming of nonwords was attributable to items that were either phonologically or orthographically similar to real words. They failed to find evidence in support of this idea.

Evidence suggesting that phonological similarity to real words plays a role in nonword priming has been reported by Cermak, Verfaellie, Milberg, Letourneau, and Blackford (1991), using the same sort of perceptual identification procedure as employed previously by Cermak et al. (1985). In one experiment, amnesic patients and control subjects studied a list comprised of words, nonwords, and pseudohomophones (nonwords with the same pronunciation as a real word; e.g., phaire). Amnesics showed some, but impaired, priming for both nonwords and pseudohomophones. Although these data are inconclusive, in an additional experiment, a list consisting solely of pseudohomophones was studied, and amnesic patients now showed intact priming. Haist et al. (1991) suggested that the differences between their data and those of Cermak et al. (1991) are attributable to the use of explicit memory by normal subjects in the Cermak et al. mixed list condition.

In summary, although the literature on nonword priming in amnesic patients is rather unsettled, with both positive and negative findings reported, the message from recent work is that conditions do indeed exist in which amnesics show robust and even normal priming effects for nonwords. Note also that two of the studies that failed to observe significant nonword effects, at least by a standard criterion of priming (Gordon, 1988; Smith & Oscar-Berman, 1990), used a lexical decision task. This task has often failed to show nonword priming effects in normal subjects (e.g., Bentin & Moscovitch, 1988; Forbach et al., 1974; Fowler et al,, 1985), so the noisy data obtained with amnesic patients are not entirely surprising. The possible use of explicit memory strategies by control subjects under certain experimental conditions has also been suggested as a reason for apparently impaired priming of nonwords by amnesics. This suggestion has some plausibility, particularly because studies of nonword priming in normal subjects have typically failed to produce dissociations between priming and explicit memory of the sort that could rule out the use of intentional retrieval strategies by control subjects (see Schacter et al., 1989, for more extensive discussion of this general point). Nevertheless, it is not satisfactory to invoke the use of explicit strategies by normal subjects whenever amnesic patients fail to show intact priming; the problems of circular reasoning inherent in such an approach should be clear enough. This sort of explanation carries some force only when there are good reasons to believe that a particular priming paradigm invites the use of explicit strategies by control subjects, and when appropriate implicit/explicit dissociations that could rule out the use of such strategies have not been obtained with normal subjects (Schacter et al., 1989).

Priming of New Associations.   A second major domain in which priming of novel verbal information has been assessed involves the analysis of implicit and explicit memory for newly acquired associations, using a cued stem completion task developed and explored in a series of studies by Graf and Schacter (1985, 1987, 1989; Schacter & Graf, 1986a, 1986b, 1989). In these studies, subjects studied unrelated word pairs (e.g., WINDOW–REASON) and were then given a stem completion test in which word stems are preceded either by the paired word from the study list (e.g., WINDOW-REA_____; same context condition), or by some other unrelated word (e.g., OFFICER-REA_____; different context condition). Numerous experiments with normal subjects have revealed significantly higher levels of completion performance in the same context than in the different context condition, thereby demonstrating priming for newly acquired associations. However, in contrast to priming effects with familiar words, which are generally insensitive to levels of processing manipulations (cf. Bowers & Schacter, 1990; Graf & Mandler, 1984; Jacoby & Dallas, 1981), priming of new associations tends to be observed only following some degree of elaborative study processing (Graf & Schacter, 1985; Schacter & Graf, 1986a; but see Micco & Masson, 1991). Furthermore, some evidence indicates that associative priming in college students is observed only in those subjects who exhibit some awareness of the relation between the completion task and the study list, whereas priming of familiar words can be observed in subjects who exhibit no such awareness (Bowers & Schacter, 1990). However, experimental conditions do exist in which college students and elderly adults can show associative priming in the apparent absence of test awareness (Howard, Fry, & Brune, 1991).

Several studies have examined whether associative priming effects on stem completion performance can be observed in amnesic patients. In their initial study, Graf and Schacter (1985) tested 12 amnesic patients of varied etiologies, 12 matched control subjects, and 12 college students. They found associative priming effects of comparable magnitude in all three groups. However, in a subsequent re-analysis of these data, it was observed that the associative effect—more priming in the same- than in the different-context condition—was observed only in patients with relatively mild disorders; severely amnesic patients showed priming, but there was little difference between same- and different-context conditions. A similar pattern of results was observed in a subsequent study that compared priming of new associations in groups of mildly and severely amnesic patients (Schacter & Graf, 1986b).

Subsequent studies that have used the Graf and Schacter paradigm with amnesic patients have revealed a quite mixed pattern of results. Cermak, Bleich, and Blackford (1988) reported no evidence of associative effects in severely amnesic Korsakoff amnesics, but Cermak, Blackford, O'Connor, and Bleich (1988) found that a densely amnesic encephalitic patient (S. S.) exhibited more priming in the same- than in the different-context condition. Shimamura and Squire (1989) replicated the Cermak et al. finding of no associative effects in Korsakoff patients, but found trends for associative priming in patients with presumed or demonstrated damage to the medial temporal region: these amnesic patients showed an 8.7% context effect, whereas matched control subjects showed a 10.5% context effect. In addition, Shimamura and Squire (1989) found a positive correlation between the amount of associative priming that was exhibited by individual patients and their score on the General Memory index of the Wechsler Memory Scale (Revised), thus replicating and extending Schacter and Graf's (1986b) finding that associative priming is related to severity of amnesia. Finally, Mayes and Gooding (1989) found little evidence of associative effects in a mixed group of amnesic patients.

In view of the finding that associative priming effects on stem completion performance in college students often depend on elaborative study processing and test awareness, it is tempting to suggest that the phenomenon might be attributable to the use of explicit memory strategies, thereby accounting for why associative effects are not consistently observed in amnesic patients. However, this idea has difficulty accommodating the fact that several experiments that have produced experimental dissociations between the associative effects on stem completion and associative effects on cued-recall performance under conditions in which the cues on the two tests were the same and only instructions (implicit vs. explicit) were varied. For example, manipulations of degree and type of elaborative study processing, as well as proactive and retroactive interference, had no effect on priming of new associations despite large effects on explicit memory (Graf & Schacter, 1987, 1989; Schacter & Graf, 1986a; Schacter & McGlynn, 1989). By contrast, study/test modality shifts nearly eliminated the context effect on priming but had little or no effect on cued-recall performance (Schacter & Graf, 1989). If associative priming is a simple consequence of intentional retrieval, it should not have been possible to obtain such dissociations in normal subjects under conditions in which nominal cues were held constant on implicit and explicit tasks, and only test instructions were varied.

Evidence concerning priming of new associations in amnesic patients has been obtained with two additional paradigms. Tulving, Hayman, and Macdonald (1991) reported an extensive case study of a severely amnesic head-injured patient, KC, who exhibits essentially no episodic memory. KC showed normal levels of priming on a fragment completion test for previously studied low frequency words, and these priming effects were quite long-lasting. However, when target words were paired with associatively unrelated phrases and pictures, KC showed no more priming when these contextual cues were reinstated during the fragment completion test than when they were not. KC was able, however, to acquire novel associations after extensive repetitions (Tulving et al., 1991), a finding that confirms and extends previous reports that with extensive repetition, KC can learn, and retain over long retention intervals, complex new associations and knowledge (Glisky & Schacter, 1988; Glisky, Schacter, & Tulving, 1986a, 1986b).

A further paradigm that has been used to investigate priming effects for unrelated word pairs in amnesic patients was developed by Moscovitch, Winocur, and McLachlan (1986). Subjects initially read pairs of words, and then reread either the same pairs, or recombined pairs that were formed by repairing study list items. Moscovitch et al. found that following a single exposure to an unrelated word pair, amnesic patients, elderly adults, and young control subjects all read same pairs faster than recombined pairs, thus suggesting that newly acquired associative information affected reading performance in all groups. However, Musen and Squire (1990) failed to replicate this result. They found associative effects on reading time (i.e., faster reading of same than recombined pairs) only following several study-list exposures to the unrelated word pairs.

The evidence on priming of new associations in amnesic patients, then, is similar to the previously discussed evidence on priming of nonwords, inasmuch as a relatively inconsistent pattern of positive and negative results has been obtained. Although it seems unlikely that this inconsistency is attributable to the use of explicit retrieval strategies by control subjects, it is possible that the initial acquisition or setting up of novel associations depends on an episodic or declarative memory system that is damaged in amnesia (cf. Shimamura & Squire, 1989).

Priming of Unfamiliar Objects and Unfamiliar Visual Patterns

The majority of research on priming and implicit memory has focused on verbal materials; there is less evidence available on priming of nonverbal information and still less on priming of novel or unfamiliar nonverbal information (for review, see Schacter, Delaney, & Merikle, 1990). Nevertheless, studies with normal subjects have established quite clearly that priming effects can be observed for novel objects and patterns, and have further indicated that such effects can be dissociated from explicit memory. For example, Schacter, Cooper, and Delaney (1990) observed priming effects on an object decision task that requires subjects to judge whether previously studied and nonstudied novel objects are structurally possible or impossible. The priming effect was observed for possible but not for impossible objects and was not enhanced by various encoding manipulations that increased explicit memory for the novel objects (see also Schacter, Cooper, Delaney, Peterson, & Tharan, 1991). More recent work has shown that priming of novel objects was not reduced by study/test changes of object size and reflection that impaired explicit memory (Cooper, Schacter, Ballesteros, & Moore, 1992). Musen and Triesman (1990) demonstrated priming of novel dot patterns on a task that involved identifying briefly exposed patterns, and a subsequent study showed that this priming effect does not benefit from verbal encoding strategies that enhance explicit memory (Musen, 1991; for additional examples of nonverbal priming, see Kroll & Potter, 1984; Kunst-Wilson & Zajonc, 1980; Mandler, Nakamura, & Van Zandt, 1987).

Only a few studies have assessed priming of unfamiliar nonverbal materials in amnesic patients, but their results are relatively consistent. One study examined the performance of the well-known amnesic patient H. M. and control subjects with a paradigm that assessed priming of unfamiliar dot patterns (Gabrieli, Milberg, Keane, & Corkin (1990). The target materials consisted of a spatial arrangement of five dots in a 3×3 matrix that were connected by four lines to form a specific pattern. After exposing H. M. and controls to a series of these patterns, priming was assessed with a dot completion test in which subjects were asked to connect any five dots with four straight lines. A variety of possible patterns could be generated, and the key question was whether subjects showed an enhanced tendency to connect dots to form previously studied patterns—that is, whether they showed a priming effect. Gabrieli et al. found that H. M. and control subjects exhibited similar levels of priming on this task in two experiments that used slightly different procedures to estimate baseline performance. Moreover, a striking dissociation between priming and explicit memory was observed: H. M. showed intact priming despite chance levels of performance on the recognition test.

Schacter, Cooper, Tharan, & Rubens (1991) used their possible/impossible decision task to examine priming of novel three-dimensional objects in six amnesic patients, matched control subjects, and college students. During the study phase, subjects performed a structural encoding task used previously by Schacter, Cooper, and Delaney (1990) in which they judged whether objects faced primarily to the left or to the right. After a short retention interval of several minutes, they made possible/impossible decisions about briefly exposed studied and nonstudied objects, followed by yes/no recognition memory decisions. The amnesic patients showed a normal pattern of performance on the object decision task—priming for possible but not for impossible objects—despite impaired recognition memory. In a follow-up study, Schacter, Cooper, and Treadwell (in press) observed normal object decision priming in amnesic patients across a study-to-test size transformation. Musen and Squire (1992) examined amnesic patients' performance on the dot pattern identification task developed by Musen and Triesman (1990). They found that amnesics did show significant priming on this task, as expressed by more accurate identification of studied than of nonstudied dot patterns. However, the absolute magnitude of the priming effect in amnesic patients (7.6%) was nonsignificantly smaller than the magnitude of the effect (10.4%) in control subjects.

To summarize, evidence for priming of novel nonverbal information has been obtained consistently in amnesic patients, and has also been observed in normal subjects under conditions in which priming can be dissociated from explicit memory (for related research, see Cohen et al., 1986; Johnson, Kim, & Risse, 1985; Nissen & Bullemer, 1987). Accordingly, it seems safe to conclude that stronger evidence exists for normal priming of novel objects and patterns in amnesic patients than for normal priming of nonwords and new associations.

PRIMING OF NOVEL INFORMATION IN AMNESIA: THEORETICAL IMPLICATIONS

We began by noting that evidence on priming of novel information has potentially important implications for theories of implicit memory and amnesia, and then delineated some problems entailed in the conceptualization of novel information. We now return to these issues in light of the data that we have reviewed.

The main conclusion to emerge from our review is that conditions do indeed exist under which priming of novel information can be demonstrated at normal or near-normal levels in amnesic patients, at least when novel information is defined as the absence of a preexisting unit in memory that corresponds in some sense to the target item. As noted above, the strongest evidence for this conclusion comes from research on priming of novel nonverbal information. Although evidence on nonword priming is rather mixed, several studies have produced relatively clear-cut data showing normal priming of nonwords (Cermak et al., 1991; Gabrieli & Keane, 1988; Haist et al., 1991; Musen & Squire, 1991). In contrast, although data indicating some degree of priming for newly acquired associations have been obtained in certain kinds of patients with memory disorders, there is little or no evidence for intact priming effects of this kind in severely amnesic patients.

Although we cannot specify with any certitude the exact reasons for these differences, some clues are provided by considering recent accounts of preserved priming in amnesia. As noted earlier in the chapter, one view holds that priming effects on so-called data-driven implicit tests such as word completion, perceptual identification, and object decision depend on a presemantic perceptual representation system (PRS), which is composed of various cortically based subsystems (Schacter, 1990, 1992a, 1992b; Tulving & Schacter, 1990). By this view, priming effects for nonwords and for novel objects or patterns—which have been observed on data-driven tests—depend on changes occurring within PRS. In contrast, priming effects for newly acquired associations often involve semantic processing (Graf & Schacter, 1985; Schacter & Graf, 1986a), and may depend on processes outside of PRS—processes that may be impaired in amnesic patients and are hence unable to support the normal acquisition of novel semantic information (Schacter, Cooper, Tharan, & Rubens, 1991). Stated slightly differently, PRS may be able to function independently of the episodic or declarative memory system that is supported by the hippocampus and related structures, and hence novel perceptual representations can be acquired normally by amnesic patients. However, the acquisition of novel semantic associations may depend to a large extent on hippocampal and other limbic structures that are typically impaired in amnesic patients (cf. Musen & Squire, 1992; Schacter, 1990; Tulving et al., 1991).

The foregoing line of analysis leads to the suggestion that amnesic patients should show robust priming of novel information as long as a priming phenomenon depends primarily on perceptual processing and does not require extensive semantic analyses. It would be interesting in this regard to determine whether normal priming of new perceptual associations could be observed in amnesic patients—that is, to assess whether amnesic patients would show normal performance on an implicit memory test in which associative effects are observed following study tasks that focus attention on perceptual relations among target items. As stated earlier, associative effects on the stem completion paradigm used by Graf and Schacter are typically observed following semantic study tasks (although associative priming apparently can be observed following study tasks that do not explicitly require semantic analysis; Micco & Masson, 1991). An important task for future research would be to devise paradigms in which priming of new associations can be demonstrated following study tasks that restrict processing to the perceptual level. If the failure to observe consistently normal priming of new associations in amnesic patients is attributable to the dependence of such priming on semantic-level processing, then it should be possible to observe intact priming of novel perceptual associations.

Whatever the ultimate resolution of this issue, the positive results that have been obtained would appear to cast serious doubt on the activation theories of amnesia discussed earlier that hold that priming in amnesics is observed only for materials with preexisting memory representations (cf. Diamond & Rozin, 1984; Graf et al., 1984; Mandler, 1980). However, the force of this conclusion depends on the view of word and object representation that one holds. If the lexical view is adopted, where words or objects are represented by a single entry or unit, then the data on priming of nonwords and novel objects are difficult for an activation theory to handle. If, on the other hand, a sublexical view of word and object representation is held, where words or objects are represented in terms of connections between lower level units, then some form of activation theory can accommodate the priming data.

In addition to providing a way for activation theories to account for some of the data that we have considered, this latter idea highlights again the question of what constitutes novel information: If items that are novel at one level of analysis (i.e., word or object level) are to be defined as combinations of features that already exist at a lower level, then it is no longer clear how to determine what qualifies as a novel word, object, or pattern, or even whether it is sensible to make a distinction between novel and preexisting representations. From an empirical standpoint, the distinction is sensible as long as the data suggest important differences in the nature of priming effects for novel items and items that have preexisting representations; some such differences have been observed (cf. Bentin & Moscovitch, 1988; Feustel et al., 1983; Schacter, 1985; Schacter & McGlynn, 1989). More generally, however, future research on priming of novel information in amnesic patients will need to pay careful attention to the conceptual and theoretical underpinnings of the very construct that is the target of experimental inquiry.

ACKNOWLEDGMENTS

Preparation of this chapter was supported by grant RO 1 MH45938-01A3 from the National Institute of Mental Health to D. L. Schacter. We thank Dana Osowiecki for help with preparation of the manuscript.

REFERENCES

Bentin, S., & Moscovitch, M. (1988). The time course of repetition effects for words and unfamiliar faces. *Journal of Experimental Psychology: General, 117,* 148–160.

Besner, D., Twilley, L., McCann, R. S., & Seergobin, K. (1990). On the association between connectionism and data: Are a few words necessary? *Psychological Review, 97,* 432–446.

Biederman, I. (1987). Recognition-by-component: A theory of human image understanding. *Psychological Review, 94,* 115–147.

Bowers, J. S., & Schacter, D. L. (1990). Implicit memory and test awareness. *Journal of Experimental Psychology: Learning, Memory and Cognition, 16,* 404–416.

Carpenter, G. A., & Grossberg, S. (1987). Neural dynamics of category learning and recognition: Attention, memory consolidation, and amnesia. In J. Davis, R. Newburgh, & E. Wegman (Eds.), *Brain structure, learning, and memory* (pp. 233–290). Hillsdale, NJ: Lawrence Erlbaum Associates.

Carr, T. H., Brown, J. S., & Charalambous, A. (1989). Repetition and reading: Perceptual encoding mechanisms are very abstract but not very interactive. *Journal of Experimental Psychology: Learning, Memory and Cognition, 15,* 763–778.

Cermak, L. S., Blackford, S. P., O'Connor, M., & Bleich, R. P. (1988). The implicit memory ability of a patient with amnesia due to encephalitis. *Brain and Cognition, 7,* 312–323.

Cermak, L. S., Bleich, R. P., & Blackford, S. P. (1988). Deficits in the implicit retention of new associations by alcoholic Korsakoff patients. *Brain and Cognition, 7,* 312–323.

Cermak, L. S., Talbot, N., Chandler, K., & Wolbarst, L. R. (1985). The perceptual priming phenomenon in amnesia. *Neuropsychologia, 23,* 615–622.

Cermak, L. S., Verfaellie, M., Milberg, W., Letourneau, L., & Blackford, S. (1991). A further analysis of perceptual identification priming in alcoholic Korsakoff patients. *Neuropsychologia, 29,* 725–736.

Cohen, N. J. (1984). Preserved learning capacity in amnesia: Evidence for multiple memory systems. In L. R. Squire & N. Butters (Eds.), *Neuropsychology of memory* (pp. 83–103). New York: Guilford Press.

Cohen, N. J., Abrams, I., Harley, W. S., Tabor, L., Gordon, B., & Sejnowski, T. J. (1986). Perceptual skill learning and repetition priming for novel material in amnesic patients, normal subjects, and neuron-like networks. *Society for Neuroscience, 12,* 1162.

Cohen, N. J., & Squire, L. R. (1980). Preserved learning and retention of pattern-analyzing skill in amnesia: Dissociation of "knowing how" and "knowing that." *Science, 210,* 207–209.

Cooper, L. A., Schacter, D. L., Ballesteros, S., & Moore, C. (1992). Priming and recognition of transformed three-dimensional objects: Effect of size and reflection. *Journal of Experimental Psychology: Learning, Memory and Cognition, 18,* 43–57.

Diamond, R., & Rozin, P. (1984). Activation of existing memories in the amnesic syndrome. *Journal of Abnormal Psychology, 93,* 98–105.

Feustel, T. C., Shiffrin, R. M., & Salasoo, M. A. (1983). Episodic and lexical contributions to the repetition effect in word identification. *Journal of Experimental Psychology: General, 112,* 309–346.

Forbach, G. B., Stanners, R. F., & Hochhaus, L. (1974). Repetition and practice effects in a lexical decision task. *Memory & Cognition, 2,* 337–339.

Forster, K. I. (1976). Accessing the mental lexicon. In R. J. Wales, & E. Walker (Eds.), *New approaches to language mechanisms* (pp. 257–287). Oxford: North Holland.

Fowler, C., Napps, S. E., & Feldman, L. (1985). Relations among regular and irregular morphologically related words in the lexicon as revealed by repetition priming. *Memory and Cognition, 13,* 241–255.

Gabrieli, J. D. E., & Keane, M. M. (1988). Priming in the amnesic patient H. M.: New findings and a theory of intact and impaired priming in patients with memory disorders. *Society of Neuroscience Abstracts, 14,* 1290.

Gabrieli, J. D. E., Milberg, W., Keane, M., & Corkin, S. (1990). Intact priming of patterns despite impaired memory. *Neuropsychologia, 28,* 417–428.

Glisky, E. L., & Schacter, D. L. (1988). Acquisition of domain-specific knowledge in organic amnesia: Training for computer-related work. *Neuropsychologia, 25,* 893–906.

Glisky, E. L., Schacter, D. L., & Tulving, E. (1986a). Learning and retention of computer-related vocabulary in memory-impaired patients: Method of vanishing cues. *Journal of Clinical and Experimental Neuropsychology, 8,* 292–312.

Glisky, E. L., Schacter, D. L., & Tulving, E. (1986b). Computer learning by memory-impaired patients: Acquisition and retention of complex knowledge. *Neuropsychologia, 24,* 313–328.

Glushko, R. J. (1979). The organization and activation of orthographic knowledge in reading aloud. *Journal of Experimental Psychology: Human Perception and Performance, 5,* 674–691.

Gordon, B. (1988). Preserved learning of novel information in amnesia: Evidence for multiple memory systems. *Brain and Cognition, 7,* 257–282.

Graf, P., & Mandler, G. (1984). Activation makes words more accessible, but not necessarily more retrievable. *Journal of Verbal Learning and Verbal Behavior, 23,* 553–568.

Graf, P., & Schacter, D. L. (1985). Implicit and explicit memory for new associations in normal and amnesic subjects. *Journal of Experimental Psychology: Learning, Memory and Cognition, 11,* 501–518.

Graf, P., & Schacter, D. L. (1987). Selective effects of interference on implicit and explicit memory for new associations. *Journal of Experimental Psychology: Learning, Memory and Cognition, 13,* 45–53.

Graf, P., & Schacter, D. L. (1989). Unitization and grouping mediate dissociations in memory for new associations. *Journal of Experimental Psychology: Learning, Memory and Cognition, 15,* 930–940.

Graf, P., Shimamura, A., & Squire, L. (1985). Priming across modalities and across category levels: Extending the domain of preserved function in amnesia. *Journal of Experimental Psychology: Learning, Memory and Cognition, 11,* 385–395.

Graf, P., Squire, L. R., & Mandler, G. (1984). The information that amnesic patients do not forget. *Journal of Experimental Psychology: Learning, Memory and Cognition, 10,* 164–178.

Haist, F., Musen, G., & Squire, L. R. (1991). Intact priming of words and nonwords in amnesia. *Psychobiology, 19,* 275–285.

Howard, D. V., Fry, A. F., & Brune, C. M. (1991). Aging and memory for new associations: Direct versus indirect measures. *Journal of Experimental Psychology: Learning, Memory and Cognition, 17,* 779–792.

Jacoby, L. L. (1983). Perceptual enhancement: Persistent effects of an experience. *Journal of Experimental Psychology: Learning, Memory and Cognition, 9,* 21–38.

Jacoby, L. L., & Dallas, M. (1981). On the relationship between autobiographical memory and perceptual learning. *Journal of Experimental Psychology: General, 110,* 306–340.

Johnson, M. K., Kim, J. K., & Risse, G. (1985). Do alcoholic Korsakoff's syndrome patients acquire affective reactions? *Journal of Experimental Psychology: Learning, Memory and Cognition, 11,* 22–36.

Kirsner, K., & Smith, M. C. (1974). Modality effects in word identification. *Memory & Cognition, 2,* 637–640.

Kroll, J. F., & Potter, M. C. (1984). Recognizing words, pictures, and concepts: a comparison of lexical, object, and reality decisions. *Journal of Verbal Learning and Verbal Behavior, 23,* 39–66.

Kunst-Wilson, W. R., & Zajonc, R. B. (1980). Affective discrimination of stimuli that are not recognized. *Science, 207,* 557–558.

Mandler, G. (1980). Recognizing: The judgement of previous occurrence. *Psychological Review, 87,* 252–271.

Mandler, G., Nakamura, Y., & Van Zandt, B. (1987). Nonspecific effects of exposure on stimuli that cannot be recognized. *Journal of Experimental Psychology: Learning, Memory, and Cognition, 13,* 646–648.

Masson, M. E. J. (1989). Fluent reprocessing as an implicit expression of memory for experience. In S. Lewandowsky, & J. Dunn (Eds.), *Implicit memory: Theoretical issues* (pp. 123–138). Hillsdale, NJ: Lawrence Erlbaum Associates.

Mayes, A. R., & Gooding, P. (1989). Enhancement of word completion priming in amnesics by cueing with previously novel associates. *Neuropsychologia, 27,* 1057–1072.

McClelland, S. L., Rumelhart, D. E. (1986). *Parallel distributed processing: explorations in the microstructure of cognition. Volume II.* Cambridge, MA: MIT Press.

Micco, A., & Masson, M. E. J. (1991). Implicit memory for new associations: An interactive process approach. *Journal of Experimental Psychology: Learning, Memory, and Cognition, 17,* 1105–1123.

Milner, B., Corkin, S., & Teuber, H. L. (1968). Further analysis of the hippocampal amnesic syndrome: 14-year follow-up study of H. M. *Neuropsychologia, 6,* 215–234.

Mishkin, M., & Petri, H. L. (1984). Memories and habits: Some implications for the analysis of learning and retention. In N. Butters & L. R. Squire (Eds.), *Neuropsychology of memory* (pp. 287–296). New York: Guilford Press.

Morton, J. (1979). Facilitation in word recognition: Experiments causing change in the logogen model. In P. A. Kolers, M. E. Wrolstad, & H. Bouma (Eds.), *Processing models of visible language* (pp. 259–268). New York: Plenum.

Moscovitch, M. (1982). Multiple dissociations of function in amnesia. In L. S. Cermak (Ed.), *Human memory and amnesia* (pp. 337–370). Hillsdale, NJ: Lawrence Erlbaum Associates.

Moscovitch, M., Winocur, G., & McLachlan, D. (1986). Memory as assessed by recognition and reading time in normal and memory-impaired people with Alzheimer's disease and other neurological disorders. *Journal of Experimental Psychology: General, 115,* 331–347.

Musen, G. (1991). Effects of verbal labeling and exposure duration on implicit memory for visual patterns. *Journal of Experimental Psychology: Learning, Memory and Cognition, 17,* 954–962.

Musen, G., & Squire, L. R. (1990). Implicit memory: No evidence for rapid acquisition of new associations in amnesic patients or normal subjects. *Society for Neuroscience Abstracts, 16,* 287.

Musen, G., & Squire, L. R. (1991). Normal acquisition of novel verbal information in amnesia. *Journal of Experimental Psychology: Learning, Memory and Cognition, 17,* 1095–1104.

Musen, G., & Squire, L. R. (1992). Nonverbal priming in amnesia. *Memory & Cognition, 20,* 441–448.

Musen, G., & Triesman, A. (1990). Implicit and explicit memory for visual patterns. *Journal of Experimental Psychology: Learning, Memory and Cognition, 16,* 1068–1076.

Nissen, M. J., & Bullemer, P. (1987). Attentional requirements of learning: Evidence from performance measures. *Cognitive Psychology, 19,* 1–32.

O'Keefe, J., & Nadel, L. (1978). *The hippocampus as a cognitive map.* Oxford: Oxford University Press.

Parkin, A. J. (1982). Residual learning capability in organic amnesia. *Cortex, 18,* 417–440.

Polster, M. R., Nadel, L., & Schacter, D. L. (1991). Cognitive neuroscience analyses of memory: A historical perspective. *Journal of Cognitive Neuroscience, 3,* 95–116.

Richardson-Klavehn, A., & Bjork, R. A. (1988). Measures of memory. *Annual Review of Psychology, 36,* 475–543.

Roediger, H. L. III. (1990). Implicit memory: A commentary. *Bulletin of the Psychonomic Society, 28,* 373–380.

Roediger, H. L. III, & Blaxton, T. A. (1987). Retrieval modes produce dissociations in memory for surface information. In D. S. Gorfein, & R. R. Hoffman (Eds.), *Memory and cognitive processes: The Ebbinghaus centennial conference* (pp. 349–379). Hillsdale, NJ: Lawrence Erlbaum Associates.

Roediger, H. L. III, Weldon, M. S., & Challis, B. H. (1989). Explaining dissociations between implicit and explicit measures of retention: A processing account. In & F. I. M. Craik & H. L. Roediger III (Eds.), *Varieties of memory and consciousness: Essays in honour of Endel Tulving* (pp. 3–41). Hillsdale, NJ: Lawrence Erlbaum Associates.

Rosson, M. B. (1985). The interaction of pronunciation rules and lexical representations in reading aloud. *Memory and Cognition, 13,* 90–99.

Rozin, P. A. (1976). The psychobiological approach to human memory. In M. R. Rosensweig & E. L. Bennett (Eds.), *Neural mechanisms of memory and learning* (pp. 3–48). Cambridge, MA: MIT Press.

Rueckl, J. G. (1990). Similarity effects in word and pseudoword repetition priming. *Journal of Experimental Psychology: Learning, Memory and Cognition, 16,* 374–391.

Salasoo, A., Shiffrin, R. M., & Feustel, T. C. (1985). Building permanent memory codes: Codification and repetition effects in word identification. *Journal of Experimental Psychology: General, 114,* 50–77.

Schacter, D. L. (1985). Priming of old and new knowledge in amnesic patients and normal subjects. *Annals of the New York Academy of Sciences, 444,* 41–53.

Schacter, D. L. (1987). Implicit memory: History and current status. *Journal of Experimental Psychology: Learning, Memory and Cognition, 13,* 501–518.

Schacter, D. L. (1990). Perceptual representation system and implicit memory: Toward a resolution of the multiple memory systems debate. *Annals of the New York Academy of Sciences, 608,* 543–571.

Schacter, D. L. (1992a). Priming and multiple memory systems: Perceptual mechanisms of implicit memory. *Journal of Cognitive Neuroscience, 4,* 244–256.

Schacter, D. L. (1992b). Understanding implicit memory: A cognitive neuroscience approach. *American Psychologist, 47,* 559–569.

Schacter, D. L., Bowers, J., & Booker, J. (1989). Intention, awareness, and implicit memory: The retrieval intentionality criterion. In S. Lewandowsky, J. Dunn, & K. Kirsner (Eds.), *Implicit memory: Theoretical issues* (pp. 47–65). Hillsdale, NJ: Lawrence Erlbaum Associates.

Schacter, D. L., Cooper, L. A., & Delaney, S. M. (1990). Implicit memory for unfamiliar objects depends on access to structural descriptions. *Journal of Experimental Psychology: General, 119,* 5–24.

Schacter, D. L., Cooper, L. A., Delaney, S. M., Peterson, M. A., & Tharan, M. (1991). Implicit memory for possible and impossible objects: Constraints on the construction of structural descriptions. *Journal of Experimental Psychology: Learning, Memory and Cognition, 17,* 3–19.

Schacter, D. L., Cooper, L., Tharan, M., & Rubens, A. (1991). Preserved priming of novel objects in patients with memory disorders. *Journal of Cognitive Neuroscience, 3,* 117–130.

Schacter, D. L., Cooper, L. A., & Treadwell, J. (in press). Preserved priming of novel objects across size transformation in amnesic patients. *Psychological Science.*

Schacter, D. L., Delaney, S. M., & Merikle, E. P. (1990). Priming of nonverbal information and the nature of implicit memory. In G. H. Bower (Ed.), *The psychology of learning and motivation* (pp. 83–123). New York: Academic Press.

Schacter, D. L., & Graf, P. (1986a). Effects of elaborative processing on implicit and explicit memory for new associations. *Journal of Experimental Psychology: Learning, Memory and Cognition, 8,* 727–743.

Schacter, D. L., & Graf, P. (1986b). Preserved learning in amnesic patients: Perspectives from research on direct priming. *Journal of Clinical & Experimental Neuropsychology, 8,* 727–743.

Schacter, D. L., & Graf, P. (1989). Modality specificity of implicit memory for new associations. *Journal of Experimental Psychology: Learning, Memory and Cognition, 15,* 3–12.

Schacter, D. L., & McGlynn, S. M. (1989). Implicit memory: Effects of elaboration depend upon unitization. *American Journal of Psychology, 102,* 151–181.

Scoville, W. B., & Milner, B. (1957). Loss of recent memory after bilateral hippocampal lesions. *Journal of Neurology, Neurosurgery and Psychiatry, 20,* 11–21.

Seidenberg, M. S., & McClelland, J. R. (1989). A distributed, developmental model of word recognition and naming. *Psychological Review, 96,* 523–568.

Shimamura, A. P., & Squire, L. R. (1984). Paired-associate learning and priming effects in amnesia: A neuropsychological approach. *Journal of Experimental Psychology: General, 113,* 556–570.

Shimamura, A. P., & Squire, L. R. (1989). Impaired priming of new associations in amnesia. *Journal of Experimental Psychology, Learning, Memory, and Cognition, 15,* 721–728.

Smith, M. E., & Oscar-Berman, M. (1990). Repetition priming of words and pseudowords in divided attention and in amnesia. *Journal of Experimental Psychology: Learning, Memory and Cognition, 16,* 1033–1042.

Squire, L. R. (1987). *Memory and brain.* New York: Oxford University Press.

Squire, L. (1992). Memory and the hippocampus: Synthesis of findings with rats, monkeys and humans. *Psychological Review, 99,* 195–231.

Squire, L. R., Cohen, N., & Nadel, L. (1984). The medial temporal region and memory consolidation: A new hypothesis. In H. Weingartner & E. Parker (Eds.) *Memory Consolidation* (pp. 185–210). Hillsdale, NJ: Lawrence Erlbaum Associates.

Tulving, E., & Schacter, D. L. (1990). Priming and human memory systems. *Science, 247,* 301–306.

Tulving, E., Hayman, C. A. G., & Macdonald, C. A. (1991). Long-lasting perceptual priming and semantic learning in amnesia: A case experiment. *Journal of Experimental Psychology: Learning, Memory, and Cognition, 17,* 595–617.

Van Orden, G. C., Pennington, B. F., & Stone, G. O. (1990). Word identification in reading and the promise of subsymbolic psycholinguistics. *Psychological Review, 97,* 488–522.

Warrington, E. K., & Weiskrantz, L. (1968). New method of testing long-term retention with special reference to amnesic patients. *Nature, 277,* 972–974.

Warrington, E. K., & Weiskrantz, L. (1970). Organizational aspects of memory in amnesic patients. *Neuropsychologia, 9,* 67–71.

Warrington, E. K., & Weiskrantz, L. (1974). The effect of prior learning on subsequent retention in amnesic patients. *Neuropsychologia, 12,* 419–428.

Whittlesea, B. W. A., & Cantwell, A. L. (1987). Enduring influence of the purpose of experiences: Encoding-retrieval interactions in word and pseudoword perception. *Memory and Cognition, 15,* 465–472.

Wickelgren, W. A. (1979). Chunking and consolidation: A theoretical synthesis of semantic networks, configuring in conditioning, S-R versus cognitive learning, normal forgetting, the amnesic syndrome, and the hippocampal arousal system. *Psychological Review, 86,* 44–60.

Wolters, G., & Phaf, R. H. (1990). Implicit and explicit memory: Implications for the symbol-manipulation versus connectionism controversy. *Psychological Research, 52,* 137–144.

15

Are Word Priming and Explicit Memory Mediated by Different Brain Structures?

Arne L. Ostergaard
University of California, San Diego

Terry L. Jernigan
San Diego VA Medical Center and University of California, San Diego

The explicit/implicit memory distinction is one of several hypothesized memory dichotomies. As first proposed, the distinction was between tasks that require conscious recollection of experience (explicit) and tasks in which performance is facilitated by previous experience but for which recollection of that experience is not required (Graf & Schacter, 1985). As such, the distinction is neutral regarding the question of underlying memory systems. However, several authors have postulated that performance on implicit memory tasks is mediated by a different underlying memory system than performance on explicit memory tasks (Gabrieli, Milberg, Keane, & Corkin, 1990; Schacter, 1990; Squire, 1987; Tulving & Schacter, 1990), and a central question in current memory research regards the extent to which the experimental evidence requires that independent systems subserve explicit and implicit memory.

This issue has relevance not only for purely psychological memory theories but for anatomical models as well. If independent memory systems exist, then it is important to identify those brain structures comprising each of the systems. On the other hand, if implicit and explicit memory measures reflect the operation of the same underlying memory mechanisms, then discrepancies between performance on these tasks must be attributed to differing contributions by brain structures subserving nonmemory functions. Three types of evidence are advanced in support of the multiple memory systems proposal: (a) findings of stochastic independence between performance on explicit and implicit memory tasks; (b) functional independence between explicit and implicit memory tasks; and (c) evidence from brain-damaged patients, notably patients with the amnesic syndrome, indicating that performance on explicit memory tasks may be selectively impaired. In the following discussion, we review each of these lines of evidence briefly.

STOCHASTIC INDEPENDENCE

Stochastic independence refers to the relation between two events in which the probability of their joint occurrence is equal to the product of the probabilities of the occurrence of each event alone. In other words, stochastic independence is a statistical relation between two events indicating that the events occur independently of each other. In terms of measures of memory, stochastic independence is obtained when memory for the same items is tested successively on two different tests, and the probability of a correct response to an item on both tests is equal to the product of the probabilities of a correct response on each of the tests. Recently, several articles have appeared reporting stochastic independence between implicit and explicit measures of memory (Eich, 1984; Hayman & Tulving, 1989; Jacoby & Witherspoon, 1982; Light, Singh, & Capps, 1986; Musen & Triesman, 1990; Schacter, Cooper, & Delaney, 1990; Schacter, Cooper, Delaney, Peterson, & Tharan, 1991; Schacter, Cooper, Tharan, & Rubens, 1991; Tulving, Schacter, & Stark, 1982). This, it is claimed, supports the hypothesis that different memory systems mediate performance in the two kinds of tests. This argument is weakened by recent findings of stochastic independence between different word-priming (implicit) measures (Witherspoon & Moscovitch, 1989). Also, many problems are associated with the contingency analysis that forms the basis for findings of stochastic independence, such as Simpson's paradox (Hintzman, 1980), intertest biases (Shimamura, 1985), and item and subject characteristics and their interaction (Hintzman & Hartry, 1990). Furthermore, Ostergaard (1992) showed that almost invariably when stochastic dependency analyses have been carried out on data from implicit and explicit memory tasks, very little of the variance in one or both of the tasks is attributable to memory. Under such circumstances, even maximum possible dependence between the two tasks with respect to this memory-related variance will have little impact on the overall contingency analysis.

Unlike most explicit tests of memory, performance on implicit tests is substantially affected by factors other than the prior study episode (e.g., perceptual and lexical processes, familiarity with the materials, guessing, etc.). For example, in priming tasks that require subjects to identify briefly presented words, word fragments, or fragmented pictures, subjects perform better with items presented earlier than with new items. This difference between previously studied and new items is the priming effect. However, performance is generally well above chance level even with items that have not been studied, and often the priming effect is relatively small compared to overall performance level. Therefore, in such tasks, overall performance is only partly mediated by memory, with factors unrelated to the study episode (such as perceptual processes, the nature of the retrieval cues, preexperimental familiarity with the materials, guessing, etc.) making a significant contribution. However, the contingency analyses are always carried out on the overall success rates for previously presented (studied) items in the two tasks. Whether or not stochastic independence is obtained may therefore be more strongly related to the extent to which performance on the two tasks is mediated by memory than to the extent to which performance reflects the function of different memory systems.

Ostergaard (1992) developed a method for estimating the effect on the overall contingency analysis of maximum possible dependence between two tasks with respect to the memory-related variance (*maximum memory dependence*). The model of maximum memory dependence partitions the proportion of correct responses to studied items into two parts: the proportion of correct responses resulting from previous study of the items (the memory-mediated part) and a remainder proportion of correct responses due to other factors. It is then assumed that there is maximum possible dependence between the two memory measures with respect to the proportions of correct responses that result from prior study (the memory-mediated responses), and independence for correct responses due to other factors. Given these assumptions, it is possible to estimate the consequences for the overall contingency analysis of maximum possible dependence between the study-related aspects of performance on two memory tasks. When this method was applied to the data from a number of recent studies reporting stochastic independence between explicit and implicit memory tasks, it was clear that contingency analysis could not discriminate between independence and maximum memory dependence. In a large proportion of the experiments, even maximum dependence between the two tasks, with respect to the memory-related variance, would not produce an overall contingency relation significantly different from independence. Thus, such evidence from contingency analyses may reveal little about the memory processes mediating performance in implicit and explicit memory tasks.

FUNCTIONAL INDEPENDENCE

Functional independence is said to exist between two tasks when an independent variable affects performance on one but not the other task, or affects performance in both tasks but in opposite directions (Tulving, 1985). For example, level-of-processing manipulations generally affect performance on explicit memory tasks (with semantic processing producing better performance than phonemic or orthographic processing) while having little or no effect on implicit memory performance (e.g., Jacoby & Dallas, 1981). Many such dissociations between explicit and implicit measures of memory have been reported. Variables reported to affect performance on explicit and implicit tasks differently include shift of modality between presentation and test, and reading words versus generating the same words from antonyms during study (Blaxton, 1989; Jacoby & Dallas, 1981; Winnick & Daniel, 1970). However, there are many explanations for functional dissociations between two memory tasks other than that the two tasks address different memory systems. At the lowest level, dissociations between memory tasks can occur as a result of scaling or sensitivity differences. In other words, they can occur simply as a result of nonlinearities in the relations between the different measures used, for example, nonlinearities due to floor and ceiling effects (Dunn & Kirsner, 1988; Hintzman, 1990; Olton, 1989). Furthermore, different tasks by nature place demands on different cognitive processes (e.g., perceptual, attentional, and response-related processes) and consequently dissociations are to be expected whenever tasks are compared (for further discussion of this point, see Hintzman, 1990; Mandler, 1991; Roediger, 1984). Finally, single memory system or process models can also predict dissociations between memory tasks. For instance, the transfer-appropriate processing model predicts dissociations between memory tasks depending on the extent to which each task is perceptually or conceptually driven (cf. Roediger, Weldon, & Challis, 1989). Therefore, dissociations between memory tasks, although consistent with multiple memory systems, provide only weak support for functionally distinct memory systems.

In summary, findings of stochastic or functional dissociations between memory tasks, although certainly consistent with the existence of independent memory systems, represent only weak evidence for this view. Such dissociations can occur for a variety of reasons; some may be due to artifacts (e.g., scaling differences, lack of memory-related variance), whereas others may be related to differences in nonmnemonic information processing requirements (e.g., perceptual, attentional, and response-related processes). For these and other reasons, the evidence garnered from observations of amnesic patients is often regarded as the most compelling evidence for multiple memory systems. Amnesic patients, by definition, have severely impaired explicit memory without any other significant cognitive deficits. Despite their severely compromised explicit memory functions, amnesic patients often appear to perform normally on implicit memory tasks. Although such evidence represents just one of many functional dissociations between memory tasks (i.e., amnesia affects one task but not the other), the evidence is particularly compelling regarding priming. With priming tasks, it is possible to study explicit and implicit memory for similar materials studied under identical conditions. The evidence for spared priming in amnesia will be discussed in some detail because it is central to hypothesized relations between brain structures and specific memory functions.

IS PRIMING SPARED IN AMNESIA?

Descriptions and characterizations of which learning and memory functions are impaired and which are spared in amnesia have appeared in several recent reviews (Mayes, 1988; Shimamura, 1986; Squire, 1987). Frequently, the spared and impaired functions have been linked to different underlying memory systems with presumed distinct anatomical bases. Among proponents of the multiple memory system approach, there is broad agreement about the main divisions of memory. Recent views advanced by Schacter (Schacter, 1990; Schacter, Cooper, Tharan, & Rubens, 1991), Tulving (Tulving, 1985; Tulving, Hayman, & Mac-Donald, 1991; Tulving & Schacter, 1990), Gabrieli (Gabrieli et al., 1990; Keane, Gabrieli, Fennema, Growdon, & Corkin, 1991), and Squire (Squire, 1987; Squire & Zola-Morgan, 1988; Zola-Morgan & Squire, 1990) and their colleagues all distinguish between an explicit/declarative memory system, which is affected in amnesia, and an implicit/nondeclarative memory system, which is intact. Explicit/declarative memory is presumed to be crucially dependent on the function of mesial temporal and diencephalic structures consistently found to be damaged in amnesia. There also seems to be broad agreement that implicit/nondeclarative memory consists of a number of more or less well-defined subsystems, most if not all of which are spared in amnesia, and therefore these systems are thought to be independent of the mesial temporal and diencephalic structures.

Warrington and Weiskrantz (1968, 1970; Weiskrantz & Warrington, 1970), in their classical early studies, showed that amnesic patients demonstrated remarkably good retention of words and pictures when cued with fragmented versions of the items. On recall and recognition memory tasks with these materials, the patients' performance was very impaired compared to control subjects. Subsequently, these findings have been interpreted as possibly the first demonstration that priming may be spared in amnesia. Recently, numerous reports have appeared of normal or near normal performance on repetition priming tasks by amnesic patients who at the same time demonstrate severely deficient explicit memory for the same materials (Cave & Squire, 1992; Cermak, Talbot, Chandler & Wolbarst, 1985; Diamond & Rozin, 1984; Gardner, Boller, Moreines, & Butters, 1973; Graf, Squire, & Mandler, 1984; Haist, Musen, & Squire, 1991; Jacoby & Witherspoon, 1982; Schacter, Cooper, Tharan, & Rubens, 1991). This evidence, which has been reviewed extensively elsewhere (Shimamura, 1986; Richardson-Klavehn & Bjork, 1988), has led to the suggestion that priming represents a form of implicit memory that is spared in amnesia. However, there are reasons to suspect that such a conclusion is premature, since findings of impaired priming in amnesia are far more common than generally acknowledged.

Even in the original studies by Warrington and Weiskrantz there was evidence that priming was not entirely spared in amnesia. The amnesic patients did evidence remarkably good retention when tested with the fragment cues. However, Warrington and Weiskrantz (1968) pointed out that less information was retained from session to session by the amnesic patients than by normal control subjects. This deficit in the amnesics was found to be statistically significant at retention intervals of 1 and 24 hours (Weiskrantz & Warrington, 1970). In other words, although the amnesic patients evidenced priming, the size of the priming effect appeared not to be entirely normal. Milner, Corkin, and Teuber (1968) reported similar findings when they administered the Gollin incomplete picture task to the famous amnesic case, H. M. This type of fragmented picture task is now widely regarded as a priming task. An hour after the learning trials, H. M., like the amnesics in Warrington and Weiskrantz's study, evidenced good retention of the pictures when tested with the fragmented cues. This appeared in sharp contrast to his inability to recall or recognize previously presented pictures after even a relatively short interval. However, as pointed out by Milner et al. (1968), H. M. did produce considerably more errors on the retest than did controls. Thus, in priming terminology, H. M. did evidence priming but he evidenced less priming than normal controls.

Cohen and Squire (1980) and Martone, Butters, Payne, Becker, & Sax (1984) reported that amnesic patients acquired the general skill of reading mirror-reversed words at the same rate as control subjects. The patients, however, did not benefit as much as normal subjects from repetition of specific words, which may be interpreted as indicating impaired item-specific priming in the amnesic patients.

Gabrieli, Cohen, Huff, Hodgeson, and Corkin (1984) investigated memory and priming in the amnesic patient H. M. and found that H. M. showed less priming than control subjects in two different experiments. One experiment involved repetition effects in a lexical decision task, whereas the other measured priming in terms of biasing of the spelling of homophones.

Cermak, O'Connor, and Talbot (1986) investigated priming in amnesic patients and control subjects with a homophone biasing task. The homophones used were words that sound the same but have different meanings and spellings (e.g., sun and son). The homophones were first presented in a context that emphasized one meaning, and therefore spelling, of the homophone. Subsequently, the subject was asked to write (spell) to dictation a number of words, including the previously encountered (biased) homophones. In all of the three separate experiments reported by Cermak et al. (1986), the amnesic patients evidenced significantly less priming on the spelling test than did control subjects. That is, although the amnesic patients showed a tendency to spell the homophones in accordance with meaning induced during the study phase, this tendency was significantly smaller than that seen with control subjects.

Squire, Shimamura, and Graf (1987) reported normal priming effects in amnesic patients in one word-stem completion experiment involving word stems that had many possible solutions. However, in two other experiments, Squire et al. (1987) found reduced priming effects in amnesic patients compared to controls. These completion experiments employed word stems and word fragments having only one possible solution.

Tulving et al. (1991) studied priming over a 12-month period with a word-fragment completion task in a single head-injured patient with memory defects.

In only one of the several test sessions (immediate test) did they include data from normal control subjects. However, in two of the four cuing conditions at this immediate test, Tulving et al. (1991) noted that the patient's performance was notably poorer than that of the normal subjects.

Ostergaard (1993) investigated priming in amnesic patients, patients with Alzheimer's disease (AD), and normal control subjects in two tasks: one involving identification of tachistoscopically (very briefly) presented words, and another involving identification of visually degraded words. In absolute terms, there was no difference between the priming effects produced by control subjects and amnesic patients. Both groups identified previously seen words more easily than new words. However, in the tachistoscopic task, the amnesic patients evidenced significantly higher overall identification threshold than control subjects—that is, they required longer exposure times than control subjects to identify the words. Because baseline identification threshold and the size of the priming effect were positively correlated, such baseline differences between the groups had to be taken into account when evaluating the priming effects. When this was done, either by using multiple regression analysis or by carefully matching amnesic and control subjects, the amnesic patients evidenced significantly less priming than the controls.

The studies discussed so far all used familiar words or pictures of familiar objects as stimulus materials. Several studies have reported reduced priming in amnesic patients when nonwords or pseudowords are used (Cermak et al., 1985; Cermak, Verfaellie, Milberg, Letourneau, & Blackford, 1991; Diamond & Rozin, 1984; Smith & Oscar-Berman, 1990; Verfaellie, Cermak, Letourneau, & Zuffante, 1991). Similarly, priming for newly formed associations between otherwise unrelated words has also been found to be impaired in amnesia (Schacter & Graf, 1986; Shimamura & Squire, 1989). Finally, Verfaellie, Milberg, Cermak, and Letourneau (1992) reported impaired priming for novel nonverbal patterns in a group of Korsakoff amnesics compared to alcoholic control subjects.

Proponents of the view that priming and explicit memory depend on different memory systems generally maintain that when impaired priming is observed in amnesic patients, it is because the priming task was contaminated by the use of explicit memory strategies (cf. Cermak et al., 1985; Squire et al., 1987; Tulving et al., 1991). The argument is that the normal control subjects employ explicit/episodic/declarative strategies in the priming tasks and that these strategies are not available to the amnesic patients.

The tendency toward circularity is clear here; the decision as to whether a priming measure addresses explicit was well as implicit memory systems depends to a degree on the outcome of experiments testing predictions about explicit and implicit memory in amnesia. For instance, on the basis of available evidence, there is little reason to expect that word completion taps one memory system when the stems or fragments have many possible solutions and another or both when they have only one solution, as was argued by Squire et al. (1987).

Completion of word fragments with only one solution shows many of the dissociations from recognition memory that are the basis for multi-memory-system hypotheses, such as effect of modality shift (Roediger & Blaxton, 1987), reading versus generating words during study (Blaxton, 1989), and stochastic independence (Tulving et al., 1982). Furthermore, Roediger, Weldon, Stadler, and Riegler (described in Roediger, Srinivas, & Weldon, 1989) directly compared tasks involving word stems with many solutions to tasks involving word fragments with just one solution. They found that the word stems and word fragments produced similar patterns of performance in relation to a number of manipulated variables.

The circle was completed in a study of priming of random patterns by Gabrieli et al. (1990). The patient, H. M., and control subjects were first asked to copy random patterns consisting of straight lines connecting five dots in a 3 by 3 matrix. Subsequently, the subjects were given only the 3 by 3 dot patterns. In one condition, they were asked to draw any figure that came to mind onto the dot patterns (priming condition). In another condition, the subjects were told to use the dot patterns as cues to draw from memory the patterns that they had copied earlier (explicit memory). It was found that H. M. evidenced as much priming on this task as controls, but surprisingly, when given explicit cued recall instructions, his performance was also equivalent to, indeed a little better than, that of control subjects. In this case Gabrieli et al. (1990) argued that the cued recall task, which, a priori, had been expected to be an explicit memory task, must in effect have been a priming task.

The danger of this kind of argument is that a real impairment of priming in amnesia may be missed. If the performance of amnesic patients is used as a criterion for defining memory tasks as explicit or implicit, then the performance of such patients on these same tasks should not be taken as evidence for multiple memory systems. The evidence that priming is spared in amnesia represents failure to reject the null hypothesis of no difference between patients and controls. Such failure may result from a lack of sensitivity of the priming measure. Priming measures vary greatly in their sensitivity to experimental manipulations, such as delay between study and test, number of times the primed items are presented, and level of processing (Graf et al., 1984; Jacoby, 1983; Jacoby & Dallas, 1981; Ostergaard, 1993; Scarborough, Cortese, & Scarborough, 1977; Squire et al., 1987). Therefore, it should perhaps not be surprising that such priming measures show different sensitivity to the experimental variable "amnesia." In other words, when no significant difference is found between amnesic patients and control subjects on a given measure, it is possible that the measure is not sensitive to a real underlying impairment.

Unfortunately, it is difficult to evaluate the power of the statistical analyses reported in most studies of priming effects in amnesic patients. Indices of dispersion (variance, standard deviation, standard error) of the relevant measures are rarely reported or are only shown as error bars on figures that cannot be read with

TABLE 15.1
Sensitivity of Priming and Recognition Memory Measures

	Priming		Recognition Memory	
	Control Mean	Difference Required for P < .05	Control Mean	Difference Required for P < .05
Haist et al. (1991)				
Words	126.0 msec	128.0 msec	85.5%*	6.0%
Nonwords	64.0 msec	84.0 msec		
Cave and Squire (1992)				
Experiment 1	95.1 msec	83.5 msec	72.2%*	4.6%
Paller et al. (1991)				
Familiar/same	190.0 msec	168.0 msec		not tested
Familiar/different	129.0 msec	186.0 msec		not tested
Unfamiliar/same	198.0 msec	279.0 msec		not tested
Unfamilar/different	91.0 msec	220.0 msec		not tested
Cermak et al (1986)				
Experiment 1	76.0%*	6.6%	75.0%*	4.5%
Experiment 2	72.0%*	7.1%	72.0%*	3.8%

Note. The priming measures in Haist et al. (1991), Cave and Squire (1992), and Paller et al. (1991) are response latency difference scores between studied and new items. The priming scores reported by Cermak et al. (1986) are percent of homophones to which the spelling changed as a result of study. Recognition memory scores reported by Cave and Squire (1992) are percent correct (i.e., hits plus correct rejections), those reported by Haist et al. (1991) are percent correct on two-alternative forced choice (words and nonwords analyzed together), and those reported by Cermak et al. (1986) are percent hits, with false positive rates reported to be very close to zero.
*Amnesic patients found to be significantly impaired compared to the control subjects.

the precision required for power estimation. Furthermore, actual t or F values are commonly not reported for nonsignificant differences. Consequently, it is in many cases impossible to evaluate the sensitivity of a test that produced a nonsignificant difference between control subjects and amnesic patients. This is particularly unfortunate because such null findings are used to draw conclusions about memory processes and the relative preservation of certain functions in amnesia. However, the relevant dispersion indices or actual t or F values were reported, at least for some measures, in the studies shown in Table 15.1. The table shows mean priming and recognition memory (when available) reported for control subjects, and it shows how different the mean of the amnesic patients would have to be from the control mean to produce a statistically significant difference. These differences were calculated on the basis of the error variance in the studies using a liberal one-tailed test with a 5% significance level. The error variance was calculated either from reported measures of dispersion or from reported group means and the corresponding t or F values. Although different scales of measurement are used in the different studies and in priming and recognition memory measures, the table clearly illustrates the problem of lack of sensitivity in some of the priming measures. For several of the response latency measures, the amnesic patients would have had to produce negative priming effects to be significantly different from the controls. Indeed, on none of these latency measures could the patients have shown significant priming effects that were still significantly inferior to those of the control subjects. Although different scales of measurement are involved, this is clearly not the case for the recognition memory measures nor for the priming measures in the Cermak et al. (1986) study. On these measures, it was possible for the patients to show a significant study effect that was significantly smaller than that of the control subjects. Indeed, on these measures the amnesic patients were found to be significantly impaired. Thus, failure to find a significant difference between priming effects obtained with control subjects and amnesic patients may to some extent be due to lack of sensitivity of the priming measures.

The challenge for memory studies using modern brain imaging techniques is to help resolve these issues. If performance on different memory measures is consistently associated with degree of damage to different brain structures, this would represent evidence for multiple memory systems.

THEORIES ABOUT THE NEURAL BASES OF PRIMING

Proponents of independence between implicit and explicit memory functions interpret the evidence for spared implicit memory in amnesia as critical for localization hypotheses about priming and other implicit memory functions. Thus, for these authors, neural structures mediating priming must, by implication, lie outside of those brain regions damaged in amnesic patients (Squire and Zola-Morgan, 1988). It is therefore useful to enumerate the structures reasonably excluded by such hypotheses.

Well before the advent of modern brain imaging techniques, careful observation by neurologists and neuropathologists had revealed the most common sites of cerebral damage in classically amnesic patients. Sir Charles Symonds (1966) and, later, J. B. Brierley (1977) summarized many cases in which, by various means, damage occurred to mesial temporal lobe or diencephalic structures, bilaterally, and the patients were known to have selective loss of recent and in some cases remote memory. Among temporal lobe structures, the hippocampus and parahippocampal gyrus were especially often implicated, while the roles of the amygdala and the uncus were less clear, because surgical lesions of these areas usually spared memory functions. Diencephalic lesions associated with memory impairments were most often observed in alcoholic amnesics, as a result of infarction, or in tumor or trauma cases. These lesions were seldom limited to a single diencephalic structure, though the mammillary bodies were very frequently damaged. Thus, although diencephalic structures lying near the third ventricle, such as the mammillary bodies, adjacent hypothalamic structures, the anterior nuclear group of the thalamus, and the dorsomedial thalamic nucleus, were frequently affected in amnesic patients, little specificity within this group of structures could be established. Interestingly, although the work of Victor, Adams, and Collins (1971) suggested a critical role in amnesia for dorsomedial nucleus damage, Spiegel, Wycis, Orchinik, and Freed (1955) found that bilateral stereotactic lesions of this nucleus produced inconsistent and often transient symptoms.

Additional cases have, of course, been reported since these reviews appeared. These have served to confirm the earlier observations implicating the hippocampal formation (notably Zola-Morgan, Squire, & Amaral, 1986), to focus further attention on the basal forebrain structures within the diencephalon (Alexander & Freedman, 1984; Damasio, Graff-Radford, Eslinger, Damasio, & Kassell, 1985), and to provide evidence that neither mammillary body nor dorsomedial nucleus damage is required for diencephalic amnesia (Mair, Warrington & Weiskrantz, 1979; Mayes, Meudell, Mann, & Pickering, 1988). In summary, those structures most likely to play a critical role in explicit memory function include those of the basal forebrain, hypothalamus, anterior and dorsomedial thalamus, and the structures on the mesial surface of the temporal lobe.

Most hypotheses about the localization of specific implicit memory functions are based on evidence from group studies of brain-damaged patients. Heindel, Salmon, Shults, Walicke, and Butters (1989) and Butters, Heindel, and Salmon (1990) reported a double dissociation between motor-skill learning and word-stem completion priming in patients with Huntington's disease (HD) and patients with Alzheimer's disease (AD). The AD patients evidenced impaired word-stem priming, although the HD patients performed normally on this task. However, the opposite pattern was observed in a pursuit rotor task. On this task, the performance of the AD patients improved at a normal rate from session to session, whereas the HD patients showed little or no learning on this task. Neuropathological and neuroradiological evidence from other studies suggests that HD patients suffer disproportionate damage to subcortical structures such as the basal ganglia (particularly the caudate nucleus), whereas AD patients have more extensive neocortical damage. Heindel et al. (1989) and Butters et al. (1990) therefore suggested that association cortices may play a crucial role in word priming, whereas the basal ganglia may be critical for motor skill learning. It should be noted, however, that the observed double dissociation may not reflect a dissociation between different memory processes. The dissociation could be between language and motor functions—that is, the AD patients may have more severe linguistic (and therefore word priming) deficits whereas HD patients may have impaired motor functions (and therefore show deficient pursuit rotor learning).

Specific predictions for localization of priming effects have also been made by other authors. Gabrieli and colleagues distinguish between a system involved in perceptual priming, which they suggest resides in occipital cortex, and another involved in lexical-semantic priming, localized in temporo-parietal association cortex (Gabrieli et al., 1990; Keane et al., 1991). These predictions are based on their own evidence for spared perceptual priming but impaired lexical-semantic priming in AD patients, and evidence from functional imaging studies showing that occipital lobe metabolism is relatively intact in such patients whereas temporo-parietal function is consistently affected.

Schacter and colleagues (Schacter, Cooper, Tharan, & Rubens, 1991; Polster, Nadel, & Schacter, 1991) also speculated that a presemantic perceptual representation system, within which priming effects occur, may consist of posterior cortical structures, particularly in inferior temporal areas, extrastriate occipital lobe, or parietal lobe, depending on the kind of representations primed.

In none of the studies reviewed so far were concurrent measures of word priming, explicit memory function, and degree of damage to different implicated brain structures presented. Thus, it has not been demonstrated that the amount of damage to mesial temporal or diencephalic structures is associated with the severity of explicit memory deficits, but not measured priming, in the same subjects. Nor has it been shown that measures of damage to posterior cortical structures predict the severity of priming deficits. Studies providing such data could yield very useful evidence pertinent to the localization hypotheses described here, provided that an adequate degree of variability on the critical measures was present within the study sample. In vivo brain imaging techniques provide the first opportunity to obtain such evidence.

AN ANATOMICAL STUDY OF WORD PRIMING

Previous studies of memory impairment employing brain imaging techniques have adopted the neuropathology model; that is, patients with severe, isolated memory deficits have been examined with brain imaging techniques in an attempt to determine the location of the pathology. Although this approach is likely to yield much useful information, it has potential limitations for the purpose of linking the degree of structural damage directly to the severity of memory deficits. For example, if, within a group of amnesic patients, measurable damage is present in more than one structure, evidence specifically implicating one of these on the basis of group comparisons is weak. The fact that measured damage to one of the structures may be greater than that in another provides little specific evidence, because scarcely anything can be assumed about the function relating a given unit of structural damage to memory impairment. Thus, a particular pathological process may cause severe damage to one structure, which has little consequence for memory function, and less damage to a second structure, which is, however, highly significant for memory function. Also, discrepancies can occur due to simple differences in measurement sensitivity, that is, damage to one structure may appear to be more severe because one's measure of that structure is more sensitive than one's measures of other structures. Evidence for specificity would be stronger if the measured variability in the degree of damage to a structure could be shown to be related in an orderly way to the severity of memory impairment. Unfortunately, in typical studies of amnesics, all patients have severe explicit memory deficits (often many patients are near chance on recognition memory tests), and thus there is little scope for observing direct correlations with measured structural damage.

We recently conducted a study that was an initial attempt to link priming and explicit memory function to the amount of damage present in specific brain structures (Jernigan & Ostergaard, 1993). We began by examining the caudate nuclei, the mesial temporal lobes, and the posterior temporo-parieto-occipital cortex, using magnetic resonance imaging, in a group of subjects within which a large degree of variability existed on priming and explicit memory measures. The 30 subjects included AD patients, HD patients, alcoholic Korsakoff's (AK) patients, patients with amnesia due to anoxic episodes, and normal subjects spanning the age range of the other subjects. This was not a study of the behavioral and anatomical abnormalities in various diagnostic groups. On the contrary, the subjects were regarded as a single group spanning the full range from normal to severely impaired on both the memory measures and the anatomical indices. It was reasoned that if the extent of damage to a specific structure is associated with degree of impairment of a specific function, then this relationship should be observable, regardless of the diagnosis of the subjects. By employing subjects from several diagnostic groups, we obtained a range of levels on both performance and anatomical measures, which is usually lacking in group studies, and which enabled us to detect quantitative relations between performance and anatomical measures. The anatomical measures obtained were estimated volumes of the caudate nucleus, the combined mesial temporal lobe (temporal limbic) structures, and the more lateral temporo-parieto-occipital neocortex. Figure 15.1A shows a set of three representative, digitally processed images from the same individual in which the region designated as caudate is highlighted in black. The temporo-parieto-occipital cortical volume was defined as all cortical grey matter falling posterior to a stereotactically placed coronal dividing plane that bisected the corpus callosum. Cortical surfaces of the mesial temporal lobe were, however, excluded from this measure. The areas designated as within this posterolateral region are shown in black in Fig. 15.1B. The computed images shown in Fig. 15.1C illustrate the regions included in the mesial temporal lobe volume: They were the uncus, amygdala, hippocampus, and parahippocampal gyrus.

Priming effects were measured in a tachistoscopic identification threshold task in which the subject tried to identify words presented very briefly. Each word was initially presented for only 16 msec and immediately followed by a random pattern mask. Exposure duration was then gradually increased until the subject was able to identify the word. This exposure duration was the identification threshold. Repetition priming and recognition memory were measured with this

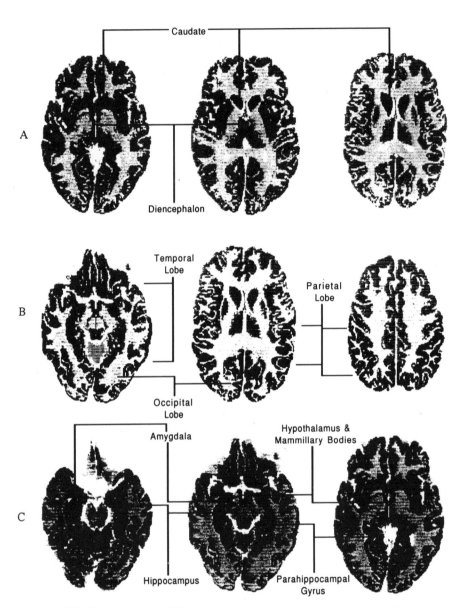

FIG. 15.1. Processed MR images from one individual illustrating definition of anatomical regions. Three representative axial sections through each region are shown, moving superiorly from left to right through each region and with frontal lobes pointing upward. Pixels within caudate nuclei (A), temporo-parieto-occipital neocortex (B), and temporal limbic cortex (C) highlighted in black. The locations of some of the structures mentioned in the text are also indicated.

task as follows: The subjects read aloud a list of words presented on a computer screen. After a delay, the identification threshold was measured for some of the words from the list and some new words. Also, throughout the task, after each word identification, the subject was asked if the word was on the studied list. The measure of repetition priming was the difference between the mean identification threshold for all old-word trials and the mean for all new-word trials. The measure of recognition memory was the number of correct classifications of words as on or off the list (i.e., number of hits plus number of correct rejections). We examined the relationships between the anatomical measures and three measures of performance on the memory tasks, namely, mean identification threshold for all new-word trials (i.e., the subject's efficiency at processing the lexical stimuli), repetition priming, and recognition memory.

Each task measure was predicted by the three anatomical measures in a separate simultaneous multiple regression analysis. This analysis was used because intercorrelation of the anatomical measures was expected, and the goal of the analyses was to estimate the specific contributions to the different memory impairments made by damage to each of the target structures.

The regression results are summarized in Table 15.2. Although all of the anatomical measures were correlated with recognition memory, only the temporal limbic loss showed a significant specific association with poor recognition memory. The simple correlations of the anatomical measures with priming did not reach significance; however, the multiple regression analysis revealed significant contributions by both the caudate and the temporal limbic measures. However, the effects were in opposite directions: Caudate volume loss was associated with increased priming, whereas temporal limbic loss was associated with de-

TABLE 15.2
Brain Structural Correlates of Task Measures

	Criterion Variable					
	Recognition Memory		Priming		Identification Threshold for New Words	
	r	β	r	β	r	β
Caudate	.49**	.17	-.35	-.54*	-.58***	-.38*
Posterolateral neocortex	.50**	.16	-.09	-.08	-.48**	-.17
Temporal limbic cortex	.66***	.49**	.17	.48*	-.53**	-.25
	R = .70***		R = .53*		R = .66**	

Note. r = Pearson correlation coefficient for simple correlation; β = standardized regression coefficient from simultaneous multiple regression; R = Multiple R from simultaneous multiple regression.
* p < .05.
** P < .01.
*** p < .001.

creased priming. Such results in multiple regression analyses are often referred to as *suppressor* effects. In other words, the association of higher priming performance with caudate damage acted to suppress the correlation between poor priming and temporal limbic loss. For the new-word threshold, again, all simple correlations were significant; however, it appeared from the regression analysis that the caudate losses were most strongly related to inefficient lexical processing (as reflected in increased threshold).

The latter result suggested a possible explanation for the unexpected priming correlations. In normal subjects, several manipulations that make processing of lexical items more difficult result in increased priming for those items. For example, low-frequency words and visually degraded stimuli produce larger priming effects (Norris, 1984; Scarborough et al., 1977). We reasoned that perhaps impairment in the perceptual and lexical processing of the stimuli, associated with caudate damage, acted in a similar way to increase the priming effects of some of the subjects within the sample. In fact, a significant correlation between poorer processing of the new items and increased priming did occur within the sample. If caudate losses result in poor lexical/perceptual processing, then such damage alone, like stimulus degradation, may actually increase priming effects. On the other hand, when temporal limbic losses occur in isolation, this might decrease priming effects. This would have resulted in the regression results shown in the table for the priming measure. Also, if this explanation were correct, then a measure of priming which controlled for the subjects' performance on the new-word (baseline) threshold should show a relationship to the temporal limbic measure. Such a residual priming score, removing variance associated with baseline threshold, was computed, and this score was correlated with each anatomical measure. The results suggested that, indeed, only temporal limbic losses were significantly correlated with this measure of priming.

As we expected, the results of this study suggested that, relative to caudate and posterior neocortical damage, volume loss in the structures of the mesial temporal lobe was specifically related to poor recognition memory. Damage to the caudate, on the other hand, seemed particularly to affect perceptual/lexical processing of the words.

An analysis of the relationship between priming, identification threshold for new words, and recognition memory in this study revealed that the correlation between priming and recognition memory was virtually zero; however, recognition memory and new-word threshold both contributed significantly to the prediction of priming in a multiple regression analysis, with good recognition memory and slowed new-word processing both associated with increased priming. Of particular interest is the fact that slower word identification predicted larger priming effects. This has important implications for the finding of intact priming in patients who may have slowed perceptual/lexical function. Clearly, baseline levels on tasks such as these must be taken into account in the assessment of priming.

The lack of correlation between the priming and recognition memory scores is quite consistent with the view that they measure completely independent memory-related processes. However, the result of the regression in which both the new-word threshold and recognition memory predict priming suggests a different interpretation. Apparently, priming variability on this task is comprised of a significant memory-related component and an independent perceptual/lexical processing component. Limbic damage may affect the memory component and thereby reduce measured priming. However, if damage in other areas affects lexical or perceptual processing, this may increase measured priming effects and therefore mask the reduced priming resulting from the limbic damage. These results are consistent with those from Ostergaard's study (Ostergaard, 1993), reviewed previously, showing that when priming scores were adjusted for baseline threshold, the amnesics showed impaired priming. The anatomical study suggests that such impairment may have been due to temporal lobe limbic damage.

It should be noted that the correlation of priming and temporal limbic damage in our anatomical study cannot easily be explained by postulating that the subjects used explicit memory strategies in the word identification task (i.e., that when identifying the very briefly presented words, they consciously attempted to retrieve candidates from the original list of words). On the simple measure of priming (i.e., not accounting for baseline performance), there was complete overlap between the group of normal subjects and the group of amnesic subjects, whereas there was no overlap between these two groups on the recognition memory measure. This result replicates many previous findings of seemingly normal word priming in amnesia. However, if, in our study, priming was to a significant extent increased by explicit memory strategies, then the normal subjects would have shown greater priming effects than the amnesic patients, because the normal subjects' recognition memory was clearly superior to that of the amnesic patients.

Ultimately, however, it is impossible to rule out the possibility that both an explicit memory system and an implicit memory system contributed in concert to priming performance. The important point is that observations of spared priming have been taken as evidence for the existence of an independent implicit memory system. When such sparing can be attributed to baseline effects, as in our study, and when the residual priming variability cannot be dissociated from recognition memory performance nor from damage to the mesial temporal lobe, then such observations provide no evidence for a separate memory system.

On the basis of our studies, we have suggested that at least two factors influence measured priming: one related to memory and one related to processing efficiency. The memory-related component is revealed by removing the variance due to processing efficiency (baseline) from the priming measure. This memory-related component of priming is related to recognition memory and, like recognition memory, is affected by the extent of mesial temporal lobe damage. The component related to processing efficiency could, in the results of our anatomical study, be observed directly (as a correlation between baseline threshold and measured priming). Perhaps a subject's efficiency at stimulus processing determines how a given amount of actual priming will affect a priming measure. If the subject's processing is highly efficient, the actual priming may result in little facilitation of performance and thus relatively little measured priming. If, on the other hand, the subject's stimulus processing is inefficient, there may be more scope for improvement. The same amount of actual priming of the words may produce larger measured priming effects.

This interpretation receives support from a recent study by Randolph (1991), who investigated priming and cued recall with a word-stem completion task in AD, HD, and normal control subjects. He found that, in absolute terms, the HD patients evidenced normal and the AD patients significantly reduced priming compared to controls. However, he also found a significant correlation between cued recall (explicit memory) and priming in all three subject groups. When an analysis of covariance was employed to remove the cued-recall variance from the priming scores, the AD patients evidenced normal priming while HD patients evidenced significantly increased priming compared to control subjects. In other words, the priming impairment of the AD patients, with presumed temporal limbic damage, could be attributed to a defect of memory-related priming (as reflected in their cued-recall performance), because when this variance was removed these patients showed normal priming. The hyperpriming evidenced by the caudate-damaged HD patients (after cued-recall variance was removed) may be the result of inefficient lexical/perceptual processing. This is consistent with our data indicating that temporal limbic damage is associated with memory impairments and reduced priming, whereas caudate damage is associated with impaired lexical/perceptual processing and increased measured priming.

In a study of word-stem priming and word-stem cued recall using positron emission tomography (PET), Squire, Ojemann, Miezin, Petersen, Videen, and Raichle (1992) found that blood flow in the right hippocampus was significantly higher in a cued-recall condition ($p < .001$) and in a priming condition ($p < .05$) than in the baseline condition. Blood flow in the right lingual gyrus (mesial occipital) was also significantly lower in the priming condition ($p < .05$), and almost significantly lower in the cued-recall condition ($p < .07$). Right prefrontal flow was significantly augmented in the cued-recall condition. Because the hippocampal flow increase was significantly greater in the cued recall than in the priming condition, the authors interpreted the results to mean that the hippocampus was critically involved in cued recall, and that decreased activity in the mesial occipital area underlies priming. However, these findings are equally consistent with the argument advanced here, because hippocampal activity increased in both the priming and the recognition memory condition, albeit to different degrees. Similarly, reductions in the mesial occipital region appeared to accompany both retention conditions. Therefore, the pattern of results may reflect the different processing requirements of the two tasks rather than the activation of different memory systems.

CONCLUSIONS

When interpreting priming studies two factors must be taken into account: (a) the sensitivity of the priming measures, and (b) interactions between processing requirements and measured priming effects. As discussed, amnesic patients often demonstrate normal priming, but impaired priming has also been reported in several studies. Patients with AD often show reduced priming compared to controls (Heindel, Salmon, and Butters, 1989; Salmon, Shimamura, Butters, & Smith, 1988; Shimamura, Salmon, Squire, & Butters, 1987). On the other hand, normal priming has also been reported (Grosse, Wilson, & Fox, 1990; Moscovitch, 1982; Ober & Shenaut, 1988), and in one study both normal and impaired priming effects were obtained with AD patients (Keane et al., 1991). Such conflicting results may partly be a consequence of differential sensitivity of the priming measures. However, they may also to some extent reflect the degree to which processing deficits interact with measured priming. We have found that some perceptual/lexical processing impairments, associated with caudate damage, may increase measured priming. This is consistent with findings that patients with HD, who have disproportionate damage to the basal ganglia, may actually show increased priming compared to controls (e.g., Heindel, Salmon, & Butters, 1990; Randolph, 1991). However, it should be noted that other patient groups with severe memory defects, such as amnesics and AD patients, also show variable degrees of damage to basal ganglia structures (Jernigan, Salmon, Butters, & Hesselink, 1991; Jernigan, Schafer, Butters, & Cermak, 1991; Shimamura, Jernigan, & Squire, 1988). This observation implies that, in such patients, factors that increase measured priming may play a role, and seemingly normal priming effects should perhaps not be taken to establish the presence of an intact memory system.

ACKNOWLEDGMENTS

This work was supported by NIA Grants AG06849 to Dr. A. L. Ostergaard and AG05131 to Dr. R. Katzman, and by the Medical Research Service of the Department of Veterans Affairs to Dr. T. L. Jernigan.

REFERENCES

Alexander, M. P., & Freedman, M. (1984). Amnesia after anterior communicating artery aneurysm rupture. *Neurology, 34*, 752–757.

Blaxton, T. A. (1989). Investigating dissociations among memory measures: Support for a transfer of appropriate processing framework. *Journal of Experimental Psychology: Learning, Memory, and Cognition, 15,* 657–668.

Brierley, J. B. (1977). Neuropathology of amnesic states. In C. W. M. Whitty & O. L. Zangwill (Eds.), *Amnesia* (pp. 199–223). London: Butterworths.

Butters, N., Heindel, W. C., & Salmon, D. P. (1990). Dissociation of implicit memory in dementia: Neurological implications. *Bulletin of the Psychonomic Society, 28*(4), 359–366.

Cave, C. B., & Squire, L. R. (1992). Intact long-lasting repetition priming in amnesia. *Journal of Experimental Psychology: Learning, Memory, and Cognition, 18,* 509–520.

Cermak, L. S., O'Connor, M., & Talbot, N. (1986). Biasing of alcoholic Korsakoff patients' semantic memory. *Journal of Clinical and Experimental Neuropsychology, 8,* 543–555.

Cermak, L. S., Talbot, N., Chandler, K., & Wolbarst, L. R. (1985). The perceptual priming phenomenon in amnesia. *Neuropsychologia, 23,* 615–622.

Cermak, L. S., Verfaellie, M., Milberg, W., Letourneau, L., & Blackford, S. (1991). A further analysis of perceptual identification priming in alcoholic Korsakoff patients. *Neuropsychologia, 29,* 725–736.

Cohen, N. J., & Squire, L. R. (1980). Preserved learning and retention of pattern-analyzing skill in amnesia: Dissociation of knowing how and knowing that. *Science, 210,* 207–210.

Damasio, A. R., Graff-Radford, N. R., Eslinger, P. J., Damasio, H., & Kassell, N. (1985). Amnesia following basal forebrain lesions. *Archives of Neurology, 42,* 263–271.

Diamond, R., & Rozin, P. (1984). Activation of existing memories in anterograde amnesia. *Journal of Abnormal Psychology, 93,* 98–105.

Dunn, J. C., & Kirsner, K. (1988). Discovering functionally independent mental processes: The principle of reversed association. *Psychological Review, 95,* 91–101.

Eich, E. (1984). Memory for unattended events: Remembering with and without awareness. *Memory & Cognition, 12,* 105–111.

Gabrieli, J. D. E., Cohen, N. J., Huff, F. J., Hodgeson, J., & Corkin, S. (1984). Consequences of recent experience with forgotten words in amnesia. *Society for Neuroscience Abstract, 10,* Part 1, 383.

Gabrieli, J. D. E., Milberg, W., Keane, M. W., & Corkin, S. (1990). Intact priming of patterns despite impaired memory. *Neuropsychologia, 28,* 417–428.

Gardner, H., Boller, F., Moreines, J., & Butters, N. (1973). Retrieving information from Korsakoff patients: Effects of categorical cues and reference to the task. *Cortex, 9,* 165–175.

Graf, P., & Schacter, D. L. (1985). Implicit and explicit memory for new associations in normal and amnesic patients. *Journal of Experimental Psychology: Learning, Memory, and Cognition, 11,* 501–518.

Graf, P., Squire, L. R., & Mandler, G. (1984). The information that amnesic patients do not forget. *Journal of Experimental Psychology: Learning, Memory, and Cognition, 10,* 164–178.

Grosse, D. A., Wilson, R. S., & Fox, J. H. (1990). Preserved word-stem-completion priming of semantically encoded information in Alzheimer's disease. *Psychology and Aging, 5,* 304–306.

Haist, F., Musen, G., & Squire, L. R. (1991). Intact priming of words and nonwords in amnesia. *Psychobiology, 19,* 275–285.

Hayman, C. A. G., & Tulving, E. (1989). Contingent dissociations between recognition and fragment completion: The method of triangulation. *Journal of Experimental Psychology: Learning, Memory, and Cognition, 15,* 228–240.

Heindel, W. C., Salmon, D. P., & Butters, N. (1990). Pictorial priming and cued recall in Alzheimer's and Huntington's disease. *Brain and Cognition, 13,* 282–295.

Heindel, W. C., Salmon, D. P., Shults, C., Walicke, P., & Butters, N. (1989). Neuropsychological evidence for multiple implicit memory systems: A comparison of Alzheimer's, Huntington's and Parkinson's disease patients. *Journal of Neuroscience, 2,* 582–587.

Hintzman, D. L. (1980). Simpson's paradox and the analysis of memory retrieval. *Psychological Review, 87,* 398–410.

Hintzman, D. L. (1990). Human learning and memory: Connections and dissociations. *Annual Review of Psychology, 41,* 109–139.

Hintzman, D. L., & Hartry, A. L. (1990). Item effects in recognition and fragment completion: Contingency relations vary for different subsets of words. *Journal of Experimental Psychology: Learning, Memory, and Cognition, 16,* 955–968.

Jacoby, L. L. (1983). Perceptual enhancement: Persistent effects of an experience. *Journal of Experimental Psychology: Learning, Memory, and Cognition, 9,* 21–38.

Jacoby, L. L., & Dallas, M. (1981). On the relationship between autobiographical memory and perceptual learning. *Journal of Experimental Psychology: General, 110,* 306–340.

Jacoby, L. L., & Witherspoon, D. (1982). Remembering without awareness. *Canadian Journal of Psychology, 36,* 300–324.

Jernigan, T. L., & Ostergaard, A. L. (1993). Word priming and recognition memory both affected by mesial temporal lobe damage. *Neuropsychology, 7,* 14–26.

Jernigan, T. L., Salmon, D. P., Butters, N., & Hesselink, J. R. (1991). Cerebral structure on MRI, Part II: Specific changes in Alzheimer's and Huntington's diseases. *Biological Psychiatry, 29,* 68–81.

Jernigan, T. L., Schafer, K., Butters, N., & Cermak, L. S. (1991). Magnetic resonance imaging of alcoholic Korsakoff patients. *Neuropsychopharmacology, 4*(3), 175–186.

Keane, M. M., Gabrieli, J. D. E., Fennema, A. C., Growdon, J. H., & Corkin, S. (1991). Evidence for a dissociation between perceptual and conceptual priming in Alzheimer's disease. *Behavioral Neuroscience, 105*(2), 326–342.

Light, L. L., Singh, A., & Capps, J. L. (1986). Dissociation of memory and awareness in young and older adults. *Journal of Clinical and Experimental Neuropsychology, 8,* 62–74.

Mair, W. P. G., Warrington, E. K., & Weiskrantz, L. (1979). Memory disorders in Korsakoff's psychosis. *Brain, 102,* 749–783.

Mandler, G. (1991). Your face looks familiar but I can't remember your name: A review of dual process theory. In W. E. Hockley & S. Lewandowsky (Eds.), *Relating theory and data: Essays on human memory in honor of Bennet B. Murdock* (pp. 207–225). Hillsdale, NJ: Lawrence Erlbaum Associates.

Martone, M., Butters, N., Payne, M., Becker, J. T., & Sax, D. S. (1984). Dissociations between skill learning and verbal recognition in amnesia and dementia. *Archives of Neurology, 41,* 965–970.

Mayes, A. R. (1988). *Human organic memory disorders.* Cambridge: Cambridge University Press.

Mayes, A. R., Meudell, P. R., Mann, D., & Pickering, A. (1988). Location of lesions in Korsakoff's syndrome: Neuropsychological and neuropathological data on two patients. *Cortex, 24,* 367–388.

Milner, B., Corkin, S., & Teuber, H.-L. (1968). Further analysis of the hippocampal amnesic syndrome: 14-Year follow-up study of H. M. *Neuropsychologia, 6,* 215–234.

Moscovitch, M. A. (1982). A neuropsychological approach to perception and memory in normal and pathological aging. In F. I. M. Craik & S. Trehub (Eds.), *Aging and cognitive processes. Advances in the study of communication and affect* (Vol. 8, pp. 55–78). New York: Plenum.

Musen, G., & Treisman, A. (1990). Implicit and explicit memory for visual patterns. *Journal of Experimental Psychology: Learning, Memory, and Cognition, 16,* 127–137.

Norris, D. (1984). The effects of frequency, repetition and stimulus quality in visual word recognition. *Quarterly Journal of Experimental Psychology. A, Human Experimental Psychology, 36,* 507–518.

Ober, B. A., & Shenaut, G. K. (1988). Lexical decision and priming in Alzheimer's disease. *Neuropsychologia, 26,* 273–286.

Olton, D. S. (1989). Inferring psychological dissociations from experimental dissociations: The temporal context of episodic memory. In H. L. Roediger & F. I. M. Craik (Eds.), *Varieties of memory and consciousness: Essays in honour of Endel Tulving* (pp. 161–177). Hillsdale, NJ: Lawrence Erlbaum Associates.

Ostergaard, A. L. (1992). A method for judging measures of stochastic dependence: Further comments on the current controversy. *Journal of Experimental Psychology: Learning, Memory and Cognition, 18,* 413–420.

Ostergaard, A. L. (in press). Dissociations between word priming effects in normal subjects and patients with memory disorders: Multiple memory systems or retrieval. *Quarterly Journal of Experimental Psychology.*

Paller, K. A., Mayes, A. R., Thompson, K. M., Young, A. W., Roberts, J., & Meudell, P. R. (1992). Priming of face matching in amnesia. *Brain and Cognition, 18,* 46–59.

Polster, M. R., Nadel, L., & Schacter, D. L. (1991). Cognitive neuroscience analyses of memory: A historical perspective. *Journal of Cognitive Neuroscience, 3,* 95–117.

Randolph, C. (1991). Implicit, explicit, and semantic memory functions in Alzheimer's disease and Huntington's disease. *Journal of Clinical and Experimental Neuropsychology, 13*(4), 479–494.

Richardson-Klavehn, A., & Bjork, R. A. (1988). Measures of memory. *Annual Review of Psychology, 39,* 475–543.

Roediger, H. L. III. (1984). Does current evidence from dissociation experiments favor the episodic/semantic distinction? *Behavioral Brain Sciences, 7,* 252–254.

Roediger, H. L. III., & Blaxton, T. A. (1987). Effects of varying modality, surface features, and retention interval in word fragment completion. *Memory & Cognition, 15,* 379–388.

Roediger, H. L. III., Srinivas, K., & Weldon, M. S. (1989). Dissociations between implicit measures of retention. In S. Lewandowsky, J. C. Dunn, & K. Kirsner (Eds.), *Implicit memory: Theoretical issues* (pp. 67–84). Hillsdale, NJ: Lawrence Erlbaum Associates.

Roediger, H. L. III., Weldon, M. S., & Challis, B. H. (1989). Explaining dissociations between implicit and explicit measures of retention: A processing account. In H. L. Roediger & F. I. M. Craik (Eds.), *Varieties of memory and consciousness: Essays in honour of Endel Tulving* (pp. 3–41). Hillsdale, NJ: Lawrence Erlbaum Associates.

Salmon, D. P., Shimamura, A. P., Butters, N., & Smith, S. (1988). Lexical and semantic priming deficits in patients with Alzheimer's disease. *Journal of Clinical and Experimental Neuropsychology, 10,* 477–494.

Scarborough, D. L., Cortese, C., & Scarborough, H. S. (1977). Frequency and repetition effects in lexical memory. *Journal of Experimental Psychology: Human Perception and Performance, 3,* 1–17.

Schacter, D. L. (1990). Perceptual representation systems and implicit memory: Toward a resolution of the multiple memory systems debate. In A. Diamond (Ed.), *The development and neural bases of higher cognitive functions* (pp. 543–571). New York: New York Academy of Sciences.

Schacter, D. L., Cooper, L. A., & Delaney, S. M. (1990). Implicit memory for unfamiliar objects depends on access to structural descriptions. *Journal of Experimental Psychology: General, 119,* 5–24.

Schacter, D. L., Cooper, L. A., Delaney, S. M., Peterson, M. A., & Tharan, M. (1991). Implicit memory for possible and impossible objects: Constraints on the construction of structural descriptions. *Journal of Experimental Psychology: Learning, Memory, and Cognition, 17,* 3–19.

Schacter, D. L., Cooper, L. A., Tharan, M., & Rubens, A. B. (1991). Preserved priming of novel objects in patients with memory disorders. *Journal of Cognitive Neuroscience, 3,* 117–130.

Schacter, D. L., & Graf, P. (1986). Preserved learning in amnesic patients: Perspectives from research on direct priming. *Journal of Clinical and Experimental Neuropsychology, 8,* 727–743.

Shimamura, A. P. (1985). Problems with the finding of stochastic independence as evidence for multiple memory systems. *Bulletin of the Psychonomic Society, 23,* 506–508.

Shimamura, A. P. (1986). Priming effects in amnesia: Evidence for dissociable memory function. *Quarterly Journal of Experimental Psychology, 38A,* 619–644.

Shimamura, A. P., Jernigan, T. L., & Squire, L. R. (1988). Korsakoff's syndrome: Radiological (CT) findings and neuropsychological correlates. *Journal of Neuroscience, 8*(11), 4400–4410.

Shimamura, A. P., Salmon, D. P., Squire, L. R., & Butters, N. (1987). Memory dysfunction and word priming in dementia and amnesia. *Behavioral Neuroscience, 101,* 347–351.

Shimamura, A. P., & Squire, L. R. (1989). Impaired priming of new associations in amnesia. *Journal of Experimental Psychology: Learning, Memory, and Cognition, 15*, 721–728.

Smith, M. E., & Oscar-Berman, M. (1990). Repetition priming of words and pseudowords in divided attention and in amnesia. *Journal of Experimental Psychology: Learning, Memory, and Cognition, 16*, 1033–1042.

Spiegel, E. A., Wycis, H. T., Orchinik, L. W., & Freed, H. (1955). The thalamus and temporal orientation. *Science, 121*, 771–772.

Squire, L. R. (1987). *Memory and brain.* Oxford: Oxford University Press.

Squire, L. R., Shimamura, A. P., & Graf, P. (1987). Strength and duration of priming effects in normal subjects and amnesic patients. *Neuropsychologia, 25*, 195–210.

Squire, L. R., Ojeman, J. G., Miezin, F. M., Petersen, S. E., Videen, T. O., & Raichle, M. E. (1992). Activation of the hippocampus in normal humans: A functional anatomical study of human memory. *Proceedings of the National Academy of Sciences, 89*(5), 1837–41.

Squire, L. R., & Zola-Morgan, S. (1988). Memory: Brain systems and behavior. *Trends in Neurosciences, 11*, 170–175.

Symonds, C., Sir. (1966). Disorders of memory. *Brain, 89*(4), 625–644.

Tulving, E. (1985). How many memory systems are there? *American Psychologist, 40*, 385–398.

Tulving, E., Hayman, C. A. G., & MacDonald, C. A. (1991). Long-lasting perceptual priming and semantic learning in amnesia: A case experiment. *Journal of Experimental Psychology: Learning, Memory, and Cognition, 17*, 595–617.

Tulving, E., & Schacter, D. L. (1990). Priming and human memory systems. *Science, 247*, 301–306.

Tulving, E., Schacter, D. L., & Stark, H. A. (1982). Priming effects in word-fragment completion are independent of recognition memory. *Journal of Experimental Psychology: Learning, Memory, and Cognition, 8*, 336–342.

Verfaellie, M., Cermak, L. S., Letourneau, L., & Zuffante, P. (1991). Repetition effects in a lexical decision task: The role of episodic memory in the performance of alcoholic Korsakoff patients. *Neuropsychologia, 29*, 641–657.

Verfaellie, M., Milberg, W. P., Cermak, L. S., & Letourneau, L. (1992). Priming of spatial configurations in alcoholic Korsakoff's amnesia. *Brain and Cognition, 18*, 34–45.

Victor, M., Adams, R. D., & Collins, G. H. (1971). *The Wernicke-Korsakoff syndrome.* Oxford: Blackwell.

Warrington, E. K., & Weiskrantz, L. (1968). New method of testing long-term retention with special reference to amnesic patients. *Nature, 217*, 972–974.

Warrington, E. K., & Weiskrantz, L. (1970). Amnesic syndrome: Consolidation or retrieval? *Nature, 228*, 628–630.

Weiskrantz, L., & Warrington, E. K. (1970). A study of forgetting in amnesic patients. *Neuropsychologia, 8*, 281–288.

Winnick, W. A., & Daniel, S. A. (1970). Two kinds of response priming in tachistoscopic recognition. *Journal of Experimental Psychology, 84*, 74–81.

Witherspoon, D., & Moscovitch, M. (1989). Stochastic independence between two implicit memory tasks. *Journal of Experimental Psychology: Learning, Memory, and Cognition, 15*, 22–30.

Zola-Morgan, S., & Squire, L. R. (1990). The neuropsychology of memory: Parallel findings in humans and nonhuman primates. In A. Diamond (Ed.), *The development and neural bases of higher cognitive functions* (pp. 434–456). New York: New York Academy of Sciences.

Zola-Morgan, S., Squire, L. R., & Amaral, D. G. (1986). Human amnesia and the medial temporal region: Enduring memory impairment following a bilateral lesion limited to field CA1 of the hippocampus. *Journal of Neuroscience, 6*(10), 2950–2967.

Author Index

Subject Index